CONFESSIONS

A New Translation

AUGUSTINE

Translation and Notes by
PETER CONSTANTINE

Foreword by Jack Miles

LIVERIGHT PUBLISHING CORPORATION
A Division of W. W. Norton & Company
Independent Publishers Since 1923
New York   London

For information about permission to reproduce selections from this book,
write to Permissions, Liveright Publishing Corporation, a division of
W. W. Norton & Company, Inc., 500 Fifth Avenue, New York, NY 10110

For information about special discounts for bulk purchases, please contact
W. W. Norton Special Sales at specialsales@wwnorton.com or 800-233-4830

Manufacturing by LSC Communications, Harrisonburg
Book design by JAM Design
Production manager: Lauren Abbate

Library of Congress Cataloging-in-Publication Data

Names: Augustine, of Hippo, Saint, 354–430, author. | Constantine, Peter, 1963–
translator, editor. | Miles, Jack, 1942– writer of foreword.
Title: Confessions : a new translation / Augustine ; translation and notes by Peter
Constantine ; foreword by Jack Miles.
Other titles: Confessiones. English
Description: First edition. | New York : Liveright Publishing Corporation, 2018. |
Includes bibliographical references.
Identifiers: LCCN 2017051892 | ISBN 9780871407146 (hardcover)
Subjects: LCSH: Augustine, of Hippo, Saint, 354–430. | Christian saints—Algeria—
Hippo (Extinct city)—Biography. | Hippo (Extinct city)—Biography.
Classification: LCC BR65.A6 E5 2018 | DDC 270.2092 [B]—dc23
LC record available at https://lccn.loc.gov/2017051892

ISBN 978-1-63149-600-4 pbk.

Liveright Publishing Corporation, 500 Fifth Avenue, New York, N.Y. 10110
www.wwnorton.com

W. W. Norton & Company Ltd., 15 Carlisle Street, London W1D 3BS

1 2 3 4 5 6 7 8 9 0

CONFESSIONS

CONTENTS

FOREWORD

Jack Miles

News that a great classic like Augustine's masterpiece, the *Confessions*, has found a brave new translator is momentous news indeed, for the masterworks of literature take our measure as much as we take theirs. I still remember the long walk I took on a damp November afternoon in 1962, having ditched class to finish *War and Peace*. My measure had been taken. I would never be quite the same. Or another timeless moment, on a sunny morning a year later, alone at my desk in the dormitory of a Jesuit seminary, when I finally finished reading the *Aeneid* in Latin. To have finished the great work in the original was something to be proud of, and yet I was emotionally defeated.

The world's most serious writers demand that we give to the reading as much as they gave in the process of writing, which is to say that these works demand a kind of surrender. Translation is that surrender in its most abject form. What Augustine demanded of Peter Constantine in this accomplished new translation was that he become a reader taken captive and, like a prisoner of war, turned into a writer in his captor's service. Moreover, for the widely translated classics of Western literature, perhaps particularly the classics of Western spirituality, a prisoner like Constantine is never alone.

For these monumental works, an encounter with the original untouched by the influence of prior translations is scarcely to be had and not necessarily even to be desired. Sarah Ruden, a prolific translator of Greek and Latin classics (including her own translation of Augustine's *Confessions*), remarked in a recent study of biblical translation: "I bring from the translation of pagan literary works a great reluctance to write what everybody else has written, commonsensical and well supported as it may be."[1] But Ruden, in her breezy and candid manner, heads the very paragraph where she makes this observation "Sheer Pigheaded Egotism," and she may be right to do so.

Saying this, I invoke the memory of a giant among modern translators, my dear friend the late Michael Henry Heim.[2] Mike—who translated Anton Chekhov, Günter Grass, and Milan Kundera, among others in a dozen modern languages—once commented to me that novelty at all cost was often the translator's worst enemy. It was, if I recall his phrase correctly, "the curse of cleverness." A modest man but with something like perfect emotional pitch on the page, Mike was determined above all not to show off. His translations were almost always the first ever to appear of the works he took in hand; yet when a great work is already in print in many translations, the temptation to difference, for difference's own showy sake, must surely lurk around every corner.

Those who resist the temptation are those who are so utterly smitten by the original that they are compelled, almost despite themselves, to share as faithfully as they can what they believe *they* alone have grasped. There is an erotic dimension to this compulsion that puts me in mind of the poem "When You Are Old" by W. B. Yeats. A beautiful woman, addressed in the poem, has made many conquests in her day. The poet knows that he is only one among them. But he knows something about her, feels something for her, that he is certain has escaped her other lovers. And now that she is "old and gray and full of sleep and nodding by the fire," he is bold to say that "But one man loved the pilgrim soul in you, / And loved the sorrows of your changing face." That he loved her thus did not win her. His love was finally unrequited. In the way of a great beauty with her lovers, she may have known quite well that he loved the sorrows of her changing face, whether or not he ever said it. Yet even in the twilight of her life, even in this moment of poignant vindication for him, she remains invincibly beyond his reach.

The masterworks are invincible in that way, and so the heroism of translation is a poignant heroism. A labor of love, we casually call it, knowing not just how little it usually pays but also how eclipsed the translator, the lover, must ever be by the beloved author, the *belle dame sans merci*. But the love within the labor has other deep costs as well, hidden costs, and we readers are fed by that love, learning most from repeated translations of the greatest works. The classics do not just reward but may even demand repeated reading. Have you had your measure taken once? Have it taken again, my friend. Something about you may have escaped it the first time. You may need to suffer a deeper test.

As Peter Brown once memorably put it, "Augustine's back is turned to us throughout the *Confessions*. His attention is elsewhere. He is speaking with his God." Each of the thirteen component books would have taken approximately one hour in the kind of public recital that Augustine clearly anticipated, Brown estimates, and "those who first heard it would have found themselves listening to a stunning, yet disturbingly 'modern' piece of Latin verbal music."[3] With this, Peter Constantine is in warm agreement:

Part of Augustine's journey toward conversion was to reject what he saw as the sophisticated language of pride, and to embrace all that is simple and straightforward, the *sermo humilis*, humble speech, or the *sermo piscatorius*, the fisherman's language of the Apostles, who spoke frank and forthright truths that all men and women could understand. The stylistic mastery of *Confessions* is that Augustine, the sophisticated rhetorician and Latin stylist, who had been the Rhetorician of Milan (the seat of the Roman emperor), distilled his language into a beautiful and mellifluous simplicity.

Unique among contemporary translations of the *Confessions* into English, Constantine's is the work of a translator whose mother tongue is Greek. His first encounter with the work came through a translation into *katharevousa*, the refined neoclassical Greek first fostered by nineteenth-century Greek nationalists. This was a latter-day Greek equivalent of the Latin *sermo sublimis* that Augustine had quite deliberately left behind. Only later did Constantine read the work for a second time in Demotic Greek—the everyday *sermo humilis* that has become the official language of the Hellenic Republic. The reading experience of the translator, to this extent, recapitulated the writing experience of the author.

My own first encounter with that simplicity came in a curiously out-of-sequence way. First as a high school boy, and then as a Jesuit seminarian, I had studied Latin classics in what was at the time the established order: Caesar's *Gallic Wars*; Cicero's *Catiline Oration* and other orations and essays; then Virgil's *Aeneid* and, for a select few, the *Odes* of Horace. Toward the end of that parade, however, I turned against Latin and hatched (very briefly) the truly perverse scheme of so mastering the language that I could irrefutably demonstrate that there was no reason any longer to study it. On the inside cover of my secondhand Latin grammar, someone had written what I took to be an immemorial lament:

Latin is a dead language.
It's dead as it can be.
It killed all the Romans,
And now it's killing me.

I fantasized a British (or maybe Irish) schoolboy as the anonymous author of that jingle. At seventeen, I embraced him as my brother.

Alas, in a way that perhaps Augustine might appreciate, God had other plans for me. Four years later, in 1964, I was seated as a seminarian in a philosophy classroom at the Pontifical Gregorian University in Rome, where lectures and textbooks were all in Latin, and all examinations were oral examinations, also in Latin. This was Latin immersion, to be sure, but only to a point. After school, I was immersed not in Latin but in Italian, intoxicated to be talking and hearing at last a *living* language with living and wonderfully lively Italian friends. During my summers, I went to Germany and grew at least as excited about that language and about the several cultures of the German *Sprachgebiet*. It was only after all that—that is, after three full years as an American abroad in Europe and Israel—that I happened by chance upon an edition of the *Confessions* in Latin. Somewhat to my surprise, I found that I could make pretty good sight-reading sense of it, but—a much stronger surprise—I had the sudden and simultaneous sense that this wasn't classical literature at all. This . . . this was *European*!

That was how I experienced what Peter Brown calls, in quotes, the "modern" quality of Augustine's Latin, the quality that Peter Constantine characterizes as Augustine's "mellifluous simplicity." But is it fair to declare Augustine's Latin European? I think one could more easily argue that Western Europe's languages are Augustinian. More concretely, one could argue that they are all marked by what happened to the Latin language in Augustine's hands. The case for this bold claim would rest on Augustine's vast influence as the mediator to Western Europe of the classical rhetorical tradition in an inextricable intellectual tangle with Christian ideas and, above all, in a stylistic tangle with the artful artlessness of biblical prose and poetry.

The emotional range of the Greco-Roman classics is enormous, and the meditational mode is certainly represented. One thinks, for example, of Marcus Aurelius in *De rerum natura*, and Constantine mentions Marcus Aurelius in his introduction. But does any classical poem, including that one, *confide* in the way that some of the Psalms do, and that Paul then does, and that Augustine— turning, as it were, a folk tune into a symphony—does at length in the *Confessions*? I doubt it, and it is by such elusive and aesthetic means as these that the mentality of one culture evolves into the mentality of another or that the encounter of two cultures gives birth to a third.

In watching a great actor onstage, one can be impressed with his technique, his complete mastery of his part, and his intelligent awareness of how his part, whatever its size, functions within the play. Yet the most powerful of dramatic moments can sometimes come when normal control fails and the part seems to possess the actor. This is the dramatic equivalent of the literary surrender that I speak of above. There are times when Augustine, as the author of the *Confessions*, seems all too self-consciously in control of his performance, but there are peak moments when the role of penitent sinner turned ecstatic worshipper ceases to be a role and becomes simply the naked truth of the man himself. In such moments, the involuntary, almost helpless sincerity of the author requires a difficult answering sincerity in the translator.

The deep strength of Peter Constantine's translation is that he has matched Augustine's sincerity with his own. Listening as closely as I can in this translation for the false note, the faked note, the show-off note, the note of preening insincerity or accursed cleverness, I hear none.

NOTES

1 Sarah Ruden, *The Face of Water: A Translator on Beauty and Meaning in the Bible* (New York: Pantheon Books, 2017), 122.

2 Cf. *The Man Between: Michael Henry Heim and a Life in Translation* (Rochester, NY: Open Letter/University of Rochester Press, 2014). The book, edited jointly by several friends of Heim's after his death, contains essays on the subject of translation as well as appreciations of and work by Heim himself.

3 Peter Brown, introduction to *Confessions*, by Augustine, trans. F. J. Sheed, ed. Michael P. Foley, 2nd ed. (Indianapolis: Hackett Publishing Company, Inc., 2006), xvii–xviii.

TRANSLATOR'S INTRODUCTION

> What strikes me is that my *Confessions* affected me as much
> when I wrote them as they do now as I read them. What
> others who have read them might have understood, only they
> can tell; but I do know that my *Confessions* have greatly
> pleased and still please many of my brothers.
>
> From Augustine's *Retractiones* (Revisions) 2.6.1,
> written in his early seventies before his death in 430 CE

*A*ugustine's *Confessions* (397–398 CE) has remained among the
most original works of world literature. It is like no work before it, and
there has been no work like it since. It is the world's first autobiography in the modern sense, and it is also the first philosophical study
of an individual's inner life, the first study of human nature and the
soul, the first analysis of love, of sensory perception, of memory, of
time. It is the first modern biblical exegesis, its critical examination
of the Scriptures opening new paths for modern Christian thought.
In over one and a half millennia, *Confessions* has maintained a per-
sistent and intense relevance for readers throughout the world.

A radical new species of writing, *Confessions* opened the door
for all subsequent premodern and modern autobiographers, from
Montaigne to Rousseau, from Virginia Woolf to Gertrude Stein.
There had been autobiographical works before *Confessions*, but they
had been mainly didactic, homiletic, or apologetic, writings limited

to self-promotion or serving as paradigmatic examples for readers to follow. Some eight centuries earlier in Greece, in the fourth century BCE, Isocrates had written his autobiographical *Antidosis* as a fictional courtroom defense—since a courtroom defense in the Classical Greek world was the only acceptable form of a sustained personal narrative in which one could also list one's virtues. "For I hoped that this would be an excellent way of making the facts about my person known, leaving this work as a memorial to myself much finer than any statues in bronze," Isocrates wrote.[1] Among the Romans, Emperor Marcus Aurelius (121–180 CE) had composed his autobiographical *Meditations* as a reminder to himself and his readers what an exemplary life is and ought to be. The opening lines list the desired virtues:

> From my grandfather Verus I inherited morals and restraint; from the glory and remembrance of my father, modesty and manliness; from my mother, piety and generosity, as well as abstemiousness, not only from evil deeds, but also from evil thoughts, and furthermore frugality in life, casting aside the ways of the wealthy.

While Marcus Aurelius keeps a distance between himself and his readers, Augustine is the first autobiographer to achieve a warm and intimate bond with his audience, creating the first confessional intimacy of modern autobiography that brings the reader into the private and personal sphere of the writer. The interesting twist, however, is that *Confessions* is technically not written for a mortal reader; it is in the form of an intimate prayer to God. The "You" in *Confessions* is always addressed to God, except for some rare cases when Augustine, perhaps inadvertently, directly addresses a mortal readership.

Among *Confessions'* many innovations is that it is not a clear-cut linear narrative of a life with beginning, middle, and end. For many centuries, readers, particularly present-day readers, have found its structure puzzling. The autobiography of *Confessions* is a spiritual examination of the self, the narrative of a life that moves over bypaths toward a great change: the momentous conversion, the turning back to God, the narrative of a struggle that Augustine contends all true Christians must make since Adam and Eve turned away from God. The autobiographical journey in *Confessions* moves toward Augustine's growing understanding that he is a mutable being engaging and embracing God, who is immutable. In the first nine books of *Confessions*, Augustine's narrative takes us from the time of his birth to his mother's death in 387 CE, when he was thirty-three. This is where the autobiographical narrative of *Confessions* ends. The abrupt shift away from the narrative of the first nine books is what many modern readers find difficult to understand. At the core of Book X is a philosophical analysis of memory that might strike readers as irrelevant to the first nine books, but is in fact Augustine's natural spiritual progression from remembering his life to exploring the nature of memory that gives context to his remembrance. In Book XI, Augustine progresses from exploring memory to exploring time and eternity, and Books XII and XIII progress to an exploration of the first Book of Genesis and the Creation. *Confessions* draws to a close, still in the form of a prayer to God, with Augustine imparting to his readers the religious insight he has achieved, both as a result of his journey toward conversion and as the Christian thinker and bishop that he has become since that journey. As Augustine sums up more succinctly in his book *Retractiones* (Revisions), "From Book I to Book X, I write about myself, while the last three books are about the holy Scripture."[2]

AUGUSTINE WAS BORN IN 354 CE in the small North African Berber–Roman town of Thagaste in the Roman province of Numidia, today the city of Souk Ahras in Algeria. His mother, Monnica, was a Christian of Berber origin, and his father, Patricius, was of Roman background and a pagan, working as a minor civil servant. Monnica, revered today in the Catholic Church as the patron saint of wives and victims of abuse, had been Augustine's first Christian inspiration, drawing her son to her creed despite her husband's wishes. As Augustine writes about Christ in Confessions: "This name of my Savior, Your Son, my infant heart had devoutly imbibed with my mother's milk, drinking it and preserving it deep within me."[3]

Augustine had been "a poor man born of poor parents," at times compelled to wear threadbare clothes, as he pointed out in one of his Sermons,[4] but his family had gone to great lengths to secure him a traditional and sound Roman education in Madaura, a university town not far from his birthplace, and later in Carthage. This education placed much emphasis on effective rhetorical expression, which would lead to wealth and success in the Roman world. "My supposedly respectable studies had the aim of achieving excellence in the courts of litigation, where the greater the deceit, the greater the praise. Such is the blindness of men that they glory in blindness. And I was the foremost pupil in the school of rhetoric. I was puffed up with pride and rejoiced in vanity."[5] And Augustine was to become an accomplished orator and professor of rhetoric. Delight in Latin and in the great Latin classics made men of Augustine's class wary of the simple translations of the Old and New Testaments with their awkward Latin; the canon of the Bible was still very much in flux. The simplicity of the Scriptures seemed off-putting and even risible to men, like the young Augustine, who prized and recited by heart entire works of Cicero and Virgil. Part of Augustine's journey toward conversion was to reject what he saw as the sophisticated language of pride, and to embrace all that is simple and straightforward, the sermo humilis, humble speech, or the sermo piscatorius, the fisherman's language of the Apostles, who spoke frank and forthright truths that all men and women could understand. The stylistic mastery of Confessions is that Augustine, the sophisticated rhetorician and Latin stylist, who had been the Rhetorician of Milan (the seat of the Roman emperor), distilled his language into a beautiful and mellifluous simplicity. His contemporary readers would have been amazed and transported not only by what Augustine imparted in *Confessions* but by how he imparted it. As *Confessions* is Augustine's private prayer to God, on which we the readers are permitted to eavesdrop, Augustine would address God not in complex and elaborate Ciceronian Latin but in words that had all the simplicity of authentic feeling and sincerity.

And yet, to the great amazement of many generations of Augustine's readers, it was Cicero's work that first set Augustine on his path to conversion. Augustine, a young man of nineteen, had come across *Hortensius*, one of Cicero's works that has survived only in fragments. *Hortensius*, in the form of a dialogue among Cicero's friends, extols philosophy, with Cicero arguing that happiness can only be achieved by developing reflection and reason so that they will supersede the passions. As Augustine wrote later, "[*Hortensius*] altered my state of mind and my prayers, making them turn to You, Lord, changing my longings and desires. Suddenly every vanity became worthless, and with a fire raging in my heart I longed for the immortality of wisdom, rousing me to return to You. . . . How I burned, my God, how I burned to soar up to You from earthly things, though I did not know what You would do with me. For with You is wisdom."[6]

It was also in his nineteenth year that Augustine became a Manichaean devotee, his affiliation lasting for almost a decade. Manichaeism was fast becoming one of the most widespread religions in the world, and by Augustine's day was a serious threat to Christianity and other established religions. The founder of the Manichaean sect was the Persian mystic Manichaeus (216–c. 274 CE), also known as Mani; his doctrine brought together elements of Christianity, Zoroastrianism, and Buddhism, among others. Mani had pronounced himself Supreme Illuminator and Apostle of Jesus Christ, promising salvation through knowledge, without the elements of blind faith on which other Christian sects insisted. The Manichaean emphasis on intellectual discourse and eloquence drew in many brilliant young men like Augustine, whose Roman education and intellectual curiosity rejected the unquestioning fideism on which the local Catholic churches insisted. In fact, the Manichaeans considered themselves true Christians, accusing the Christian sects of North Africa of paganism. As Augustine quotes the Manichaean Bishop Faustus in *Against Faustus the Manichaean*: "They have temples, sacrifices, and altars, a priesthood and all the services and ceremonies, the same rites as the pagans, only more superstitious."[7] Throughout his twenties Augustine was to remain affiliated with the Manichaeans, and through their connections he moved to Rome in 383, and then the following year to Milan, where he was to be the Imperial Rhetorician. Though he was to renounce Manichaeism in no uncertain terms, his Manichaean affiliations and connections were to haunt him, and he had to fend off accusations of heresy for the rest of his life. One of the important goals of *Confessions*, and the other works he was writing in 396 and 397 CE, was to vigorously clarify his Catholic position and to renounce and denounce the Manichaeans.

The final intellectual turning point in Augustine's path toward Christianity was his discovery in 386 CE of Neoplatonic philosophy. The Alexandrian philosopher Plotinus (205–c. 270 CE) had developed a deep, original, and complex metaphysics from Plato's concepts, at the core of which lay the principle that everything in the universe derives from a transcendent "One" that is ineffable and immutable. Augustine writes in *Confessions*:

> Having now read the books of the Platonists that taught me to seek an incorporeal truth, I saw that Your invisible nature was to be understood through the things You have created. Yet, downcast, I also realized that the darkness in my soul would not let me behold clearly, though I was certain that You exist and are infinite, that You are not diffused over spaces that are finite or infinite, and that You truly are, and are always the same, varying

in no part or motion, and that all other things are from You, as is proven by the single unshakable fact that they exist. I was certain of these things, but too uncertain to delight in You.[8]

As we will see in *Confessions*, his path to Christianity had led him from the Manichaeans to astrology, to Academic skepticism, to Neoplatonism, and then drawn him nearer to the Church as a catechumen, a new member who was being prepared for initiation into the sacred mysteries, attending the church of the Nicene Christian community under Bishop Ambrose, who would later be canonized as Saint Ambrose. Then, on a late-summer day in 386, in a garden in Milan, beneath a fig tree, Augustine experienced a sudden and dramatic conversion that began with a spiritual collapse that left him desperate and in utter agony, but from which he ecstatically soared, resolved to embrace celibacy and Christianity.

On Easter morning of 387 CE, Augustine was baptized by Bishop Ambrose of Milan after months of Bible study, preparations, and intricate baptismal rites. He was baptized in an octagonal pool within an octagonal baptistry in the Basilica Nova, Milan's main church. It was a group baptism, and with him were also his teenage son, Adeodatus, and his close friend Alypius, who like Augustine had once been a Manichaean.

How I wept at Your hymns and canticles, deeply moved by the sweet-sounding voices of Your Church! The voices flowed into my ears, distilling the truth into my heart. My feelings of devotion streamed forth and my tears flowed, and they brought me contentment.[9]

A decade had passed from the moment the autobiographical narrative of *Confessions* ends before Augustine began writing the work. He was now the new Bishop of Hippo, a Roman port city in North Africa, today the town of Annaba in Algeria. He was forty-three, and five years into his vocation as a man of the church. He had come to a half-way point in his long life, but in that era few people lived past their forties. A third-century Roman jurist, Ulpian, who studied the population of Rome and is credited with having drawn up the first demographic mortality table, concluded that a person's life expectancy at the time began to decline significantly after the age of twenty.

Augustine might have considered *Confessions* his last work, a final testament of his Christian devotion. His letters from the period when he began writing *Confessions* reveal that he was gravely ill, and perhaps thought he might be dying. To his friend Bishop Profuturus of Cirta he wrote, "I am confined to my bed and can neither walk, nor stand, nor sit, because of the pain and swelling of my pustules and sores. . . . Pray that though I walk through the valley of the shadow of death, the Lord will be with me so that I will fear no evil."[10] Despite his recurring illness as he wrote *Confessions*, he had an extremely busy schedule as bishop and was simultaneously writing a number of other works: *Expositions on the Psalms, Sermon on Christian Discipline*, and several anti-Manichaean polemics: *Against the Fundamental Epistle of Manichaeus, Against Faustus the Manichaean, Against Felix the Manichaean*. But although Augustine was walking "through the valley of the shadow of death," as he had written to Bishop Profuturus, he was to live another thirty-four years, gaining in his day world renown as a charismatic and pious man of the church, and writing some seventy more works, which would make him one of the most prolific Latin authors. There was never to be a time when his books were not circulated or, with the invention of the printing press, available in print, first in Latin editions, and then in many translations.

NOTES

1 *Antidosis* 15.6.
2 *Retractiones* (Revisions) 2.6.1.

3 *Confessions*, Book III, 4.8.

4 *Sermons* 356.13.

5 *Confessions*, Book III, 3.6.

6 *Confessions*, Book III, 4.7–8.

7 *Against Faustus the Manichaean* 20.4.

8 *Confessions*, Book VII, 20.26.

9 *Confessions*, Book IX, 6.14.

10 *Epistola* 38.1.

ACKNOWLEDGMENTS

I would like to thank Michael Lynch and the Humanities Institute at the University of Connecticut for their support and for introducing me to the Homer Babbidge Library, with its holdings that were very helpful for the annotation of this translation.

I am particularly grateful to Robert Weil, my editor at Liveright, for his initial suggestion that I translate *Confessions*, and for his encouragement and expertise in editing this complex text. I am also thankful to Liveright's Marie Pantojan for her editorial advice and tireless help. I would also like to thank my agent, Jennifer Lyons, for her encouragement and support as I worked on the translation.

My very special thanks to Burton Pike, who inspired, helped, and advised me throughout the project.

NOTES ON THE TEXT

*T*he oldest manuscripts of *Confessions* divide the work into thirteen books; with the onset of the new printing presses of the fifteenth century, the first printed editions of the work added chapter numbers, and the first collected edition of Augustine's works, published in Paris in 1679 by the Benedictines of the Abbey of Saint-Maur, added paragraph numbers. Modern editions of *Confessions* number its books, chapters, and paragraphs following the practice of those editions.

Throughout *Confessions*, Augustine delicately weaves Biblical lines into his prose, particularly verses from the book of Psalms. Sometimes a phrase or verse from the Bible appears intact, but more often Augustine's quotations are slightly altered. The Biblical texts Augustine knew were the first Latin translations of the Bible, a number of different translations of varying quality used by the Roman Church before St. Jerome's Vulgate translation became the standard Latin Bible. (Jerome was working on his translations throughout the decade of the 390s CE, the time when Augustine was writing *Confessions*.) One marked difference between the first Latin translations of the Bible and Jerome's Vulgate is that the older translations, particularly of the book of Psalms which Augustine quoted so extensively, were based on the Septuagint, the Greek translations of the Old Testament that had been prepared by Greek Jewish scholars in the 3rd century BCE, while Jerome primarily used Hebrew texts as his source for the Vulgate; consequently, the various versions of the

Biblical verses often differed in nuance, which is still reflected today in the various English versions of the Bible. Throughout my translation of *Confessions* I have footnoted Augustine's biblical quotations and allusions, giving the name of the Scripture's book, chapter, and the verse number. It is fascinating to see how Augustine has integrated the biblical verses into his text and their interaction with his prose and style, and so I have also at times provided in the footnotes an English text of these verses from one of the modern English bibles, such as the New King James Bible or the Douay-Rheims 1899 American Bible. As there is often a marked variance between the English translations, I chose the version that most closely reflected Augustine's quotation or allusion. The book of Psalms has traditionally been numbered differently in the Septuagint translation, which the Old Latin bibles and Vulgate followed, from the numbering in the Hebrew Bible that most modern English bibles use. In the Septuagint and Latin bibles, the psalms—starting from Psalm 10 through Psalm 148—are numbered at one number less than the Hebrew Bible, since in these versions Psalm 9 and Psalm 10 form one psalm. To help readers locate psalms in different bibles I have provided both numberings in my footnotes: for instance, Psalm 53:8 (Vulgate), 54:6 (other translations).

CONFESSIONS

BOOK I

[1.1] You are great, O Lord, and worthy of the highest praise; great is Your power, and Your wisdom incalculable.[1] Seeking to praise You is a man, part of Your creation, a man bearing with him his mortality,[2] bearing evidence of his sin and evidence that You oppose the proud.[3] But still this man, part of Your creation, seeks to praise You; You inspire in him delight in praising You, for You have made us for Your sake, and our hearts are restless until they rest in You. Grant me, O Lord, to know and understand what is first: to appeal to You or to praise You, and whether knowing You must come before appealing to You. But who can appeal to You when he does not know You, for in not knowing You he might mistakenly appeal to another. And yet, do we not appeal to You so that we may know You? But how can man appeal to one in whom he has not believed? Or how shall he believe if You have not been proclaimed? Those who seek the Lord will praise Him: for those who seek Him shall find Him, and those who find Him shall praise Him. I will seek You, O Lord, by appealing to You, and appeal to You believing in You, for You have been proclaimed to us. My faith, O Lord, is appealing to You, the faith that You have given me, with which You have inspired me through the incarnation of Your Son, and through the labor of Your preacher.[4]

[2.2] But how shall I appeal to my God, my God and Lord, since when I appeal to Him I will be calling Him into myself? But what place is there within me into which my God can enter, where God can enter into me, God Who made heaven and earth? Is there, Lord my God, anything in me that can contain You? Can heaven and earth, which You have created and in which You have created me, contain You? Since all that exists would not exist without You, does whatever exists contain You? And as I too exist, why do I pray that You enter into me, as I would not exist at all if You were not within me? I am not in Hell, though You are there, for were I to descend to Hell You would be present. Thus I would not exist, my God, not exist at all if You were not in me. Or should I say I would not be, if I were not in You of Whom all things are, by Whom all things are, in Whom all things are? It is thus, Lord, it is thus. To where am I calling You if I am within You? From where would You come to me? Where should I go beyond heaven and earth so that my God, Who has said, "I fill heaven and earth," may come to me?

[3.3] Since You fill heaven and earth, do they contain You? Or do You fill them and more of You still remains because they cannot contain You? And where does the rest of You pour out when heaven and earth are filled? Or have You, Who contain all things, no need to be contained, since what You fill You fill by containing it? The vessels filled with You do not give You form, since even if they were to break, You would not pour out. And were You to pour out over us, You would not pour onto the ground but would uplift us; You would not be dispersed, but would gather us together. In filling all things You fill them with the whole of You. But if all things cannot contain You entirely, do they contain part of You, and all things the same part at once, or does each thing contain a certain part, the greater thing a greater part, the smaller thing one that is smaller? Is then one part of You greater and another smaller, or are You entirely present everywhere, no thing containing You entirely?

[4.4] Who then are You, my God, who, I ask, if not the Lord God? For who is lord if not the Lord, and who is god if not our God?[5] O most high, most good, most powerful, most mighty, most merciful and most just, most mysterious and most present, most beautiful and most strong, steadfast and ungraspable; immutable but all-changing, never new, never old, You Who are all-renewing[6] and Who bring age upon the proud unawares; You Who are ever active, ever at rest, gathering all and needing nothing, supporting and filling and protecting; creating, nourishing, and bringing to perfection, seeking though You lack nothing. You love but without fire, are jealous and calm; You repent and do not grieve, are angry and serene. You change Your works but not Your plan; You recover what You find but have never lost. Never in need, You rejoice in Your gains; never covetous, You exact interest; we give You more than You demand so that You will owe us; but who has anything that is not Yours? You pay debts without owing, and forgive debts without losing. But what have we said, my God, my Life, my holy Sweetness? What can any man say when he speaks of You? Yet woe to those who speak not of You, for though full of words, they are mute.

[5.5] If only I could find rest in You, if only You were to enter my heart and intoxicate it so that I might forget all that is bad in me and embrace the one good, which is You! What are You to me? Have mercy on me so I can speak. What am I to You Who command my love, and, if I do not give it, You are angry with me and threaten me with momentous woes? Is it a slight woe if I do not love You? O Lord my God, in all Your mercy, tell me who You are to me. Tell my soul: "I am your salvation."[7] Tell me so that I can hear. Behold the ears of my heart before You, Lord. Open them and say to my soul, "I am your salvation." I will run after this voice and seize You. Do not hide Your face from me. Let me die so that I do not die, so that I may see it.

[5.6] The house of my soul is too narrow for You to enter; make it wider, O Lord! It is in ruins; repair it! It has what must offend Your eyes; I acknowledge this and know it. But who will cleanse it? To whom besides You should I call out, "Cleanse me, O Lord, from my hidden faults, and spare Your servant from others."[8] I believe, and therefore I speak. Lord, You know. Have not I, my God, declared my transgressions to You to my disfavor, and have You not forgiven the impiety of my heart? I do not contend with You,[9] Who are the truth; I do not want to deceive myself, lest my iniquity be its own lie.[10] Therefore I do not contend with You, for if You would take note of the iniquities, O Lord, O Lord, who could bear it?[11]

[6.7] But let me speak to Your mercy, I, dust and ashes, let me speak, since I speak to Your mercy and not to a man, who would deride me. You too perhaps deride me, but You will turn and have compassion upon me. For what do I wish to say, Lord, except that I do not know from where I came into what I call this dying life, or living death; I do not know. But the consolation of Your mercies uplifted me, as I heard from the father and mother of my flesh, out of whom and in whom You formed me at the appropriate time, for I do not remember it myself. I was embraced by the comforts of human milk, but neither my mother nor my nurses filled their own breasts for me. It was You Who through them gave me the food of my infancy according to Your ordinance and the riches spread throughout the essence of all things. You also granted me to want no more than You gave, and granted that my nurses wanted to give me what You had given them, for they sought to give me by divine ordination what they had received in abundance from You. But the good that came to me from them was also good for them, though it did not come from them but through them; for from You, O God, come all good things, and from my God is my entire salvation.[12] This I learned only later, when, through all the inner and outer things You bestow, You called to me; for then I only knew how to suckle, content in what was pleasurable and crying at what offended my flesh, and nothing more.

[6.8] Later I began to smile—first in sleep, then waking. At least that is what I was told about myself, and I believe it, for this is what we see in infants, though I do not remember it about myself. Gradually I began to perceive where I was, and to want to express my needs to those who could fulfill them; but I could not express them, for the needs were inside me, and the other people outside; nor were they able with any of their senses to enter my soul. So I kicked and shouted; these were the few signs I could make that resembled my wishes, though they did not really resemble them. And when I was not obeyed, either because I was not understood or because what I wanted might harm me, I became indignant with the adults for not submitting to me, indignant with those who were not my slaves for not serving me, and avenged myself by crying. That is how infants are, as I learned from those I have been able to observe; the infants who knew nothing showing me better than my experienced nurses that I too had been like that.

[6.9] My infancy is long dead, yet I am alive. But You, Lord, Who live forever and in Whom nothing dies, You existed before the beginning of the ages, before all that can be called "before," and are God and Lord of all You have created. In You are the constant causes of all inconstant things, and all mutable things have in You their immutable beginnings; in You live the eternal reasons for all things unreasoning and temporal. Tell me, Your suppliant, O God, in pity for Your wretch, tell me, did another period, now dead, precede my infancy? Was it the period I spent in my mother's womb? For about that I have heard some things, and have myself seen pregnant women. But what about before that, my Sweetness, my God, was I anywhere or anyone? No one can tell me, neither father nor mother, nor the experience of others, nor my memory. Do You mock me for asking You this, and command me to praise and confess to You with what I do know?

[6.10] I confess to You, Lord of heaven and earth; I praise You for my beginnings and the infancy I do not remember, for You have granted that man should conjecture about himself from what he sees in others, and believe much about himself that is based on what he has heard from simple women. I existed and had life then too, and at the end of my infancy sought for signs with which I could make known to others what I thought. From where could such a creature come, if not from You, Lord? Can anyone be his own creator? Or is it some vein from elsewhere through which being and life flow into us that comes not from You Who have created us, O Lord in Whom being and life are not two separate things, because the most supreme being and the most supreme life are one? For You are the highest and do not change, nor does in You the present day end, and yet it does come to an end, for all these things are within You. They would have no way to change from one thing to another if You did not set boundaries for them, and since Your years have no end,[13] Your years are all a single today. How many of our days and those of our fathers have passed through Your today and received from it their measure and form of existence, and still others will pass through it and receive their measure and form of existence. But You always remain the same, and You will make into today, have made into today, everything that will be tomorrow and beyond, and everything that was yesterday and before. What is it to me if someone does not understand this? Let him rejoice and ask, "What is this?" Let him rejoice and be glad to find You by not seeking You, rather than seeking You and not finding You.

[7.11] Hear me, O God! Alas for man's sin! A man is saying this, and yet You pity him, for You made him, though You did not make the sin in him. Who reminds me of the sins of my infancy, since no one in the world is without sin before You, not even the infant whose life is a single day upon the earth? Who reminds me? Does not any infant do so in whom I see things about myself that I do not remember? And what had been my sin? Was it that, crying, I grasped for the breast? For if I grasped that way now—not for the breast but for food appropriate to my age—I would be rightly derided and rebuked. What I did in my infancy was worthy of rebuke; but since I was not able to understand the rebuke, neither custom nor reason permitted me to be rebuked. As we grow we cast off such ways, and does anyone ever knowingly cast off things that are good? Or was it good in the period of infancy to cry for things that would be harmful to me? Was it good to be indignant that free people, adults, those who gave birth to me, and many people of experience, would not submit to me at my whim, whom I would strike and try to injure as much as I could for not obeying my commands which it would be harmful to obey? Hence it is merely the feebleness of infant limbs that is innocent, not the infant's mind. I myself have seen and observed a jealous baby: he could not yet speak, but turned pale and glared at the other infant being breastfed along with him. Who has not encountered such things? Mothers and nurses tell us that they respond to these things with all kinds of remedies. Can it in truth be innocence in the infant when the fountain of milk flows freely, even abundantly, and the infant cannot endure sharing it with his brother, even if his brother is in extreme need, his life depending on that very nourishment? We regard these things with indulgence, not because they are slight or insignificant, but because they disappear with age. Though you might accept such behavior in the case of the infant, it proves utterly unacceptable when encountered in those of mature years.[14]

[7.12] You then, Lord my God, Who have given life to the infant and the body, providing it, as we see, with senses, joining its parts, adorning its form, and instilling in it all the impulses of life for its wholeness and safety, You, O Lord, command me to praise You in these things and confess to You and sing Your name, O Most High.[15] For You are God, almighty and good, even if You had done nothing but this that none but You could do, You Who are one, and from Whom every manner of being comes, O most finely formed Who form all things, and by Your law place all things in their order. But it pains me to count as part of my life in this world, O Lord, that period I do not remember, a period I have taken at others' word and have conjectured—a very likely conjecture—from infants that I have observed. It belongs to the darkness of what I have forgotten, such as my life in my mother's womb. But if I was conceived in iniquity, and my mother nurtured me in her womb in sin,[16] then where, I beseech You, my God, where, O Lord, or when, was I, Your servant, innocent? But I will say no more about that time; what use is it when I can recall no trace of it?

[8.13] On my way to the present I passed from infancy to boyhood. Or is it not that boyhood came to me, succeeding infancy? Not that infancy departed, for where would it have gone? Yet suddenly it was no more, for I was no longer an infant who could not talk but had become a boy speaking. This I remember; but how I learned to speak I found out only later. I was not taught to speak by adults presenting me with words in a certain fixed order, as they would do somewhat later with letters. But with the mind that You gave me, my God, I myself learned, through cries and all kinds of sounds and motions of my limbs, to express the feelings of my heart so that my wishes would be fulfilled. But I was not able to express everything I wanted to express to whomever I wanted. I managed to remember whenever adults called a thing something; and when, along with their voice, they moved their bodies toward a certain object, I would see and retain the sounds with which they expressed the object. Moreover, what they wanted to express was clear from their gestures, which are the natural language of all races and are expressed in the face, the eyes, and movements of the limbs, and tones of voice that indicate the state of a person's mind as it strives toward, takes hold of, rejects, or shuns a thing. In this way, by repeatedly hearing words as they were positioned in various sentences, I gradually connected them with the things they signified, and so trained my mouth to express my desires through these signs. In this way I communicated the signs of my desires to the people I was among, and so entered into the tempests of society; yet I was still dependent on the authority of my parents and the will of the adults around me.

[9.14] O God, my God, what miseries I now experienced, what follies, when as a boy it was put before me that the only way of living right was to obey those who were instructing me to excel in this world by using the skill of language to secure worldly honors and spurious wealth. I was sent to school to learn to read and write, the uses of which, poor wretch that I was, I did not know, and whenever I lagged in my studies I was beaten. This was extolled by adults, many previous generations having laid out the difficult path we were made to tread, increasing the toil and suffering of the sons of Adam. But, Lord, we also came upon men who prayed to You, and from them we learned, as far as we were able, to imagine You as some great being who, though we could not see You, would hear and help us. Thus I began as a boy to pray to You, my aid and refuge, and invoking You unraveled the knots of my tongue, a small boy but with great love, praying to You that I not be beaten in school. And when You did not hear me—which saved me from the folly of praying to You for trifles—the adults, including my parents, laughed, though not unkindly, at the beatings I received, which at the time were a great and heavy sorrow to me.

[9.15] Is there anyone, O Lord, any mind so great, so close to You in powerful love? Is there anyone, I ask, so close to You in piety and magnanimous love that he will think lightly (and not because his wits are dull) of the racks and hooks and other torments that men in this world pray to You with such dread to escape, but who mock the torments they so bitterly fear, just as our parents mocked the torments our tutors inflicted on us as boys? For we did not fear our torments less, nor did we pray less to You to escape them. But still we transgressed, for we wrote, read, and studied less than was demanded of us. Not that we lacked the ability or memory, O Lord, which You willed us to have in ample measure for our age. But we delighted in amusements, for which we were punished by those who also delighted in amusements—yet the amusements of adults are called "business," while those of children are punished by the adults, and no one pities either the children or the adults. Perhaps some fine arbiter might approve of my having been beaten because my playing with a ball hindered the pace of the learning that I was to use as an adult to play reprehensible games. Was he who flogged me any better? If a fellow tutor should trump him on some trifling matter, was he any the less angry or jealous than I was when a play-mate beat me at ball?

[10.16] And yet I was sinning, Lord God, Creator and Orderer of all things in nature, though when it comes to sins You only put them in order but do not create them. I was sinning, Lord my God, by going against the rules set by my parents and tutors, but later I was able to put my knowledge to good use, regardless of their motives in mak-ing me acquire it. I was disobedient not because I chose something better, but out of love for play, loving the pride of victory in con-tests and having my ears tickled with false myths that made them burn even more ardently. The same curiosity drew me increasingly to the grand spectacles and games of adults.[17] Those who sponsor these spectacles are held in such high esteem that almost everyone wishes the same for their children; yet they willingly allow their children to be flogged if those same spectacles keep them from the studies that the parents hope will one day enable their children to sponsor such spectacles themselves. O Lord, look with mercy on these things and deliver us who are appealing to You, as well as those who have not yet appealed to You, that they turn to You and You will deliver them.

[11.17] As a boy I had already heard of an eternal life promised us through the humility of the Lord our God Who stooped to our pride, and when barely out of my mother's womb I was marked with the sign of the cross and blessed with salt,[18] for she put great trust in You. You saw, O Lord, how when I was still a boy a pain in my stomach had me burning with fever and close to death. You saw, my Lord and God, for You were already my keeper, with what fervor and faith I begged for the baptism of Your Christ, how I begged for it, appealing to my mother's piety and that of Your Church, the mother of us all. The mother of my flesh was distraught, laboring in the birth of my eternal salvation even more lovingly, her heart pure in Your faith. Had I not soon recovered, she would have hastened to arrange for my initiation and washing in the sacraments of salvation so that I could confess to You, Lord Jesus, for the forgiveness of my sins. My cleansing was postponed, as if it were inevitable that should I live I would pollute myself, for it was thought that if I were to sin after the holy washing, the pollution would be greater and more perilous. So I was already a believer, along with my mother and the whole household. But my father, though he did not believe, did not contest my right to follow my mother's devotion, and did not forbid me to believe in Christ because he himself was not yet a believer. For my mother strove that You, my God, should be my father rather than him, and in this You helped her prevail over her husband, to whom, though his better, she was subjected, and so was also subjected to You and Your command.[19]

[11.18] I beg You, my God, I want to know, if You will it, why my baptism was delayed, and if it was for my good that the reins of sin, so to speak, were loosened? Or were they not loosened? How is it that one still hears everywhere, "Let him be, let him do what he wants; he is not yet baptized?" And yet when it comes to the well-being of a body we never say, "Let him be wounded more, for he is not yet healed." How much better it would have been for me had I been quickly healed, and then through my family's and my own striving gained the salvation of my soul that would then have been safe under the protection You would have granted it. It would truly have been better. But my parents foresaw the threat of so many great waves of temptation after my boyhood; my mother knew what these temptations were, and preferred to expose to them the mere clay from which I would be formed rather than expose to them the final image.[20]

[12.19] Yet even in childhood, when my family feared less for me than in my youth, I did not like to study, and hated being forced to do so. But I was forced, and it was good for me. Not that it was I who was doing good, because I would not have studied had I not been compelled to. No one does good when he does it against his will, even if he is doing a good thing—yet neither were they who were forcing me doing good. What was good came to me from You, my God, for they did not consider how I should later use what they forced me to learn other than to satiate the insatiable desires of an impoverished wealth and an ignominious glory. But You, Who number the hairs of our head,[21] used for my good the error of all those who urged me to learn; and You used my own error in not wanting to learn to punish me, a punishment I deserved, so small a boy and yet so great a sinner. You did me good through those who did not do good, and for my own sin You exacted a just retribution: for You have commanded, and it is so, that every disordered soul will be its own punishment.

[13.20] I have still not managed to fathom the reasons why I hated Greek, which I studied as a boy. Yet Latin I truly loved; not what my first masters taught me, but what I later learned from the men we call grammarians. For I considered my first lessons of reading, writing, and arithmetic as great a burden and punishment as any Greek lesson. And yet, as I was flesh, a passing breath that does not return,[22] did this not come from the sin and vanity of life? The first lessons were in fact better than the later ones, because they were more sound. Through them I acquired, and still retain, the ability to read whatever I find written and to write whatever I want; whereas in my later lessons I was forced to retain the strayings of an Aeneas I did not know, forgetting my own, and to weep over a dead Dido who killed herself for love; while I, without a tear, was prepared to pitiably die away from You through such works, my God, my life.

[13.21] What is more pitiable than a pitiful being who does not pity himself but weeps at the death of Dido for love of Aeneas; a pitiful being who does not weep over the death he is suffering because he does not love You, O God, light of my heart, bread of the mouth deep within my soul, vigor that impregnates my mind and the vessel of my thoughts. I did not love You, and fornicated against You, and as I did so I heard from all around cries of "Well done! Well done!" for the friendship of this world is fornication against You; and "Well done! Well done!" is what they shout in order to shame a man who is not like them. For all this I did not weep, but wept for Dido, "who with a dagger did the lowest ends pursue,"[23] just as I, having forsaken You, pursued the lowest of Your creations, dust turning to dust.[24] Had I been forbidden to read these works, I would have suffered at not being able to read what made me suffer. And such foolishness is considered a higher and better education than that by which I learned to read and write.

[13.22] But now may my God call out in my soul, Your Truth proclaiming to me, "This is wrong, this is wrong! Your first lessons were better by far!" For I would readily forget the strayings of Aeneas rather than forget how to read and write. The doors of the grammarians' schools are indeed hung with precious curtains, but this is not so much a sign of high distinction as a cloak for their errors. Let not those whom I no longer fear cry out against me while I confess to You what my soul seeks, finding peace in condemning my evil ways and loving Your good ways. Let not the sellers and buyers of high learning cry out against me. If I ask them whether it is true that Aeneas once came to Carthage, as the poet says, the less learned will reply that they do not know, while the more learned will say that he never did. But if I ask with what letters the name "Aeneas" is written, everyone who has learned this will answer me correctly, according to the agreement and decision that men have reached concerning these signs. Likewise, if I should ask which was the greater inconvenience, forgetting how to read and write or forgetting those poetic fictions, who would not know what answer someone in possession of his senses would give. Thus as a boy I sinned, preferring empty learning to learning that was more useful, going so far as to love the former and hate the latter. "One plus one is two, two plus two is four" was a hateful incantation, while the sweetest dream of my vanity was the wooden horse filled with armed men, the burning of Troy, and even the ghost of Creusa.[25]

[14.23] So why did I hate Greek literature, which also sings of such feats? Homer too is skilled at weaving such tales, delusive in the sweetest way, and yet when I was a boy he was bitter to my taste, as I suppose Virgil might be to Greek boys forced to study him as I was forced to study Homer. Clearly it was the difficulty of learning a foreign tongue that sprinkled as if with gall the sweetness of the Greek heroic tales. I did not know a word of Greek, and to make me learn, my tutors goaded me with fierce threats and punishments. As an infant I had not known a word of Latin either, but I learned it from cooing nurses and their jesting and laughing and happy games; I learned it by paying attention, without torment or dread. I learned Latin without the threat of punishment, for my heart goaded me to bring its concepts to life, something I could not have done had I not already learned a few words—not from tutors, but from those who talked to me, and in whose ears I also strove to bring forth what I thought and felt. This clearly proves that free curiosity has a greater power to make one learn than severe enforcement. And yet enforcement curbs the unbridled wandering of that curiosity by way of Your laws, O God, Your laws from the tutor's cane to the martyr's trial, Your laws that mix for us a wholesome but bitter potion, calling us back to You from the pestilent delight that has drawn us away from You.

[15.24] Lord, hear my prayer: that my soul not falter under Your discipline, nor that I falter in avowing before You the mercies through which You have rescued me from my most evil ways; I pray that You become sweet to me beyond all the seductions I pursued, that I may love You most fervently and clasp Your hand with all my heart, and that You will rescue me from all temptation, even to the end. O Lord, my King and God, may whatever I learned that was useful in my childhood serve You: my speaking, writing, reading, and counting. For when I was learning all that was worthless You gave me Your discipline and forgave my sin of delighting in those vain things. These things did give me many useful words, though they can also be learned in things that are not worthless, the safe path along which children should walk.

[16.25] But woe to you, torrent of human custom! Who can resist you? When will you run dry? How long will you drag the sons of Eve down to that vast and dreadful sea which even those who cling to wood can barely cross?[26] Did I not read in you of Jupiter the thunderer and adulterer—he surely could not have been both, but was presented as such so that a fictitious thunder might mimic and pander to real adultery. For who among our robed orators will lend a sober ear to a colleague from his own forum crying out: "These are Homer's inventions, transferring human qualities to the gods; how much better if Homer had transferred divine qualities to us!" It would have been truer to say that these are indeed Homer's inventions, but that he is attributing a divine nature to dissolute men so that their shameful acts will no longer be shameful, and that those who commit them are seen to be imitating not fallen men but celestial gods.

[16.26] And yet, O infernal torrent, it is into you that the sons of men are cast along with the fees for their studies, in order for them to learn all that is worthless; and it is given great importance when publicly, in the forum, within sight of the inscriptions of the laws decreeing the tutors' salaries from public funds, the pupils' extra fees to their tutors are decreed.[27] Infernal torrent, you lash at your rocks and roar: "This is why words are learned, this is why eloquence is acquired, the eloquence so vital to inducing others to do one's will and implement one's purpose." It is as if we would not have known expressions such as "shower of gold," "lap," "deceiving," "temples of heaven," had not Terence in his play brought a lewd young man onto the stage who takes Jupiter as his model for debauchery as he gazes at a mural "that shows the god sending forth, as in the legend, a shower of gold into Danae's lap," and so deceiving the woman.[28] And look how the young man is incited to wanton lust through celestial guidance: "Such a great god!" he says. "He rocks the temples of heaven with his thunder! And I, little man that I am, should not do as he did? I did so, and with pleasure." Words are certainly not learned more easily with the help of such vileness, but through such words vileness is committed with greater confidence. I do not reproach the words, for they are precious and exquisite chalices, but I reproach the wine of error that was offered us in these chalices by drunken tutors; and if we did not drink this wine of error we were beaten, and had no sober judge to whom we could appeal. And yet, my God, before Whom I now recall this without fear, I learned all this readily, and, wretch that I was, delighted in what I was learning, and was called a boy of great promise.

[17.27] Permit me, my God, also to say something about my innate talent, Your gift, and the foolishness on which I squandered it. I was set a task that greatly worried me because of the prospect of praise or shame, and the dread of being beaten: the task was to speak the words of Juno as she raged and grieved, unable as she was to "keep the Prince of Troy from seeking the shores of Italy,"[29] even though I knew she had never spoken such words. But we were forced to go astray in the footsteps of those poetic creations, and to say in plain speech what Virgil had said in verse. The declaimer who was most praised was the one who best brought forth, shrouded in the most fitting words, the grandeur of the feigned characters in their passion of rage and grief. What is it to me, my God and true life, that my declamation was applauded over that of so many of the pupils of my age and in my class? Is all this not smoke and wind? Was there nothing else on which to exercise my talent and my tongue? Your praises, Lord, Your praises through Your Scriptures, would have trellised the young vines of my heart, and foolish nonsense would not have snatched at it, vile prey for winged scavengers. There is more than one way for man to pay homage to fallen angels.[30]

[18.28] Was it a wonder that I lost myself in vain trifles, moving away from You, when I was given men to imitate who would have been mortified if, while describing their deeds, albeit good deeds, they were caught using a barbarism or a solecism, while if they spoke with pure grammar and ornate style of something licentious they had done, they were applauded and proud? You see these things, O Lord, but remain silent, patient, and abundant in mercy and truth. Will you remain silent forever? Even now you pluck from colossal depths the soul that seeks You, the soul that thirsts for Your delights, whose heart says to You, "I have sought Your countenance, and Your countenance, Lord, I shall seek."[31] Far from Your countenance I am steeped in dark passions. One does not leave You or return to You through walking or movement. Nor did the prodigal son seek horses or chariots, or ships, or fly on visible wings, or use his legs so that in a distant land he would dissipate in lavish living all that You gave him at his departure, a gentle Father when You gave, and gentler still when he came back in need. To be far from Your countenance is to be steeped in lustful and dark passions.

[18.29] Lord God, look with patience, as You always do; see how carefully the sons of men observe the rules of letters and syllables received from those who spoke the language before them, and yet neglect the eternal rules of everlasting salvation received from You. If he who learns or teaches the old rules of sound were to pronounce, contrary to grammatical precepts, the word *homo*, man, without an aspiration of the first syllable, he would offend men more than if, contrary to Your precepts, he were to hate a man despite being a man himself; as if an enemy could be more pernicious than the hatred that has flared up within him, or as if he could wound the man he is pursuing more deeply than he wounds his own heart through his own enmity. Certainly, no knowledge of letters can be as deep-rooted as the conscience inscribed in us that we should not do to others what we would not wish to suffer ourselves.[32] How mysterious You are, dwelling in silence on high, O God, Who alone are great, and by an unflagging law strew blindness as punishment for forbidden desires. A man seeking the fame of eloquence will rise before a human judge surrounded by a human multitude and inveigh against his enemy with prodigious hatred, all the while taking the utmost care that his tongue will not slip and say "humanness" instead of "humanity," and yet not caring if his raging spirit were to remove the man forever from among his fellow humans.

[19.30] It was on the steps of such a school of morals that I was abandoned, a wretched boy, in an arena in which the rules of the game led me to fear more a barbarous slip of the tongue than, having committed one, fearing the sin of hating those who had not. I say this and confess to You, my God, that I was praised by those who in those days I had thought it a virtue to please. I did not see the chasm of infamy into which I was cast far from Your eyes. What was more loathsome before Your eyes than I, who was deceiving my tutor, my masters, and my parents with innumerable lies out of love of play and a zeal to see worthless spectacles, eager to imitate what I saw there? I also committed theft, stealing from my parents' cellar and table, partly from gluttony but also so that I would have something to give the other children to bribe them to play with me, though they enjoyed playing as much as I did. Even in these games I strove to win by cheating, overcome by the vanity of desiring to be superior. And yet there was nothing I hated more, nothing I rebuked so fiercely as catching others doing what I did. And if I myself was caught cheating, I preferred to quarrel bitterly rather than yield. Is that the innocence of childhood? No, Lord, it is not. Am I not right, my God? For this same deceit that begins with tutors and masters, marbles, balls, and sparrows progresses with advancing years to prefects and kings, gold, estates, and slaves, just as the cane is succeeded by more severe punishments. It is the humility of which the small size of children is an emblem that You, our King, commended when you said, "Of such is the Kingdom of heaven."[33]

[20.31] And yet to You, O Lord, most supreme and good creator and governor of the universe, to You our God I give thanks, even if I had not lived beyond boyhood. For even in those years I existed and lived, and strived for my preservation, a sign of the most mysterious unity that had created me. Through my inner senses I guarded the wellbeing of my outer senses, and in trifling thoughts and matters I already rejoiced in the truth. I did not want to be deceived, I had a good memory, was schooled in speech, and warmed by friendship; I shunned sorrow, dejection, and ignorance. Was not such a creature worthy of admiration and praise? But all these qualities were gifts from my God—it was not I who gave them to myself. These gifts were good, and all of them were part of me. So He Who created me is good, and He is my good, and before Him I exult[34] in all the good that was already in me as a boy. For I sinned in that it was not in God I sought delights, pure thoughts, and truth, but in his creatures—myself and others—and was immersed in pain, confusion, and error. I thank You, my God, my Sweetness, my Honor, my Trust, I thank You for Your gifts; keep them safe for me, and thus keep me safe. What You have given me will expand and grow, and I shall be with You, for Your gift to me is that I exist.

꒰ꗃ꒱

NOTES

1 Psalm 47:2 (Vulgate), 48:1 (other translations); Psalm 146:5 (Vulgate), 147:5 (other translations).

2 2 Corinthians 4:10.

3 James 4:6; 1 Peter 5:5.

4 It is unclear which preacher Augustine is referring to: Christ, Saint Ambrose, or perhaps Saint Paul.

5 Psalm 17:32 (Vulgate), 18:31 (other translations). "For who is God but the Lord? or who is God but our God?" (Douay-Rheims Bible)

6 Wisdom 7:27.

7 A quotation from Psalm 34:3 (Vulgate), 35:3 (other translations).

8 Psalm 18:13–4 (Vulgate), 19:13–4 (other translations).

9 Jeremiah 2:29.

10 Psalm 26:12 (Vulgate), 27:12 (other translations).

11 A quotation from Psalm 129:3 (Vulgate), 130:3 (other translations).

12 Psalm 34:3 (Vulgate), 35:3 (other translations).

13 Psalm 101:28 (Vulgate), 102:27 (other translations).

14 The *Confessions* having been written as Augustine's private communication with God, this is one of the few moments in which Augustine directly addresses a mortal readership.

15 Psalm 91:2 (Vulgate), 92:2 (other translations).

16 Psalm 50:7 (Vulgate), 51:5 (other translations).

17 Such as theatrical performances, races, and fights, which wealthy individuals subventioned in order to secure civic honors.

18 Blessing with salt was one of the initiation rites of a catechumen, an individual who was being prepared for Christianity but who had not yet been baptized.

19 Augustine's father, Patricius, was baptized on his deathbed (see Book IX, 22). Augustine's mother, though bound by duty and convention to be

subservient to her husband, prevailed—with God's help, as Augustine stresses—over her husband in matters of Christianity and Augustine's religious upbringing.

20 Figuratively, the "mere clay" is Augustine in an unformed state before his baptism, the "final image" being Augustine as a Christian man. Augustine's mother felt that as a young man he was bound to give in to sinful temptations, which might prove less dangerous to his soul if he was not yet baptized.

21 Matthew 10:30.

22 Psalm 77:39 (Vulgate), 78:39 (other translations).

23 Virgil, *Aeneid* 6.456–57.

24 Genesis 3:19.

25 The wife of Aeneas and daughter of King Priam of Troy. In Virgil's *Aeneid*, Creusa attempts to flee burning Troy with Aeneas but is separated from him; Aeneas returns to Troy to look for her but finds only her ghost.

26 Wisdom 14:5. *Lignum*, a piece of wood, can help one float on the sea, but Augustine also uses it here to refer to the wood of the cross.

27 The texts of the laws on salaries were inscribed in the Forum. A fixed annual salary for tutors had been introduced, the idea being that this would cover their living expenses (*salarium*, "money for salt"). Pupils were to supplement this salary by paying tuition, which led to corruption.

28 Augustine first quotes single words from Terence's comedy *The Eunuch* (from lines 583–90), in which young Chaerea justifies his rape of Pamphilia by claiming that he is following Jupiter's example, and then, almost verbatim, Augustine quotes line 585 of the play.

29 Augustine is quoting a line from Virgil that is slightly altered (*Aeneid* 1.38).

30 In *The City of God* (2.24), Augustine equated fallen angels with Classical Greek and Roman deities. The implication is that one of the ways in which Augustine had been led to pay homage to these demons is his having been forced as a young man to study Classical works that glorified these deities.

31 Psalm 26:8 (Vulgate), 27:8 (other translations).

32 Matthew 7:12.

33 Matthew 19:14.

34 Psalm 2:11.

BOOK II

[1.1] I recall my past impurity and the carnal corruptions suffered by my soul, not because I love them but so that I may love You, my God. It is out of love for Your love that in the bitterness of my memory I seek to recall the most terrible things I did, so that Your sweetness will flow into me, O God, O Sweet One Who never fails, Sweet One serene and untroubled, Who gathered up the pieces into which I had been scattered when I turned away from You, the One, only to waste myself among the many. For in my youth I burned fervently to satisfy my hellish desires, wallowing in sensual and shadowy loves, my beauty wasting away; before Your eyes I was putrid, while I sought pleasure for myself and to please the eyes of others.

[2.2] What was it that I delighted in, if not loving and being loved? But there was no path from soul to soul, no luminous links of friendship; it was only vapors rising from the slimy lusts of the flesh and the gushings of puberty that beclouded my heart, so that I was not able to discern the bright serenity of love from the hazy mists of lust. Both love and lust raged in turmoil within me, dragging me in my weak youth into the chasms of sin, plunging me into the raging abyss of disgrace. Your wrath was growing, though I did not know it. The clanking chains of my mortal flesh had rendered me deaf, punishing me for the pride of my soul, and I strayed ever further from You, and You let me. I was hurled and scattered in all directions, dissipating myself in my fornications, while You, O my belated joy, were silent! You were silent then, and in proud degradation and restless despondence I strayed ever further from You, the seed of my sorrow ever more sterile.

[2.3] Who would have set my disarray in order, putting to use the fleeting beauty of Your lowliest creations? Who would have set limits to their charms, so that if the surging tides of my youth could not have been calmed, they might at least spill onto the shores of matrimony, content with the aim of procreation as Your law prescribes, O Lord, You Who in this way form the progeny of our death, Your mild hand softening the thorns excluded from Your paradise?[1] For Your omnipotence is not far from us even when we are far from You. I ought to have paid more heed to the voice resounding from Your clouds: "The flesh of the married will be troubled, but you I will spare."[2] And: "It is good for a man not to touch a woman."[3] And: "He who is without a wife reflects on the things of the Lord, how he may please the Lord; but he who is bound in marriage thinks of the things of this world, how he may please his wife."[4] I should have listened to these words more carefully and, castrated for the sake of the kingdom of heaven,[5] should have awaited in bliss your embraces.

[2.4] But inside me, poor wretch, everything was surging, following the rush of my own tide, forsaking You, transgressing all Your laws, though not escaping Your scourges—what mortal can?—for You were always present, stern in Your mercy, pouring extreme bitterness on my illicit delights so that I would seek delights that were innocent. Wherever I would have succeeded I would have found nothing but You, O Lord, nothing but You, Who teach us through pain[6] and strike us so we will heal, and slay us so we do not die away from You.[7] Where was I, how far was I exiled from the delights of Your House, in that sixteenth year of the age of my flesh? The madness of lust raised its scepter over me and I had relinquished myself to it entirely, condoned as it was by the turpitude of man, yet forbidden by Your laws. Meanwhile, my family did not seek through marriage to keep me from plunging into the abyss; their only concern was that I should learn to excel in discourse and be persuasive as an orator.

[3.5] But that year my studies were interrupted. I was brought back from Madaura, a nearby town where I had been sent in order to learn letters and oratory, so that funds could be gathered for a longer course of study in Carthage; more an impetuous idea of my father's rather than one based on his limited means, as he was only a modest citizen of Thagaste. But to whom am I telling this? Not to You, my God, but before You I declare this to my own kind, to mankind, even if only a small part of mankind will come upon these writings. And why? So that I and whoever reads these words will give thought to the depths out of which we must call out to You.[8] For what is closer to Your ear than a confessing heart and a life of faith? Everyone praised my father, who, despite his limited means, strove to provide his son with all that was necessary for a long course of study far away. Many fellow citizens of his who were far wealthier than he did not do as much for their children; yet this same father was not concerned about the way in which I was maturing before You or how chaste I was, as long as I was cultivated, even if that meant not being cultivated by You, my God, Who are the only true and good Lord of my heart, Your field.

[3.6] That year, when I was sixteen, our lack of means forced me to break off my studies for a while and live at home with my parents, in such idleness that the brambles of lust rose above my head with no hand in sight to rip them out by the roots. In fact, it was quite the opposite; when at the baths my father caught sight of my maturing, aroused adolescence, he told my mother, rejoicing as if the sight were reason enough to hope for grandchildren, rejoicing in the drunkenness in which the world forgets You, its creator, and instead loves Your creation;[9] the drunkenness of the invisible wine of a perverse inclination to what is most base. But in my mother's breast You had already laid the foundation of Your temple and the cornerstone of Your holy abode, while my father was still just a catechumen, which he had only recently become. Though I was not yet baptized, my mother shook in pious fear, dreading the tangled paths along which those walk who turn their backs to You, not their faces.[10]

[3.7] O my Lord and God, do I dare to say that You remained silent while I strayed further from You? But were You really silent? Whose words, if not Yours, were the words that through my mother, Your faithful servant, You let ring in my ears? Yet none of those words sank into my heart; I paid them no heed. For my mother begged me, and I remember her taking me aside and with great solicitude, warning me not to commit fornication, and especially never to defile another man's wife. To me these seemed womanish warnings that I would have blushed to heed, but they were Your warnings, though I did not know it, thinking that You were silent and that it was my mother speaking, though it was You Who were speaking through her. You were not silent, and yet through my mother I scorned You, I, her son, the son of Your handmaid, Your servant.[11] But I did not know and threw myself headlong into sin, with such blindness that I would have been ashamed had my actions been any less shameful than those of my companions, hearing them boast of their lustful deeds. And the greater their sins, the more they vaunted them, while I relished not only the pleasure of my lustful deeds but the praise I received for them. What is worthy of reproach if not depravity? But so I would not be reproached I made myself more depraved, and whenever I could not match my companions in sin I pretended I had done things that I had not, so that I would not appear to be too contemptible by being too innocent, or too vile for being too chaste.

[3.8] Such were the companions with whom I roamed the streets of Babylon, wallowing in its filth as if it were a bed of cinnamon and precious perfumes. And so that I would be tied even more tightly to Babylon's navel, the invisible fiend trampled and seduced me, seducible as I was. Even my mother, though she had hastened to flee the midst of Babylon,[12] was still lingering on its outskirts: for although she urged me to be chaste, she did not consider what my father had told her about me to be noxious or dangerous enough for my future to see to it that marriage would quell my lust, if my lust could not otherwise be cut to the quick. She did not consider arranging a marriage for me, for she feared that a wife might prove an impediment to their hopes for me—not the hopes she had set in You and in the world to come, but their hopes of my studying, to which both of my parents fervently aspired: my father barely thinking of You, and thinking of me only out of vanity; my mother believing that a customary course of study would not be a detriment to me but might even open up a path for me to reach You. This at least is what I surmise, as I recall, to the extent I can, the attitudes of my parents. In the meantime the reins had been slackened, and unchecked by even a minimum of strictness I indulged myself in dissolute acts of every kind, a dark mist cutting me off from me the brightness of Your Truth, O my God, iniquity bursting out as if from my entrails.[13]

[4.9] Your law punishes theft, O Lord,[14] as does the law written in the hearts of men that even wickedness cannot erase, for what thief will gladly bear another thief robbing him, even if he is rich and the one robbing him is in need? But I wanted to steal and I did, driven not by any need, but by a lack of regard for justice and an abundance of wickedness. For I stole something of which I had plenty and far better; nor did I seek to enjoy what I had stolen, only the theft and the sin itself. Near our vineyard was a pear tree heavy with fruit that did not tempt with either color or taste. Late one night, I and some wicked youths, still seeking fun in our usual haunts, as was our foul habit, set about to shake the pears off the tree and carry them away, taking with us a huge load, not to eat, but to throw to the pigs. If we ate a few of the pears, it was only to relish the wrongness of what we had done. Such was my heart, O God, such was my heart, which You took pity on in the profoundest depths of the abyss. Let my heart tell You now what it sought there, being wicked for no reason and having no cause to do ill except wickedness itself. It was detestable, but I delighted in it. I delighted in my undoing, I delighted in my eclipse, not that for which I was eclipsed but the eclipse itself, a depraved soul falling from Your firmament to its destruction, not seeking anything through my shamefulness but shame itself.

[5.10] Just as beauty can be seen in lovely objects, in gold and silver and such things, and just as the harmony of objects is vital to our sense of touch, each of our other senses have their own response. Transient honor too, such as the powers of ruling and command, has its splendor, which also gives rise to man's urge to claim his rights. And yet in our quest for these things we must not depart from You, O Lord, nor deviate from Your law. The life we live in this world also has its appeal through a certain beauty of its own and a harmony with all the beautiful things here below, as does friendship, tied with its sweet and precious knot that unites many souls. Yet all of this can lead to sin when through an unrestrained urge for good things that are the lowest things of Your creation, forsaking things that are better and higher, forsaking You, our Lord God, Your Truth, and Your Law. For the lower things have their delights, but not like my God, Who made all things, and in Whom those who are righteous delight, and Who is the joy of those upright in heart.[15]

[5.11] When we ask why a crime was committed, we tend not to believe the answer unless there seems to have been a desire to obtain—or a fear of losing—some of the things I have called a lower good. This lower good is beautiful and appealing, though when compared with higher and blessed good, it is base and vile. A man has committed a murder; why did he do it? Perhaps he loved the murdered man's wife, or his property, or he robbed the man to secure his livelihood, or feared that he might be robbed of his livelihood by the man he murdered; or, wronged, he burned to be avenged. Would anyone commit murder for no reason, simply delighting in murder? Who would believe such a thing? Yet it has been said of a certain crazed man of boundless cruelty that he was cruel and evil without cause, though a reason was also cited: lest through idleness his hand or heart should wilt.[16] And yet we should ask, why was this man so cruel? It was so that through his acts of crime he might seize Rome and attain honors, power, and wealth, and free himself from fear of the laws, the dangers of poverty, and the offenses he had committed. Hence not even this man, Catiline, loved his deeds, but loved something else for the sake of which he did them.

[6.12] Wretch that I was, what did I love in you, my theft, O deed committed in that night of my sixteenth year? It is not that you were beautiful, for you were a theft. Are you even a thing, that I can speak to you? Beautiful were the fruits we stole, for they were Your creation, O Most Beautiful of all, Creator of all, O God that is good, God the highest Good and my true Good. Beautiful were those fruits, but it was not them that my wretched soul desired, for I had plenty better, and the ones I plucked I plucked only so that I might steal. No sooner had I plucked them than I threw them away, my sin being the only feast I rejoiced in. And the few bites of fruit that did enter my mouth were seasoned with sin. And now, O Lord my God, I ask You what it was in that theft that delighted me. It had no beauty: I do not mean beauty as in the beauty of justice or judiciousness, nor such beauty as is in the mind of man, in the memory, the senses, or blossoming life; nor as the stars are beautiful and splendid in the sky, nor as the earth and sea are filled with new life, through birth replacing what has died; not even the false beauty lurking in shadows that belongs to vice.

[6.13] This too is the way that pride imitates lofty elegance, whereas You alone are God, exalted above all. What does vanity seek but honors and glory? Whereas You alone are to be honored and glorious in eternity. The cruelty of powerful men aims to be feared, but who is to be feared other than the one and only God? What can be seized or robbed of his power—when, where, how, or by whom? Tender caresses aim to spark love, yet nothing is more tender than Your love, nor is anything loved with more wholesomeness than Your Truth, beautiful and bright above all. Curiosity poses as a desire for knowledge, whereas You Who are above all know all. Ignorance and foolishness hide behind the names of simplicity and innocence, but there is no greater simplicity than You, no greater innocence, for sinners are harmed by their own deeds. Idleness poses as a desire for calm, but what calm is there other than the Lord? Extravagance strives to be called abundance and plenty, but You are plenitude and the unfailing plenteousness of imperishable delight. Prodigality seeks to array itself in the glow of generosity, but it is You Who are the supremely abundant giver of all good. Greed seeks to possess much, but You possess all. Jealousy strives for excellence, but what is more excellent than You? Anger seeks revenge, but who avenges with greater justice than You? Fear recoils from things that are unaccustomed and unexpected, things that endanger what is beloved, and fear takes precautions for the safety of what it loves. But to You what is unaccustomed? What is unexpected? Who can take from You what You love? Where other than with You is enduring safety? Sadness pines for things lost in which cupidity delighted, insisting that nothing be taken from it, just as nothing can be taken from You.

[6.14] Thus the soul that turns away from You fornicates, seeking outside You that which is clear and pure, but which it can only find when it returns to You. All those have erred who seek to imitate You perversely, having distanced themselves from You and extolling themselves in pride against You. But even by seeking to imitate You they admit that You are the creator of the entire universe and that it is not possible for them to distance themselves from You entirely. What then did I love in that theft, and how did I, albeit perversely and in error, imitate my Lord? Did I delight in breaking Your law at least furtively, as I lacked power, like a slave who steals with impunity, attaining a shadowy semblance of omnipotence? Behold the servant fleeing his Lord and seeking a shadow! O putridness! O monstrous life and chasm of death! Was I drawn to what was forbidden just because it was forbidden?

[7.15] What shall I render to the Lord[17] that as my memory recalls these things they do not frighten my soul? I will love You, Lord, and give You thanks and praise Your name[18] because You have forgiven me my evil and nefarious deeds. It is to Your grace and mercy that I attribute Your melting my sins away like ice.[19] To Your grace also I attribute whatever evils I did not do; for what might I not have done, I who loved an evil deed that I did for no reason? Yet everything has, I avow, been forgiven me: both the evils I committed of my own free will and the evils that, with Your guidance, I did not commit. What man pondering his weaknesses would dare ascribe his purity and innocence to his own strength so that he should love You less, as if he were less in need of the mercy with which You forgive the sins of those who have turned to You? For whoever is called by You and follows Your voice, and avoids the things he reads me recalling and confessing here, should not scorn me who was sick but who was cured by that physician through whose ministrations I was no longer sick, or, rather, less sick. He should therefore love You as much, or even more, since he must see that the one who saved me from the great ravages of sin is also the one who has saved him from those ravages.

[8.16] What reward did I, wretch that I was, gain from those things at remembering which I can now only blush with shame?[20] Particularly that theft in which I loved only the theft and nothing else, the theft itself so trifling, and I therefore the greater wretch for loving it. But I would not have committed it alone—I remember my state of mind at the time—I would certainly not have committed it alone. In that theft I also loved the company of those with whom I committed it. So could I have loved nothing but the theft? Yes, I did love nothing, for that company itself was nothing. What was this really? Who can tell me except He Who illumines my heart, shedding light on its shadows? What drives my mind to question, examine, and seek? For had I loved the fruits I stole and wanted to enjoy them, I could have done it alone had committing the evil deed been sufficient to attain my pleasure, nor would I have needed accomplices to rouse the heat of my cravings. But as my pleasure was not in those pears, it was in the evil deed itself, done in the company of a sinful group.

[9.17] What was my state of mind? What is certain is that it was quite despicable and a woe to me. Who can understand sin?[21] Yet what was this state of mind? It was a matter of mockery, as if our hearts were titillated that we could trick those who would never believe us capable of such deeds and would have been horrified. Why then was I so delighted but still would not do the deed alone? Because nobody easily mocks alone? Indeed, no one does. And yet men are sometimes gripped by laughter when they are alone, when no one else is present, if they perceive something ridiculous. But I would most definitely not have done this alone. Here, my God, before Your eyes, is the vivid recollection of the state of mind I was in; alone, I would not have committed the theft in which I did not like what I stole, but that I stole. Committing the theft alone would not have appealed to me, nor would I have done it. O fiendish friendship! Unfathomable seducer of the mind! O desire to do evil for sport and jest, thirsting to harm what belongs to another without seeking any gain for myself or desiring revenge. One hears one's companions calling: "Let us go! Let us do it!" and is ashamed not to be shameless.

[10.18] Who can unravel this twisted and tangled knot? It is detestable; I do not wish to dwell on it, I do not want to think further about it. What I want is You, O Clemency and Innocence of unsating satiety, so beautiful and glorious to honest eyes. With You is utter peacefulness and imperturbable life. Whoever enters into You enters into the joy of his Lord[22] and shall have no fear, and will find himself exalted. In my youth I drifted away from You and erred, my God, straying far from Your steadfastness, becoming to myself a desert of dire want.

∞

NOTES

1   Genesis 3:17–18.

2   A quotation from 1 Corinthians 7:28.

3   A quotation from 1 Corinthians 7:1.

4   1 Corinthians 7:32–33.

5   Matthew 19:12. "There are eunuchs who have made themselves eunuchs for the kingdom of heaven's sake." (New King James Bible)

6   Psalm 93:20 (Vulgate), 94:20 (other translations).

7   Deuteronomy 32:39.

> "*There is* no God besides Me;
> I kill and I make alive;
> I wound and I heal;
> Nor *is there any* who can deliver from My hand." (New King James Bible)

8   Psalm 129:1 (Vulgate), 130:1 (other translations). "Out of the depths I have cried to You, O Lord." (New King James Bible)

9   Romans 1:25.

10   Jeremiah 2:27.

> "They and their kings and their princes, and their priests and their prophets,
> Saying to a tree, 'You *are* my father,'

And to a stone, 'You gave birth to me.'
For they have turned *their* back to Me, and not *their* face.'" (New King James Bible)

11   Psalm 115:16 (Vulgate), 116:16 (other translations). "O Lord, for I am thy servant: I am thy servant, and the son of thy handmaid. Thou hast broken my bonds." (New King James Bible)

12   Jeremiah 51:6.

"Flee from the midst of Babylon,
And every one save his life!" (New King James Bible)

13   Psalm 72:7 (Vulgate), 73:7 (other translations).

14   Exodus 20:15.

15   Psalm 63:11 (Vulgate), 64:10 (other translations).

"The righteous shall be glad in the Lord, and trust in Him.
And all the upright in heart shall glory." (New King James Bible)

16   An altered quotation of Sallust's *Catiline* (16.3): "If there was no motive at hand, he simply seized and murdered innocent people as if they were guilty, clearly choosing to be wicked and cruel without cause, lest his hand or heart should wilt through idleness." (Translation by Peter Constantine)

17   Psalm 115:12 (Vulgate), 116:12 (other translations).

18   Psalm 53:8 (Vulgate), 54:6 (other translations).

19   Ecclesiasticus 3:17 (Vulgate), Sirach 3:17 (other translations). "In the day of affliction thou shalt be remembered: and thy sins shall melt away as the ice in the fair warm weather." (Douay-Rheims Bible)

20   Romans 6:21. "What fruit did you have then in the things of which you are now ashamed? For the end of those things *is* death." (New King James Bible)

21   Psalm 18:13 (Vulgate), 19:12 (other translations).

22   Matthew 23:21.

BOOK III

[1.1] I came to Carthage and was immersed in a seething cauldron of illicit loves. I had not yet loved but was burning to experience love, and, consumed by an inner craving, was vexed at myself for not craving more. In love with love, I sought an object of love, but shunned a path that had no snares. I was consumed by hunger, deprived of inner food, deprived of You, my God, and yet it was not for You that I hungered; I lacked all desire for incorruptible sustenance, not because I was sated by it, but the emptier I was the more I disdained it. And so my soul sickened and, covered in pustules, gushed forth, wretchedly striving to be soothed by sensual objects. Yet if these objects had not had a soul they would not have been objects of love. To love and be loved was all the sweeter to me if I could delight in the body of the beloved. So I sullied the clear spring of friendship with the filth of carnality, dulling its brightness with infernal lust, and though I was base and vile, in my vanity I paraded myself as refined and urbane. So I flung myself into that love by which I so longed to be seized. My God, my Mercy! In Your goodness how much gall did You sprinkle on that sweetness! For I was loved, and secretly attained the fetters of delight, rejoicing in being enmeshed in the tangle of misery, to be scourged with the burning rods of jealousy, suspicion, fear, anger, and contention.

[2.2] I was captivated by theatrical spectacles filled with images of my miseries, which poured fuel on my fire. Why is it that man wants to sorrow by watching distressing and tragic things that he would not want to endure? And yet he wants to endure this sorrow as a spectator, and this sorrow is his delight. What is this if not utter folly? Indeed, the more a man is moved by such suffering, the less free he is of it himself, for when one is suffering it is called misery, while when one feels sympathy for the suffering of others it is called compassion. But what sort of compassion is this for things that are feigned and staged? The spectator is not summoned to help but only to grieve, and the more he grieves the more he applauds the actor of these representations. But if the misfortunes, whether of ancient times or invented, are acted in such a way that the spectator does not grieve, he leaves the theater filled with disappointment and anger, but if he does grieve he delights in his tears.

[2.3] Thus sorrows are also loved. But people want to enjoy themselves; no one likes to be miserable, even if he likes to commiserate: so do we love sorrows because commiserating cannot exist without misery? This also arises from what we might call the vein of human relations. But where does this vein lead? Where does it flow to? Why does it pour into that torrent of boiling pitch that gushes forth into the monstrous surges of hideous lust into which it has degenerated, torn from heavenly serenity by its own proclivities? So should compassion be cast aside? By no means. One can at times love sorrows, but beware of impurity, O my soul, under the protection of my God, the God of our fathers who is to be praised and exalted above all for eternity, beware of impurity! Not that I have ceased to feel pity, but in those days, in the theaters, I shared in the delight of the lovers when they enjoyed one another in disgraceful acts, though what they were doing was imaginary and on the stage, and when they lost one another it was as if I grieved with them in pity; I enjoyed both their delights and their sorrows. But today I have far more pity for him who takes pleasure in shameful acts than for him who believes he is suffering through lack of some pernicious delight, or because he has lost out on some pitiable stroke of luck. This is certainly the truer compassion, but sorrow does not delight in it. For even if a person who grieves for those in distress is commended for his charity, he who is genuinely compassionate would prefer there to be nothing for him to grieve for. Only if there were such a thing as malevolent benevolence, which cannot be, would a person who truly and sincerely pities wish that there were pitiable wretches for him to pity. Hence there is pain that is laudable, but not pain that can be loved. For You, O Lord God, Who love souls and have compassion far purer than ours, You have pity that is more unchangeable since You are never beset by sorrow. Who is sufficient for such things?[1]

[2.4] But in those days, wretch that I was, I loved that grief, and looked for occasions at which to grieve. In the actor's feigned and conjured sorrows, the spectacle pleased me all the more, and more ardently, when it brought me to tears. Is it a wonder that a luckless sheep, impatient of Your oversight, strays from Your flock only to be beset by festering pustules? This was the source of my love for sorrow; not the kind of sorrow that penetrated deep within me, for I did not long for the suffering I saw on the stage, but only the kind that would scratch me lightly; but just as with the scratches of fingernails, there are inflamed swellings, pus, and putrefaction. My life being such, was it a life, my God?

[3.5] But from afar Your mercy, so constant, hovered over me. With how many sins did I consume myself in my quest for sacrilegious knowledge that led me, who had forsaken You, into a perfidious abyss, to the deceitful allegiance of devils to whom I offered up my evil deeds? And in all I did you scourged me. During solemnities celebrated within the sanctuary of Your church I even dared to lust and bring about something worthy of the fruit of death. For this you lashed me with great punishments, though not in proportion to my guilt, O my God, You Who are my greatest mercy, Who are my ref-

uge from the terrible evils among which I proudly strode, only to
wander further from You, loving my path and not Yours, loving the
troubled liberty of the fugitive slave.

[3.6] My supposedly respectable studies had the aim of achieving
excellence in the courts of litigation, where the greater the deceit,
the greater the praise. Such is the blindness of men that they glory
in blindness. And I was the foremost pupil in the school of rhetoric. I was puffed up with pride and rejoiced in vanity, though I was
more restrained by far than my fellow students, Lord, as You know,
keeping my distance from the destructiveness of the Destroyers, who
sported this sinister and devilish name as a sign of urbanity.[2] I lived
among them shamelessly ashamed that I was not like them. I was
with them, and at times enjoyed their friendship, though I always
abhorred the deeds with which they shamelessly persecuted shy new
students, attacking them and jeering at them for no reason, feeding
their own malicious delight. Nothing resembles the actions of devils
more than theirs, so what better name can there be for them than
"the Destroyers," destroyed and corrupted as they are by the deceitful
spirits that secretly deride and waylay them with the same deeds with
which they taunt and deceive others.

[4.7] Its was among them, at my tender age, that I studied the books
of eloquence by which I longed to distinguish myself, driven by
delight in human vanity, a damnable and empty aim. In the course
of my studies I had come upon a book by a certain Cicero, whose
tongue almost everyone admires, though not so much his heart. The
book is called _Hortensius_[3] and contains an exhortation to study philosophy. It altered my state of mind and my prayers, making them
turn to You, Lord, changing my longings and desires. Suddenly every
vanity became worthless, and with a fire raging in my heart I longed
for the immortality of wisdom, rousing me to return to You. I did
not immerse myself in this book to perfect my style, something I was

pursuing in those days when I was nineteen with my mother's funds, as my father had died two years before. No, it was not to perfect my style, for it was not the book's style that swayed me but its words.

[4.8] How I burned, my God, how I burned to soar up to You from earthly things, though I did not know what You would do with me. For with You is wisdom. But the love of wisdom is called in Greek "philosophy," and it was that with which Cicero's book inflamed me. There are those who use philosophy to lead people astray, shading and coloring their errors by means of that great and honored word, and almost all the philosophers who in Cicero's day and in former ages were of that kind were listed and described in his book. Clear also is the salutary advice of Your Spirit, which You sent through Your good and pious servant Paul: "Beware lest anyone cheat you through philosophy and empty deceit, according to the tradition of men, according to the basic principles of the world, and not according to Christ, for in Him dwells all the fullness of the Godhead bodily."⁴ At that time, as You know, O light of my heart, the words of the apostle were still unknown to me, but one thing that attracted me was Cicero's exhortation not to embrace this or that doctrine, "but to prize and pursue wisdom whatever it be, to achieve, understand, and embrace it."⁵ The only thing in Cicero's book that dampened my blazing fervor was that the name of Christ was not in it. For Christ's name, by Your mercy, Lord, this name of my Savior, Your Son, my infant heart had devoutly imbibed with my mother's milk, drinking it and preserving it deep within me, and whatever work did not contain that name could not grip me entirely, no matter how learned, refined, or sincere it might be.

[5.9] I was therefore determined to apply my mind to the Holy Scripture in order to see what it was, and what I saw was something not discernible by the proud, nor open to the young, its entrance modest but its inner halls exalted and veiled with mysteries. I was not one who was able to enter or to bow my head and proceed. I did not feel then when I approached the Scripture what I feel now, but it struck me as unworthy of comparison to the distinction of a Cicero. My strutting pride shunned the simplicity of the Scripture, my eye not keen enough to penetrate its interior. Yet the Scripture is such that it grows with those who are simple. But I disdained the thought of being simple and, swollen with pride, perceived myself as great.

[6.10] That was why I fell in with men who were deluded with pride. These men were lascivious and silver-tongued, their mouths filled with the Devil's snares limed with the syllables of Your name, those of the Lord Jesus Christ and the Paraclete our comforter, the Holy Ghost.[6] These names came from their mouths only as empty sounds, as noises of the tongue, for their hearts were empty of truth. And yet they kept exclaiming: "Truth, Truth!" They talked much about truth, but truth was not within them. They told lies, not only about You, Who truly are Truth; they even lied about the elements of this world, Your creation. Out of love for You, my Father, Who are supremely good, and the beauty of all things beautiful, I should also have cast aside the philosophers, even if they said things that are true about the elements of Your creation.[7] O truth, truth! Even in those days the marrow of my soul deep within me was longing for You, when these men, so often and in so many ways, with so many weighty books, kept holding forth about You. Such were the dishes that they served me who was hungering after You, placing before me not You but the sun and the moon, beautiful works of Yours but only Your works, not You, nor Your first works, for Your spiritual works came before Your corporeal works, even if these were celestial and shining.[8] But I hungered and thirsted not after those first works of Yours but after You, after You Who are Truth and in Whom there is no variation or shadow of alteration.[9] But the dishes those men paraded before me contained splendid phantasms, than which it would have been bet-ter to worship the sun itself, which at least is real to our eyes, than to worship such phantasms that through our eyes deceive our mind. Mistaking them for You I partook of them, not avidly, for You did not taste to me as You are; nor were You in these empty figments, nor was I nourished by them, but exhausted. Food when one dreams resembles food when one is awake, but those who are dreaming are not nourished, for they are asleep. Yet those phantasms did not resemble You in any way, as I realized now that You have spoken to me, for they were physical apparitions, false bodies, while the true bodies that we behold with our own eyes, whether celestial or terrestrial, are far more certain. We see them just as animals of the earth and birds of the air see them, and they are more certain than the way we imagine them to be. Yet we imagine them with more certainty than when, through them, we imagine other bodies vaster and more infinite that do not exist. That was the emptiness I was being fed, but I was not nourished. But You, my Love, for Whom I fade that I may be strong, are not those bodies that we see, though they be in heaven, nor those we cannot see, which You have created, though You do not deem them among the highest of Your creations.[10] How far You are from those imaginings that I had had, imagining bodies that do not exist; far more certain than these are the images of the bodies that do exist, and still more certain are the bodies themselves, of which You are none; nor are You the soul that is the life of the bodies and therefore, as the life of the bodies, better and more certain than the bodies themselves. For You are the life of souls, the life of lives, You are self-sufficient and unchangeable, O life of my soul.

[6.11] Where in those days were You to me, and how far away? I strayed so very far from You, barred even from the husks I fed to pigs,[11] for how much better are the fables of poets and grammarians than those snares? Verses and poems, and "Medea flying,"[12] are certainly more useful than the five elements colored according to the five caverns of darkness,[13] which do not exist, but which slay those who believe in them. After all, I can turn verses and poems into

nourishment, and though I declaimed "Medea flying," I did not claim
that it was true, nor when I heard it declaimed did I believe its words.
And yet I believed in those other things. Woe, woe! By what steps
was I brought down to the depths of hell, suffering and uncertain
through lack of truth, since I sought You, my God (to You I confess
it, who had mercy on me before I had yet confessed), not through the
mind's powers of understanding, in which You willed that I should
surpass the beasts, but sought You through the sense of the flesh. You
were more inward to me than my innermost part, and higher than
my highest. I had come upon a brazen woman, a woman from one of
Solomon's proverbs, sitting on a stool at her door, calling out: "You
will eat hidden bread with far greater pleasure and drink sweet stolen water."[14] She seduced me because she found me living within the
eye of my flesh, outside my soul, redevouring what through that eye
I had devoured.

[7.12] I did not know any other truth, and was cleverly persuaded
to concur with the foolish deceivers when they asked me: "Where
does evil come from?" "Is God bound within a bodily shape? Does
he have hair and nails?" "Are those with many wives and who have
killed men and sacrificed animals to be deemed just?" Ignorant as
I was I was confused, and straying from the truth thought that I
was approaching it, for I still did not know that evil was simply an
absence of good, that evil has no existence in itself. How could I see
clearly, as my sight was only with my eyes and reached only objects,
my mind only phantasms? I did not know God to be a Spirit,[15] that
He did not have limbs that had length and breadth, that He did not
have mass, since any mass is less in its part than in its whole. Even
if that mass were infinite, it must be less in any part that is bound by
a certain space than it is in its infinitude, and consequently cannot
be everywhere in its entirety as a Spirit, as God. I simply had no idea
what it is within us that makes us exist, and as the Scripture affirms,
makes us in God's image.

[7.13] I also did not know the true inward justice that does not judge
according to custom but according to the most rightful law of God
Almighty. Through this law the customs of places and times were
adapted to those places and times, while the law itself always and
everywhere remained the same, not being one thing in one place or
time and something else in another; consequently Abraham, Isaac,
Jacob, Moses, David, and all those who were commended by the
mouth of God were just, but they were judged as unjust by ignorant men who judged by human judgment,[16] measuring the mores
of the entire human race by their own. These men are like someone
ignorant of armor who is unaware of what part fits which limb and
so seeks to cover his head with shin guards or shod himself with a
helmet, complaining that nothing fits. It is as if on a public holiday, when business is prohibited by law in the afternoon, one were
angered at not being permitted to continue trading simply because
it had been permitted in the morning. Or as if one notices a slave
touch something that he who serves the wine may not touch; or as if
something is permitted behind the stables but prohibited in the din-
ing room and one is angry that what is allowed in one home might
not be allowed everywhere and to everyone. Such are those who are
resentful when they hear that something was granted to the righteous in former ages that is not granted now; or that God, for temporal reasons, commanded people of former ages one thing and people
of today another, though both had to obey the same justice: whereas
one may see on a single day and in a single household that certain
things are fit for one member and not another, and that a thing that
a short while ago was permitted may not be allowed an hour later.
What in one corner might be permitted or even mandatory might
in another be forbidden and punished. Is then justice varying or
changeable? No, it is not. The times over which justice presides do
not flow evenly, for that is the nature of time; but man's life on earth
is brief, and so people cannot connect the causes of things in former ages and other nations, of which they have no experience, with

causes of which they have experience, whereas in a single body, day, or home, people easily see what is fitting for which limb and which moment, or which part or person. In the one case they are offended; in the other they acquiesce.

[7.14] In those days I neither knew nor had noticed such things; all around my eyes fell on them, but I did not see them. When I composed poetry I was not allowed to place this or that metric foot just anywhere, but had to put different feet in different meters, and even in the same line not always the same foot in all places. But the art itself by which I composed did not have different rules at different points, but the same rules throughout. Yet I could not discern that the justice, which good and holy men had to obey, contained in far greater and sublime perfection without varying in any way all those things that God commanded, though it prescribed different things at different times, distributing and commanding what was apt at those times. Blind as I was, I found fault with the holy fathers, not only that they acted as God commanded and inspired them, but also for prophesying the future as God revealed it.[17]

[8.15] Can it at any time or place be wrong to love God with all your heart and all your soul and all your mind and love your neighbor as yourself?[18] Sinful acts against nature, such as those of the Sodomites, are to be detested and punished everywhere and at all times. Even if all peoples should commit such acts, they would stand accused of the same crime by the divine law that did not make men so that they should use one another in this way. Even the bond that should exist between God and us is violated when man's nature, of which God is the author, is polluted by the perversion of lust. Sinful acts contrary to the customs of men are thus to be avoided in the light of the diversity of these customs, so that the agreement within a city or a people that is established by custom or law in any city or nation will not be violated at the lawless pleasure of any citizen or foreigner.

Any part that does not fit the body it belongs to is offensive. But when God commands something that goes against the customs or agreement of a people it must be done, even if it has never been done before, and if it has been neglected it must be restored, and if it was never instituted it must be instituted now. It is, after all, permitted a king to command within the state over which he reigns what no one before him has commanded, nor even he himself until then. Obeying his command does not go against the social agreement; in fact, it would be contrary to the agreement not to obey it, for obeying kings is a general contract of society. This being so, how much more must God, the ruler of all He has created, be obeyed in all that he commands. For just as among the magistrates of society the higher magistrate is obeyed before the lower, so must God be obeyed above all.

[8.16] The same is true of crimes that are driven by the desire to hurt another through insult or injury, crimes committed either out of revenge, such as one enemy attacking another; or in order to gain another's property, such as a bandit attacking a traveler; or in order to avoid an evil, such as attacking someone who is feared; or crimes committed because of envy, when someone less fortunate attacks one whose fortunes are better, or if one who has experienced success attacks one he fears might soon reach his status or already be his equal. Or someone might attack another for the mere pleasure at the other's pain, as we see with the spectators of gladiators, or those who like to deride and mock others. These are the foremost of the sins; they spring from the lust for domination, the lust of the eye and of the flesh,[19] either as one lust, or two, or all lusts at once. Those who live in evil are sinning against the three and seven of Your commandments,[20] that psaltery of ten strings, Your Decalogue, O God most high and most sweet. But what shameful acts can reach You Who cannot be defiled, what violence can be done to You Who cannot be harmed? You punish what men perpetrate against themselves, since when they sin against You they do evil to their own souls. Iniquity deceives itself[21] when men corrupt and pervert their nature, which You have created and ordained, or when they use to excess things that are allowed, or lust for things that are not allowed and are contrary to nature.[22] Or they are guilty of raging in thought and word against You, kicking against the goads,[23] or when the boundaries of society are shattered they audaciously rejoice either in the factions or the cabals, whichever pleases or displeases them. And these things are done when You are forsaken, O Fountain of Life Who are the only and true creator and ruler of the universe, or when through self-involved pride a single false part is loved above the whole. It is only through humble devotion that we return to You and You cleanse us of our evil habits and have mercy on the sins of those who confess. You hear the groans of prisoners[24] and release the chains that we ourselves have wrought, provided we do not thrust against You the horns of a false freedom, losing all by coveting more, by loving more what we take as our own than by loving You Who are the good of all.

[9.17] But among these shameful acts and deeds, and among all the other iniquities, are also the sins of those striving for success. If one is to judge rightly, they are to be condemned according to the criteria of perfection, and yet they are to be commended like green sprouts in a field in the hope of a future harvest. There are also actions resembling shameful acts and deeds which, however, are not sins because they offend neither You, our Lord God, nor society: when someone seizes an opportunity to gather goods that are needed to survive, but it is not clear whether it was done out of lust for possession, or when an official authority zealously inflicts punishment, but it is uncertain whether it was done out of a lust to inflict harm. Many actions that in men's eyes are to be censured are approved by Your testimony, and many actions that men praise are condemned by Your testimony, because the appearance of an action is often quite disparate from the intent of him who commits the action, and the circumstances at the time are unknown to us. But when You suddenly command something unusual and unexpected, even though You might have forbidden it before, and for a time You hide the reason for this command, then who will doubt that what You command must be done, even if the command goes against the compact of a society? For the only society that is just is a society that serves You. Blessed are they who know that it is You Who are the one Who issued the command! For all things done by Your servants show what must be done in the present or what is to be done in the future.

[10.18] Not knowing all these things, I ridiculed Your holy servants and prophets. But what did I gain by ridiculing them other than to make myself ridiculous to You? Without realizing it I was gradually drawn to folly, such as believing that a fig weeps when it is plucked, and that the tree, its mother, sheds milky tears. But if the fig is eaten by some saint, plucked by another's guilt and not his own, and digested by the saint's innards, he would breathe out angels, or rather, as he mumbled in prayer he would burp out particles of God.[25] Had they not been released by the tooth and belly of this elect saint, these particles of the most high and true God would have remained bound within that fig. And I, wretch that I was, believed that more mercy was to be shown to the fruits of the earth than to men for whom these fruits were created. If a hungry man who was not a Manichaean asked for a morsel of food, that morsel was thought to be condemned to capital punishment if it was given him.

[11.19] But You reached out Your hand from on high[26] and drew my soul up from that profound darkness, for my mother, Your faithful servant, wept for me before You more than mothers weep over the bodies of their dead children; through the faith and spirit she had from You she could see my death, and You heard her, Lord. You heard her, and did not despise her tears that streamed forth, watering the ground before her eyes wherever she prayed. You heard her.

From where else could have come that dream through which You comforted her, so that she allowed me to live with her once more and sit at the same table, which she had refused me, shrinking from the blasphemies of my errors which she abominated? In her dream she saw herself standing on a measuring stick, a shining youth coming toward her smiling full of joy, while she grieved and was overwhelmed by her grief. He asked her the reason for her sorrow and the tears she shed every day, not as a question but, as happens in visions, to instruct her. She replied that she was mourning my perdition, and he bade her not to despair but to look up and see that where she was, I was too. And when she looked up, she saw me standing next to her on the same measuring stick. Where could this vision have come from but that Your ears were close to her heart, O You Who are good and almighty, Who care so much for every one of us as if You were caring for him alone, and so care for all of us as if we were one!

[11.20] From where else could that dream have come? When she told me of her vision, I tried to interpret it as meaning that she should not despair of one day being what I was, but she immediately and without hesitation said to me: "No, for I was not told 'Where he is, there you too shall be,' but 'Where you are, there he too shall be.'"

I confess to You my memories, O Lord, to the extent that I can recollect them. What moved me most—and this is a matter I have often addressed—was Your response through my vigilant mother, who did not let herself be waylaid by the lie of my skewed interpretation, and immediately saw what had to be seen (which I certainly had not seen before she uttered her words). I was moved more by Your response than by the dream itself, which for this pious woman foretold joys that lay still far in the future but that consoled her in her present anguish.[27] Almost nine years were to pass in which I was to wallow in the mire of dark falsehood, often trying to emerge but sinking ever deeper, while that chaste, pious widow, the kind You love, fired on by hope but still unrelenting in her tears and supplications, did not cease her hours of prayer lamenting to You about me. Her prayers reached You, but still You suffered me to flounder in darkness.

[12.21] In the meantime You gave my mother another answer that I call to mind, for I am passing over much as I hasten on to the matters that compel me more to confess to You, and there is much that I do not remember. You gave her another answer through a priest of Yours, a certain bishop raised in Your Church who was well versed in Your books. When my mother begged him to condescend to speak to me and show me my errors, to wean me from what was evil and teach me what was good (for he always did this when he found a suitable person), he declined, wisely, as I later realized. He said that I was not yet ready to be taught, filled as I was with the novelty of the Manichean heresy, and I had already, as she had informed him, pestered a number of less experienced individuals with trifling questions. "Leave him as he is," he told my mother, "but pray to God for him. In reading, he himself will understand what an error and how great an impiety it is."

At the same time he told her how he himself, when he was a boy, had been handed to the Manicheans by his beguiled mother, and had not only read almost all their books but had even copied them out, and so, without being contradicted or converted by anyone, had come to see how much that sect was to be avoided, and he had avoided it. Though he spoke these words, my mother would still not acquiesce, continuing to insist with copious tears that he should see me and speak with me. "Leave me be," he told her, somewhat peeved, "and God bless you, for it is not possible that the son of tears such as yours will perish."

She embraced this answer, as she later often mentioned to me, as if it had come from heaven.

NOTES

1 2 Corinthians 2:16. "To the one *we are* the aroma of death *leading* to death, and to the other the aroma of life *leading* to life. And who *is* sufficient for these things?" (New King James Bible)

2 The *Eversores* (literally "destroyers" or "topplers") were a rowdy fraternity of senior students who terrorized teachers and younger students.

3 Cicero wrote *Hortensius* (of which only fragments have survived) as an introduction to his philosophical writings of 46–45 BCE. In *Hortensius*, Cicero argued that the path to happiness was overcoming one's passions and embracing philosophy and reason.

4 A quotation from Colossians 2:8–9.

5 A possible quotation from Cicero's lost work *Hortensius*, though more probably a general paraphrase.

6 Augustine had come under the influence of the Manicheans, whose religious sect had become extremely influential in the Roman Empire and a threat to the early Christian Church. Manichaeism had a Gnostic foundation, incorporating many Christian and Zoroastrian elements, and its intellectual and mystical aspects had attracted the young Augustine.

7 Augustine states that he should have cast aside the teachings of the ancient philosophers, which, despite containing certain truths about the world, fall short of God's truth.

8 Manichaeans believed that the cosmos consisted of a well-ordered mixture of light (a good force) and darkness (an evil force). The sun and the moon were thought of as vessels of pure light. Augustine assumes that God's first creation was spiritual: heaven, according to Genesis, having been created before the earth.

9 James 1:17. "Every best gift, and every perfect gift, is from above, coming down from the Father of lights, with whom there is no change, nor shadow of alteration." (Douay-Rheims Bible)

10 According to Genesis 1:6, God first created heaven and earth and then the firmament.

11 A reference to Luke 15:16: "And he would gladly have filled his stomach with the husks that the swine ate, but no one gave him anything." The husks are pagan texts, and the pigs are the students to whom Augustine had had to teach these texts.

12 A reference to the image of Medea flying up toward the sun in her chariot in Ovid's *Metamorphoses* 8.

13 The number five was important in Manichean doctrine. There were five categories of animal life, five bodily substances, five senses, five stages of a soul's ascent, and, on a more cosmic scale, five elements within five caverns or repositories of darkness and evil.

14   See Proverbs 9:13–17.

15   John 4:24. "God *is* Spirit, and those who worship Him must worship in spirit and truth." (New King James Bible)

16   1 Corinthians 4:3.

17   The Manicheans rejected the Old Testament prophesies of Gospel events.

18   Matthew 22:37–40.

19   1 John 2:16.

20   The first three of the Ten Commandments are concerned with man's duty to God, the other seven with men's duties to one another.

21   Psalm 26:12 (Vulgate), 27:12 (other translations).

22   Romans 1:26.

23   Acts 26:14.

24   Psalm 101:21 (Vulgate), 102:20 (other translations).

25   The Manichean "saints" or "elect" led ascetic and celibate lives and were subjected to strict dietary rules. They believed that there were particles of God in everything, and that if they plucked fruit or vegetables they would be injuring God. Consequently, their acolytes gathered their food for them. It was believed that the elect, pure in body as they were, could release particles of God that were trapped within the food they ate. See Book IV, 1.

26   Psalm 143:7 (Vulgate), 144:7 (other translations).

27   The joy of Augustine's mother was to be his conversion to Christianity in 381/2 CE.

BOOK IV

[1.1] During that time of nine years, from when I was nineteen to twenty-eight, in the grip of many passions, I misled and was misled, I deceived and was deceived. Publicly I practiced the arts we call liberal; secretly I practiced a false religion.[1] In my public role I was proud, in my religion superstitious, and in both roles empty. Publicly I sought hollow glory, even to the applause of the stage, the prizes for verse, the contests for grass garlands, the foolish spectacles, and the excesses of lust. In my religion I sought to be purged from all that filth by gathering food for those who were called "Elect" and "Holy," so that in the laboratory of their stomachs they could forge angels and gods through whom we would be liberated.[2] These are the things I pursued and practiced with my friends, who were beguiled by me and with me. Let the proud mock me, the proud who have not been cast down and crushed by You, my God, for their good, but I will still confess to you my disgrace as it is to your praise. Allow me, I beseech You, grant me in my present memory to wander through the strayings of my errors, and to offer you the sacrifice of thanksgiving.[3] For what am I to myself without You but a guide to my own downfall? What am I at best but one imbibing the milk that You give, a nourishment that never perishes? And yet what kind of man can any man be, being but a man? Let the strong and mighty laugh at us, but we, the weak and helpless, will confess to You.

[2.2] During those years I taught the art of rhetoric, selling the craft of eloquence and victorious argument, driven as I was by cupidity. Yet as You know, Lord, I wanted pupils who were good, or what is considered good, and I, without artifice, taught those pupils artifice, not of the kind intended to be used against the lives of the innocent, but sometimes to save those who were guilty. And You, God, watched me from afar as I stumbled on that slippery ground, and within the smoke You saw a spark of the honesty I manifested in my teaching of those who prized deception and lies, I myself being one of them. In those years I was with a woman, not in what is called a lawful marriage, but a woman my weak and errant passion had found. Yet she was the only one, and I remained faithful to her, experiencing personally the great difference between the convention of marriage that one enters in order to create a family, and the pact of sensual love, in which children are born against their parents' wishes, though once born they compel their parents to love them.[4]

[2.3] I remember how when I took part in a poetry competition in the theater, some diviner asked me how much I would give him in order to win. But I, disgusted by such foul mysteries, answered with outrage that even if the garland were of imperishable gold, I would not want a single fly to be killed so I could win it, for he was going to kill living creatures in his sacrifices and through such gifts ensure the demons' support for me. And yet I did not spurn such evil out of the purity of my love for You, O God of my heart, for I did not know how to love You, and as in those days could only conceive of material light.[5] Does not a soul longing for such fictions commit fornication against You, trusting in lies and feeding the winds?[6] Though I did not want sacrifices to be offered to demons for me, I sacrificed myself to them through that false religion. For what else is it to feed the winds than to feed the demons, and by erring become their derision and delight?

[3.4] Therefore I continued to consult those deceivers we call astrologers, and they did not seem to offer sacrifices or pray to any spirit to conduct their divinations. Yet true Christian piety always rejects and condemns what they do. It is a good thing to confess to You, Lord, and to say: "Have mercy upon me, heal my soul, for I have sinned against You."[7] Nor must I abuse Your indulgence, seeing it as a license to sin, but must remember the words of Christ: "Behold, you have been healed, sin no more, lest something worse befalls you."[8] But all who proclaim, "The firmament is the inescapable cause of your sinning; it is Venus that has done this, or Saturn, or Mars!" are striving to destroy the Lord's healing. This way, man, who is flesh, blood, and proud corruption, remains blameless, while the Creator and Orderer of heaven and the stars is made to bear the blame. And who is this but our God, the sweetness and source of justice, You Who render to every man according to his works[9] and never spurn a broken and humble heart.[10]

[3.5] There was at that time a man who was wise, and skilled in the art of medicine, for which he was renowned. Yet it was not as a physician but as the acting proconsul that he placed the garland of the poetry contest upon my ailing head, since the disease that I had only You alone can cure, You Who oppose the proud and give grace to the humble.[11] But even with this venerable man You did not fail me or desist from healing my soul, for he and I became friends, and I would listen eagerly and attentively to his conversation, which, though not phrased with elegance, was vigorous and delightful in the earnest opinions he expressed. When he gathered from our conversations that I was devoted to astrological books, he advised me in a warm and fatherly manner to cast them aside and not waste on such foolish things the effort and work I could use for something useful. He told me that in his youth he himself had studied astrology, thinking he might make it his profession, for if he could understand Hippocrates, he had felt, he could surely understand the works of the astrologers. And yet he had abandoned astrology and chosen medicine, for no other reason than that he found astrology to be an utter sham, and that he, a sound man, did not wish to make a living by deluding people. "But you," he told me, "can sustain yourself by teaching rhetoric, and are dedicating yourself to these deceitful arts not out of a need to earn your keep but out of your own zeal. You should believe me all the more as I had striven to learn astrology perfectly so I could earn my living by it." I asked him how it could be that in astrology so many true things were foretold, and he replied that from what he could tell this happened because there was a force of chance spread throughout the course of things. One might happen to glance at the pages of a poet, a verse miraculously coming to the fore that fits one's concerns, even if the poet was singing and thinking of something quite different; should one then wonder if from out of man's soul, through some higher instinct unaware of what takes place within it, a voice should emerge, not by art but by chance, which harmonizes with the concerns and actions of him who is enquiring?

[3.6] This truth You conveyed to me from, or rather through, that venerable man, tracing onto my memory the things I would later examine for myself. But at that time neither he nor my dearest Nebridius, a youth who was so good and so very pure and who derided the whole genre of divination, could persuade me to cast these things aside; the authors' authority inspired me more than the authority of my friends, and as yet I had not come upon the definitive proof by which it would be clear to me without any ambiguity that what had been foretold correctly by the astrologers was the result of chance, and not of the art of studying the stars.

[4.7] In those years when I first began to teach rhetoric in the town in which I was born,[12] I made a friend who was very close to me because of our shared interests, a young man of my age and who like me was in the flower of youth. We had grown up together as boys, had been at school and had played together. But he had not yet been as close a friend as he was to be later, even though it was not to be a true friendship even then, for a friendship cannot be true unless it is one that You, Lord, bond together between those who adhere to You in a love that has been poured into our hearts by the Holy Spirit who was given to us.[13] Yet it was an exceedingly sweet friendship, deepened through a passion for the same pursuits. But I was also to lead him astray from the true faith, which because of his youth had not truly and deeply taken hold, waylaying him to embrace those superstitious and pernicious fables over which my mother wept so many tears on my account. And so this man strayed with me in mind and soul; nor could my mind and soul be without him. But You, Lord, were there, close at the heels of those fleeing You, God of vengeance[14] but also Fountain of Mercies, who turn us to You by wondrous means. Lord, You took that man out of this life when our friendship had barely filled a year, a friendship sweet to me above all the sweetness of my life.

[4.8] Who can count all Your praiseworthy acts that he has experienced on himself alone? What did You do then, my God, and how unfathomable are the depths of Your judgments?[15] My friend was beset by a fever, and lay long unconscious in the sweat of death, and when all hope was abandoned he was baptized without his knowing; I did not particularly mind, as I presumed that his soul would rather retain what it had learned from me and not what was done to his body without his knowing. But this proved not to be the case. He recovered, was restored to health, and as soon as I could speak to him (and I could do so the moment he was able, since I never left his side as we clung so much to one another), I tried to joke with him about the baptism that had taken place when he was entirely absent in mind and feeling, but which he now knew he had undergone. I was certain that he too would laugh, but he shrank back from me in horror as if from an enemy, and with sudden and surprising candor told me that if I wanted to remain his friend I must stop saying such things. I was stunned and confused, but suppressed all my emotions until he should recover and was strong once more, when I could act as I pleased. But he was torn away from my folly so that he might be preserved at Your side for my consolation; a few days later, while I was away, the fever returned and he succumbed.

[4.9] What pain darkened my heart, and everywhere I looked I saw death. My town was a torment to me, my house a misery. Whatever I had shared with him became without him a monstrous torture. My eyes sought him everywhere but did not find him. I hated everything, for he was not there; nor could I be told, "Here he is, he is coming!" as when he was alive and had been away. I became a great enigma to myself, and I asked my soul why it was so sad and why it perturbed me so much, but my soul did not know what answer to give. And if I said, "Trust in God," my soul did not obey, and rightly so, because the beloved man it had lost was more real and good than the phantasm[16] I was bidding my soul to trust. Only tears were sweet to me, as they took the place of my friend in my soul's delights.

[5.10] Now, Lord, all these things have passed and time has soothed my wound. May I hear from You, Who are Truth, and bring my heart's ear to Your mouth so You can tell me why weeping is sweet to those in misery? Or have You, though You are present everywhere, cast our misery far from You, and remain within Yourself while we are tossed about in trials? And yet if we do not weep into Your ear, no remnant of hope would remain for us. From where, then, is the sweet fruit of the bitterness of life plucked: from groaning and weeping, sighing and lamenting? Or is it only sweet in that we hope that You hear us? This is also true of our prayers, because in them is the longing to draw near to You. But why was I so overcome in my grief and sorrow for what I had lost? For I neither hoped he would return to life, nor did I seek it with my tears; I only wept and grieved, for I was miserable and had lost my joy. Or is weeping also a bitter thing that delights us through our turning from of the things we enjoyed before but now abhor?

[6.11] But why am I speaking of all this? Now is not the time to weigh these things, but to confess to You. I was wretched; and wretched is every soul bound by friendship to what is mortal and torn to pieces when it is lost, then first sensing the wretchedness that was there before the mortal things were lost. That is how it was with me, and I wept bitterly, and found solace in bitterness. So I was in misery and held that miserable life dearer than my friend. For though I wanted to change that life, I was less willing to part with it than with him, and I do not even know if I would have parted with it for him, as is said of Pylades and Orestes, if it is not a myth, that they would gladly have died for one another or together, since not staying alive together was for them far worse than death. But a kind of feeling entirely contrary to this had arisen in me, a great weariness of life and a fear of death. I believe that the more I loved him, the more I hated and feared death, as if death were the cruelest enemy who had taken him from me, and I imagined that death would soon consume all mankind, since it had consumed him. That was how things were with me, as I remember them. Behold my heart, O God, behold within; see all I remember, O my Hope, You Who cleanse me from the impurity of such affections, directing my eyes toward You and drawing my feet out of the snare. For I wondered that other mortals were alive when he whom I loved as if he would never die was dead, and wondered even more that I, who was a second self to him, could live though he was dead. A man once said fitting words about his friend that he was half his soul, for I felt that my soul and his soul were "one soul in two bodies,"[17] and therefore life was a dread to me, because I did not want to live halved, and thus I perhaps also feared dying, lest he should then wholly die whom I had loved so much.

[7.12] O madness that does not know how to love man as man should be loved! O foolish mankind that encounters man's fate with such immoderation! That was my predicament. How I raged and sighed, wept and floundered, with neither rest nor purpose, for within me I bore a shattered, bleeding soul that could not bear being borne by me, and yet I could not find a place for it to rest. Not in shady groves, not in amusements, nor in song could my soul find repose, nor in fragrant gardens or sumptuous feasts, nor in the pleasures of bed and couch, nor in books or poetry. Everything repelled me, even light itself. Everything was irksome and vile that was not what he was, everything except for laments and tears, since it was in those alone that I found a little solace; but when my soul was averted from these, a great weight of misery smothered me. It is to You, Lord, that I should have raised my soul to be cured, something I knew but neither could nor would do; this, since to me You were not something definite or substantial when I thought of You. It was not of You that I thought but of a false phantasm, and my error was my God. If I sought to rest my soul with that false phantom, to give it respite, it slid through the void and once more came rushing down upon me. I had become an unhappy place to myself in which I could neither abide nor which I could abandon, since where could my heart flee to from my heart? Where should I flee to from myself, where not pursue myself? And yet I fled the town in which I was born, since my eyes would seek him less where they did not expect to see him. And so, leaving the town of Thagaste, I came to Carthage.

[8.13] Time does not rest, nor does it flow idly through our senses, but does strange things to our minds. Time came and went, day by day, and in coming and going infused other hopes and other memories into my mind, gradually healing me once more with my former delights, to which my sorrow yielded. But these delights were succeeded, if not by other sorrows then by the causes of other sorrows, for how had that former sorrow penetrated me so easily and so profoundly if not because I had poured my soul onto the sand, by loving one who was mortal as if he were immortal? It was the solace of other friends that renewed and restored me most, friends with whom I loved what I loved instead of You: a vast myth and prodigious lie, by whose false caresses our minds, with eager ears, were being corrupted.[18] But for me that false myth would not die, even when one of my friends did. There were other things that occupied my mind when I was with my friends: talking and laughing together, being kind to one another, reading beautiful books together, talking nonsense or talking earnestly, disputing at times but without anger, as one might dispute with oneself, and flavoring with the very rarity of these disputes our many agreements; to teach something to one another or learn from one another, to long for those absent with distress, and receive those returning with joy. These and the like signs from the hearts of those who love and are loved in turn, signs expressed through the face, the tongue, the eyes, and a thousand pleasing gestures, were like fuel that inflamed our minds and out of many made but one.

[9.14] This is what is loved in friends, and loved in a way that a man's conscience condemns itself if he does not love him who loves him in return, or does not love in return the one who loves him, seeking nothing from that person but signs of his love. Hence the grief if he dies, the darkness of sorrow, the sweetness turning to bitterness as the heart is steeped in tears, and with the loss of life of the dying comes the death of the living. Blessed is he who loves You, Lord, and loves his friend in You, and his enemy because of You. He alone loses no one who is dear to him, for all are dear in the one who cannot be lost, and who is it who cannot be lost but our God, our God Who made heaven and earth and fills them, because by filling them he created them?[19] No one loses You unless he abandons You, for in abandoning You where can he go or flee except from Your gentleness to Your anger? Where will he not find Your law in his punishment? And Your law is Truth, and Truth is You.

[10.15] O God of Hosts, make us turn and show us Your face and we shall be whole.[20] For wherever the soul of man turns, unless it turns to You, that soul is fixed upon sorrows, even if it be fixed on beautiful things outside You and outside itself, things that are nothing unless they are from You; things that rise and set, and by rising begin to be, so to speak, and grow so they may be perfected, and once perfect they grow old and perish, though not all do grow old, but all do perish. So when things rise and strive to be, they grow all the quicker so that they may be, and hasten all the more not to be. That is their limit, that is what You have allotted them, for they are parts of things that do not exist all at once, but by death and succession they all create the universe of which they are the parts. This is also how our speech comes about through voiced sounds, and our speech too would not be whole if a word would not pass away once it has voiced its part so that another may succeed. For these things let my soul praise You, God, creator of all, but do not let my soul be bonded to them by love through the senses of the body. For they go where they have always gone, to where they will not be, and they tear apart the soul with pestilent desires; for the soul wants to exist, but loves to repose in what it loves. Yet there is no place for repose in these things, for they do not stay, they flee; and who can follow them with the senses of the flesh? Who can grasp them when they are present? For the sense of the flesh is slow because it is the sense of the flesh; that is its limit. It suffices for what it was created, but does not suffice to grasp things that flow from their allotted beginning to their allotted end. For in Your Word, by which they are created, they hear: "From here" and "Up to here."

[11.16] Do not be vain, O soul, nor let the din of your vanity deafen you through your heart's ear. You, too, must listen: the Word itself calls you to return. That is the place where imperturbable repose is, and where love is not forsaken if it does not forsake. Behold how these things pass away so that others may succeed them, and how this low universe comes together in all its parts. "But do I depart for anywhere else?" says the Word of God. O soul, set your dwelling where God is, and there put in trust all that you possess, now that you at least have tired of deceit. Entrust to Truth whatever has come to you from Truth and you will lose nothing, and all that had decayed in you shall blossom once again, and all your ills will be healed, and all that is perishable within you restored and renewed and tightly bound to you; nor will these pull you down to their depths but will stand fast with you, and abide before God, Who forever stands fast and abides.

[11.17] Why then are you, O soul, perversely following your flesh? Turn around, and let it follow you. Whatever you discern through your flesh is incomplete. You do not know the whole of which these are parts, and yet they delight you. But if the sense of your flesh were able to comprehend the whole, and had not justly been restricted to a part of the universe through your punishment, you would want whatever exists in this present to pass, so that the whole, in its entirety, might better please you. For what we speak you also hear through the same sense of the flesh, and yet you would not want those syllables to stay fixed but to fly away, so that other syllables may come and you can hear the whole thing. And so it is always with a whole made up of many single things (that do not all exist at the same time); they delight more as a whole than they do in parts, if one could see them as a whole. But far better is He Who made the whole, and He is our God; nor does He pass away, for nothing succeeds Him.

[12.18] If God's creations please you, praise God for them and turn your love to their creator, lest in these things that please you, you displease Him. If souls please you, let them be loved in God, for they too are mutable, though in God they become unchanging; otherwise they would move on and perish. In God let them be loved, and seize and bring to Him whatever souls you can, and say to them, "Him let us love: He made these things; nor is He far away, for He did not make these things only to depart, for they are from Him and within Him. Behold, He is where truth prevails. He is deep within the heart, but our heart has strayed from Him. Return, sinners, to your heart[21] and adhere to Him Who made you. Stand with Him, and you shall stand fast. Rest in Him, and you shall be at rest. Where are you going to along such harsh ways? Where are you going? The good that you love is from Him; but it is through Him that it is good and sweet, and justly will it turn bitter, because unjustly loved is anything that is from God if God is to be forsaken for it. Why would you insist on walking such difficult and laborious paths? There is no rest where you seek it. Seek what you seek, but it is not where you are seeking it. You seek a blessed life in the land of death; it is not there. For how can there be a blessed life where there is no life?

[12.19] But He Who is our life itself descended and endured our death, and struck death down with the abundance of his life, and He thundered, calling for us to return to Him, to that secret place from which He came to us, first into the Virgin's womb in which He united with human creation, mortal flesh, so that it would not forever be mortal. Then He came forth like a bridegroom emerging from his chamber, a hero rejoicing to run his course.[22] For He did not linger but ran, calling out through words, deeds, death, life, descent, ascension, calling out that we return to him. And He departed from our sight so that we might return to our heart[23] and find Him there. For He departed, and, behold, here He is. He did not want to be with us long, but He did not leave us, for He departed to where He never left, because the world was made by Him,[24] and in this world He was and into this world He came to save sinners.[25] It is to Him my soul confesses and is healed by Him, for it has sinned against Him.[26] "Sons of men, how long will your hearts be heavy?[27] Will you not, after life has descended to you, ascend and live? But where will you ascend to when you are on high and set your mouth against heaven?[28] Descend so that you may ascend, and ascend to God, for you have fallen by ascending against God." Tell the souls this so that they may weep in the valley of tears, and carry them up to God with you, because by His Spirit you speak these things to them, if you speak burning with the fire of love.

[13.20] I did not know these things then and loved the beauties of this world and was falling into the depths, and said to my friends, "Do we love anything except what is beautiful? What then *is* beautiful, and what is beauty? What is it that attracts and wins us over to the things we love? If they did not have beauty and attraction they could not have drawn us to them." And I noticed and discerned in the objects something like a whole that was beautiful, and something else that was beautiful because it fit well, like a part of the body with the whole, or a shoe with a foot. This consideration sprang up in my mind from my inmost heart, and I wrote *On the Beautiful and the Fitting*, in two or three books, I think. You know, my God, though I have forgotten, for I no longer have the books; I have lost them, though I do not know how.

[14.21] But what is it that moved me, Lord my God, to dedicate these books to Hierius, an orator of Rome, whom I did not know as a person but admired for the fame of his learning that was so celebrated? I had heard words of his that I liked, and admired him most because others admired him and greatly praised him, amazed that a man from Syria who had first learned fluent Greek would then become a brilliant Latin orator and exceptionally learned in philosophy. A man can be praised and loved even when we do not know him. Does this love enter the heart of the hearer from the mouth of the extoller? It does not. But an admirer will kindle the admiration of another. This is how an extolled person comes to be admired, when the extoller's praise is heartfelt, that is, when he who admires him praises him.

[**14.22**] For in those days I admired men through the judgment of men, not through Yours, my God, in Whom no one is deceived. And yet why did I not admire them as I might a famous charioteer, or a notorious gladiator who battles beasts in the arena, but admire them quite differently and more earnestly and so that I myself would be praised? For I did not want to be praised or admired as actors are, though I myself praised and admired them, but would rather have been unknown than known in the way that they are, and would rather have been hated than admired in that way. Where are the balances in a single soul of such diverse and contradictory kinds of love? How is it that I would admire in another what I would hate in myself, renouncing and casting it away, and yet we are both men? For it is not like a good horse being loved by a man who would not want to be a horse himself, even if he could be one; the same can be said of an actor, who shares our nature. Do I then admire a man whom I would hate to be, though I am a man? Man himself has a great depth; You number his very hairs, O Lord, and none can be lost within You.[29] And yet the hairs of his head are easier to be numbered than his feelings and the movements of his heart.

[**14.23**] But the orator Hierius was of the kind that I admired in such a way that I wanted to be like him, and I erred because of my pride and was tossed about with every wind,[30] but I was still secretly steered by You. So how is it that I know and confess to You with such certainty that I had admired him more on account of the admiration of his extollers than because of the things for which he was extolled? The reason is because had he not been praised, had the same men criticized him, berating and deriding him, my admiration and fervor would not have been aroused, would not have been sparked. And yet nothing would have been different, nor would he have been another man: the only thing different would have been the estimation of those men. Behold where the weak soul, not yet bolstered by the solidity of truth, is cast! Just as the winds of tongues blow from the breast of those who voice opinions, so is the soul thrown this way and that, turned and whirled, clouds hindering it from seeing light, from seeing truth; and yet behold: truth lies right before us. It was a vital thing to me that my discourse and studies be known to that orator, for if he commended them I would have been kindled even more, but if he rejected them, my empty heart, void of Your firmness, would have been deeply wounded. And yet *On the Beautiful and the Fitting*, which had been the reason I had written to Hierius, was a topic which I delighted in reflecting on and contemplating, esteeming it even if others did not join me in that estimation.

[15.24] But I had not yet seen that the crux on which this truly great subject hinges is Your creation, Almighty God, You Who alone create miracles.[31] My mind had perused corporeal forms, and I defined "beautiful" as being that which is beautiful in itself, distinguishing it from "fitting" as being that whose beauty lies in its harmony with something else, and I built up this notion through examples from the physical world. I then reflected on the nature of the mind, but the false idea I had of spiritual things did not allow me to discern the truth. Truth was pouring into my eyes with all its force, but I turned my reeling mind from incorporeal things to shapes, colors, and large and solid things. And as I was unable to see these things in my mind, I thought I could not see my mind. And whereas in virtue I loved peace and in vice despised discord, in the former I observed unity, while in the latter I observed a kind of division. And in that unity I foolishly perceived the rational mind as well as the nature of truth and of supreme good, while in that division I believed there to be some unknown substance of irrational life as well as the nature of supreme evil, which should be not simply a substance but real life as well, and yet not derived from You, my God, You Who are the source of all things. The former I had called a "monad," as if it were a sexless mind, but the latter a "duad," anger in cruelty, lust in passion. I did not know what I was talking about, for I had not known or learned that evil was not a substance, nor that our mind is not the supreme and unchangeable good.

[15.25] For just as cruelty is sparked if the emotion of the soul where passion arises is corrupted and becomes contrary and unruly, and lust is sparked when the affection of the soul is not restrained where carnality is sparked, so too do errors and false opinions defile life if the rational mind is corrupted. This was the case with me at the time, as I did not know that the mind must be enlightened by another light in order to partake of truth, as it is not itself the nature of truth, for You will light my lamp, Lord my God, You will lighten my darkness, and of Your bounty we have all received, for You are the true light that lights every man who comes into this world; for in You there is no changing or shadow of change.[32]

[15.26] I strove toward You, but You rejected me so that I would taste death, for You oppose the proud. And what greater pride than for me to claim with wondrous madness that I am by nature that which You are? For while I am mutable, which was clear to me by my wish to become wise—to change from worse to better—I preferred to imagine You as mutable too, rather than think myself not to be that which You are. So You rejected me and opposed my stiff-necked vanity, and I imagined corporeal forms, and, myself flesh, I accused You of being flesh as well. I was a wandering breeze[33] and did not return to You, but kept wandering on to things that are not, that are neither in You nor in me nor in the body, things that were not created for me by Your Truth but formed by my vanity out of the corporeal. I used to address the humble who were faithful to You, fellow citizens from whom, unknown to myself, I stood exiled, and I would say to them, prattling and foolish as I was, "How can a soul that God created err?" And yet I did not want to be asked, "How can God err?" I used to contend that Your immutable substance is compelled to err rather than admit that my mutable substance had erred of its own accord, and that its punishment was now to wander.

[15.27] I must have been about twenty-six or twenty-seven years old when I wrote those volumes, steeped in imagined corporeal entities that were droning in the ears of my heart, which I had turned toward Your inner melody, my God, Who are sweet truth, as I thought about the beautiful and the fitting and longed to stand still and hear You, and rejoice at the voice of the Bridegroom.[34] But I could not, for through the voices of my own errors I was being impelled to external things, and through the weight of my own pride I was sinking into what was lowest, for You did not let me hear joy and gladness; nor did my bones rejoice, for they had not yet been humbled.[35]

[16.28] What good did it do me that when I was not yet twenty a book of Aristotle came into my hands that people call *Ten Categories* (whose very title my rhetoric master at Carthage spoke with cheeks puffed out with pride, as did others who were considered learned, so that I longed with great and divine suspense to read it), and that I then read and understood this book without the aid of another? And on my conferring with those who said that they had only understood it with great difficulty after reading it with accomplished tutors who had not only explained it to them but had drawn many things in the sand, they could not tell me more than I had learned from reading the book on my own. The book appeared to me to speak quite clearly of substances, such as "man" and what constitutes him, such as the form of a man and what kind of form it is, his stature and how many feet high that is, and his relationship to others, such as whose brother he is, or where he is situated, or when he was born, and whether he is standing or sitting, wearing shoes or armor, whether he is doing something or whether something is being done to him, and the innumerable things that can be classed under the nine categories of which I have given some examples, or under the chief category of substance.[36]

[16.29] So what good did this do me when in fact it did me harm, and, believing that all that exists is gathered within those ten categories, I tried to understand even You, my God, Who are miraculously simple and immutable, as if You had been subjected to Your beauty and magnitude and they existed in You as in a body, as qualities of a subject, whereas You Yourself are Your own beauty and magnitude. A body, on the other hand, is not great or beautiful just by being a body: even if it were less great or less beautiful it would nevertheless still be a body. What I thought of You was false, not true, a figment of my misery, not the firmament of Your beatitude. For You had commanded, and it was done, that to me the earth would bring forth thorns and thistles, and that with toil I would earn my bread.[37]

[16.30] And what good did it do me that I, the most worthless slave of evil lusts, had read and understood on my own all the books I could find on the so-called liberal arts? I delighted in them, but did not know the source of all that was true and certain in them, for I had my back to the light and my face to the things that were illuminated, so that my face, with which I could discern all that was illuminated, remained in the dark. I could understand without great difficulty or the help of a tutor whatever was written on the art of speaking or disputing, on the measures of forms, of music, and of numbers. This You know, Lord my God, because both quickness of mind and acumen in discerning have been Your gift to me, though that did not lead me to offer them up to You, so they did not bring me good but brought me ruin, since I did much to keep a great part of my gift to myself. I did not keep my wealth for You, but strayed from You to a distant land to dissipate it in lustful harlotry.[38] For what good did it do me to have something good that I did not use well? I did not realize how difficult these arts were to understand even by those who were studious and clever until I attempted to teach these arts to them, when the best student was the one who was not too slow in following my explanations.

[16.31] But what good did it do me to believe that You, Lord God and Truth, are a bright immense body and I a fragment of that body? What perverseness! But that was how I was, and I do not blush, my God, to avow before You Your mercies toward me, and appeal to You now, when I did not blush then to profess to men my blasphemies and to bark like a dog against You.[39] What good to me then was it that my agile intellect understood those doctrines of learning, and that without the help of a human tutor I could unknot all those knotted texts, while in the doctrines of piety I erred so disgracefully and with such sacrilegious infamy? Or what harm came to Your children whose intellect was slower, since they did not wander so far from You, so that in the nest of Your Church they might sprout feathers in safety, and nourish the wings of love with the food of a sound faith? O Lord our God, under the cover of Your wings we have hope. Protect us and carry us, for it is You Who carry us when we are small and until our hair turns white;[40] for our strength when it is You is true strength, but when it is our own, it is weakness. Our good is to abide at Your side forever; having turned away, we were ruined. Let us now return, Lord, so that we will not be overturned, because our unblemished good abides at Your side, You being our good, and we do not fear that there is nowhere for us to return, because it is from there that we fell: while we were away our House, Your eternity, did not fall.

NOTES

1   The Manichaean religion.

2   It was believed that Manichean "saints" or "elect"—the elders of the Manichaean religion—could release particles of God that were trapped within food by digesting what they ate. See Book III, 10.18.

3   Psalm 26:6 (Vulgate), 27:6 (other translations).

4   Augustine had a son, Adeodatus, from this union.

5   The Manichaean spiritual world of light.

6   Proverbs 10:4. "He that trusteth to lies feedeth the winds: and the same runneth after birds that fly away." (Douay-Rheims Bible)

7   A quotation of Psalm 40:5 (Vulgate), 41:4 (other translations).

8   From John 5:14. Jesus speaks these words to an invalid he had healed.

9   A quotation of Romans 2:6.

10 Psalm 50:19 (Vulgate), 50:17 (other translations).

11 James 4:6; 1 Peter 5:5. See Book I, 1.1.

12 Thagaste.

13 Romans 5:5. "Now hope does not disappoint, because the love of God has been poured out in our hearts by the Holy Spirit who was given to us." (New King James Bible)

14 Psalm 93:1 (Vulgate), 94:1 (other translations).

15 Romans 11:33.

16 Augustine was still Manichaean at the time, and his understanding of God was not yet Christian.

17 Ovid, *Tristia* 4.4.72.

18 2 Timothy 4:3–4.

19 Jeremiah 23:24.

20 A quotation from Psalm 79:8 (Vulgate), 80:7 (other translations).

21 Isaiah 46:8.

22 A quotation from Psalm 18:6 (Vulgate), 19:5 (other translations).

23 Isaiah 46:8.

24 John 1:10.

25 1 Timothy 1:15.

26 Psalm 40:5 (Vulgate), 41:4 (other translations).

27 Psalm 4:3 (Vulgate), 4:2 (other translations).

28 Psalm 72:9 (Vulgate), 73:9 (other translations).

29 Matthew 10:30.

30 Ephesians 4:14.

31 Psalm 135:4 (Vulgate), 136:4 (other translations).

32 James 1:17. "Every best gift, and every perfect gift, is from above, coming down from the Father of lights, with whom there is no change, nor shadow of alteration." (Douay-Rheims Bible)

33 Psalm 77:39 (Vulgate), 78:39 (other translations).

34 John 3:29. The Bridegroom is Christ.

35 Psalm 50:10 (Vulgate), 51:8 (other translations).

36 Aristotle's chief categories: substance, quantity, relations, quality, place,
     time, position, state, action, and affection.

37 Genesis 3:18–19. God's punishment of Adam.

38 Luke 15:13.

39 Judith 13:15.

40 Isaiah 46:4.

BOOK V

[1.1] Accept the sacrifice of my confessions from the hand of my tongue[1] that You have formed and have stirred to praise Your name,[2] and heal all my bones[3] so they will proclaim, "Lord, who is like You?" For he who confesses to You does not inform You of what takes place within him; Your eye is not shut out from a closed heart, nor can Your hand be repulsed by the harshness of man, for You can crush it in pity or in vengeance, and nothing can escape Your fire.[4] But let my soul praise You so that it may love You, and acknowledge Your mercies to You so that it may praise You. Your whole creation neither ceases nor is silent in praising You, nor is the spirit of all that lives in silence, their voices directed to You, nor creation animate or inanimate through the voice of those who contemplate these creations, so that our soul will rise from its weariness toward You, propping itself on what You have created to reach You Who wonderfully made these creations, and having reached You our soul will be restored and given true strength.

[2.2] Let the restless and the wicked depart and flee from You, but still You see them, You pierce the shadows. And behold, everything about them is beautiful though they are ugly. How have they wronged You? How have they dishonored Your rule that from the heavens to the lowest depths is just and unblemished? Where did they flee when they fled from Your countenance?[5] Where will You not find them? But they fled so that they would not see You see-

ing them and, blinded, would stumble against You, for You forsake
nothing You have created; the unjust stumble against You and justly
flounder: withdrawing from Your gentleness, they collide with Your
rectitude and fall at Your severity. It is clear that they do not know
that You are everywhere, that no place can encompass You, and that
You alone are near even to those who believe that they are far from
You. Let them turn and seek You, for You have not forsaken Your
creation as they have forsaken their creator. Let them turn and seek
You, and behold, You are in their hearts, in the hearts of those who
confess to You and rush toward You, and weep on Your breast after
the many arduous paths they have trodden. You gently wipe away
their tears,[6] and they weep more and rejoice in their tears; for it is
You, Lord, not a man of flesh and blood but You, Lord, Who made
them, and Who remakes and consoles them. But where was I when I
was seeking You? You were before me, but I had departed from myself
and could not find myself, much less find You.

[3.3] I will speak of my twenty-ninth year openly before my God. A
certain bishop of the Manicheans had come to Carthage, Faustus[7]
by name, a great trap of the Devil,[8] and many were ensnared by the
lures of his delightful eloquence that I admired, though I could see
that his words diverged from the truth of the things about which
I was eager to learn: nor did I consider the ornate plate containing his discourse so much as I did the knowledge that this Faustus,
so praised among the Manicheans, set before me to feed upon. His
fame, that he was supremely skilled in all the esteemed disciplines,
particularly the liberal disciplines, preceded him, but as I had read
and kept in my memory much of the philosophers, I compared some
of their teachings with the tangled fictions of the Manicheans, and
I found that what the philosophers said was more probable, for at
least they prevailed in appraising the world, though they were unable
to discover its Lord.[9] For You are great, Lord, and keep the humble in Your sight, though You regard the lofty from afar.[10] You only

draw near to crushed hearts; You are not found close to those whose hearts are proud, not even if by assiduous skill they could count the stars and the grains of sand and measure the constellations and track the courses of the stars.

[3.4] With the minds and intellect You bestowed upon the philosophers they have discovered many things, predicting many years ahead the eclipses of those bright celestial bodies, the sun and the moon, what day and what hour, and the degree of their eclipse, their calculations not falling short. Things came to pass as they foretold. They wrote down the rules they had ascertained, and today these rules are read and predictions made in what year and what month of the year, on what day of the month and at what hour of the day, and what fraction of the light of the moon or the sun will be eclipsed, and it comes to be as it is foretold. People who are not versed in this science marvel and are amazed, and those who are versed in it exult and are exalted, and by their impious pride they depart from You and desert Your great light. They can foresee an eclipse of the sun in the future, though they cannot see their own eclipse in the present, for they do not search piously the source of the intellect that has granted them this understanding. Discovering that You made them, they do not give themselves to You to save what You made, nor slay in sacrifice to You what they have made of themselves. Nor do they slaughter their pride that soars like a bird, nor their own prying curiosity that, like a fish of the sea, wanders through the hidden paths of the abyss, nor do they slaughter their own lust that is like that of the beasts of the field, so that You, Lord, a devouring fire, may consume their decaying mortal cares, and recreate them immortal.

[3.5] But they did not know the way—Your Word—by which You made these things that they measured, or made them who did the measuring, or made the perception with which they perceived what they measured and the mind with which they measured; nor did they know that Your wisdom is immeasurable.[11] Jesus, the Only-Begotten, was Himself made for our wisdom and righteousness and sanctification,[12] and was numbered among us and paid tribute to Caesar.[13] They did not know the way to descend from themselves to Him, and through him to ascend to him. They did not know this way, and regarded themselves as exalted among the stars and constellations, and behold, they fell crashing to the earth[14] and their foolish hearts were rendered dark.[15] The Manicheans say much that is true about the creation, but the Truth, the Author of the creation, they do not seek with piety and so cannot find Him, or if they do find Him, recognizing God, they do not honor Him as God, or give thanks, but stray in their ideas, and call themselves wise, attributing to themselves what is Yours; and consequently with perverse blindness they strive to attribute to You what is theirs, bestowing lies on You Who are Truth, and changing the glory of incorruptible God into the image of corruptible man, and bird, and four-footed beast, and creeping things, changing Your Truth into a lie, worshipping and serving creation rather than the Creator.[16]

[3.6] Yet I did retain many true things that the Manicheans asserted about the creation itself. I took into consideration the system of calculations and the sequencing of time and the visible evidence of the stars; comparing these with the assertions of Mani, who had written much and in ravings on these matters, I did not come upon any system for the solstices or equinoxes, or the eclipses of the heavenly bodies, nor anything of the kind I had learned from books of temporal knowledge. I was commanded to believe, but Mani's teachings did not correspond to the system of calculations and what I had put to the proof with my own eyes, but was decidedly different from these.

[4.7] Lord God of truth, does he who knows these things please You? Unhappy is the man who knows all this yet does not know You, but happy is he who knows You though he does not know any of this.

And whoever knows You and these things as well is not the happier on account of them, but only on account of You, if in knowing You he glorifies You for being You and gives thanks and does not stray in his own ideas. For he is better who knows that he owns a tree and gives thanks to You for its use, though he does not know how many cubits high the tree is or how wide it spreads, than the man who measures the tree and counts all its branches but neither owns the tree nor knows or loves its Creator. This is also true of a faithful believer to whom all the wealth of this world belongs and yet possesses all as if he owned nothing[17] by clinging to You, Whom all things serve, even if he does not know the course of the Great Bear. It would be foolish to doubt that this man is better than the one who can measure the heavens and count the stars and weigh the elements, but disregards You Who have arranged all things in number, weight, and measure.[18]

[5.8] But yet who bade this fellow Mani write on matters not necessary for learning piety? For You have said to man, "Behold, piety is wisdom,"[19] a concept of which Mani could well be ignorant even if he had perfect knowledge of other things. But brazenly daring to teach a thing of which he truly knew nothing shows clearly that he did not know piety. For it is vanity to profess these worldly things even when one knows them, while to confess to You is piety. Therefore he strayed in speaking so much of these things, exposed as he was by those who truly understood them, from which the limits of his understanding of more recondite matters are clear. He did not want to be thought insignificant, and so endeavored to persuade people that the Holy Ghost, the comforter and enricher of those faithful to You, was personally within him with full authority. When, then, Mani was discovered to have erred in what he said of the heaven and the stars, and of the movement of the sun and moon, though these matters do not pertain to religious doctrine, his sacrilegious audacity was revealed, seeing that he not only asserted with raging vanity things about which he was ignorant but also lied, striving to attribute them to himself as if he were divine.

[5.9] When I hear a brother Christian who is ignorant of one or another matter and who thinks that something is true when it is not, I regard him with patience as he expresses his opinion, but I would not perceive his ignorance of the aspect and order of physical creation as harmful to him so long as he does not believe anything unworthy of You, Lord, Creator of all things. But it is harmful if he declares that his opinion pertains to religious doctrine, and obstinately dares assert things that he does not know. Such a weakness in the infancy of faith is endured with motherly solicitude until the new man grows into a complete man and is not blown this way and that by every wind of doctrine.[20] But when a man has dared to present himself as a teacher, a founder, the leader and prince of those he has persuaded of his ideas, so that they who follow him believe that they are not following a mere man but Your Holy Spirit, then who among us, once that man has been exposed for teaching lies, would not condemn his actions as a great madness that is to be detested and cast aside? But I had not yet clearly determined whether Mani's teachings did not perhaps explain the changes of longer and shorter days and nights, the change of day and night itself, the eclipses of the heavenly bodies, and whatever other phenomena of this kind I had read of in books: so long as his concepts remained a possibility, I was not certain whether the truth lay with him or with the philosophers; but, trusting in his reputed sanctity, I was prepared to place his authority above what I believed.

[6.10] For almost the entire nine years in which, with roving mind, I had listened to the Manicheans, I had waited with great yearning for the coming of this man named Faustus. Whenever the other Manicheans I met with were unable to answer my questions, they promised me that once this Faustus came and he and I conversed, he would easily and clearly explain these questions, and even greater questions I might want to ask. When he finally did come, I found him to be a man of agreeable and pleasant words, who said all the same things the others said, except that his prattling was far more affable. But of what use to my thirst was an ornate but empty cup offered me by a pleasing cupbearer? My ears were already cloyed with all those ideas; nor did they seem any better to me because they were better said, nor truer because they were more expertly put, nor the mind wise because the face was fair and the speech graceful. Those who had held this man out to me had little judgment, which was why they thought him knowledgeable and wise merely because he charmed them with his speech. I have also known a different kind of people who become suspicious of truth and refuse to accept it if it is delivered in speech that is adorned and rich. But You, my God, had already taught me through wonderful and secret ways, and I believe what You have taught me because it is true; nor is there any teacher other than You of truth, wheresoever or from wherever it may illuminate us. It is from You that I had learned that nothing must be thought to be spoken truly merely because it is spoken eloquently, nor falsely merely because the words from the speaker's lips are not smooth, but then again also not simply true because the words are spoken without refinement, and not simply false because the discourse is exquisite. For wisdom and folly are like nourishing and unnourishing food, while adorned or unadorned phrases are like plates made of gold or brass: either kind of food can be served on either kind of plate.

[6.11] The fervor with which I had waited so long for that man to come was heightened by the passion and feeling with which he discoursed and the elegant and quick words in which he clothed his ideas. I was delighted, and praised and extolled him as much as many others did and even more, though I was grieved that in the assembly of his audience I was not permitted to ask questions and warmly converse and dispute with him, sharing with him what troubled me. When this did become possible, and I and my friends managed to engage him at a moment when it was not inappropriate for us to converse, I expressed some of the things that troubled me and found him quite ignorant of the arts and sciences, except for grammar, and that merely in the ordinary way. But because he had read some of Cicero's orations, very few books by Seneca, some works of the poets, and whatever books of his own sect had been written well in Latin, and because he practiced speaking in public every day, he had acquired an eloquence that proved all the more agreeable and seductive, tempered as it was by his intelligence and a kind of natural gracefulness. Is it not as I recall it, Lord my God, judge of my conscience? Before You are my heart and my remembrance, You Who had led me then by the hidden mystery of Your providence and set my shameful errors before my eyes[21] that I might see them and hate them.

[7.12] For after it became clear to me that Faustus was unversed in the sciences in which I had thought he excelled, I began to despair of his answering and solving the questions that troubled me. One can of course be ignorant and attain true piety, but not if one is a Manichaean, for their books are filled with tangled fictions about the heaven and the stars, the sun and the moon. I no longer thought him able to give me the answer to the question I had been so longing for: whether the calculations contained in the books of Mani were in any way comparable to those I had read elsewhere or whether they were better. When I proposed that we examine and discuss the matter, he refrained with sound modesty from contending with the burden. He knew that he did not know these things, and was not ashamed to confess it. He was not one of those loquacious men, so many of whom I have had to endure, who ventured to instruct me but had nothing to say. This man did have a heart, though it was not directed toward You, but still it was not entirely unreflective upon itself. He was not altogether ignorant of his own ignorance; nor was he rashly prepared to become enmeshed in a debate from which he could neither extricate himself nor prevail. This led me to like him all the more, for the modesty of a mind that confesses is of greater worth than the questions for which I sought an answer. This is how I found him to be when it came to all the more difficult and subtle questions.

[7.13] My zeal for the writings of Mani had been broken, and I despaired even more of the other Manichean teachers when Faustus, who was so renowned among them, had fallen short in the many questions that troubled me. But I began to spend time with him, for he too was a lover of literature, which as a rhetorician I was teaching young men in Carthage at that time, and I began to read with him either what he desired to hear or what I considered amenable to his intellect. But for the rest, all the efforts with which I had intended to advance higher in that sect came to an end once I got to know him. Not that I removed myself from the Manicheans entirely, but remained as one who has found nothing better, resolved in the meantime to content myself with what I had somehow stumbled into, unless by chance something greater should shine forth. Thus Faustus, who was for so many a snare of death,[22] had begun, though neither willingly nor wittingly, to loosen the trap that was ensnaring me. For in Your secret providence, my God, Your hands did not forsake my soul. Out of my mother's heart's blood, and through the tears she wept night and day, a sacrifice was offered for me to You, and You led me forth in wondrous ways. You led me, my God, for it is the Lord Who directs the steps of man, and the Lord Who determines his path.[23] For how can salvation be attained but from Your hand, remaking what You have made?

[8.14] You led me so that I should be persuaded to go to Rome, to teach there what I was teaching in Carthage, and I will not omit confessing to You how I was persuaded to this, because in that too

Your most profound recesses and Your mercy most present to us must be reflected on and confessed. I did not want to go to Rome simply because my friends urged me to, assuring me that in Rome I would garner greater profit and honor, though those things did influence my mind at the time. My main, and almost my only, reason was that I had heard that young men studied there more peaceably and were subjected to more rigorous discipline, not all rushing wildly into the class of a master whose pupils they were not; in Rome they were not even admitted into a class without a master's permission. In Carthage, on the other hand, there is an uncouth and unruly excess among pupils. They brazenly interrupt classes, and with crazed rowdiness bring turmoil to the order that the masters have established for the good of their students. With surprising foolishness they wreak mayhem that would be punishable by law if custom did not protect them, and they are the more wretched in that they do as lawful what will never be lawful by Your eternal law; and they believe that they are doing this with impunity, whereas they are punished with the blindness by which they do it, and suffer incomparably worse consequences than what they wreak. Such practices, which as a student I had refused to engage in, I had to endure in others as a teacher, and so I was happy to go to a place where those who knew assured me that such things were not done. But it was in truth You, my hope and my portion in the land of the living,[24] who wanted me to change my earthly dwelling for the salvation of my soul, and in Carthage You goaded me so that I would tear myself away from it, and for Rome You placed before me enticements that would draw me there with the advice of Manichean friends who loved a dead life, doing mad things in this life, hoping for vain things in the next. To set my steps aright, You secretly used their and my perverseness; for those who disturbed my calm were blinded by a disgraceful frenzy, while those who summoned me away loved only this world. Yet I, who detested true misery here, sought false happiness there.

[8.15] You knew, God, why I left Carthage and went to Rome, but You did not reveal the reason either to me or to my mother, who bitterly lamented my leaving and followed me as far as the shore. She clung to me in desperation, seeking either to keep me there or to come with me, but I deceived her, pretending that I had a friend I was seeing off with whom I had to wait until he had a good wind to sail. I lied to my mother—lied to such a mother—and so escaped. This too You have mercifully forgiven me, I who was filled with abhorrent foulness, preserving me from the waters of the sea for the waters of Your grace that would cleanse me and dry my mother's streaming eyes, with which she daily watered before You the ground on which she stood. But she refused to return home without me, and I barely managed to persuade her to stay that night in a place near our ship where there was a sanctuary in memory of the blessed Saint Cyprian. But that night I secretly departed without her as she remained behind, weeping and praying. What was she asking of You with so many tears, my God, but that You would not let me sail? Yet You, in Your high mindfulness, hearing the core of her desire, did not heed what she was asking, so that You could make out of me exactly what she had always asked. The wind blew and swelled our sails, and the shore receded from our sight, and on the following morning my mother came there raving with sorrow, filling Your ears with complaints and lamentations to which You paid no heed, while You allowed me to be transported by my desires in order to extinguish those desires, and my mother's earthly longing for me was rightly chastened by the scourge of sorrow. For she loved my being with her, as mothers do, though much more than many others, and she did not know what great joy You were preparing for her by my absence. She did not know, which is why she wept and sobbed, and through these torments she manifested the inheritance of Eve, seeking as she did with pain what with pain she had brought forth.[25] And yet, after accusing me of deception and cruelty, she again turned to interceding for me with You, and went back home while I went on to Rome.

[9.16] But behold, in Rome I was welcomed by the scourge of sickness, and I set out on a descent to hell, carrying with me all the sins I had committed against You, against myself, and against others, many and grievous sins beyond the shackles of original sin whereby we all die in Adam.[26] For You had not forgiven me any of these sins in Christ, nor by His Cross had He delivered me from the wrath I had incurred in You through my sins. For how could He deliver me by the crucifixion of a specter, which I believed him to be? As false as the death of His flesh seemed to me, so true was the death of my soul, and as true as the death of His flesh, so false was the life of my unbelieving soul. As my fever grew worse, I was dying and departing forever. But had I then set forth, where would I have set forth to but into fire and torment such as my deeds deserved within Your order of truth? My mother did not know this, but, absent, prayed for me. But You, everywhere present, heard her where she was, and had compassion for me where I was, so that my body should recover and become sound once again despite my unsound sacrilegious heart. For notwithstanding the great danger I was in, I did not desire Your baptism; I had done better as a boy, when I had begged it of my pious mother, as I have recollected earlier and confessed. But I had grown in shamefulness, and I madly mocked the counsel of Your medicine, You Who would not let me, being in the state I was in, die this double death. My mother's heart pierced by such a wound would never have healed, for I cannot put into words what she felt for me and how much greater her torment was now, in giving birth to my spirit, than it had been when she had given birth to me in the flesh.

[9.17] As my dying unbaptized would have pierced the inner depths of my mother's love, I cannot see how she could have recovered; but all her many prayers, so unceasing and profuse, had only been to You and You alone. But would You, merciful God, have spurned the crushed and humbled heart of the chaste and sober widow who was so generous in giving alms, so obedient in her service to Your saints, never missing a day to take communion at Your altar—twice a day, morning and evening—never failing to come to Your church, not in order to listen to foolish tales or the gossip of old women, but that she might hear You in Your words, and You might hear her in her prayers. Could You, through Whose gift this woman was as she was, disdain and refuse Your succor to the tears with which she was beseeching You not for gold or silver, nor for any fickle or flimsy benefit, but for the salvation of her son's soul? Never, Lord. Of course You were at her side, hearing and providing within the order You had predestined that her prayers be fulfilled. It is unthinkable that You would deceive her in visions, and the answers she kept in her faithful breast, some of which I have mentioned, others not, and, always praying, presented to You as a note of promise written in Your own hand. For as Your mercy endures through the ages,[27] You condescend to become the debtor through Your promises to those all of whose debts You forgive.

[10.18] And so You had me recover from that illness, healing the son of Your servant, but only in body for the time being, so that You would grant him a better and more enduring health. At that time in Rome I also joined those deceiving and deceived Manichean saints, not only their disciples, among whom was the man in whose house I had fallen ill and recovered, but also those they call "Elect."[28] For I still thought that it was not we who sin, but that some other nature was sinning within us. It delighted my pride to be free of blame and not to have to confess when I did evil, so that You might heal my soul because it had sinned against You. I was delighted to excuse myself and accuse that other thing within me, a thing that was not I. But in fact it was entirely I; my impiety had divided me against myself, and my sin was the more incurable in that I did not judge myself a sinner. It was an execrable iniquity that I preferred to have You, Almighty God, You, subjugated within me to my destruction, than to have myself subjugated within You to my salvation. You had not yet posted a guard before my mouth and a door of restraint about my lips so that my heart would not stray with evil words, making excuses for sins committed with those who sin, which is why I was still close to the Manicheans' Elect, though I now despaired of advancing in that false doctrine; and though I had resolved to follow it if I should find no better, I did so now halfheartedly and with indifference.

[10.19] The thought had also arisen in me that the philosophers who are called the Academics might be more judicious than the rest, proposing that everything was to be doubted, determining that truth lay beyond man's comprehension. This, as was commonly believed, clearly seemed to me to be their doctrine, though I had not yet discerned their true intent. Nor did I refrain from openly discouraging my host from the excessive confidence I saw him to have in the fables that filled the books of Mani. Yet I remained closer to the Manicheans than I did to others who were not of this heresy, but I no longer defended it with as much vehemence. Still, my closeness to that sect (Rome conceals a great number of Manicheans) deterred me from searching for anything else, especially as I despaired of finding truth in Your Church from which they had diverted me, Lord of heaven and earth, Creator of all things visible and invisible.[29] It seemed to me a disgrace to believe You to have a form of human flesh and to be bound by the physical lines of our limbs. And because when I strove to think of my God I did not know what to think of but a physical mass, for I thought that whatever was not a physical mass could not exist, this was the greatest and almost sole cause of my inevitable error.

[10.20] Thus I also believed evil to be a physical substance of a kind with its own repulsive and misshapen mass, whether solid, which they called earth, or dilute and delicate like the body of the air, which they imagined to be creeping over the earth like a malignant mind. And because my piety, such as it was, hindered me from believing that our good God would ever create an evil nature, I determined that there had to be two masses opposing one another, each boundless, but the evil mass more contracted and the good mass more vast. From these first pestilent ideas other sacrileges followed, for when my mind strove to return to the true faith, I was driven back, since the true faith was not as I had thought it to be. O God Whose mercies have made my confessing possible, I thought myself more devout if I believed You unbounded on all sides except for the side where the mass of evil was opposed to You (even if in this way I was driven to profess You bounded), rather than if I believed You bounded on all sides by the form of a human body. And it seemed to me better to believe You to have created no evil (that to me, ignorant as I was, seemed not only some sort of substance but a corporeal substance, since I could not conceive of a mind being anything but a delicate substance spreading over space) than to believe that the nature of evil as I conceived it to be came from You. I even imagined our Savior, Your Only-Begotten Son, to have emerged from the mass of Your luminous substance for our salvation, refusing to believe of him anything other than what in my vanity I could imagine. Furthermore, I believed that a nature such as his could not be born of the Virgin Mary without being mingled with flesh, and I could not see how what I had imagined could be mingled without being polluted. I was therefore afraid to believe him born in flesh, lest I be compelled to believe him defiled by flesh. Your true followers will laugh with indulgent compassion if they read these confessions of mine; but that is how I was.

[11.21] I also did not believe that what the Manicheans refuted in Your Bible could be defended, but there were times when I did long to confer upon particular points with an expert in the Bible, putting his notions to the test. Already in Carthage the words of a certain Helpidius, who spoke and debated against the Manicheans, had begun to unsettle me in that he had produced from the Scrip-

tures things that could not easily be questioned, to which the Manicheans' response struck me as weak. Nor would they offer their
responses openly in public but only to us in private, asserting that
the Scriptures of the New Testament had been corrupted by someone who sought to graft the law of the Jews upon the Christian
faith, though the Manicheans were unable to produce any uncorrupted texts. But the main thing that fettered and choked me, suffocated me, was my conception of those physical masses, smothered
beneath which I could not breathe in the air of Your pure and
untainted truth.

[12.22] I now began assiduously to teach rhetoric, for which I had
come to Rome, first gathering at my house some pupils to whom
and through whom I began to be known. But I soon discovered that
pupils in Rome did things beyond what I had had to bear in Carthage. It was true that, just as my friends had assured me, the destruction wreaked by dissipated young men[30] was not practiced in Rome,
but to avoid paying a master's fee, I was now told, many young men
would suddenly group together and conspire to change to another
master, betraying trust, shunning justice for love of money. I hated
these youths, though not with a perfect hatred,[31] because I hated
more what I would suffer through them than the unlawful things
they did to everyone. Truly, these are base individuals who commit
fornication against You,[32] loving the fickle wantonness of temporal
things and the besmirched profit that defiles the hand that grasps
it, embracing the fleeting world and despising You Who abide, and
Who call back and forgive the meretricious souls of men that return
to You. Now, too, I hate such perverse and twisted men, though I
love them if they will reform so as to prefer the learning they acquire
over wealth, and prefer You over learning, God Who are the truth
and richness of assured good and purest peace. But in those days I
shunned these evildoers more for my sake, rather than wanting them
to become good for Yours.

[13.23] When, therefore, an epistle came from Milan to the Prefect of Rome requesting that they be provided with a master of rhetoric for their city, who, furthermore, was to travel there at public expense, I proposed myself through those very men filled with Manichaean untruths, though neither I nor they were aware that my going there would free me of them. I first had to give an oration on a proposed topic before Symmachus, who at the time was the Prefect of Rome, and he then sent me to Milan. I came to that city to Bishop Ambrose, known throughout the world as among the best of men, devout in his worship of You, his eloquence powerfully ministering to Your people the flour of Your wheat,[33] the gladness of Your oil,[34] and the sober intoxication of Your wine.[35] I was unknowingly led by You to him, so that by him I might knowingly be led to You. This man of God received me as a father and welcomed me with the true kindness of a bishop, and I began to be greatly drawn to him, at first not as a teacher of the truth, of which I cherished no hope at all in Your Church, but as a man who showed kindness toward me. I listened attentively to him speak before the people, not with the purpose for which I ought to have listened, but examining, as it were, his eloquence to see whether it matched its reputation or whether its flow was greater or lesser than had been reported. I hung intently on his words, but was indifferent and disdainful of what he said; I was delighted by the sweetness of his speech, which was more learned than that of Faustus yet less ebullient and honeyed in manner. But in the content there was no comparison, for Manichean delusions led Faustus astray, while Bishop Ambrose soundly taught salvation. But salvation is far away from sinners such as I was then, and yet gradually and unconsciously I was drawing nearer.

[14.24] I made no effort to learn what he spoke about, but only to hear how he spoke it, for only this empty care was left to me as I despaired of a path attainable to man that leads to You. But together with the words that I regarded, I now began to take in the substance that I had disregarded, for I could not separate them from one another. And as I opened my heart, noting how eloquently he spoke, I also began to note how truly he was speaking. I now started to see for the first time that everything he said was defendable, and that the true faith, which I had believed could not prevail against the Manicheans' objections, could be upheld without shame, especially after I heard him resolve one enigmatic passage after another from the Old Testament where my literal interpretation had slain me spiritually.[36] After many of those passages had been spiritually explained, I blamed myself for having despaired that the Law and the Prophets could be defended against those who hated and derided them. Yet even so I did not feel that I ought to choose the path of the True Faith simply because it needed its own knowledgeable defenders, who could powerfully and without absurd reasoning counter its detractors; nor did I feel that my former beliefs should be condemned on account of both sides being defendable. Though I did perceive the True Faith as not defeated, it still did not appear to me triumphant.

[14.25] But now I put my mind more vigorously to the task of seeking through definite proof to convict the Manichaeans of falsehood. Had I been able to conceive of the existence of a spiritual substance, all their contrivances would have come undone and been cast utterly from my mind; but I could not conceive of such a thing. Nevertheless, concerning the physical world and the whole of nature that our senses of the flesh can touch, the more I considered and compared, the more I judged the notions of most of the philosophers to be far more probable than those of the Manicheans. And so I followed the Academic philosophers' practice of doubting everything, as they are said to do. I wavered between the conflicting ideas and came to the conclusion that I would abandon the Manicheans. I decided that though I was still only in doubt, I would not continue to remain with that sect over which I already preferred some of the philosophers, even if I refused to entrust the curing of my ailing soul to these philosophers, as they were without Christ's saving name. I therefore decided for the time being to be a catechumen in the Christian Church to which my parents had entrusted me until a clear light should shine onto the path I was to follow.

NOTES

1 Proverbs 18:21.
2 Psalm 53:8 (Vulgate), 54:6 (other translations).
3 Psalm 6:3 (Vulgate), 6:2 (other translations).
4 Psalm 18:7 (Vulgate), 19:7 (other translations).
5 Psalm 138:7 (Vulgate), 139:7 (other translations).
6 Isaiah 25:8; Revelation 7:17, 21:4.
7 "Faustus" means "fortunate" or "auspicious" in Latin.
8 1 Timothy 3:7.
9 Wisdom 13:9.
10 Psalm 137:6 (Vulgate), 138:6 (other translations).
11 Psalm 146:5 (Vulgate), 147:6 (other translations).
12 1 Corinthians 1:30.
13 Matthew 22.
14 Isaiah 14:12.
15 A quotation from Romans 1:21.
16 Romans 1:21–25.
17 2 Corinthians 6:10.
18 Wisdom 11:21 (Vulgate), 11:20 (other translations).
19 Job 28:28.
20 Ephesians 4:13–14.
21 Psalm 49:21 (Vulgate), 50:21 (other translations).
22 Psalm 17:6 (Vulgate), 18:5 (other translations).
23 A quotation from Psalm 36:23 (Vulgate), 37:23 (other translations).
24 Psalm 141:6 (Vulgate), 142:5 (other translations).
25 Genesis 3:12.
26 1 Corinthians 15:22. "And as in Adam all die, so also in Christ all shall be made alive." (Douay-Rheims Bible)
27 Psalm 117:1(Vulgate), 118:1 (other translations).
28 See note 25, page 50.

29 Colossians 1:16.

30 The *Eversores*, a rowdy fraternity of senior students. See Book III, 3.6.

31 Psalm 138:22 (Vulgate), 139:22 (other translations).

32 Psalm 72:27 (Vulgate), 73:27 (other translations).

33 Psalm 80:17 (Vulgate), 81:16 (other translations).

34 Psalm 44:8 (Vulgate), 45:7 (other translations).

35 Bishop Ambrose's hymn "Splendor of the Father's Glory" ("Splendor paternae gloriae"), line 23.

36 2 Corinthians 3:6.

BOOK VI

[1.1] O God, my hope from my youth,[1] where were You, and to where had You withdrawn from me? Had You not created me and set me apart from the four-footed beasts and the birds of the sky, making me wiser?[2] And yet I was walking in darkness and on slippery paths,[3] seeking You outside myself, but not finding the God of my heart. I had reached the depths of the sea,[4] and despaired of ever finding truth. Strong in her piety, my mother had now come to me, following me over sea and land, confident in You in every danger she faced, and even on the perilous sea she comforted the sailors, who are more used to reassuring frightened passengers unaccustomed to the sea. She promised them a safe arrival, for You had assured her of this in a vision. She found me in great peril and in despair that I would ever find truth, but when I revealed to her that I was no longer a Manichean though not yet a true Christian, she did not leap with joy as if my words were unexpected. But she was now reassured concerning that part of my misery for which she had wept over me as one dead, though to be reawakened by You, and on a bier of her thoughts she offered me to You that You might say to the son of this widow, "Young man, I say to you, arise!"[5] And her son would come to life again and begin to speak, and You would deliver him to his mother. Thus no tempestuous exultation shook her heart when she heard that what she had prayed to You for every day with lamentations had already in so large a part come about, and though I had not yet attained truth, I had been rescued from falsehood. But as she was certain that You would grant the rest, since You had promised the whole, she replied to me with great calm, her breast filled with confidence, that she believed in Christ and that before she left this life she should see me a true and faithful Christian. That is what she said to me. But to You, Fountain of Mercies, her prayers and tears surged more profusely that You would quicken Your help and enlighten my darkness; and she hurried all the more zealously to church and hung on Bishop Ambrose's lips, praying for the fountain of water that springs up into eternal life. She cherished that man as if he were an angel of God, because she knew that it was through him that I had been brought for the time being to that state of wavering and doubt through which she foresaw with certainty that I would pass from sickness to health, with more severe danger in the interim that physicians call the turning point.

[2.2] My mother brought cakes, bread, and wine to the memorial shrines of the saints as she used to do in Africa,[6] but when she was stopped by the sexton and heard that Bishop Ambrose prohibited such offerings, she embraced the bishop's wishes with such piety and obedience that I marveled at how readily she faulted her own practice rather than dispute his prohibition. Thirst for wine did not beset her spirit, nor did love of wine incite her to a hatred of the truth, as happens with many men and women who are as repelled by a sermon of sobriety as drunkards are by watery wine. But when my mother would bring her basket with the customary ceremonial fare to the sanctuaries, to be first tasted by herself and then shared with others, she never offered more than a small cup of wine diluted according to her own sober taste, of which she would partake in piety. And if there were many shrines of the departed saints to be honored, she brought to them only that one cup to be offered everywhere, and this cup of wine, which was not only watery but also unpleasantly warm from being carried about, she distributed to the people there by small sips, for she had come to the sanctuary seeking piety, not pleasure. And my mother refrained with delight when she learned that the preeminent preacher and pious preceptor forbade such offerings, even to those who offered them in sobriety, lest an opportunity for excess be given to drunkards, for these offerings to the dead very much resembled the superstitions of heathens. Instead of a basket filled with fruits of the earth, my mother now learned to bring to the shrines of the martyrs a heart filled with untainted vows and to give what she could to the poor, so that the communion of the Body of the Lord might be celebrated there where in imitation of His Passion the martyrs had been sacrificed and crowned. And yet it seems to me, Lord my God—and my heart believes this before Your presence—that perhaps she would not have acquiesced so readily in relinquishing this custom had it been forbidden by another whom she did not cherish as she cherished Bishop Ambrose. She loved him beyond measure on account of my salvation, while he cherished her for the deep devoutness with which in good works and fervent spirit[7] she always came to the church, so that when he saw me he often sang her praises, congratulating me at having such a mother, though he did not know what a son she had in me, who doubted all these things and believed that the path to life could not be found.

[3.3] Nor did I yet in my prayers cry out for You to help me, but my mind was striving to learn and impatient to dispute. I considered Ambrose a happy man in the eyes of the world, as he was greatly respected by so many men of power. Only his celibacy seemed to me a heavy burden, but I could neither surmise nor had I ever experienced the hopes that he bore, his struggles against the temptations that beset his very perfection, or what solace he had in adversity, or the delicious joy as the hidden mouth of his heart partook of Your bread. Nor did he know of the fiery ferment within me or the perilous pit before me, for I could not ask him what I wanted to ask, nor in the way I wanted to ask it, kept as I was from asking him all my ques-

tions and hearing all his answers by the bustling throngs of people
to whose infirmities he ministered; and when he was not occupied
by these people, which was only for brief periods, he either restored
his body with essential nourishment or his mind with reading. But
when he read he ran his eyes across the page, his heart culling the
meaning though his voice and tongue remained at rest. Often when
we visited him (for no one was prohibited from entering, nor did he
expect that those who visited should be announced to him), we saw
him reading soundlessly, never in any other way, and after we sat
for a long time in silence (for who would dare intrude on such rapt
attention?) we would depart, assuming that he would not want to be
disturbed in this brief interval he had found to restore his thoughts,
free from the clamor of other people's cares. Perhaps his reason for
reading in silence was to avoid having to explain to a chance listener
who might interrupt him to ask the meaning of a difficult passage
he was reading or to discuss some of the harder questions: spending
his time in discussion, he could not read through as many scrolls as
he desired, though probably his wish to preserve his voice, which
tired so easily, might be the truer reason for his silent reading. But
whatever motive led him to read in this way, it was definitely a good
motive in a man like him.

[3.4] I did not, however, find an opportunity to ask the questions
I wanted to of that most holy oracle of Yours, his heart, unless
what I asked could be answered briefly; but to pour out the fiery
ferment within me required him to have much time, which he
never had. Yet I did hear him every Sunday rightly preaching the
Word of truth[8] among the people; and it became ever more clear
to me that all the knots of ingenious trickery that the Manichean
deceivers had devised against the Holy Scriptures could be unraveled. I now learned for certain that Your spiritual sons, who by
Your grace have been born again through our Mother the true
Church, do not interpret man as having been made by You in Your

own image[9] to mean that they conceived You as being bound by a human form (though I did not have the slightest, dimmest notion of what a spiritual substance might be). I blushed with dismay, but was also delighted that for so many years I had railed not against the Christian Church, but against the fictions of imagining You as corporeal. I had been so impetuous and impious that what I ought to have learned with inquiry I had pronounced upon with condemnation. For You, most high and most near, most hidden and most present, Who do not have some limbs that are larger and some that are smaller, who are entire everywhere and not limited to one place, You are not of a corporeal shape such as ours, and yet have made man after Your own image, but behold, man from head to foot is in one place.

[4.5] Ignorant of what Your image consisted, I ought to have knocked[10] and asked how it was to be believed, not opposed it with insults as if what I imagined was in fact believed. Thus distress as to what I should hold for certain gnawed more sharply at my innards the more ashamed I was that for so long I had been deluded and deceived by the promise of certainty, ranting as I had done with childish error and audacity against so many uncertainties as if they were certain. That they were falsehoods became clear to me later. But I was sure that they were uncertain and that I had once held them for certain, when, with blind disputes, I had accused Your true Church. Even if I did not yet know that that Your Church taught the truth, at least I knew that it did not teach that of which I had so gravely accused it. Hence I was confused, and turned toward You, and I rejoiced, my God, that the one true Church, the body of Your only Son, in which the name of Christ had been instilled in me as a child, was not inclined to childish trifles; nor did its sound doctrine maintain any precept that should confine You, the Creator of all, within a space however vast and wide, constraining You on all sides within the limbs of a human form.

[4.6] I was also filled with joy that I could now read the Law and the Prophets of the Old Testament with a different eye, to which before they had seemed absurd, and I had censured Your saints for doctrines that they did not in fact espouse. I was delighted to hear Ambrose in his sermons to the people assiduously commend as a rule, "The letter kills, but the Spirit gives life,"[11] drawing aside the mystic veil and revealing spiritually that which, when understood literally, seemed to teach something perverse. He did not say anything I could not accept, though I did not yet know whether what he said was true, for I kept my heart from assenting, fearing that I would fall. But in hanging suspended as I was, I was all the more suffocated. I wanted to be as certain of the things I could not see as I was certain that seven and three are ten. I was not so mad as to think that even that could not be comprehended, but I wanted to have other things just as certain, whether they be corporeal things not present to my senses, or spiritual things that I did not know how to imagine other than in a corporeal way. But I could have been cured by believing, so that my mind's vision would be cleared and in some way guided to Your Truth, which always abides and never forsakes. But as happens with one who has had a bad physician and is afraid of entrusting himself to one who is good, so it was with my soul that could not be healed except by believing, and out of fear that it might believe falsehoods, it refused to be healed, resisting Your hands, You Who have prepared the medicines of faith and applied them to the illnesses of the entire world, giving them such great power.

[5.7] From this time on, however, I began to prefer the true Christian doctrine, and thought it more restrained and honest in its call to believe things that could not be proven (either because they could not be understood by those present despite their being provable, or because they could not be proven at all), while the Manicheans brashly promised knowledge, mocking faith as credulity, only then to command that we believe most whimsical and absurd things because they could not be proven. Then little by little, Lord, with Your most tender and merciful hand, You touched and appeased my heart. I now reflected on the innumerable things I believed that I had not seen or that had occurred when I was not present: the many things in the history of the world, the many reports of places and cities I had never seen, the many things I had heard from friends, from physicians, from so many other men, things which if we did not believe we would do nothing in this life at all. And then there was that firm assurance with which I believed of what parents I had been born, something I could not know unless I had believed what I had heard. Thus You persuaded me that those were not to blame who believed Your Scriptures, which You have established with such authority among nearly all peoples, but that those who did not believe them were to blame. You persuaded me that I must not listen to those who might say to me, "How do you know that those Scriptures have been bestowed upon mankind by the Spirit of the one true and truthful God?" For this of all things is most to be believed, since no belligerence of deceitful questioning, so much of which I had read in all the philosophers who contradicted one another, could wrench from me the belief that You are what You are, even if I knew not what You are and that the governance of all things human lies with You.

[5.8] My belief in this was at times stronger, at times weaker, but I always believed both that You exist and that You watch over us, though I neither knew what was to be thought of Your substance, nor what path led to You or led back to You. Since we were too weak to discover the truth through clear reason, we needed the authority of the Holy Writ, and I now began to believe that You would never have given such exalted authority in all lands to the Bible, had You not willed us through it to believe in You and seek You. Since I had heard explained many of the incongruities in the Bible, incongruities that in the past I could not accept literally, I now ascribed them to the depth of its mysteries. Its authority seemed to me the more venerable and worthy of holy faith in that, while it was open for all to read, it preserved the grandeur of its mysteries within its profounder meaning. There is great clarity in the Bible's words and humility in its style, but it also rouses the concentration of those who are not light of heart,[12] and so receives all people in its embrace. Through its narrow gates[13] it sends to You a few souls, yet many more than if it did not loom with such great authority, nor draw such crowds to its bosom through its holy humility. These were my thoughts and You were with me, I sighed and You heard me, I wavered and You led me, and I wandered through the wide paths of the world and You did not forsake me.

[6.9] I strove for honors, riches, marriage, and You laughed at me. In pursuing these desires I underwent the most bitter difficulties, and You were the more compassionate the less You allowed anything that was not You to delight me. Look at my heart, Lord, You Who will me to remember and confess to You. May my soul cling to You now that You have freed it from the viscous birdlime of death. How wretched was my soul, and You inflamed the pain of the wound so that abandoning all else it might be directed toward You, Who are above all things and without Whom all things would be nothing, so that it might be directed toward You and healed. How wretched I was, and how You made me feel my wretchedness on that day when I was preparing to recite a panegyric on the emperor, in which I was to lie profusely and, in lying, gain the favor of those who knew I was lying. My heart was smothered with distress and boiling with the fever of pestilential thoughts. As I walked along a street in Milan I noticed an indigent beggar, who was probably drunk; he was joking and happy. I sighed, and said to my friends who were accompanying me how we suffered on account of foolish ambitions such as those I was striving for, and how I was dragging behind me the burden of my own wretchedness, goaded by the honors I lusted after, the load growing as I dragged it along. And yet all we wanted in our lives was to attain that carefree joy which the beggar had attained, though we had not and would perhaps never attain it, since what the beggar had achieved by means of the few coins he had begged for—the joy of temporary happiness—I was struggling to achieve through many anguished detours and deviations. It is not that this beggar had true happiness, but I, with my thirst for honors, was striving for a happiness that was far more untrue. He was filled with joy, and I was filled with anxiety; he was untroubled, and I was distressed. If anyone had asked me whether I would rather be elated or downcast, I would have answered: elated. And yet had I been asked whether I would rather be what he was or what I was at the time, I would have chosen to be myself even though I was beset by trouble and fear. But would I not have made that choice rather out of perverseness than out of truthfulness? For I ought not to have set myself above the beggar simply because I was a man of greater learning, considering that my learning gave me no joy. With that learning I strove to find favor with men, not to instruct them, but only to cull favor, for which You broke my bones with the staff of Your instruction.

[6.10] I turn my back on those who say to me, "There is a difference in the source of a man's happiness: the beggar delights in drunkenness, you delight in glory." But what glory is there, Lord, when it is not in You? Just as the beggar's happiness was false, so too was my glory, and this preyed on my mind all the more. The beggar dispelled his drunkenness that very night, but I slept and rose again with mine, and was to sleep and rise with it again for You know how many days. But I was aware that there is a difference in the sources of man's delight, and a delight in faith lies far ahead of a delight in vanity, just as the beggar stood far ahead of me: he was much happier than I, not only because he was drenched in mirth and I disemboweled with worry, but he had acquired his wine by wishing people well, while I strove for prideful honors with lies. I said much about this to my friends at the time, and I also realized on other occasions such as this what my state was, a state I found to be base, and I suffered and doubled the baseness; and if good fortune smiled upon me I refrained from reaching out, since almost before I could grasp it, it flew away.

[7.11] We friends who lived together lamented all this, but I discussed it in greater depth and friendship with Alypius and Nebridius, Alypius having been born in the same town as I, to a family of the highest rank, though he was younger than me. He had studied under me when I first taught in our town, and later in Carthage as well, and he held me in great esteem as he considered me kind and learned, while I prized him for his exceeding innate virtue that had been manifest from his youngest years. Yet the whirl of Carthaginian life, with all those foolish spectacles that people followed with such fervor, had drawn him into the lewd frenzy of the circus arena. While Alypius was caught up in this deplorable whirl, he was not yet attending the public classes in rhetoric that I was teaching, because of some rancor that had arisen between his father and me. But I had discovered Alypius' dire passion for the circus arena, and was deeply anguished that he was about to, or already had, cast away a future of such promise. Yet I could not admonish or somehow restrain him, not with the goodwill of a friend nor with the authority of a teacher, for I assumed that he thought of me the same way his father did; but this was not the case. Disregarding his father's wishes, he began to greet me, and sometimes would come into my auditorium to listen for a while and then leave.

[7.12] I neglected to tend to him so that his blind and rash fondness for vain diversions would not ruin his excellent qualities. But You, Lord, Who steer and govern all that You have created, had not neglected him who was to be a bishop of Your sacrament among Your children;[14] and his correction must be entirely attributed to You, even if You brought it about through me, who was unaware of Your design. For one day, as I was sitting at my usual place with my students before me, he entered, greeted me, sat down, and applied his mind to what I was instructing. As I was explaining a certain passage, an example from the lewd circus arena occurred to me that I felt would make what I was explaining to the students clear through biting ridicule of those who were under the sway of that madness. You know, God, that it had not been my intention to cure Alypius of that pestilence, but he took what I said entirely upon himself and thought I had said it only on his account, and while another might have been angered at me, this honest youth took it as a reason to be angered at himself, cherishing me all the more. For You had once said, and placed it in Your Scriptures: "Admonish a wise man and he will love you."[15] Yet it was not I who had admonished him, but You made of my heart and tongue fiery coals with which You scorched away the disease in his mind of great promise and so cured it, You Who make use of everyone whether they are aware or unaware, and all within an order that You discern, and that order is just. Let him not sing Your praises who considers not Your mercies,[16] which I avow before You from my inmost depths. For after I had spoken those words Alypius soared forth from the deep pit into which he had so willingly plunged, blinded by its bizarre delights, and with great forbearance he shook out his soul, whereupon all the filth from the circus flew off, nor did he ever go there again. He now overcame his father's opposition to my becoming his tutor; his father yielded and agreed, and Alypius began to attend my lessons once more, becoming along with me entangled in the same superstitions, esteeming in the Manicheans their show of austerity, which he supposed to be true and sincere, whereas it was one that was deceptive and seductive, an austerity that captured precious souls[17] who were not yet able to reach the heights of virtue and were easily beguiled by appearances of what was merely a feigned and false virtue.

[8.13] Alypius had not turned his back on the worldly path his parents had beguiled him into pursuing, and had left before me for Rome

to study law. There, in an unbelievable way and with unbelievable
passion, he was drawn to the arenas of the gladiator fights. While he
had shunned and detested such spectacles, one day he chanced upon
some friends and fellow students coming from a dinner, and though
he vehemently objected and resisted they persevered, as friends will,
and dragged him by force to the amphitheater during the season of
the cruel and deadly games. "You can drag my body to that place and
keep me there," he protested, "but you cannot make me look at such
spectacles or accept them. I will be present but absent, and so I shall
prevail against both you and them." Still, his friends dragged him to
the amphitheater, probably to see whether he would really manage to
do as he intended. They arrived and took whatever seats they could,
and soon the whole crowd was roaring with violent delight. But Alypius shut his eyes tightly, forbidding his mind to encounter so much
evil; if only he had stopped his ears as well! For when during the fight
a mighty cry from the whole audience struck him with vehemence,
he was overcome by curiosity and, certain that even if he looked he
would disdain and surmount whatever it was he saw, he opened his
eyes. He was struck in his soul with a deeper wound than the body
of the man in the arena. Alypius fell more wretchedly than the man
whose fall had caused the clamor that had entered his ears and pried
open his eyes so that his soul could be smitten and cut down, a soul
courageous rather than strong, but the weaker in that it had relied
on itself rather than relying on You. For as soon as he beheld the
blood, he drank in its savagery; he did not turn away but fixed his
gaze, imbibing the frenzy, blind to all else, and exulted in that sinful
contest, intoxicated with blood-drenched delight. He was no longer
the same man he was before but one of the crowd, a true companion of the youths who had dragged him there by force. In brief, he
watched, yelled, flared up, and took away with him the frenzy that
would drive him to return again, not only with the youths who had
first dragged him there but even without them, bringing others with
him. But Your hand of supreme power and mercy raised him out of

this misery, and You taught him to have confidence not in himself, but in You; yet this was much later.

[9.14] This remained in his memory as a medicine for the future, as was also the following incident that took place when he was still a student and studying under me in Carthage. At noon one day in the market forum, he was thinking through what he would be declaiming, as students of rhetoric do, and you suffered him to be arrested as a thief by the forum guards. I believe that You, our God, permitted this for no other reason than that he who in the future was to be so great should begin to learn that when a man is to be judged, he must not be rashly condemned by another man. For while Alypius had been pacing up and down in front of the tribunal with his writing tablet and stylus, another student of rhetoric—the actual thief—suddenly appeared, furtively carrying an ax. Unseen by Alypius, he made his way over to the lead railings above a row of silversmithies and began to hack away at the metal. But the silversmiths below the railings heard the sound of hacking. They began to whisper among themselves and sent some men to seize the culprit. The student heard their voices and ran away, leaving his ax behind as he was afraid to be caught with it. Alypius, who had not seen him enter but now saw him run off, wanted to know what was going on and went inside; finding the ax, he stopped and wondered why it was there. Suddenly the men who had been sent to catch the thief found him there alone, holding the ax whose noise had roused them to come. They now seized Alypius and dragged him away and, gathering all the tenants of the forum, boasted of having caught a thief in the act, after which Alypius was brought before the judges.

[9.15] But this was the extent of Alypius' instruction, for immediately, Lord, You came to the aid of his innocence, to which You alone were witness. As the tenants of the forum were leading him either to prison or his punishment, they were met by the architect responsible for the supervision of public buildings. They were delighted to see this man, as he had always suspected them of stealing materials from the forum; now at last they could show him who the true malfeasant was. But the architect had met Alypius a number of times at the house of a certain senator to whom he often paid his respects, and recognizing him the architect immediately took him aside and asked him the reason for all this trouble. Alypius told him what had happened, and the architect bade the yelling, menacing crowd to come with him. They all followed him to the house of the youth who had done the misdeed, where they found a slave boy outside the door who was so young that he thought he could reveal the entire truth without any harm coming to his master. The boy had in fact accompanied his master to the forum, and Alypius remembered him and told the architect that he had seen him there. The architect now showed the ax to the boy and asked him whose it was. "It is ours," the boy replied, and being asked further questions revealed everything. With the deed now falling on the owner of that house, the crowd that had been marching in triumph with Alypius fell into confusion, and he who would one day be the dispenser of Your Word and an examiner of many cases in Your Church went on his way, having learned and experienced much.

[10.16] Thus I had found Alypius again in Rome, and his bond to me was so strong that he followed me to Milan to be at my side and to practice in the law, which he had studied at his parents' wish rather than his own. He had sat three times as an assessor, and had done so with a restraint that others wondered at, while Alypius wondered even more at those who preferred gold to honesty. His character was tested not only with the enticements of gain but also with the spurs of fear. In Rome he had been assessor to the Keeper of the Italian Treasury,[18] and in those days there was a powerful senator to whom many were bound through favors and fear. This senator, as was his usual practice, sought to apply his influence so he could do what the laws did not permit; Alypius resisted. A bribe was promised, but Alypius scorned it. Threats were made, but Alypius trampled on them. Everyone marveled at his extraordinary spirit, which neither sought the friendship nor feared the enmity of a man so renowned for the countless ways in which he could benefit or harm another. The judge himself whose assessor Alypius was did not wish to grant the senator's demands, yet refrained from rejecting them openly, shifting the accountability onto Alypius, alleging that Alypius would not consent to his granting the demand. And it was true that if the judge had acquiesced to the senator, Alypius would have resigned his post. The only thing that almost led Alypius astray was his passion for literature, which tempted him to have manuscripts copied out for him by Praetorian scribes; but deliberating on the justice of this he chose the better path, judging as more rewarding the fairness that prohibited such an action rather than the power that permitted it. This might be a small matter, but he who is true in what is minor is also true in what is great,[19] nor can ever be empty that which came forth from the mouth of Your Truth:[20] If a man has not been true in unrighteous wealth, who will grant him true riches?[21] And if you have not been true in that which belongs to another man, who will grant you that which belongs to you?[22] Such was the friend who clung to me, and with me wavered in what course of life ought to be embraced.

[10.17] Nebridius too left his place of birth near Carthage, and Carthage itself where he had spent so much time, leaving behind the fine home and lands of his father, and leaving his mother, who was not to follow him. He had come to Milan for no other reason than to live with me in an ardent search for truth and wisdom. Like me he sighed and like me he wavered, an ardent seeker of the blessed life and an adamant explorer of the most difficult questions. Ours were three starving mouths calling out our hunger to one to another and turning to You that You might give them food in due season.[23] We sought the reason for our suffering in all the bitterness that, by Your mercy, followed the worldly things we did, but we encountered only darkness and turned away in pain, asking, "How long will this continue?" We were often to ask this question, and though we asked it we did not forsake those worldly things, for nothing certain had yet shone forth that, in forsaking these things, we could embrace.

[10.18] I myself was struck when I contemplated how much time had passed since my nineteenth year, when I had begun to burn with a desire for wisdom, planning to abandon all the vain hopes and false foolishness of inane desires. And here I was now in my thirtieth year, still stuck fast in the same mire,[24] hungering to enjoy the fleeting things of the present that were dissipating me, while I said to myself, "Tomorrow I shall find that wisdom; it will appear before me and I shall grasp it; lo, Faustus will arrive and explain everything! O great Academic philosophers, can really nothing be determined for certain about how an ordered life is to be lived? But no, let us seek with greater diligence, and let us not despair. Things in the Holy Writ no longer seem absurd as they once did, and can be understood differently and in a virtuous way. I will take my stand where as a child my parents placed me until the clear truth be discovered. But where is the truth to be sought? Ambrose has no time; we have no time to read. Where are we even to find the books, when and from where are we to obtain them? From whom are we to borrow them? Time must be allocated and certain hours assigned for the health of our soul. A great hope has arisen: the True Faith does not teach what we had thought it taught and had vainly accused it of teaching; its experts consider it a sin to believe that God is bounded by the shape of a human body. Why do we hesitate to knock at the door that will open out to all else?[25] Our pupils take up our mornings, but what do we do for the rest of the day? Why not dedicate that time to this? But when would we then pay our respects to exalted friends whose favors we seek? When would we prepare what our pupils pay us for? When would we restore ourselves, relaxing our minds from the strain of worry?

[11.19] "Let all this perish, let us dismiss all these empty and futile things, and let us dedicate ourselves to the search for truth! Life is wretched, death uncertain: if it should suddenly surprise us, in what state will we depart? Where will we learn all that we neglected, and will we not have to face the punishment for this neglect? What if death itself cuts off and ends all cares along with our senses? This too must be examined. But let us put that aside! It is no vain and empty thing that the great and exalted authority of the Christian Faith has been spread throughout the world. Never would our deity have wrought so much and such great things for us, if with the death of the body the life of the soul were to be destroyed. So why then do we hesitate to abandon worldly hopes and dedicate ourselves entirely to seeking God and a happy life? But wait: worldly things are delightful too, and have a considerable charm of their own. We cannot turn away from them lightly, for it would be shameful to return to them again. See how simple it is to attain a position of honor: what more can we wish for in this world? We have a great number of powerful friends; if we are determined and persist, we can even secure ourselves the governorship of a province and a wife with some money so that our expenditures will not weigh on us. This would be the bounds of our desires. Many great men most worthy of imitation have dedicated themselves to the study of wisdom while they were married."

[11.20] Alternating winds drove my heart this way and that as I weighed these things; time was passing, and I delayed turning to the Lord and deferred from day to day[26] to live in You, but did not defer dying every day in myself. I yearned for a happy life, but feared seeking it where it dwelled, and sought it by fleeing from it. I considered myself wretched if I was to be deprived of the embrace of a woman, but did not think that the medicine of Your mercy could cure that infirmity, as I had not tried it. I believed continence to be within our own power, though I was not conscious of such a power within me, being so foolish as not to know that as it is written, none can be continent unless You grant it,[27] and that You would grant it if with inner cries I knocked at Your ears and with firm faith cast my care on You.[28]

[12.21] It was in fact Alypius who kept me from taking a wife, always saying that we would not be able to continue living in carefree ease together in the pursuit of wisdom, as we had so long desired to do. He was even then entirely chaste, which was all the more admirable since he had experienced sexual pleasure in his early youth, though he had not let it trap him, afflicted by his deed and spurning it, living from then on in utter continence. But I always countered with examples of those who had cultivated wisdom as married men and were pleasing to God[29] and who had remained faithful and loving to their friends, though I fell far short of their greatness of spirit. Fettered by the deadly sweetness of the disease of my flesh, I dragged my chains behind me, dreading to be freed, and, as if Alypius had struck my wound, I repulsed his good words as if they were the hands that were unchaining me. Moreover, it was through me that the serpent spoke to Alypius, my tongue scattering sweet snares along his path to entangle his chaste and unfettered feet.

[12.22] Alypius was surprised that I, for whom he had such great regard, was so firmly caught in the birdlime of sensuality as to declare whenever we discussed the matter that I could never lead a life of celibacy. And I, seeing his surprise, argued in my defense that there was a great difference between the hurried and secret encounter that he could now barely remember and so could easily scorn, and the continuing delights with which I was so familiar, delights to which, if the honest name of marriage were to be linked, he should not be surprised that I would embrace such a life. He now also began to long for marriage, not because he was overcome with a desire for such sensuality, but out of curiosity, for he said he wanted to know what it could be, without which my life, so agreeable to him, seemed to me not a life but a punishment. For his mind, free from such chains, was amazed at my enslavement, and that amazement led to his desire to try it, and then, experiencing it, perhaps fall into the enslavement that amazed him, seeing that he wanted to make a pact with death,[30] and he who loves danger will fall into it.[31] But neither he nor I gave more than slight thought to the matter that the virtue of matrimony lay in fulfilling the duties of marriage and raising children. For me, above all, the habit of satiating an insatiable lust was what kept me captive and tormented, while for him it was wonderment that had caught and enchained him. That was our condition until You, Most High, not forsaking our lowliness, taking pity on our pitifulness, came to our aid in wondrous and secret ways.

[13.23] I was continually being urged to take a wife. I made a proposal and it was accepted, largely through my mother's efforts, for she hoped that once I was married, baptism with its salvation would cleanse me, and she was delighted that I was more receptive with every day, and she saw that her prayers and Your promises were being fulfilled in my faith. At my bidding and through her longing she begged of You every day, with cries from her heart, that You reveal to her in a vision something about my future marriage, but You never did. What she saw were empty and fantastic visions fueled by the passion of the human spirit striving for answers; she told me about these visions, discounting them, as she did not have the same confidence in them that she had when it was You Who sent them. For she said that she could discern by some strange sensation, which she could not explain in words, the difference between Your revelations and the dreams of her own soul. Nevertheless, the pressure on me to marry continued, and a maiden was asked for in marriage; she was two years under marriageable age, but as she was thought suitable all were prepared to wait.

[14.24] We were a group of several friends who detested the turbulence and trouble of life, and we discussed and debated and had almost resolved to live in contemplation far removed from the bustling crowd, and this was how we intended to attain such a life: we would bring together whatever each of us was able to contribute, and from that create a single household, so that in our true friendship nothing would belong only to one person or another but would be a single possession gathered from all, and as a whole would belong to each, and all to all. We concluded that we could bring some ten men into this fellowship, some of whom were very wealthy, especially our townsman Romanianus, whom the burdensome tangle of his affairs had brought to the courts, and who from childhood had been a close friend of mine. He was the most zealous advocate of this plan, and his voice was of great weight because his wealth far exceeded that of any of us. We had also decided that two of us would be elected every year, the way magistrates are, to attend to everything, the rest of the group remaining free from such cares. But when we began to give thought as to whether wives, which some of us already had and others were hoping to attain, would agree to what we were planning with such care, it fell to pieces in our hands, and, our plans crushed, we cast them aside. And so we returned to our sighs and laments, our steps following the broad and well-trodden paths of the world, for many thoughts were in our hearts,[32] but Your counsel abides in all eternity.[33] And yet through that counsel You laughed at our designs and prepared Your own to grant us nourishment in due season and fill our souls with blessing.[34]

[15.25] In the meantime my sins were multiplying,[35] and when the woman with whom I shared my bed was torn from my side for being an impediment to my marriage, my heart that clung to her was rent and bled. She returned to Africa,[36] vowing before You never to know any other man, leaving with me the natural son I had had by her. But wretch that I was, I could not follow that woman's example. Impatient at the delay of my marriage, since it would be two years before I could have what I wanted, I procured for myself another woman, though not a wife; for I was not a lover of marriage but a slave to lust, so that the sickness of my soul was sustained and prolonged, remaining intact, even heightened, so that my habit could be guarded and tended until I reached the state of matrimony. Nor had the wound made by the parting with my former lover healed, but after inflammation and piercing pain it festered, and though the pain dulled, it also became more desperate.

[16.26] Praise to You, glory to You, Fountain of Mercies! As I grew more wretched, You drew nearer. Your right hand was ever ready to raise me out of the mire[37] and wash me, but I did not know it; nor did anything draw me back from an even deeper abyss of carnal pleasures except the fear of death and of Your judgment to come, a fear that through all my changing beliefs never left my heart. And as I discussed the nature of good and evil with my friends Alypius and Nebridius, I felt that Epicurus would have won the wreath of victory had I not believed that after death there remained the life of the soul and the consequence of our deserts, something which Epicurus refused to believe. And I wondered, if we had been immortal and able to live in perpetual sensual pleasure without the fear of having to relinquish it, why should we not be happy? What else would we want? I did not realize that my profound wretchedness, steeped in blindness as I was, lay in that I could not discern the light of virtue and beauty that was to be embraced for its own sake, and that the eye of the flesh could not see but could only be seen from within. Nor did I, wretch that I was, reflect from what vein sprang the delight of conversing with my friends, even on such base matters, nor could

I be happy without friends despite being steeped in a profusion of carnal pleasures as I then was. But these friends I loved for themselves alone, and felt that it was for myself alone that I was beloved by them. What winding paths! Woe to my audacious soul that hoped that by receding from You it might find some better thing, turning this way and that, on its back, its sides, and its belly, yet all was hard, for You alone are respite. And behold, You are here and deliver us from our wretched strayings and place us on Your path; You comfort us, and say: "Run, I will carry you and will bring you through, and I will still carry you."[38]

NOTES

1 Psalm 71:5 (Vulgate), 70:5 (other translations).
2 Job 35:11.
3 Psalm 34:6 (Vulgate), 35:6 (other translations).
4 Psalm 67:23 (Vulgate), 68:22 (other translations).
5 Luke 7:14 (Vulgate), Luke 7:12 (other translations).
6 The Roman provinces of North Africa.
7 Romans 12:11.
8 2 Corinthians 2:15.
9 Genesis 1:26.
10 Matthew 7:7.
11 2 Corinthians 3:6.
12 Ecclesiasticus (Sirach) 19:4.
13 Matthew 7:13.
14 Alypius was to become Saint Alypius, Bishop of Thagaste.
15 Proverbs 9:8.
16 Psalm 106:8 (Vulgate), 107:8 (other translations).
17 Proverbs 6:26.
18 The *comes largitionum italicianarum* was an official of the Imperial Treasury in charge of finances in the Italian provinces of the Roman Empire.
19 Luke 16:10.
20 Isaiah 55:11.
21 Luke 16:11.

22   Luke 16:12.

23   Psalm 103:27 (Vulgate), 104:27 (other translations). Also in Psalm 144:15 (Vulgate), 145:15 (other translations).

24   Terence's play *Phormio*, line 780.

25   Matthew 7:7.

26   Ecclesiasticus 5:8 (Vulgate), Sirach 5:7 (other translations).

27   Wisdom 8:21.

28   Psalm 54:23 (Vulgate), 55:22 (other translations).

29   Hebrews 13:16.

30   Isaiah 28:18.

31   Ecclesiasticus 3:27 (Vulgate), Sirach 3:26 (other translations).

32   Proverbs 19:21.

33   Psalm 32:11 (Vulgate), 33:11 (other translations).

34   Psalm 144:15 (Vulgate), 145:15 (other translations).

35   Ecclesiasticus 23:3 (Vulgate), Sirach 23:3 (other translations).

36   The Roman provinces of North Africa.

37   Psalm 39:3 (Vulgate), 40:2 (other translations).

38   Isaiah 46:4.

BOOK VII

[1.1] My bad and impious youth was now dead and I passed into manhood, but the older I grew the baser the emptiness within me became, as I was not able to imagine the existence of any substance that could not be seen with the eyes. Yet I did not, O God, think of You as being within the figure of a human body, for since I began to learn something of the philosophers, I avoided thinking this and rejoiced at having found that the faith of our spiritual mother, Your Church, espoused this too. But I did not know how else to conceive of You. I, a man—and such a man that I was—sought to think of You, the sole, supreme, and true God, and from the bottom of my heart I believed You incorruptible, inviolable, and immutable, and although I did not know how or why, I saw clearly and was certain that that which can be corrupted must be inferior to what cannot be corrupted, and I preferred without hesitation that which cannot be violated to that which is violable, and knew that what was immutable was better than what had to undergo change. My heart cried out passionately against all the images conjured up by my mind, and with this single blow I tried to drive away from my mind's eye the fluttering sullied swarm,[1] but barely had the swarm scattered when, in the twinkling of an eye, it came teeming back, flailing against my face so that I could not see. Thus, though I did not think of You in the form of a human body, I was still driven to think of You as occupying a space, whether infused in the world or infinitely diffused outside it.[2] But I did think of You as incorruptible, inviolable, and immutable, which I preferred to the corruptible, the violable, and the mutable. Because it seemed to me that whatever was deprived of such space had to be nothing, absolutely nothing, not even a void, as if a mass had been withdrawn from a place and the place remained empty of any mass at all, of earth or water, air or heaven, and that it would remain a void place, a spacious nothing.

[1.2] My heart calloused,[3] and myself not clear even to myself, I considered to be utterly nonexistent whatever was not extended over space, either diffused, or concentrated, or expanding, or whatever did not or could not adopt any of these qualities. The same forms over which my eyes moved, my mind sought as well, but I did not realize that the same energy by which I fashioned those images also had no body, and yet this energy could not have formed these images had it not in itself been something, and something great. I imagined even You, life of my life, as vast within infinite space, penetrating the entire essence of the world and in all directions beyond through boundless infinity, so that the earth should have You, the heaven should have You, all things should have You, and they would be finite within You but You infinite. As the body of the air, the air that is above the earth, does not hinder the light of the sun from penetrating it, and does not slice or shatter light but is filled by it entirely, so I conceived of You as permeating not only the heaven and the air and the sea, but also the earth, so that Your presence can penetrate all its greatest and smallest parts, Your secret breath governing from within and without all the things You have created. This was what I assumed, as I could not imagine anything else. But it was wrong, for this way a greater part of the earth would contain a greater part of You, and a lesser part would contain less. All things would be filled with You in such a way that the body of an elephant would contain more of You than the body of a sparrow, to the degree in which the elephant is larger and occupies more space. This way, You would have portioned out Your presence in the world in fragments that are large for the large and small for the small. It is not so, but You had not yet enlightened my darkness.[4]

[2.3] It would have been enough, Lord, for me to counter those deceived deceivers and dumb prattlers, from whose mouths Your Word does not ring forth, with an argument Nebridius had used long ago in Carthage at which all of us who heard it were amazed: "What could this supposed race of darkness that the Manicheans claim as an adverse force against You, our God, have done to You had You refused to fight it? If the Manicheans are to reply that it would have done You harm, this would be saying that You are subject to violation and corruption. But if they were to say that it could not do You harm, there would have been no reason that they could put forward for Your fighting it, and fighting it in a manner in which a certain part or member of You, or the offspring of Your substance, should be mingled with the adverse forces and with natures not created by You, and thus be corrupted and changed by them for the worse, turned from blessedness into wretchedness, needing help to be rescued and purified. This would then be the soul that in its enslavement would be rescued by Your Word which is free, rescued in its pollution by Your Word which is pure, rescued in its corruption by Your Word which is whole. If this were so, Your Word itself would be corruptible because it was from one and the same substance. So if You, whatever You are—Your substance, that is, by which You are—are incorruptible, then everything the Manicheans proposed was false and deplorable; and if they maintained that You *are* corruptible, then their argument is false and revolting to the core." This argument of Nebridius was sufficient against those who deserved to be vomited out from my bulging insides for thinking and speaking of You in a way that is a terrible sacrilege of heart and tongue.

[3.4] I firmly felt and asserted that You cannot be polluted or changed or in any way altered, our God, our true God, who made not only our souls but our bodies, and not only our souls and bodies but all beings and all things; and yet the cause of evil was not yet clear and incontrovertible to me. But whatever it was, I knew it had to be sought out in a way that would not constrain me to believe our unalterable God to be alterable, lest I myself turn into the evil I was examining. So I examined it coolly, certain that what the Manicheans said was not true, my mind and soul shunning them, for as I was examining the origin of evil I saw that they themselves were filled with evil, since they preferred to believe that Your essence suffers evil rather than believe that their own essence commits it.

[3.5] I endeavored to discern what I kept hearing, that the free choice of our will was the cause of our doing evil, and Your just judgment[5] the cause of our suffering, but I was unable to discern this clearly. Striving to draw my mind's eye out of the abyss, I again plunged into it, and every time I strove I again fell back into it. But what raised me toward Your Light was that I knew with certainty that I had a will and that I was alive, so that whenever I wanted or did not want a thing, I was entirely certain that I and no other wanted or did not want it. I now realized that there was where the cause of my sin lay. I also saw that whatever I did against my will I endured rather than did, and I judged this to be not my fault but my punishment, and as I held You to be just, I acknowledged myself immediately as one not unjustly punished. But again I asked: "Who made me? Was it not my God, who is not only good but who is goodness itself? How is it then that I want what is bad and do not want what is good? Is it so that I may be justly punished?[6] Who planted this in me and thus implanted this seed of bitterness,[7] seeing that I was entirely created by my most sweet God? If the Devil had been the author, where did the Devil come from? And if the Devil himself, by his own perverse will, turned from a good angel into a Devil, from where came that evil will through which he became a Devil when the entire angel he had once been had been made by the supremely good Creator?" Through such thoughts I was again dragged down and smothered, but not brought down to that hell of error where no one confesses to You,[8] as they believe that You suffer evil rather than that man does it.

[4.6] In this manner I now sought to discover the remaining truths, as one who had already discovered that the incorruptible had to be better than the corruptible, and You therefore, whatsoever You were, I avowed to be incorruptible, for no mind has ever been able to conceive, or shall ever be able to conceive, of anything that might be better than You Who are the highest and foremost good. But since, as I now believed, it is entirely true and certain that the incorruptible is preferable to the corruptible, my thoughts could only have reached something better than my God had my God not been incorruptible. Thus it was where I saw the incorruptible as preferable to the corruptible that I ought to have sought You, and from there found out where evil is, in other words, the origin of corruption, by which Your substance cannot be violated, since corruption can in no way violate our God: by no act of will, by no compulsion, by no sudden chance, for He is God, and what He determines for Himself is good, and He Himself is that good, while to be corrupted is not good. Nor are You constrained against Your will to anything, since Your will is not greater than Your power, which it could only be if You were greater than Yourself: for the will and the power of God is God Himself. And what can be unforeseen by You Who know all? The universe only exists because You know it. But what need is there to say so much about God's essence not being corruptible, since if it were corruptible it would not be God?

[5.7] So I sought the origin of evil, but sought it in a wrong way and could not see the error in my searching. Before my mind's eye I set up the entire creation, whatever we can see, such as the earth and the sea, the air, the stars, the trees, and the mortal creatures, but also whatever we cannot see, such as the firmament of heaven above and all its angels and spiritual beings. But my imagination arranged these beings within space as though they were bodies, and I made one great mass of Your creation, varied according to the kinds of body, some being real bodies, and others bodies my mind had invented for spirits. I made this mass great, not as great as it was, for I could not know that, but as great as I thought it might well be, and finite on all sides. But You, Lord, I imagined as encompassing and penetrating it from all sides, though infinite in all directions as if there were a sea everywhere and all around throughout boundless infinity, a single sea that had a sponge within it that was vast but finite, and that that sponge in all its parts was filled by that boundless sea.[9] That was how I imagined Your creation, finite but filled with You the Infinite, and I said, "This is God and this is what God has created, and God is good and most mightily and incomparably excels all this: but yet He, the Good, created all this to be good, and behold how He encompasses and fills it. But where then is evil? How and from where did it creep in? What is its root and what its seed? Or does it not exist at all? Why then do we fear and avoid something that does not exist? Or if we fear it in vain, then is not that fear itself evil as it tortures and torments the heart for no reason, and all the greater an evil as what we fear does not exist, and yet we fear it? Hence either evil is what we fear, or else it is evil that we are in fear. Where then does this evil come from, since our God, who is good, has created all these things to be good? Indeed, the greater and supreme Good has created lesser goods, yet still both the Creator and the created are good. Where did evil come from? Had the matter of which our God made good things been evil before, and in giving this matter form and order had He left something in it that He did not convert into good? Why would He have done that? Did he not have the might, though He is almighty, to change and transform the entire substance so that no evil would remain within it? And finally, why did He want to make something out of that matter at all, and not, by the same almightiness, cause it not to be? Was it possible that it existed against His will? Or if it had existed in all eternity, why did He allow it to be as it was through infinite spaces of time, and only so much later decided to create something out of it? Or, if the Almighty suddenly decided to create something out of it, would He not have preferred that this evil not exist, and that He alone existed, the ultimate true, supreme, and infinite Good? Or, since it was not good that He who was good should make and create something that was not good, could he not have removed that evil matter and reduced it to nothing, replacing it with good matter out of which to create all things? For He would not be almighty if He was unable to create something good without the aid of a matter that He Himself did not create." Such thoughts whirled through my wretched mind, fraught as I was with the gnawing fear that I might die without having found the truth. But the faith through the True Church in Your Christ, our Lord and Savior, was firmly fixed in my heart, a faith that in many points was still unformed and wavering in the rule of doctrine, but my mind, far from forsaking it, drank it in more and more with every passing day.

[6.8] I had already rejected the deceptive divinations and impious nonsense of the astrologers. Here too, from my innermost soul, I thank You, God, for Your mercies,[10] You, and You alone, for who else calls us back from deadly error if not the Life that knows no death and the Wisdom that enlightens humble minds, but needs no light and governs the universe down to the falling leaves of trees? You cured the obstinacy with which I opposed Vindicianus, a sagacious old man, and Nebridius, a young man with a wonderful mind, Vindicianus affirming vehemently, and Nebridius saying hesitantly but repeatedly, that astrology is not a science through which one can foresee the future, but that men's reading its signs has the same power as casting lots. As these astrologers say so much, some of what they say is bound to come to pass, not because they know something, but because by constantly talking they stumble upon the truth.

Thus You cured my obstinacy through a friend who was an eager consulter of the astrologers, and though he had not studied their works, he did consult these astrologers with avidity. But he knew one thing about this art that he had heard from his father, though he was unaware how far it went in overturning the reputation of that science. My friend—his name was Firminus, a well-educated man trained in rhetoric—consulted me as his dearest friend about certain affairs of his in which his worldly hopes had risen, and asked me my opinion concerning his so-called horoscope. I had already begun to incline toward Nebridius' views, but did not refrain from conjecturing and telling Firminus what came into my wavering mind, though I did add that I was now almost persuaded that this was all ridiculous and futile. He told me that his father had been extremely interested in astrological works and had a friend who was just as zealous, the two men fanning the flames of their passion for this nonsense with equal fervor. They went so far as to note the times when the animals in their households had their young, observing the positions of the stars in the heavens in order to gather facts for this so-called science. Firminus said that his father had told him that when his mother had been pregnant with him, a female slave of his father's friend was also heavy with child, a matter that could not escape her master, who strove with painstaking meticulousness to note even the births of his dogs. And so it came to be that the two men, with careful observation, began to count the days and hours, and even the minutes—the one man for his wife, the other for his slave—both women giving birth at the same moment, so that the men had to calculate the same horoscope down to the minutest detail, the one man for his son, the other for his infant slave. For as soon as the women went into labor, each man sent word to the other as to where things stood in his household, and messengers were kept at hand so they could immediately inform each other of the birth: as each man lived on his own estate, it was simple enough for them to notify one another without delay. The messengers they dispatched, Firminus said, had met at the exact midpoint between the two houses, so that neither man could note any difference in the configuration of the stars or the precise moment in time; and yet Firminus, born to a high position, was to walk the shining paths of life, his wealth increasing, the highest offices at his command, whereas the slave, as Firminus who knew him revealed, was still serving his masters, his neck under the yoke.

[6.9] When I heard this story—a story I believed, since Firminus was a man of such worth—my reluctance to abandon astrology fell away, and I strove to turn him from his passion for it. I told him that if on inspecting his horoscope I could have predicted correctly, I would have been able to see that his parents were eminent among their kin, a noble family of their city, of high birth, good education, and liberal ideas. But if the slave had consulted me about the same horoscope, since his and Firminus' were identical, I should have been able to tell him in all truth of his abject origins, his status as a slave, and everything else that was so different and so removed from Firminus' condition. Consequently, by looking at the identical horoscopes, if I were to speak the truth I would have had to give different accounts, or if I gave the same account I would be lying; therefore it followed with utter certainly that whatever truth was predicted when studying a horoscope was not predicted by skill in astrology but by chance, and whatever error there was was not the result of ignorance in the discipline but the trickery of chance.

[6.10] This gave me a powerful argument against astrology, but I began to weigh other situations of the kind, since the madmen who cast horoscopes as a trade, and whom I longed to attack and expose with ridicule, might counter that Firminus had deceived me with his tale, or his father him. I thought about men who are born twins and almost always come out of the womb so close to one another that the minuscule interval, even if astrologers claim that it has a great effect within the scheme of nature, escapes human observation and cannot be reflected in the signs they inspect in order to forecast true things. But they will not be true; for examining the same signs the astrologer would have had to predict the same for Esau and Jacob, whereas entirely different things befell them.[11] The astrologer would have foretold false things, or if he were foretelling what was true he could not have foretold the same things, despite inspecting the same signs. Thus he would predict correctly not by skill in astrology but by chance. For You, Lord, supremely just Ruler of the Universe, through Your hidden inspiration—unbeknownst to the consulters and the consulted—lead the consulter to hear what according to the hidden merits of souls he ought to hear from the great depths of Your just judgment,[12] to Whom let no man say, "What is this? Why is that?" Man must not say it; he must not say it, for he is just a man.[13]

[7.11] And so You, my Rescuer, freed me from those chains, but I was still seeking the origin of evil, though I could not find it. Yet in the fluctuations of my thoughts You did not suffer me to be carried away from the faith by which I believed that You exist and that Your substance is immutable, the faith by which I believed that You watch over and judge mankind, and that with Christ, Your Son and Our Lord, and the Holy Scriptures which the authority of Your True Church placed before us, You have laid out the path of mankind's salvation to the life that will come after death. Though these principles were safe and unshakeable in my mind, I still zealously sought the origin of evil. What anxious torments filled my heart, what cries, my God! But though I did not know it Your ears did hear me, and while I fervently sought the answer in silence, the silent grief of my soul called out loudly to Your mercy. Only You knew what I suffered; no man knew. I poured so little of all this into the ears of even my closest friends, for how could the great tumult of my soul have ever reached them, when neither time nor words could have sufficed to express it? But everything reached Your ears, everything I roared out with the cries of my heart; my desire was before You, and the light of my eyes had gone from me.[14] It was within, but I was outside: nor was it in a place, yet I was fixed on things contained within a place, but there I could not find a place to rest, nor a place that would receive me so that I could say: "This is sufficient, this is fine!" Nor was I sent forth to return to where it was sufficient and fine for me. My place was above these things but below You, and You are my true joy, subjected to You as I am, and You have subjected to me all that You have created below me.[15] This was the middle ground and the mean for my deliverance, remaining in Your Image, and by serving You becoming master of my body. But when I rose in pride against You and ran against the Lord with the thick bosses of my shield,[16] even everything that was inferior rose over me and pressed me down, and nowhere could I find respite or breath. Wherever I looked, it seethed around me in towering masses, and in my thoughts the images of corporeal objects hindered my return to You, as if they were calling out to me: "Where are you going, base and unworthy wretch?" And all this had spawned from my wound, for You cut down like a vanquished man him who is proud,[17] and I was separated from You by my festering pride, my face so swelled that I could not open my eyes.

[8.12] But You, Lord, abide in eternity,[18] yet are not angry with us for eternity[19] for You pity our dust and ashes,[20] and it was pleasing in Your sight to reform my deformities, and through inner prods You goaded me so that I would be impatient for You to become certain to my inner eye. And so by the hidden hand of Your medicine my swelling abated, and my mind's eye that had been clouded by troubles and shadows was cured day by day through Your stinging tincture of healing pain.

[9.13] First You set out for me how You oppose the proud but offer grace to the humble,[21] and the great mercy with which You have shown men the path of humility in that Your Word became flesh and dwelt among men.[22] You brought before me, through a man who was puffed up with monstrous pride, certain books of the Platonists that had been translated from Greek into Latin.[23] And in them I read, not in the exact words but to the same purpose, exhorted by many and diverse reasons, that in the beginning was the Word, and that the Word was with God, and the Word was God, and was with God in the beginning; that all things were made by Him, and without Him nothing was made; I read that that which was made in Him is life, and life was the light of men, and the light shines in the darkness, and the darkness did not comprehend it.[24] I read that the soul of man bears witness to the light, but is not itself that light,[25] for the Word, which is God, is the true light that gives light to every man who comes into the world,[26] and I read that He was in the world and that the world was made by Him, and the world knew Him not.[27] But what I did not read in those books of the Platonists was that He came unto His people and that they received Him not, and that to as many as received Him, to those who believed in His name, He gave the power to become the sons of God.[28]

[9.14] I also read in those books of the Platonists that the Word, which is God, was born not of flesh nor of blood, nor of the will of man nor of the will of the flesh, but of God; yet I did not read that the Word became flesh[29] and dwelt among us. As I searched through those Platonic works I found it said in many and varying ways that the Son, being in the form of the Father, did not consider it a usurpation to be equal with God,[30] for his nature was the same. Yet those books did not write that He had laid down his glory taking the form of a bondservant and appearing in the likeness of man, and being found in appearance as a man, He humbled Himself and became obedient to the point of death, even the death of the Cross, wherefore God exalted Him from the dead and gave Him the name which is above every name, so that at the name of Jesus every knee should bend—of those in heaven, of those on earth, and of those under the earth—and that every tongue should confess that Jesus

Christ is Lord, to the glory of God the Father.[31] In those books it is written that before all times and above all times Your Only-Begotten Son abides immutably coeternal with You, and that souls receive of His fullness[32] that they may be blessed, and that by participating in that wisdom abiding in them they are renewed so that they will be wise. Yet it is not written in those books of the Platonists that at the right time He died for the impious,[33] and that You did not spare Your Only Son, but delivered Him up for us all.[34] For You hid these things from the wise and revealed them to babes,[35] so that those who toil and carry heavy burdens might come to Him and He restore them, because He is gentle and humble in heart,[36] and those who are gentle He directs in judgment and the docile He teaches His ways,[37] beholding our lowliness and trouble, and forgiving all our sins.[38] But those strutting in the loftier realms of a learning which is supposedly more sublime do not hear Him saying, "Learn from Me, for I am gentle and humble in heart, and you will find rest for your souls."[39] Though they know God, they do not glorify Him as God or give him thanks but are immersed in their thoughts, their foolish hearts darkened; professing themselves wise, they have become fools.[40]

[7.15] I also read in those books how they had changed the glory of Your incorruptible nature into idols and diverse effigies, into the likeness of corruptible man and bird and beast and serpent, indeed into that Egyptian food for which Esau lost his birthright,[41] since Your firstborn people worshipped the head of a beast instead of You, turning their hearts back toward Egypt,[42] and bowing their soul, Your image, before the image of a calf that feeds on hay.[43] These things I found in those books but did not feed on them, for it pleased You, Lord, to take away from Jacob the reproach of being the younger brother, that the elder should serve the younger,[44] and You called the pagans into Your inheritance; I had come to You from among the pagans, and I set my mind upon the gold which You willed Your people to bring from Egypt, as it was Yours, wheresoever it was.[45] And You had said to the Athenians through Your Apostle that it is in You that we live, move, and exist, as one of their own poets had said,[46] and furthermore it was from Athens that the books of the Platonists had come. But I did not set my mind on the Egyptians that they served with Your gold, changing the Truth of God into a lie, worshipping and serving the created rather than the Creator.[47]

[10.16] And being thus admonished to return to myself, I entered my innermost self with You as my Guide, and I was able to do this as You had made Yourself my Helper; I entered, and with the eye of my soul, such as it was, beheld the immutable light that was above the eye of my soul, above my mind; not the ordinary light that all flesh may look upon, nor somehow a greater light of the same kind, as though its brightness should be so many times brighter, taking up all space with its greatness. This light was not such but different, very different. Nor was it above my soul as oil is above water, nor as heaven is above earth, but was above because it made me, and I was below because I was made by it. He who knows the truth knows what that light is, and he who knows it knows eternity. Love knows it. O eternal Truth and true Love and beloved Eternity, You are my God; it is for You I long day and night, and when I first knew You, You lifted me up that I might see that there was something to see but that I was not yet one who could see. And You caused the weakness of my sight to rebound with the vehement radiance of Your Light, and I trembled with love and dread.[48] I found myself to be far away from You in the region of unlikeness, as if I heard Your voice from on high: "I am the food of grown men; grow and you will feed upon Me; nor will you change Me like the food of your flesh into you, but you will be changed into Me." And I learned that You discipline man for iniquity, and You made my soul dwindle away like a cobweb.[49] And I said: "Is Truth then nothing because it is not diffused through finite or infinite spaces?" And You called to me from afar: "Truly I AM WHO I AM."[50] And I heard, as one hears in one's heart, and there was no doubt: I would have sooner doubted that I am alive than doubted that Truth exists, for it can clearly be seen and understood through all that has been created.[51]

[11.17] And I contemplated the other things below You and saw that they neither completely are nor completely are not; for they are since they are from You, but are not since they are not what You are, for what truly is is that which abides immutably. But it is good for me to adhere to God,[52] for if I do not abide in Him, I cannot abide in myself either, but He by abiding in Himself renews all things.[53] You are the Lord my God, since You do not need my goodness.[54]

[12.18] And it was revealed to me that things that are corruptible are good,[55] things which could not be corrupted if they were supremely good or not good at all, for if they were supremely good then they would be incorruptible, and if not good at all there was nothing in them to be corrupted. Corruption does harm, but unless it were to diminish goodness it would not do harm. Consequently, either corruption does no harm, which cannot be, or, as is entirely certain, all things that are corrupted are deprived of some good. But if they are to be deprived of all good they will cease to exist. For if they were to exist and then could no longer he corrupted, they would be better than before because they would last incorruptibly, and what could be more monstrous than to maintain that things become better by losing all their good? Therefore, if they will be deprived of all good they will no longer exist. And therefore, as long as they exist they are good. Therefore, whatsoever exists is good, and the evil whose origins I was inquiring into is not a substance, for were it a substance it should be good. For either it would be an incorruptible substance and so a great good, or a corruptible substance which, if it were not good, could not be corrupted. I therefore saw, and it was revealed to me, that You made all things good, nor is there any substance at all that You did not make, and as You did not make all things equal, all things taken singly are good, and taken together are very good, because our God has made all things very good.[56]

[13.19] For You there is no evil, not only for You but also for Your entire creation, because there is nothing outside it that can break in and corrupt the order You have imposed on it. But in the different parts of Your creation some things, because they do not stand in harmony with other things, are considered evil, yet those same things are in harmony with yet other things and so are good, and are in themselves good. And all these things that are not in harmony fit with the lower part of creation that we call earth, harmonizing with its sky that is beset by clouds and winds. Far be it from me that I should exclaim: "If only they were not!" For if I were to see them and them alone, I would indeed long for something better, but I would still have to praise You for them too; for that You are to be praised is shown on earth by the dragons and all the abysses, the fire and hail, the snow and ice, and the stormy wind, all rendering Your Word, the mountains and all the hills, the fruitful trees and all the cedars, the beasts and all the cattle, the reptiles and winged birds, the kings of the earth and all the peoples, the princes and all the judges of the earth, the youths and maidens, the old and young: let them praise Your Name.[57] But You are also to be praised from the heavens; they are to praise You, our God, all Your angels on high, all Your Celestial Choir, the sun and the moon, all the stars and the light, the Heaven of Heavens and the waters above the heavens praise Your Name.[58] And I no longer sought for things that were better, because I now thought of all things together, and with sounder judgment considered that though the things above were better than those below, all things taken together are better than those that are above by themselves.

[14.20] There is no soundness in those who find fault with any part of Your creation, as there was no soundness in me when I found fault with much that You created; and because my mind did not dare find fault with my God, it would not accept as Your creation whatever found fault with it. That was how my mind had come to the idea of two substances, but it found no peace, and held forth with concepts not its own, and, turning away, had created for itself a God filling infinite areas of all space, and thought it to be You, and placed it in its heart, and had again made itself the temple of its own idol, an abomination to You. But after You had caressed my head unbeknownst to me, and had closed my eyes that they should not behold vanity,[59] I retreated a little from my stance, and my madness was lulled into a slumber, and I awoke in You and saw You infinite in another way, and this way of seeing did not arise from the flesh.

[15.21] And I turned and examined other things, and I saw that they owed their existence to You and that they were all finite within You, but in a different way; not within a space, but because through Your Truth You hold all things within Your hand, and all are true insofar as they exist; nor is anything false, unless something is thought to exist but does not. And I saw that things fit not only within their places but also within their time, and that You, Who alone are eternal, did not begin to act after immeasurable lengths of time, since all time—that which has passed and that which will pass—can neither come nor go except by Your acting and abiding.

[16.22] Experience has taught me that it is not strange that bread which tastes revolting to a sickly palate can taste delicious to a palate that is robust, and light which is hateful to sore eyes can be a delight to eyes that are sound. Thus Your justice displeases the wicked, as do the vipers and reptiles that You have created good and that fit in with the lower part of Your creation, where the wicked themselves fit in too, the more so as they are unlike You: though the more

they become like You the more they can fit in with Your higher creation. When I now asked what iniquity was, I found that it was not
a substance but the perversion of the will that turned away from
You, God, the Supreme Substance, toward what is lower, spewing out
what is within[60] while outwardly puffing itself up.

[17:23] I was amazed that I now loved You and not a phantasm in
Your stead, yet in delighting in my God I was not standing on solid
ground but was wrested up to You by Your beauty, only to be wrested
back down by my weight, sinking moaning into the depths. This
weight was my habit of lust, but the memory of You remained within
me, nor did I in any way doubt that there was a Being to Whom I
should cling; but I knew that I was not yet able to do so, for the body
that is corrupted weighs down the soul, and the earthly abode weighs
down the mind with a host of thoughts.[61] I was entirely certain that
Your invisible nature can be clearly seen, being understood by the
things You have created,[62] even Your eternal Power and Divinity. I
asked myself by what measure I approved the beauty of celestial or
terrestrial bodies, and on what grounds I could pass judgment on
mutable things, saying: "This should be thus, this not." And it was
when I asked myself how I could pass such judgments that I found
the immutable and true eternity of Truth to be above my mutable
mind. And so, step by step, I passed from bodies to the mind that
perceives through the body, and from there to the mind's internal
power to which the senses of the body report what is external, which
is the extent of what beasts can do also; and from there I passed to
the power of reasoning, to which what the body receives from the
senses is brought for judgment. This I discovered to be a mutable
thing within me, and as my mind rose to an understanding of itself
it drew my thoughts away from its habits, withdrawing itself from
those swarms of contradictory phantasms, so that it might find out
what light had pervaded it when it had cried out without any doubt
that the immutable was preferable to the mutable. It was here that

my mind had encountered the immutable itself: if it had not come to know the immutable, it could not have known with certainty to prefer it to the mutable. And so with the flash of a shuddering glance it reached That Which Is. It was then that I finally saw that Your invisible nature was to be understood through the things You have created,[63] but I could not fix my gaze. Driven back by my weakness, I again sank into my usual habits, carrying with me only a loving memory and a longing for a dish whose aroma I had smelled but of which I had not been able to partake.

[18:24] And I sought a way of obtaining sufficient strength to delight in You, but did not find it until I embraced that Mediator between God and men, the Man Jesus Christ who is God and above all things, hallowed in eternity,[64] calling out: "I am the way, the truth, and the life."[65] The food of which I was unable to partake He mixed with flesh, for the Word became flesh[66] so that Your Wisdom, through which You created all things, might provide milk for us infants. I was not yet humble enough to possess my humble Lord Jesus, nor did I yet know what His weakness was meant to teach us. For Your Word, the Eternal Truth, far above the higher parts of Your creation, raises up the submissive to Itself; but in the lower parts of your creation Your Word built for Itself a humble dwelling out of our clay, whereby to release from themselves those who will submit to Him and so bring them to Himself.[67] Thereby Your Word would heal their swelling pride and feed their love, so that in their confidence in themselves they would not move away from Him, but rather become weak when they saw before their feet the Divinity, itself weak, sharing with us our coat of skin, and that in their weariness they might prostrate themselves before the Divinity, so that It, rising, might raise them too.

[19.25] But I myself thought otherwise. I perceived my Lord Christ merely as a man of excellent wisdom whom no one could equal; above all, his miraculous birth from a Virgin struck me as an example of immortality attained by disdaining temporal things, his divine care for us assuring him great preeminence of authority. But I could not even imagine the divine mystery in the Word becoming flesh.[68] All I had understood of Christ from the Scriptures that had come down to us was that he ate and drank, slept and walked, was joyful and sorrowful, that he conversed, and that his flesh did not cleave to Your Word without a human soul and mind. Everyone who knows the immutability of Your Word knows this, and then, to the extent that I could, I knew it as well, nor did I in any way doubt it. To move the limbs of the body at will and then not move them, to be roused by an affection and then not, to express wise opinions and then remain silent, are all part of the mutability of the mind and the soul. If the things written about Christ were false, then all the rest could also be accused of being a lie, nor would there remain any salvation in faith for mankind in the Scriptures. But since the Scriptures are true, I acknowledged Christ to be a man in entirety, not merely having the body of a man, nor a body and a soul without a mind, but fully being a man. It was not as the embodiment of Truth that I believed that Christ should be preferred before others, but because of the excellence of His human nature and His perfect wisdom. Alypius, for his part, imagined the Christians to believe that God was arrayed in flesh, so that beside God and flesh there was within Christ no soul and mind of man, and because Alypius was convinced that Christ's actions as narrated could only have been performed by a living, rational creature, he was more reluctant to move toward the Christian Faith; but when he later came to realize that this was the error of the Apollinarian heretics,[69] he embraced the True Faith with joy. It was somewhat later, I confess, that I was to learn how, in maintaining that the Word became flesh, the Christian truth distinguishes itself from the falsehood of Photinus.[70] Indeed the rejection of heretics brings to the fore the creed of Your Church and what sound doctrine affirms, for there must also be heresies so that what is approved can be made clear to the weak.[71]

[20.26] Having now read the books of the Platonists that taught me to seek an incorporeal truth, I saw that Your invisible nature was to be understood through the things You have created.[72] Yet, downcast, I also realized that the darkness in my soul would not let me behold clearly, though I was certain that You exist and are infinite, that You are not diffused over spaces that are finite or infinite, and that You truly are, and are always the same,[73] varying in no part or motion, and that all other things are from You, as is proven by the single unshakable fact that they exist. I was certain of these things, but too uncertain to delight in You. I held forth as if I were an expert, but as I had not sought Your way in Christ our Savior I was not an expert, but one who had lost his way. I now began seeking to appear wise. I was filled with torment, but instead of weeping was puffed up with knowledge.[74] Where was that love that builds upon the foundation of humility that is Jesus Christ, and how could those books of the Platonists have shown it to me? I believe You intended me to come upon these books before I studied Your Scriptures so that they would remain imprinted on my memory so afterward, when I was softened by Your Scriptures, Your healing fingers having touched my wounds, I could discern and distinguish between audacity and confession, between those who see where they must go but do not see how, and those who walk the path that leads to our blessed land, not merely to behold it but to dwell in it. For if I had first been instructed by Your Holy Scriptures and You had become beloved to me through my familiarity with them, and I had then stumbled upon those other books, they might have snatched me away from the solid foundation of my piety; or, had I stood firm in the healthful state I had imbibed, I might have believed that that state might also have resulted from reading those Platonist books alone.

[21.27] So with great eagerness I embraced those venerable writings of Your Spirit, above all those of the Apostle Paul; and all the issues in which he had once seemed to me to contradict himself vanished, for in the past I had thought that the text of his discourse did not agree with the testimonies of the Law and the Prophets. The pure words now appeared to me as one single countenance, and I learned to rejoice trembling.[75] I began to read the Scriptures, and found that whatever truth I had read in the books of the Platonists appeared in the Scriptures together with the commendation of Your grace, so that whoever sees will not boast as if he had not been granted what he sees and the fact that he can see, for what does man have that he has not received from You?[76] He will be not only be urged to see You, Who are ever the same, but will also be healed so that he can adhere to You; and whoever is too far away to see can walk along the path so that he can come to You and see and hold You. For even if a man rejoices in God's law of the inner man, what will he do with the other law in his limbs that is battling against the law of his mind and leading him into captivity under the law of sin that is in his limbs?[77] For You are just, Lord, but we have sinned and committed injustice[78] and have been impious, and Your hand has grown heavy upon us,[79] and we are justly delivered to that ancient sinner the Prince of Death, because he persuaded our will to be like his, whereby he stood not in Your Truth.[80] What can wretched man do? Who will deliver him from this body of death if not Your grace through Jesus Christ our Lord,[81] whom You have begotten coeternal with You and formed in the beginning of Your ways, in whom the ruler of this world[82] found nothing worthy of death yet still killed Him, and so the decree against us was annulled?[83] Nothing of this is in the Platonists' writings; their pages do not show the face of that piety, the tears of confession, Your sacrifice, an afflicted spirit, a contrite and humbled heart, the salvation of the people, the City as a bride,[84] the pledging of the Holy Spirit,[85] the cup of our redemption. In those books no one sings: "Shall not my soul be submitted to God? From Him comes my salvation, for He is my God and my rock and my salvation, I shall no longer sway."[86] In those books no one hears Him call: "Come unto Me, all you that have toiled." They spurn learning from Him because He is meek and humble in heart,[87] for You have hidden these truths from the wise and prudent and have revealed them to babes.[88] It is one thing to see the land of peace from the mountain's wooded summit and find no way that leads to it, struggling in vain over impassible paths, beset and waylaid by fugitive deserters who are led by the lion and the dragon;[89] and it is altogether another thing to stay on the path that leads to that land, guarded by the host of the Heavenly Emperor, where none who have deserted the Heavenly Army pillage and plunder, for they flee this path as they flee torture. These things miraculously seeped through to my heart as I read the least of Your Apostles.[90] Encountering Your works, I trembled in awe.[91]

NOTES

1 Virgil, *Aeneid* 3.233. The "fluttering sullied swarm" is the harpies.
2 See Plotinus, *Enneads* 6.2, "On the Kinds of Being."
3 Matthew 13:15.
4 Psalm 17:29 (Vulgate), 18:28 (other translations).
5 Psalm 118:137 (Vulgate), 119:137 (other translations).
6 Plotinus, *Enneads* 4.3.16.
7 Hebrews 12:15.
8 Psalm 6:6 (Vulgate), 6:5 (other translations).
9 Plotinus, *Enneads* 4.3.9.
10 Psalm 106:8 (Vulgate), 107:8 (other translations).
11 Genesis 25–27.
12 Psalm 35:7 (Vulgate), 36:5 (other translations).
13 Ecclesiasticus 39:26 (Vulgate), Sirach 39:17 (other translations).
14 Psalm 37:9–11 (Vulgate), 38:8–10 (other translations).
15 Genesis 1:28.
16 Job 15:26.
17 Psalm 88:11 (Vulgate), 89:10 (other translations).

18 Psalm 101:13 (Vulgate), 102:12 (other translations).

19 Psalm 84:6 (Vulgate), 85:5 (other translations).

20 Ecclesiasticus 17:31 (Vulgate), Sirach 17:32 (other translations).

21 James 4:6; 1 Peter 5:5. See Book I, 1.1.

22 John 1:14.

23 Augustine is mainly referring to the Neoplatonist Plotinus. See Book VIII, 2.3, where Augustine mentions having read Victorianus' translations of the Platonists.

24 John 1:1–5.

25 John 1:8.

26 John 1:9.

27 John 1:10.

28 John 1:11–12.

29 John 1:14.

30 Philippians 2:6.

31 A quotation from Philippians 2:6–11.

32 John 1:16.

33 Romans 5:6.

34 Romans 8:32.

35 Matthew 11:25.

36 Matthew 11:28–29.

37 Psalm 24:9 (Vulgate), 25:9 (other translations).

38 Psalm 24:18 (Vulgate), 25:18 (other translations).

39 Matthew 11:29.

40 A quotation from Romans 1:21–3.

41 Genesis 25:29–34.

42 Acts 7:39.

43 Psalm 105:20 (Vulgate), 106:20 (other translations).

44 Romans 9:12.

45 Exodus 3:22, 11:2. Augustine's allegory is that God commands that the pagans' gold, like Platonic learning, should be put to good use.

46 Acts 17:28.

47 Romans 1:25.

48 Plotinus, *Enneads* 1.6.7.12–19.

49 Psalm 38:12 (Vulgate), 39:12 (other translations).

50 Exodus 3:14.

51 Romans 1:20.

52 Psalm 72:28 (Vulgate), 73:28 (other translations). "But it is good for me

to adhere to my God, to put my hope in the Lord God." (Douay-Rheims Bible)

53 John 15:5.

54 Psalm 15:2 (Vulgate), 16:2 (other translations).

55 Plotinus, *Enneads* 3.2.5.

56 Genesis 1:31.

57 Psalm 148:7–12.

58 Psalm 148:1–5.

59 Psalm 118:37 (Vulgate), 119:37 (other translations).

60 Ecclesiasticus 10:10 (Vulgate), Sirach 10:10 (other translations).

61 Wisdom 9:15.

62 Romans 1:20. "For since the creation of the world His invisible *attributes* are clearly seen, being understood by the things that are made." (New King James Bible)

63 Romans 1:20.

64 Romans 9:5.

65 John 14:6.

66 John 1:14.

67 God's Word—Jesus Christ—came down to live among mankind for mankind's salvation.

68 John 1:14.

69 The Apollinarians were a heretical sect of the fourth century CE that followed Bishop Apollinarius of Laodicea, who believed that Christ did not have a soul.

70 Bishop Photinus of Sirmium (d. 376 CE) was a heretic who believed that Jesus was a man adopted by God to be his son.

71 1 Corinthians 11:19.

72 Romans 1:20.

73 Psalm 101:28 (Vulgate), 102:27 (other translations).

74 1 Corinthians 8:1.

75 Psalm 2:11.

76 1 Corinthians 4:7.

77 Romans 7:22–23.

78 Daniel 3:29.

79 Psalm 31:4 (Vulgate), 32:4 (other translations).

80 John 8:44.

81 Romans 7:24–25.

82 John 12:31.

83 Colossians 2:14.

84 Revelation 21:2. "And I saw the holy city, new Jerusalem, coming down

out of heaven from God, prepared as a bride adorned for her husband."
(Revised Standard Version Catholic Edition)

85 2 Corinthians 5:5.

86 Psalm 61:3 (Vulgate), 62:1–2 (other translations).

87 Matthew 11:28–29.

88 Matthew 11:25.

89 Psalm 90:13 (Vulgate), 91:13 (other translations).

90 1 Corinthians 15:9. The Apostle Paul presented himself as the least of
    Christ's apostles. "For I am the least of the apostles, who am not worthy
    to be called an apostle, because I persecuted the church of God." (New
    King James Bible)

91 Habakkuk 3:2.

BOOK VIII

[I.I] My God, let me remember so that I can give thanks to You and avow Your mercies to me. Let my bones be bathed in Your love, and let them say, "Lord, who is like You?"[1] You have broken my chains, and I will sacrifice to You the sacrifice of praise,[2] and will now relate how You have broken them; and when people hear, let all who worship You say: "Blessed be the Lord in heaven and on earth, great and wonderful is His Name." My heart clung to Your words and I was enveloped by You. I was now certain of Your eternal life but still saw it as if through a glass, darkly.[3] I no longer doubted that there was an incorruptible substance from which all substance comes, nor did I now seek a greater certainty of You, but rather a greater steadfastness within You. As for my temporal life, all was unsteady, and my heart had to be cleansed from the old leaven.[4] I liked the Way—the Savior Himself—but was still reluctant to pass through its straits. You put into my mind, and it seemed good in my sight, to go to Simplicianus, who seemed to me a good servant of Yours, Your grace shining in him. I had also heard that since his youth he had lived in extreme devotion to You. Now he had grown old, and because of his long life spent following Your path with worthy zeal, he seemed to me a man of great learning and experience, which he truly was. For this reason I wanted to confer with him about my doubts and troubles so he would show me the best way for one in my state to walk in Your path.

[1.2] I saw the church filled with people, some having chosen one way, some the other,[5] but my own secular life vexed me. It was a harsh slavery that had become a heavy burden since I was no longer inflamed with hopes of wealth and honors. These things no longer delighted me compared to Your sweetness and the beauty of Your House that I loved.[6] But I was still tightly fettered to womankind. The Apostle Paul did not forbid me to marry, but he encouraged me to aspire to something better, very much wishing all men to be as he himself was.[7] But I, being weaker, had chosen the gentler path, and because of this alone was unsettled in other things too, weak and languishing with withering cares, because once I should have entered married life I would also have had to endure other hardships against my will. I had heard from the mouth of Truth that there were eunuchs who had castrated themselves for the sake of the kingdom of heaven, but Christ had said, "Let him who can accept it, accept it."[8] Certainly all men who have no knowledge of God are foolish, unable to find Him who exists through the good things that are visible to all.[9] But I was no longer trapped in that foolishness. I had surmounted it, and with the witness of all Your creation had found You our Creator, and Your Word that is God beside You and with You is one God, who have created all things.[10] There is another kind of impious person who, knowing God, neither glorifies Him as God nor is thankful.[11] I had also fallen among these people, but Your right hand had raised me up[12] and, carrying me away, placed me where I could be healed. For You have said to man, "Behold, piety is wisdom" and "Seek not to seem wise, because they who claimed themselves wise became fools."[13] I had now found the excellent pearl; but to buy it I would have had to sell everything, and I hesitated.

[2.3] So I went to Simplicianus, who was father confessor to Ambrose, now a bishop, whom Simplicianus had brought to Your grace and whom Ambrose truly loved as a father. I told him of my confusion and strayings, but when I mentioned that I had read cer-

tain books of the Platonists, which had been translated into Latin
by Victorinus, who had once been the Rhetorician of Rome and had
died a Christian, from what I had been told, Simplicianus expressed
joy that I had not fallen in with the writings of other philosophers
that were full of fallacies and deceptions, according to the elements
of this world,[14] whereas the Platonists in many ways had brought
God and His Word into their books. Then, to exhort me to embrace
the humility of Christ, hidden from the wise and revealed to babes,[15]
Simplicianus spoke about Victorinus, to whom he had been very
close in Rome, and I will not conceal what he told me, for it contains
great praise of Your grace and must be acknowledged in gratitude to
you. Victorinus was an aged man, an expert and greatly learned in
the liberal sciences who had read and studied a great many works of
the philosophers. He had been the tutor of many renowned senators,
and as a testament to the brilliance of his teaching a statue of him
had been erected in the Roman Forum, which men of this world
consider a rare honor. Until quite late in life he had been a worshipper of idols and had taken part in the sacrilegious rites that almost
the entire nobility of Rome, in its vainglory, pursued. He prayed to
the barking dog-headed Anubis and an abundance of monstrous
deities who had once battled Neptune, Venus, and Minerva,[16] and
whom Rome had once conquered but now worshipped, gods whom
the aged Victorinus had defended so many years with fear-inspiring
words; but Victorinus did not blush to become the servant of Your
Christ and an infant of Your fountain, bowing his neck to the yoke
of humility and submitting his forehead to the reproach of the Cross.

[2.4] O Lord, Lord, You Who lowered the heavens and descended
and touched the mountains and they smoked,[17] by what means did
You enter Victorinus' heart? As Simplicianus told me, Victorinus
used to read the Holy Writ and studied all the Christian writings
with great care, and said to Simplicianus, not in public, but in private and in confidence: "Did you know that I am already a Chris-

tian?" To which Simplicianus replied, "I will not believe it, nor will I consider you a Christian unless I see you in the Church of Christ." To which Victorinus answered wittily, "So is it walls that make Christians?" He was often to repeat that he was already a Christian, and Simplicianus as often gave the same reply, to which Victorinus repeated his quip about the walls, for he was afraid of offending his friends, proud demon-worshippers, fearing that from the heights of their Babylonian grandeur, as from the cedars of Mount Lebanon that the Lord had not yet crushed,[18] the full weight of their enmity would descend upon him. But then, after much reading and pining, Victorinus reached a firm resolution, fearing that he would be denied by Christ before the holy angels[19] if he feared acknowledging Him before men. He now felt guilty of a great crime in being ashamed of the mysteries of the humility of Your Word and not being ashamed of the sacrilegious rites of the proud demons, whose pride he had imitated when he had participated in their rites. He now became stalwart in denouncing all that was false and became meek before the truth, and suddenly and unexpectedly he said to Simplicianus, as Simplicianus told me, "Let us go to the church. I want to become a Christian." And Simplicianus, overjoyed, went with him. Not long after Victorinus had been instructed in the first mysteries of Christianity, he presented himself for baptism so that he would be reborn. Rome was amazed, the Church overjoyed. The proud saw this and fell into a rage, gnashing their teeth and melting away.[20] But the Lord God was Your servant's hope, and he did not pay heed to vanities and lying follies.[21]

[2.5] Finally the hour arrived for Victorinus to profess his faith. In Rome, those who draw near to Your grace recite words from an elevated place in the presence of all the baptized. The priests, Simplicianus told me, proposed to Victorinus that he could profess his faith more privately, an offer that was generally made to those whose shyness made them apprehensive; but Victorinus preferred to profess his salvation in the presence of the devout multitude, for what he had taught in rhetoric was not salvation, and yet he had declaimed it publicly; how much less fear should he then have in pronouncing Your Word before Your tame flock, when he had not feared delivering his own words before a crazed multitude. When he went up to the elevated place to make his profession, all those present who knew him—but who did not know him?—called out his name to one to another in a clamor of joy, a din rising from the rejoicing crowd: "Victorinus! Victorinus!" Sudden was their burst of exultation when they saw him, and just as suddenly they fell silent so they could hear him speak. He proclaimed his true faith with splendid steadfastness, and the people wanted to draw him into their hearts, and the hands with which they drew him were their love and joy.

[3.6] Righteous God, what causes a man to take greater delight at the salvation of a soul for which he had abandoned hope but which is suddenly freed from great danger, than if there had always been hope or if the danger had been less? You too, merciful Father, take greater delight in one penitent than in ninety-nine just men who need no repentance.[22] And we feel great joy whenever we hear of a shepherd whose shoulders carry back a sheep that has strayed, and the lost drachma restored to Your treasury, the neighbors rejoicing with the woman who found it;[23] and we are brought to tears by the joy of the solemnities of Your House when in Your House we hear read of Your younger son who was dead but lived again, was lost but then was found.[24] You rejoice in us and in Your holy angels, holy through holy love, for You are always the same, and know all things in the same way even though all things are not always the same, nor do they exist forever.

[3.7] What then causes the soul to be more delighted at finding or recovering things it loves than if it had always had them? Many occurrences confirm this, and witnesses everywhere cry out, "It is so!" The victorious general celebrates his triumphs, but he would not have conquered had he not fought, and the greater the danger on the battlefield, the greater his joy in the triumph. The storm pitches and tosses the seafarers, threatening them with shipwreck: all are pale with fear at their approaching death; but with the calming of the sea and sky they rejoice beyond measure, just as beyond measure they had been afraid. A loved one is ill and his pulse reveals danger, and all those at his side who long for his recovery are ill in their hearts along with him; once he is well again, though he does not have his former strength, there is joy such as there was not when he was healthy and strong. Man does not obtain the pleasures of life through unexpected and unsought difficulties, but through intentional and sought-out trouble. The pleasure of eating and drinking is null if it is not preceded by hunger and thirst; and drinkers will eat salted food to prompt a vexing heat that drink extinguishes, causing pleasure. It is also the custom that a promised bride should not be immediately given lest the husband should hold cheap the woman for whom, when he was betrothed, he did not sigh.

[3.8] This also holds true for delight that is shameful and repulsive, for delight that is permitted and lawful, for the purest and most beautiful friendship, and it also holds true for him who was dead but lived again, was lost but then was found.[25] Everywhere the joy is greater if a greater pain has preceded it. What is the meaning, Lord my God, of Your being eternal joy to Yourself, and the beings around You always rejoicing in You? What is the meaning of everything in this part of the universe alternating, regressing and progressing with clashes and conciliations? Is this a measure that You imposed when You assigned all Your good things and Your just works to their proper place and time, from the highest heaven to the lowest depths of the earth, from the beginning of ages to the end, from the angel down to the worm, from the first movement to the last? Lord, how high You are in the loftiest heights and how deep in the deepest depths! You never depart, and yet we struggle to find our way back to You.

[4.9] Come, Lord, rouse us and call us back, stir us and seize us, inflame and sweeten us! Let us love, let us run to You! Have not many returned to You out of a much deeper hell of blindness than Victorinus did? Have they not drawn near to You and were enlightened, receiving that Light from which those who are granted it receive power from You to become Your sons?[26] Yet if they are less known to a wide public, then even those who know them rejoice for them less: for when many rejoice together, the joy of each is more profuse, all being stirred and inflamed by one another, and then those who are widely known also open to many more the path to salvation, leading the way with many who follow. Therefore, all those who became Christians before them rejoice, because it is not in them alone that they are rejoicing. Far be it that in Your tabernacle the rich should be welcomed before the poor, or the noble before the humble, when You have chosen what is weak in this world to confound what is strong, have chosen what is humble and despised in this world, and chosen the things that are not, in order to bring to nothing the things that are.[27] And yet even the least of Your Apostles[28] through whose mouth You pronounced these words managed to subdue with much toil the pride of Paul the Proconsul and make him submit to the gentle yoke of Your Christ,[29] becoming a meek subject of the great King, and the Apostle, his former name having been Saul, now wished to be called Paul in token of this great victory. For the enemy suffers a greater defeat when a man is wrested from him on whom he has a greater hold, and through whom he has a hold of a great number of men; and he has a greater hold over the proud with their ranks of nobility, and through them and their power a greater hold of many others. The more esteemed Victorinus' heart had been when the devil had held it as an impregnable stronghold, and Victorinus' tongue, that sharp and mighty weapon with which he had destroyed so many, the more abundant was the exultation of Your sons that our King had bound the strong man,[30] and they saw his vessels being carried away to be cleansed and made fit for Your honor and made useful to the Lord for every good work.[31]

[5.10] When Your servant Simplicianus told me this of Victorinus, I ardently sought to imitate him, which had been the reason why Simplicianus had related it. Later he also told me how, in the days of the Emperor Julian, a law had been passed prohibiting Christians from teaching letters and rhetoric, and how Victorinus, obeying this law, preferred to forfeit the school of empty words rather than Your Word, by which You make eloquent the tongues of infants. To me, Victorinus seemed not so much resolute as lucky in having found the opportunity to dedicate himself entirely to You alone, something that I was longing for, bound as I was not by another's chains but by chains of my own making. The enemy had seized my will and had made a chain of it, binding me. A thwarted will gives rise to lust, and whoever serves lust turns it into something customary, and what is customary is not resisted but becomes necessity. It was through these links, joined together—which is why I call it a chain—that a harsh bondage was holding me fettered. Yet the new will that had begun to rise within me, the will to serve You selflessly, longing to delight in You, God, O sole Pleasure, was not yet capable of overcoming my former will, which had been hardened by age. And so my two wills, one old and the other new, one carnal and the other spiritual, collided with one another, and through their discord were scattering my soul.

[5.11] And so I came to understand through my own experience what I had read, how the flesh lusts against the spirit and the spirit against the flesh.[32] I was standing on both sides, but more on the side of what I approved of in myself than on the side of what I disapproved. What I disapproved of was no longer I,[33] for I was in large measure enduring it unwillingly rather than acting of my own free will. But it was my fault that habit was becoming so combative against me because I had willingly gone to where I did not want to be. For who can rightly speak against a just punishment following the sinner? Nor could I fall back on my former excuse that I still hesitated to disdain this world and serve You because my comprehension of the truth was still unsound, since now my comprehension had become very sound. But I was still conscripted to this world, refusing to serve You as a soldier, and I was as afraid of shedding all my burdens as I should have been afraid of shouldering them.

[5.12] The burdens of this world weighed me down in sweet sleep, and the thoughts with which I reflected on You were like the efforts of one who seeks to waken but, overcome with profound somnolence, sinks back into sleep. No one endeavors to sleep forever, and anyone with sound judgment prefers to be awake, but for the most part man defers casting off sleep when he feels a heavy torpor in his limbs, and though he is irked by this he yields to sleep with all the more pleasure, though the time to rise has passed. Thus I too knew for certain that it would be much better for me to give myself up to Your Love than to surrender myself to my passions; yet though the former course struck me as the best and the one that should triumph, the latter pleased me better and did triumph. Nor would I have known what to answer had You called to me: "Awake, you who sleep, arise from the dead and Christ will give you light."[34] Though You showed me in every way that what You said was true, I had nothing to reply except for the slow and drowsy words: "I will in a little while; just let me rest a little longer." But the "little while" kept whiling away, and the "little longer" kept being prolonged. In vain I delighted in Your law of the inner man, when in my limbs another law was battling against the law of my mind, leading me to be captive under the law of sin that was in my limbs.[35] For the law of sin is the violence of habit, through which even the unwilling mind is drawn in and held, as it deserves to be since it willingly acquiesced. Who could then deliver me, wretched as I was, from the body of this death other than Your grace through Jesus Christ our Lord?[36]

[6.13] Lord, my savior and redeemer, I will now recount and avow before You how You delivered me from the shackles of carnal lust by which I was so firmly bound, and how You delivered me from the slavery of worldly affairs. I continued living my daily life, but with increasing anxiety, and every day I longed for You. I kept attending Your Church whenever I was free from the tasks whose weight was smothering me. Alypius was living with me, unoccupied by legal work after his third term as assessor, and was waiting for someone to whom he could sell his counsel the way I sold the art of speaking, to the extent that one can impart such an art through teaching. Nebridius, for his part, had consented as an act of friendship to teach as an assistant under Verecundus, to whom we were all very close, and who was a citizen of Milan and a rhetorician there. Verecundus had urgently appealed to us in the name of friendship that one of us offer him the reliable help he so greatly needed. Nebridius was not drawn to this work by any desire for profit, for he could have earned more from his learning had he wanted to, but out of true benevolence; being a kind and gentle friend, he did not want to turn down our request. He went about his tasks with great delicacy, shying away from making himself known to figures of importance, and thus shunning the distraction of mind that this would bring, preferring to have his mind free with as many hours of leisure as was possible so he could seek wisdom through reading and listening.

[6.14] One day, a certain Pontitianus came to see me and Alypius at our lodgings on some business or other. (Nebridius happened to be absent.) He was a countryman of ours, insofar as he was from Africa,[37] and held a high office at the emperor's court. I cannot remember what he wanted from us, but we had sat down to talk when he happened to notice a book lying on a gaming table in front of us. He picked it up, opened it, and to his surprise found it to be that of the Apostle Paul, for he had imagined that it would be one of the books with which I was wearing myself out in my profession. He looked at me with a smile, commending me and expressing surprise at having found this book, and only this book, at my side. It turned out that he was a Christian and devout, bowing before You our God in frequent and extended prayer in church. When I told him I was studying these Scriptures with great care, he began to speak of Antony the Egyptian monk, whose name was so renowned among Your servants, though Alypius and I had not heard of him. When Pontitianus realized this, he continued speaking about this great man of whom we were unaware, surprised that we did not know him. We were amazed at hearing Your wonderful works confirmed so indubitably and in such recent history, almost in our own times, wrought in the true Faith and the Christian Church. We were all surprised: Alypius and I that such great wonders had occurred, and Pontitianus that we had not heard of them.

[6.15] From there his discourse moved to the communities of monks in the monasteries, and their way of life that is a sweet aroma to You, and of the fecund deserts of the hermits, about which we knew nothing. There was even a monastery in Milan outside the city walls, of which we had not heard, that was full of good brothers and under the care of Ambrose. Pontitianus spoke with fervor and at length, and we listened with intent silence. He told us how one afternoon in Trier, when the emperor was at the circus arena, Pontitianus and three companions had gone for a stroll in the gardens by the city walls, where they walked in pairs, one companion walking with him, the other two on their own, and as the other two walked they came upon an abode in which some of Your servants were living, humble in spirit, to whom the kingdom of heaven belongs,[38] and there they found a book that described the life of Saint Anthony. One of the two men had begun to read it, filled with admiration and excitement, and as he read he began to consider taking up such a life, giving up his worldly post in order to serve You. The two men were imperial administrators, and the man reading the book was suddenly filled with holy love and sober shame. In anger at himself, he looked at his friend and said: "Tell me, I beg of you, what will we achieve with all our work? What are we seeking? What is the reason for our service? Can we hope for anything more in the Imperial Court than to be a Friend to the Emperor,[39] and is that not a dangerous place to be, filled with peril? And then there are the perils we have to weather in order to reach that greater peril! And when would we finally reach it? Yet if I want to be a friend to God, I can be a friend to him right away." He spoke these words in anguish, with the birth pangs of a new life. He looked back down at the page and read on, and was changed deep inside where only You can see; his mind was stripped of the world, as was soon to become clear, for as he read, his heart was tossed about by a great surge; he raged for a while, but then saw with clarity what way he must choose and chose the better way. And having become Yours he said to his friend: "I have now broken away from our ambitions and am determined to serve God, and I will begin to do so from this moment on and in this very place. If you will not do as I do, at least do not oppose me." His companion replied that he would stay at his side in order to serve such a glorious cause. Both men were now Yours, and began to build the tower, at the fitting price of forsaking everything they had and following You.[40] Then Pontitianus and his companion, who had been strolling in other parts of the garden, came looking for them and proposed that they all return, since the day was drawing to a close. But the two companions told them their desire and intention, and how this proclivity had risen and grown strong within them, begging that if they would not join them, they should at least not hinder them. Pontitianus told us that he and his companion did not change their former way of life, but they did weep for themselves and piously congratulated the other two, commending themselves to their prayers, and so, their hearts still firmly bound to this world, they returned to the palace, while the other two, fixing their hearts on heaven, remained in the abode. Both these men had promised brides, who also dedicated their virginity to You when they heard of their resolution.

[7.16] This was the story that Pontitianus told, but, while he was speaking, You, Lord, made me turn and look at myself, coaxing me out from behind my own back to where I had retreated, unwilling to look at myself. You placed me before my face so that I could see how ugly I was, how deformed and vile, blistered and ulcerous. I looked and was horrified, but could find no place to flee from myself, and whenever I sought to turn my gaze away from myself, Pontitianus was continuing his story, and You again placed me before myself and thrust me before my eyes so that I would encounter my iniquity and hate it. I had known this, but denied it, pushing it away and forgetting it.

[7.17] But now, the more ardently I revered those young men about whose exalted state I was hearing, giving themselves wholly to You to be cured, the more abhorrence and execration I felt for myself when I compared myself to them. Many years of my life had passed since my nineteenth year—some twelve years—when I had read Cicero's *Hortensius* and was stirred to an earnest love of wisdom; but I still deferred renouncing worldly happiness and freeing myself to search for that of which not the finding but the mere seeking was preferable to all the treasures and kingdoms of mankind and to the pleasures of the body that were available all around me, and which I could have at will. But I had been a wretched young man, most wretched at the very beginning of my youth, when I had prayed to You for chastity, saying: "Grant me chastity and continence, only not yet." For I feared lest You might hear me too soon, and too soon heal me of the disease of lust which I preferred to satisfy rather than to have extinguished. And I had walked along crooked paths in a sacrilegious superstition,[41] not because I was certain of its truth, but because I preferred it to the Christian doctrine, which I did not study with piety but attacked with enmity.

[7.18] I had thought that the reason I had postponed from day to day rejecting the ambitions of this world and following only You was because I did not see anything certain by which I could set my course. But now the day had come where I stood naked before myself, and my conscience rebuked me: "Will you remain silent? Did you not say that for an uncertain truth you did not want to cast off your burden of vanity? Behold! Now the truth is certain, and yet your burden is still smothering you, while others with freer shoulders are granted wings though they did not wear themselves out with questioning, nor have they been for ten years and more meditating on all this." This was gnawing within me, and I felt confounded with horrible shame all the while Pontitianus was speaking. Having completed his story and the business he had come for, he went on his way, and I was left to myself. What things I now said against myself! With what scourges of judgment did I lash at my soul so that it would follow me as I walked after You![42] But my soul drew back and refused, though it offered no excuse; all arguments were now exhausted and refuted, and there remained only a silent trepidation, and my soul feared, as it feared death, being held back from the very flow of habit through which it was wasting away in death.

[8.19] In this great struggle of my inner self that I had stirred up powerfully against my soul in the chamber of my heart, troubled in mind and countenance, I turned to Alypius and exclaimed: "What is wrong with us? What is the meaning of all this? Did you hear Pontitianus' words? Those humble people with no learning have arisen and stormed heaven,[43] while we, with all our learning but without heart, wallow down below in flesh and blood! Should we be ashamed to follow these people because they have gone before us, or should we not rather be ashamed that we are not following them?" That is what I more or less said to Alypius, and in my fervor I tore away from him, while he stared after me in silence and astonishment. I had sounded very strange, and my forehead, cheeks, eyes, and color, and the tone of my voice, expressed more about my state of mind than the words I was uttering. Our lodgings had a small garden of which we had the use, along with the entire house, since the owner, our host, was not living there. It was to that garden that the tumult of my heart had driven me, where the heated dispute in which I was engaged with myself would be hindered by no one until it ended one way or another. You knew in which way, but I did not. I only knew that I had embraced insanity to gain sanity, embraced death to gain life. I knew how ill I was, but did not know how healed I was soon to be. I had rushed out into the garden, with Alypius following me close at heel; I did not feel my solitude disturbed when he was present, nor could he have left me to myself, distressed as I was. We sat down as far from the house as we could. My spirit was raging,[44] indignant with distressed fury that I had not entered the pact which You, my God, had willed and which all my bones cried out for me to enter[45] and praised to the skies. And we cannot reach it by ship or by cart, nor on foot, though one need not move as far as I had gone from the house to the garden in which we were sitting. For not only going but arriving was nothing more than wanting to go—but wanting ardently and entirely, not limping and turning this way and that, with the part of one's will that is seeking to rise battling the part that is clinging to the earth.

[8.20] In the fervor of my doubts I made many movements and gestures that some men want to do but cannot, either because their limbs are missing, or they are bound by shackles, impaired by infirmity, or impeded in some other way. When I tore my hair, beat my forehead, or locked my fingers to clasp my knee I wanted to do these things, and so did them. But I might have wanted to do them yet not have done them if the mobility in my limbs had not obeyed. I did so much in which my will and my power were not on a par, but did not do the one thing I wished to do more than anything else, and would have been able to do the instant I had wanted to do it providing that I really and truly wanted it, for in this both the ability to do and the will to do were on a par: and yet I did not do it. My body obeyed with greater ease the slightest will of my mind, making its limbs move at a whim, than my mind obeyed itself, when the one thing it truly willed could only be accomplished by will alone.

[9.21] How could something so aberrant come about? What was its cause? Let Your mercy shine on me that I may ask whether the answer might lie in the hidden punishment of man and the darkest contrition of the sons of Adam. How could something so aberrant come about? What was its cause? The mind commands the body and it immediately obeys, and yet the mind commands itself and is resisted. The mind commands the hand to move, and there is such readiness that one can barely distinguish the command from the compliance: and yet the mind is the mind and the hand is the body. The mind commands the mind to will a thing, and though it is commanding itself it does not comply. How could something so aberrant come about? What was its cause? I say that the mind commands itself to will, and would not command itself to do so unless it willed: and yet it does not do what it commands. It is because it does not will it entirely, and so does not command it entirely. For it commands to the extent that it wants a thing, and does not do what it commands to the extent that it does not want it, since the will is commanding itself to be a will so that there is a will: commanding not another but itself. But it does not command entirely; therefore what it commands is not done. For if the will were entire, it would not command itself to be, because it would already be. It is therefore not an aberrance partly not to will and partly to will, but an infirmity of the mind that it cannot entirely prevail even when supported by truth, since it is weighed down by habit. And therefore there are two wills, since one of them is not entire: and what is present in one is absent in the other.

[10.22] Let them perish from Your presence,[46] God, the way the vain Manichaean talkers and seducers of the mind perish, who, in observing that there are two wills when we deliberate, affirm that there are also two minds within us that have two natures, one good, the other evil. But it is they who are evil when they hold such evil tenets, though they can become good if they behold the true tenets and assent to the truth so that Your Apostle may say to them: "You were once darkness, but are now light in the Lord."[47] They do want to be light, yet not in the Lord but in themselves, imagining the nature of the soul to be what God is, thus turning themselves into an even denser darkness and receding further from You in their execrable arrogance, from You, the true Light that illumines every man coming into this world.[48] Take heed what you say, and blush! Draw near unto Him and be illumined, and your faces will not blush![49] When I was deliberating about serving the Lord my God, as had been my purpose for a long time, it was I who willed and I who did not will. It was I. I neither willed it entirely, nor did I not will it entirely, which was why I was in dispute with myself and scattering myself, and this destruction befell me against my will; yet it did not bespeak the presence of the nature of another mind,[50] but the punishment of my own. Nor was it I who had wrought it, but the sin that dwelt in me,[51] the punishment of a sin more freely committed since I was a son of Adam.

[10.23] If there were as many contrary natures as there are wills that resist themselves, there would be not only two but many. If a man were to deliberate whether he should go to a conventicle of the Manichaeans or to a spectacle, the Manichaeans would cry out, "Behold, here are two natures: one good that is leading him to our conventicle, and one bad that is leading him away. What other reason can there be for this hesitation between conflicting wills?" But I say that both are bad, the one that leads the man to them, as well as the one that leads him away. The Manichaeans, however, believe that the will that leads to them can only be good. What then if one of us Christians were deliberating, wavering as his two wills dispute whether he should go to a spectacle or to our church? Would not the Manichaeans also waver in their answer? For either despite themselves they will grant that the will that is leading to our church is good, since it leads to those who are steeped in its holy mysteries and are bound by them, or they must deem that two evil natures and two evil minds are conflicting within one man, and that what they usually say—that one will is good, the other evil—is not true, or they must be converted to the truth, and not deny that when a man deliberates he has a single soul that is being torn between opposite wills.

[10.24] So when the Manichaeans perceive two conflicting wills within one man, they must stop asserting that the conflict is between two opposing minds that are two opposing substances and two opposing principles, one good, the other bad. You, O true God, disapprove of them, refute and convict them. There is the case when both wills are bad, such as when someone is deliberating whether he should kill a man by poison or by the sword, whether he should seize one estate belonging to another or a different one if he cannot seize both, or whether he should purchase voluptuous pleasure or hoard his money in avarice; whether he should go to the circus arena or to the spectacles, if both are showing on the same day. I add a third possibility: robbing another's house if one has the opportunity, or, fourthly, committing adultery if likewise the opportunity should arise. If all these possibilities concur at the same instant and are all equally desired, though they cannot all be carried out, they

will split the mind into four conflicting wills, or even more, considering the vast variety of what man covets. But not even the Manichaeans assert that there are so many different substances. This also
holds for wills that are good. For should I ask the Manichaeans if it
is good to delight in reading the Apostle, or if it is good to delight in
a sober Psalm, or if it is good to discourse on the Gospel, they will
answer: "It is good." What if all these activities give equal pleasure,
and all concur at the same time? Will not the opposing wills tear at a
man's heart while he weighs which he would rather choose? And yet
these wills are all good though they dispute one another until one is
chosen, which must then be borne by one entire will which before
had been split into many. This is also true when eternity delights us
and draws us upward while the pleasure of a temporal good is keeping us down below: it is the same soul that wills both one thing and
the other, but not with an entire will, and so is torn with grievous
vexation, truth leading it to prefer eternity while habit will not let it
relinquish the temporal.

[11.25] This was how ill and tormented I was, accusing myself more
bitterly than ever, twisting and wrenching to break free of my chains
that were easing but still held me fast. And You, Lord, penetrated my
hidden depths with severe mercy, redoubling the lashes of fear and
shame lest I should succumb and not break the last frail fetters that
remained, allowing them to grow strong once more and bind me all
the tighter. And I said to myself deep inside, "Act now, the time to
act is now." In my words I was already resolved. I almost acted, but
did not; however, I did not fall back into my former state, but kept
close and recovered my breath. I tried once more and came even
closer, and closer; I could almost touch it, almost take hold of it, yet
I could not reach it, neither touching nor taking hold of it, hesitat-
ing to die to death and to live to life. Greater was the sway of the
evil to which I was accustomed than the goodness to which I was
unaccustomed, and the more the moment neared in which I was to

become another man, the more I was struck by horror; yet horror did not strike a decisive blow, nor did it turn me away, but held me suspended.

[11.26] I was being held in check by vain trifles and trifling vanities, my long-standing paramours tearing at my garment of flesh and whispering: "Will you send us away? From that moment on we shall never again be with you. From that moment on you will never again be allowed this and that." And what they meant by "this and that"! What were they suggesting, my God! Let Your mercy repulse it from Your servant's soul! What filth they were proposing, what infamy! Now I less than half heard them, and they did not dare come out to contradict me openly but muttered as if behind my back, plucking at me almost furtively so I would turn and look; but they managed to hold me back and delay me from tearing myself away and shaking myself free from them, and making the leap to where I was being summoned, while the force of my habits called out to me, "Do you think you can bear being without them?"

[11.27] But the force of my habit said this now quite faintly, for in the direction to which I had turned my face and to which I feared to go, Continence had now appeared before me, chaste and dignified, serene, cheerful though without allurements, beckoning me with sincerity to come and not to doubt, her holy hands reaching out to receive and embrace me with a profusion of honest examples: so many youths and maidens, so many people of every age, sober widows and aged virgins, and among them stood Continence herself, not barren but a fertile mother of children,[52] with joys granted her by You, Lord, her Husband. And she smiled, both teasing and encouraging me, as if she were saying: "Can you not do what these youths and maidens can? Do you think they managed on their own without the help of the Lord their God? The Lord their God gave me to them. Why do you persist on your own where you cannot persist?

Cast yourself upon Him; do not be afraid. He will not withdraw and let you fall. Cast yourself upon Him without fear—He will receive and will heal you." I truly blushed, for I was also still listening to the whisperings of frivolity, and so lingered and delayed, and again it was as if Continence were saying: "Shut your ears to your impure limbs that are upon the earth, so that they will be mortified.[53] They speak to you of delights, but not as does the law of the Lord your God."[54] This dispute within my heart was merely myself battling myself, and Alypius, who was at my side, waited in silence for the end of my unusual agitation.

[12.28] From hidden depths a profound introspection had gathered together and amassed all my misery before my heart's eye, and now a violent tempest arose within me, bringing a mighty shower of tears, and I got up and hastened away from Alypius so that my storm could gush forth with all its sounds and voices. Solitude seemed to me more fit for weeping, and I moved far enough away from him so that his presence would not burden me. That was the state I was in, and Alypius sensed it, for as I got up I think I said something in which my voice was choked with tears. Confounded, Alypius remained where we had sat. I collapsed beneath a fig tree, I do not remember how, and let my tears flow, streams pouring from my eyes, an acceptable sacrifice to You,[55] and I said many things to You, not in these exact words, but to this purpose: "But You, O Lord, for how long?[56] For how long, Lord? Will You be angry forever?[57] Remember not our former iniquities."[58] For I felt that these iniquities were holding me in their grip. I uttered these wretched words: "How long, how long? Ever tomorrow and tomorrow? Why not right away? Why cannot my baseness come to an end this instant?"

[12.29] I was speaking and weeping in the most bitter contrition of my heart when I suddenly heard from a nearby house a voice—that of a boy or a girl, I could not tell—repeating in a singsong, "Pick up and read, pick up and read." That instant, my countenance changed and I began to wonder intently whether there could be some kind of game in which children sang such words, but I could not remember there being such a game. I checked the torrent of my tears and rose, concluding that these words were clearly a divine command that I open the Book and read the first line I found. I had heard how Saint Anthony had come upon a reading of the Gospel and had understood the words he heard being read out as an admonition, as if they were being spoken to him: "Go, sell all you have and give it to the poor, and you will have treasure in heaven; and come, follow me."[59] With these divine words he was immediately converted to You.[60] So I hastened back to the place where Alypius was sitting, for it was there that I had laid down the volume of the Apostle when I had arisen. I seized it, opened it, and in silence read the verse upon which my eyes first fell: "Not in revelry and drunkenness, not in lewdness and lust, not in strife and envy. But put on the Lord Jesus Christ, and make not provision for the flesh in its concupiscences."[61] I neither wished nor needed to read further. Instantly, at the end of these lines, it was as if a light of serenity were pouring into my heart, and all the darkness of uncertainty dispersed.

[12.30] I shut the Book, putting my finger or some other mark between the pages, and with a calm countenance told Alypius what had happened. But he also apprised me of the change within him, of which I had not been aware. He asked to see what verse I had read. I showed it to him and he read it, and read further than I had; I did not know the verse that followed. What followed was "Receive one who is weak in the faith,"[62] and Alypius told me that he was applying this to himself. This admonition gave him strength in his pious resolution and purpose, which truly corresponded to his character, in which he had always very much differed from me for the better, and without turbulent hesitation he joined me. We go inside to my mother, we tell her, she rejoices; we recount how it had come to pass; she exults, jubilates, and praises You Who are able to do beyond that which we desire or understand.[63] She saw that You had granted her far more for me than she had begged for in her sad and tear-filled laments to You, for You had converted me to You[64] so that I now sought neither a wife nor any ambition of this world, and stood firm upon that rule of faith as You had shown me to my mother in a dream so many years before.[65] And You converted her mourning into joy[66] even more abundantly than she had hoped, and in a way that was much more precious and pure than she had sought in having grandchildren of my flesh.

ॐ

NOTES

1 This theme also appears at the opening of Book V and Book IX.

2 Psalm 115:16–17 (Vulgate), 116:16–17 (other translations).

3 1 Corinthians 13:12. "For now we see through a glass, darkly; but then face to face: now I know in part; but then shall I know even as also I am known." (King James Bible)

4 1 Corinthians 5:7.

5 Some of the people had chosen celibacy, others marriage. 1 Corinthians 7:7. "But each one has his own gift from God, one in this manner and another in that." (New King James Bible)

6 Psalm 25:8 (Vulgate), 26:8 (other translations).

7 1 Corinthians 7:7.

8 Matthew 19:12.

9 Wisdom 13:1.

10 John 1:1–3.

11 Romans 1:21.

12 Psalm 17:36 (Vulgate), 18:35 (other translations).

13 Romans 1:22.

14 Colossians 2:8.

15 Matthew 11:25.

16 Virgil, *Aeneid* 8.698–700.

17 Psalm 143:5 (Vulgate), 144:5 (other translations).

18 Psalm 28:5 (Vulgate), 28:6 (other translations). "The voice of the Lord breaks the cedars, yes, the Lord splinters the cedars of Lebanon." (New King James Bible)

19 Luke 12:9.

20 Psalm 111:10 (Vulgate), 112:10 (other translations).

21 Psalm 39:5 (Vulgate), 40:4 (other translations).

22 Luke 15:4.

23 Luke 15:8–10.

24 Luke 15:32. The younger, prodigal son in the Parable of the Lost Son.

25 Luke 15:32.

26 John 1:12.

27 1 Corinthians 1:27–8.

28 1 Corinthians 15:9. Apostle Paul.

29 Matthew 11:30.

30 Matthew 12:29.

31 2 Timothy 2:21.

32 Galatians 5:17.

33 Romans 7:17.

34 A quotation from Ephesians 5:14.

35 A quotation from Romans 7:22–23.

36 Romans 24:5.

37 The Roman provinces of North Africa.

38 Matthew 5:3.

39 Friend to the Emperor (*amicus imperatoris*) was an unofficial term for holders of high office at the imperial court.

40 Luke 14:28. "For which of you, intending to build a tower, does not sit down first and count the cost, whether he has *enough* to finish *it?*" (New King James Bible)

41 Ecclesiasticus 2:16 (Vulgate), Sirach 2:16 (other translations). The "sacrilegious superstition" Augustine is referring to is Manichaeism.

42 Jeremiah 7:9.

43 Matthew 11:12. With "people with no learning," Augustine is referring to the humble converts of Trier in Pontitianus' story.

44 John 11:33.

45 Psalm 34:10 (Vulgate), 35:10 (other translations).

46 Psalm 67:3 (Vulgate), 68:2 (other translations).

47 A quotation from Ephesians 5:8.

48 John 1:9.

49 Psalm 33:6 (Vulgate), 34:5 (other translations).

50 As Manichaean doctrine maintained.

51 Romans 7:17.

52 Psalm 112:9 (Vulgate), 113:9 (other translations).

53 Colossians 3:5.

54 Psalm 118:85 (Vulgate), 119:85 (other translations).

55 Psalm 50:19 (Vulgate), 51:17 (other translations).

> "The sacrifices of God *are* a broken spirit,
> A broken and a contrite heart—
> These, O God, You will not despise." (New King James Bible)

56 A quotation from Psalm 6:4 (Vulgate), 6:3 (other translations).

> "My soul also is greatly troubled;
> But You, O Lord—how long?" (New King James Bible)

57 A quotation from Psalm 78:5 (Vulgate), 79:5 (other translations).

58 A quotation from Psalm 78:8 (Vulgate), 79:8 (other translations).

59 A quotation from Matthew 19:21. See Athanasius, *Life of Anthony*, chapter 2.

60 Psalm 50:15 (Vulgate), 51:13 (other translations).

61 A quotation from Romans 13:13–14.

62 A quotation from Romans 14:1.

63 Ephesians 3:20.

64 Psalm 50:15 (Vulgate), 51:13 (other translations).

65 See Book III, 11.19.

66 Psalm 29:12 (Vulgate), 30:11 (other translations).

BOOK IX

[1.1] O Lord, I am Your servant, I am Your servant and the son of Your handmaid: You have broken my bonds, and I am offering up to You the sacrifice of thanksgiving.[1] Let my heart and my tongue praise You, and let all my bones say, "Lord, who is like You?"[2] Let them cry out, and You will answer me and say to my soul: "I am Your salvation."[3] Who was I and what was I? What was not evil in my deeds, and if not in my deeds, then in my words, and if not in my words, then in my will? But You, Lord, are good and merciful, Your right hand delving into the depths of my death, and from the core of my heart emptying out the abyss of corruption. And all this came to be when I no longer willed what I willed but what You willed.[4] But where had my free will been all those years, and from what profound and mysterious depths had it been called forth the instant I surrendered my neck to Your gentle yoke and my shoulders unto Your light burden,[5] Jesus Christ, my Savior and Redeemer?[6] How sweet it suddenly became to me to be free from those frivolous pleasures! What I had feared to renounce was now a joy to relinquish, for You expelled these frivolities from me, true and highest Sweetness, You expelled them, and Yourself entered in their place, more sweet than any pleasure, though not to flesh and blood; brighter than any light, though more hidden than any depth; more exalted than any honor, though not to those exalted in pride. Now my soul was free from the gnawing cares of ambition and covetousness, free from wallowing and from scratching at the prurience of lust, and my words began to pour out to You, my Brightness, my Wealth, my Salvation, Lord my God.

[2.2] And I resolved before Your presence not to tear myself away abruptly, but gently to withdraw the service of my tongue from the fairground of loquacity, so that the young men, who were not studying Your law or Your peace, but schooling themselves in deranged lying and legal insanity, should no longer purchase from my mouth the weapons for their crazed assaults. Happily there were only a few days left before the wine harvest holidays,[7] and I decided I would endure these last days so that I could formally withdraw from my post, bought free by You so I would never return to be sold. I had reached my resolution only before You and our closest friends; no one else knew, for we had agreed between us not to tell others, though You had provided us, who were now ascending from the valley of tears and singing that song of ascents,[8] with sharp arrows and destroying coals to fend off deceitful tongues[9] that, feigning advice, seek to dissuade, and, feigning love, devour us as they devour their fodder.

[2.3] You had pierced our hearts with the arrow of Your love, and we carried Your words deep within us. The examples of Your servants whom You had brought to light from darkness and to life from death accrued in our minds, burning and consuming that heavy torpor so that we would not sink into the abyss. These examples ignited us so vehemently that the gusts from the deceitful tongues of dissuasion fanned our flames all the more intensely instead of extinguishing them. Because of Your Name, which You have sanctified throughout the earth,[10] there would also have been men who would have praised my solemn pledge and resolution, but it would have seemed like ostentation not to wait for the holidays that were now so near and relinquish my public profession that was before the eyes of all; everyone would have stopped to scrutinize my action, noting how near the holidays were that I was seeking to anticipate. Much would have been said about me, accusing me of seeking to appear exalted. Would it have served a purpose that people would weigh and accuse my thoughts, and that our good would be spoken of as evil.[11]

[2.4] Moreover it had been that summer, when on account of my literary toil my lungs for the first time began to give way and I could barely breathe, and from the pain in my chest it was clear that they were wounded, hindering me from speaking at any length. At first this had troubled me, for it almost forced me to relinquish the burden of teaching, or to interrupt it for a time so that I might be cured and could recover. But when the full wish to be free and to see that You are my Lord[12] had arisen and was secure within me, as You know, my Lord, I was filled with joy that I also had that lesser excuse, that was not feigned and might soften the vexation of those who on account of their sons wished me never to be free. Filled with that joy, I continued to prevail until the interval had passed—some twenty days— but it was a struggle to bear these days, since covetousness, which in the past had helped me bear the burden of this work, had now disappeared, and I would have faltered if patience had not stepped into its place. It is possible that some of Your servants, my brothers, may say that I sinned, in that with a heart fully set on serving You I permitted myself to sit even one hour in the chair of lies, and I would not refute them. But did You not, most merciful Lord, in the holy water of baptism, pardon and also remit this sin of mine along with my other terrible and deadly sins?

[3.5] Verecundus was careworn with anxiety at the good path we were taking, for he was still held back by tight chains and saw that, not being a Christian, he would be parted from our group. Though his wife was a Christian and devout, she hindered him more resolutely than any shackles from the journey on which we had embarked, for Verecundus asserted that he would only become a Christian if he could live in unwed chastity. But he generously allowed us to remain at his estate for as long as we wished. You will reward him, Lord, at the resurrection of the just,[13] for You have already granted him the lot of the righteous. In our absence, while we were in Rome, he was seized by an illness during which he became a baptized Christian, and so departed from this life as one of the faithful. You had mercy not only on him but also on us, for we would have been tortured with intolerable pain thinking of the excellent kindness of our friend without being able to number him among Your flock. Thanks be to You, our God! We are Yours. Your exhortations and consolations attest this, for You are faithful in Your promises, and are now requiting Verecundus with the beauty of Your eternally verdant Paradise for having granted us his estate at Cassiciacum, where we found rest in You from the fever of the world; You forgave him his sins in the world upon that mountain flowing with milk, Your mountain, the mountain of abundance.[14]

[3.6] Verecundus had been careworn at our conversion, but Nebridius, on the other hand, rejoiced with us. He was not yet a Christian either, and had fallen into the pit of that most pernicious sin of believing the true flesh of Your Son to be a phantasm. But he was now emerging from that pit, and though he had not yet been steeped in the sacred mysteries of Your Church, he was a most ardent seeker of truth. Not long after my conversion and regeneration through Your baptism, Nebridius too became a true believer, serving You in perfect chastity and continence among his people in Africa,[15] and once he had made his entire household Christian You released him from the flesh, and he now abides in Abraham's bosom.[16] Whatever might be meant by "bosom," that is where my Nebridius abides, my sweet friend who from Your freed man became Your adopted son. That is where he abides. For what other place can there be for such a soul? That is where he abides, a place about which he had asked me, poor and inexperienced man that I was, so many questions. Now he no longer inclines his ear to my mouth, but inclines his spiritual mouth to Your fountain, and with eternal bliss drinks in as much wisdom as he can. But I do not believe that he is so intoxicated as to forget me, since You, Lord, whom he drinks in, are mindful of us. That was how we were then, and we comforted Verecundus' sorrow, reminding him that our friendship had endured despite our conversion, exhorting him to become a pious Christian in accordance with his state as a married man. As for Nebridius, we were waiting for him to follow us, and he was now ready to do so as my last day as a rhetorician was approaching after what seemed to me so many long days in my yearning for the freedom and time to sing to You with my entire being: "My heart has said to You: I have sought Your countenance, Your countenance, Lord, I shall seek."[17]

[4.7] And the day finally came on which I was to be freed from my post, a post from which in thought I had already been freed, and it was done. You rescued my tongue as You had already rescued my heart, and I blessed You and rejoiced, retiring with all my friends to Verecundus' estate. There I wrote works in Your service, though those works were still catching their breath from the school of pride, works that testified my disputations with others and also with myself alone in Your presence; as for my disputations with Nebridius, who was absent, my epistles to him bear witness. Never will I have enough time to commemorate all Your great mercies toward us then, especially when I must now hasten on to Your even greater mercies. My memory is bringing all this back to me, and it is delightful, O Lord, to avow before You by what inner goads You tamed me, and how You leveled me by lowering the hills and mountains of my thoughts, straightening what was crooked and smoothing my roughness;[18] and how You also subjected Alypius, the brother of my heart, unto the name of Your Only-Begotten Son, our Lord and Savior Jesus Christ,[19] whose name at first he had objected to seeing in my writings; for Alypius would rather have had my works exude the aroma of the scholars' cedars, which the

Lord has crushed, than that of the healing herbs of the Church, the remedy against serpents.[20]

[4.8] How I called out to You, my God, when I read the Psalms of David, those faithful songs and sounds of devotion that allow no pride of spirit! I was still a novice in Your true love, a catechumen spending the wine harvest holiday at the country estate with Alypius, a catechumen too, my mother at our side—in woman's garb but with a man's faith, with the serenity of age, with motherly love, with Christian piety! How I called out to You in those Psalms, and how they inflamed my love for You, rousing me to want to recite them to the whole world against the pride of man! And yet they are sung throughout the entire world, and there is none who can hide from Your heat.[21] What vehement and bitter sorrow I felt in my indignation at the Manichaeans, but I pitied them too, for they did not know the Sacraments, those remedies, and they raved against the antidote that could have healed them of their ravings. I wished that they had been somewhere near me during those days of contemplation and, without my knowing that they were there, could have beheld my countenance and heard me call out as I read the fourth Psalm and seen the effect of that Psalm upon me: "When I called, the God of my righteousness heard me; in tribulation You have strengthened me. Have mercy upon me, Lord, and hear my prayer."[22] I wish they could have heard me speak these words, and without my knowing that they were listening, lest they should think I spoke them for their sakes, for in truth I would have neither spoken these things, nor spoken them in the way I did, had I felt that they were hearing or seeing me; though if I had spoken these words, they would not have understood them in the way I spoke them by myself and for myself before You in the intimate feeling of my soul.

[4.9] I trembled with fear and burned with hope and exultation in Your mercy, Father, and all this burned in my eyes and poured forth from my voice when Your good Spirit turned to us and said, "O sons of men, how long will your hearts be burdened? Why do you prize untruths and seek lies?"²³ For I had prized untruths and sought lies. And You, Lord, had already exalted Your Holy One,²⁴ raising Him from the dead and placing Him at Your right hand,²⁵ whence from on high He sent His promise, the Comforter, the Spirit of Truth.²⁶ God had already sent Him, but I did not know it; He had sent Him, and He was now exalted, rising from the dead and ascending to heaven. For until then the Spirit had not yet been given, because Jesus was not yet glorified.²⁷ And the prophecy cries out, "How long will your hearts be burdened? Why do you prize untruths and seek lies? And know this, that the Lord has exalted His Holy One." The prophecy cries out, "How long?" It cries out, "Know this!" and I, unknowing for so long, prized untruths and sought lies, and therefore I heard these words and trembled, for they were being said to such as I remembered myself to have been, since in those illusory spirits that I had held for truths there had been untruths and lies. In the pain of my remembering I cried out many things with earnest ardor; if they who still prized untruths and sought lies had heard them, they would have surely been distraught and vomited up all the falsehoods. And You would have heard them when they cried out to You, for He Who intercedes with You for us died for us a true death in the flesh.²⁸

[4.10] I also read: "Be angry but do not sin."²⁹ How I was moved, my God, for I had now learned to be angry at myself for things past so that I would not continue to sin, and had learned to be angry with good reason, for it was not a separate nature belonging to a race of darkness that had sinned for me, as the Manichaeans who are not angry at themselves claim, and so are treasuring up wrath until the day of wrath and the revelation of Your just judgment.³⁰ Now the good I was seeking was no longer outside me, nor was it to be found with our eyes of flesh under the sun, for those who seek joy outside themselves soon waste and dissipate themselves on things seen and temporal,[31] the shadows of which their starved thoughts are licking. Oh would that their hungering had worn them out and they had said, "Who will show us what is good?" Let us then say, and let them hear, "The light of Your countenance, Lord, has been instilled in us."[32] For we are not the light that illumines every man,[33] but we are illumined by You, so that we, having been once darkness, may become light in You."[34] Oh would that they could see that the eternal is within themselves, which I had tasted and was distraught that I could not show them as long as they brought me their hearts in eyes that were turned away from You, while they said, "Who will show us what is good?" For there where I was angry at myself, within my chamber, where I had been stung by remorse, where I had slain and sacrificed the man I had been and had hoped in You as I meditated on my renewal, there I had first felt Your sweetness, and You had put joy in my heart.[35] And I cried out as I recognized within myself what I read externally. Nor did I want my worldly goods to multiply, and so waste time and be wasted by time, for in Eternal Simplicity I had found a different corn, and wine, and oil.[36]

[4.11] And with a loud cry of my heart I exclaimed words from the next verse, "O in peace!" "O in the Selfsame!" What wondrous words: "I will sleep and I will rest."[37] For who shall restrain us when the written words come to be, that "Death is swallowed up in victory?"[38] And You are supremely the Selfsame Who does not change,[39] and in You is repose that leaves all toil behind, for there is none other with You; nor are we to seek a multitude of other things that are not what You are, for You alone, O Lord, make me dwell in safety.[40] I read and I was on fire, and could not find what could be done with those who were deaf and dead, of whom I had been one, pestilent, a blind and bitter ranter against the Scriptures that are honeyed with the honey of heaven and illumined by Your luminosity, and I pined away at the enemies of the Scriptures.[41]

[4.12] How can I recollect all that happened during those holidays? But I have neither forgotten, nor will I conceal, the severity of Your scourge and the miraculous swiftness of Your mercy. You afflicted me with toothache, and when it grew so grave that I could not speak, it entered my heart[42] to prompt all my friends who were there to pray for me to You, God, Who heal both body and soul, writing my plea to them on a wax tablet and giving it to them to read. No sooner had we knelt in humble suppliance than the pain went away. But what a pain it had been, and it simply went away! I confess that I had been frightened, my Lord, my God, for since my childhood I had not experienced anything like it. Your will was deeply instilled in me, and I rejoiced in faith and praised Your Name, but this faith did not prevent my being troubled about my past sins, which had not yet been forgiven me by Your baptism.

[5.13] With the wine harvest holidays ending, I informed the Milanese that they should provide their students with another seller of words, for I had chosen to serve You and also could no longer meet the needs of that profession on account of the difficulty I had in breathing and the pain in my chest. In a series of letters I also informed Your bishop, the holy Ambrose, of my former sins and my present pledge, begging that he advise me which of Your Scriptures would be best for me to read so that I could prepare myself and become more fit to receive so great a grace. He recommended Isaiah the Prophet because, I believe, Isaiah foretells most clearly the Gospel and the calling of the Gentiles.[43] But I could not understand the initial passage, and, surmising that the entire text might be like it, I laid it aside until I was better versed in the language of the Lord.

[6.14] When the time had come for me to put my name down for baptism, we left Verecundus' estate and returned to Milan. Alypius had also resolved to join me in being reborn in You, steeped as he already was in the humility that befits Your Sacraments and a dauntless tamer of the body, treading with bare feet the frozen ground of Italy. We also took with us young Adeodatus, born of my flesh and my sin. You had formed him well; he was almost fifteen, and his intelligence surpassed that of many grave and learned men. I avow before You Your gifts, Lord my God, Creator of all, You Who are able to reform all our deformities, for I had no part in that boy other than my sin. It was You, You alone, who inspired us to raise him in Your doctrine. I avow before You Your gifts. There is a book of mine, *The Master*, in which Adeodatus and I discourse, and You know that all the ideas accredited to him in that discourse were his, though he was only sixteen at the time. I found many things in him that were admirable; his genius made me shudder with joy, and who but You could be the maker of such miracles? You were soon to withdraw his life from this world, and I think of him with greater calm, no longer fearing for his childhood, his youth, or his life as a man. He followed us on our path to baptism, and so was our peer in grace as we studied Your teachings. We were baptized together, and all our worry over our past life vanished. For me those days were filled with joyful wonder as I contemplated the profundity of Your plan for the salvation of the human race. How I wept at Your hymns and canticles, deeply moved by the sweet-sounding voices of Your Church! The voices flowed into my ears, distilling the truth into my heart. My feelings of devotion streamed forth and my tears flowed, and they brought me contentment.

[7.15] It had not been long since the Church of Milan had began to console and hearten the congregation with hymns and canticles, the brethren singing with great zeal in harmony of voice and heart. For it had been a year, or a little more, since Justina, the mother of the boy emperor Valentinian, had persecuted Your servant Ambrose in the cause of the heresy to which she had been seduced by the Arians.[44] Ambrose's pious congregation kept vigil in the church, ready to die with their bishop, Your servant. My mother, Your handmaid, was there in the forefront of those agonies and vigils, living in prayer. Even I, not yet warmed by the heat of Your Spirit, was roused by the clamor and uproar in the city. It was during these times that the practice of singing hymns and psalms in the manner of the Eastern churches had been instituted to keep the people from faltering in their agony and sorrow, and the custom has been retained from that day to this and been imitated by many, indeed almost all Your congregations throughout the world.

[7.16] During these troubles You revealed in a vision to Bishop Ambrose where lay hidden the bodies of the martyrs Protasius and Gervasius. You had kept them uncorrupted in Your secret treasury for so many years so that You might reveal them in order to contain the ire of a woman, the imperial mother of the young emperor. For when the saints had been found and disinterred, and carried with due honor to the Basilica of Ambrose, not only were people healed who had been tormented by impure spirits,[45] their demons manifesting themselves, but a man who had been blind for many years, a citizen of great note, being told the reason for the joyful clamor, jumped up and had his guide lead him to the procession, where he begged to be allowed to touch with his handkerchief the bier of Your saints, whose death is precious in Your sight.[46] And when he then laid the handkerchief on his eyes, they immediately opened. The news spread, and shining praises of You poured forth, and the mind of the hostile empress, though not changing to the salvation of belief, was at least curbed in the fury of her persecution. Thanks be to You, my God! Where from and where to have You led my remembrance that I should confess these things to You here, which though they were of such import I had forgotten to mention them where I should have? And yet then, though the aroma of Your salves was so fragrant,[47] we did not run toward You. So I wept all the more as Your hymns were sung: in the past I had yearned and sighed for You, but now I could finally breathe in the divine breeze that has entered our house of grass.

[8.17] You Who make people of like mind dwell in one house[48] brought Evodius, a young man of our home town, into our company. He had been an imperial administrator and had converted to You and been baptized before we were, relinquishing his secular service in order to serve You. We were together, and were resolved to dwell together in our holy cause. In seeking a place where we could serve You to the best purpose, we all decided to return to Africa.[49] We had just reached Ostia, by the mouth of the Tiber, when my mother died. I have passed over so much, as I have written in haste—receive my avowals and my gratitude, my God, for the countless things about which I have been silent—but I will not pass over all that my mind can bring forth concerning Your handmaid who brought me forth, both in the flesh so that I might be born into this temporal light, and in the soul so that I might be born to eternal light. I will not speak of her gifts, but of Your gifts to her, for neither did she create nor raise herself. It was You Who created her; nor did her father and mother know who it was that had been born to them, and it was the rod and the staff of Your Christ[50] that had reared her in holy fear[51]—the discipline of Your only Son—in her father's Christian household at the hand of a certain virtuous member of Your Church. She commended her mother's attentiveness for the devout training she received, but commended even more the training she received from a very old servant, who had carried her father on her back when he had been a child, in the way that children used to be carried by girls who were a little older. For this reason, and because of the servant's great age and excellent morals, she was greatly respected by the masters of that Christian household, which also accounted for the daughters of the house being left in her care. This task she undertook with great diligence, disciplining the girls with ardent and holy severity when it was necessary, and training them with profound attention. For example, beyond the hours in which they were fed with great moderation at their parents' table, though they might be burning with thirst she would not allow them to drink even water, thus forestalling an evil habit and adding these wise words: "You want to drink water now because you do not have recourse to wine, but when you come to be married and are made mistresses of your own pantries and cellars, you will dislike water, but still your habit of drinking it will remain." By this kind of instruction and the authority with which she commanded, she restrained the gluttony of tender years, and tempered the very thirst of the girls to such excellent moderation that they did not strive for anything that was not seemly.

[8.18] And yet my mother's love for wine, as she, Your handmaid, confided in me her son, her love for wine had crept up on her, for when her parents, believing her to be a temperate girl, sent her to draw wine out of the barrel, she would hold the bowl under the spigot and, before pouring the wine into the pitcher, would take a little sip with pursed lips, for more than a sip she found repellent. And yet she had not done this out of a passion for drink but out of the ebullience of youth, in which the kind of playful impulses boil over that are usually kept in check by the authority of elders. But by always adding a little more to that daily sip—for one who despises small things will fall little by little[52]—she had fallen into the habit of drinking entire cups of unmixed wine. Where then was that watchful old woman with her strict restraint? But there would have been no remedy against this hidden disease if Your healing, Lord, did not preside over us. When father, mother, and nurses are away, You are present, You Who created us, who call us, who through those placed above us induce the salvation of our souls. What did You do then, my God? How did You cure her? How did You heal her? Did You not bring forth from the soul of another a sharp reproach, like a surgeon's knife from Your secret store, and with a single slash remove all the festering putrescence? A servant with whom she used to go to the barrel happened to quarrel with her little mistress when they were alone, deriding her for her deeds with bitter insult, calling her a drunken sot. The insult stung the little girl to the quick, and she reflected on the shameful thing she had done, instantly condemning and abandoning her habit. Just as flattering friends lead to ruin, so accusing enemies often lead to reform. Yet it is not for what You do through people that You reward them, but for what people do of their own volition. The servant in her anger had sought to hurt her young mistress, not to mend her ways, and she spoke her words in secret, either in the heat of quarrel or because she might be called to account for not having said anything earlier. But You, Lord, Ruler of heaven and earth, turn to Your purposes the course of the deepest torrents, and order the turbulence of the tide of time. Through the affliction of one soul You gave health to another, and all who hear this must realize that they must not attribute a person's reform to their own powers, when someone whom they wish to reform is reformed through words they have spoken.

[9.19] So my mother was brought up in modesty and sobriety, and she was made obedient by You to her parents rather than being made obedient by her parents to You, so that as soon as she was of full age to be a bride[53] she was bestowed upon a man whom she served as her lord. And she did everything in her power to win this man over to You, speaking to him of You through the qualities by which You had made her beautiful, filling her husband with respect and love for her as well as admiration. She tolerated his infidelity so that there would never be any animosity between them, for she was awaiting Your mercy upon him, that in believing in You he might become chaste. Furthermore, he was as exceptionally kind as he was hot-tempered, but she had learned not to cross an angry husband in word or deed. It was only when his temper had settled, and he was calm and approachable, that she would explain her actions if he had happened to be too quick to flare up in anger. Many other wives who had gentler husbands bore shameful marks of beatings on their faces, and among their friends would blame their husbands' ways. But she would blame the women's tongues, giving the women as if in jest the solemn advice that the instant they had heard the marriage contract read out to them, they should have recognized that they were now slaves, and, remembering their station, it would have been more fitting for them not to take on airs before their lords. When her friends found out what a violent husband she had, they were amazed that nobody had ever heard of Patricius raising his hand to her or that she never bore the marks of a beating, and that there had never been discord among them even for a day. Asked how this could be, she told her friends her custom of responding to her husband's ire which I have mentioned above. The women who followed her example were to thank her, while those who did not suffered and remained oppressed.

[9.20] Her mother-in-law had initially been incited against her by the insinuations of malicious servants, but was assuaged by the young wife's gentle, yielding manner and her steadfast forbearance, so that she herself revealed to her son that meddling tongues had disrupted the peace in the home, causing trouble between her and her daughter-in-law, and she insisted that he punish the wrongdoers. Patricius respected his mother's wish, ensuring that discipline and peace returned to his home, and he had the maids whipped as his mother had asked, and she promised the same payment to any servant seeking to ingratiate herself by saying evil things about her daughter-in-law. As no servant now dared speak ill of her, they all lived pleasantly and amicably together.

[9.21] To this good handmaid of Yours in whose womb You created me, my God, my Mercy, You granted her another great gift, that of being a peacemaker to quarreling people whenever she could. When she heard bitter words bursting forth from both sides in bilious anger, when a friend spewed out acrid rage against an absent enemy, she would only reveal to either one whatever words might lead to their reconciliation. I might have considered this a minor gift had I not had the painful experience of encountering so many people who, by some horrendous and rampant pestilence of sin, not only disclose to an irate person what their irate enemy said about them but add things that were never said, whereas it ought to be clear to any humane person that he must not incite hostility between people through hostile words, if he cannot bring himself to use benign words to extinguish the hostility. That was how she was, for You had been the inner Teacher in the school of her heart.

[9.22] Finally, toward the very end of her husband's life on earth, she converted him to You, and once he was a believer he no longer gave her cause to lament what she had had to bear before he had become a believer. She was also the servant of Your servants, of whom all who knew her greatly praised and honored and loved You in her; they felt Your presence in her heart, which was attested by the fruits of her devout comportment, for she had been the wife of one man,[54] had honored her debt to her parents and run her house piously,[55] had testimony for her good works,[56] and had brought up children, of whom she labored as if in birth whenever she saw them straying from You.[57] Lastly she took care of all of us, Your servants, Lord, for Your gift allows me to speak on behalf of us all, who, before she closed her eyes in sleep, all lived united in You since we had received the grace of Your baptism. She cared for us as though she had given birth to us all, yet served us as though she had been the daughter of every one of us.

[10.23] With the day looming on which she was to depart this life, a day that You knew but we did not, Your hidden ways arranged that she and I would stand alone gazing out of a window that overlooked the garden of the house in which we were staying in Ostia, by the mouth of the Tiber. In this house, far from all the noise and commotion, we were recuperating from the exertions of our long journey before we set sail across the sea. She and I were talking alone, in sweet conversation, forgetting the past and reaching out for what lay ahead,[58] she and I wondering in the presence of the Truth, which You are, what the eternal life of saints would be like, which neither eye has seen nor ear has heard, nor has it entered into the heart of man.[59] The mouth of our hearts opened wide to drink in those celestial streams of Your fountain, the fountain of life,[60] which is with You, so that fortified to the extent that we could be, we might to some degree contemplate such a profound matter.

[10.24] And when in our conversation we reached the conclusion that the greatest delight of the bodily senses, the greatest corporeal light, is not worthy of comparison to the sweetness of the eternal life of saints, not worthy even of mention, we were lifted with a greater glowing love toward God, the Selfsame.[61] We rose by degrees past everything corporeal to the very heaven where sun and moon and stars shine upon the earth, and ascended even higher with our thoughts and words, with our marveling at Your works, reaching these in our minds and transcending them, coming to that region of unceasing plenty where You feed Israel in eternity with the food of truth, where life is the Wisdom through which all these things are made, all things that have been and shall be. But Wisdom is not made: Wisdom is as it has been and ever shall be. For there is no *was* or *will be* in Wisdom, only *being*, as Wisdom is eternal. For *was* and *will be* are not eternal. While we were discussing and longing for Wisdom, we touched it lightly with the most ardent effort of our hearts, and we sighed and left behind us the first-fruits of the Spirit,[62] returning to the mere sounds of our mouths, where words have a beginning and an end, and how can these words be compared to Your Word, our Lord, who remains in Himself without age and renews all things?[63]

[10.25] So we said: "If the commotion of the flesh were to fall silent in a man, silent the images of the earth and the waters and the air, and silent the heavens,[64] and the soul were silent to itself and by not thinking of itself would surpass itself, if all dreams and imaginary revelations were silent, and silent every tongue and every sign and all that exists only transiently, since if anyone could hear these things then this is what they all would say: 'We did not make ourselves, but He who abides in eternity made us.' If having said this they fell silent, having led us to open our ears to Him who made these things, and He alone would speak through Himself and not through them so that we would hear His Word not through a tongue of flesh, nor through an angel's voice, nor through the thundering sound from the clouds,[65] nor through an obscure enigma, but we might hear Him whom in these things we love, hear Him without these things, just as we now reached out and in swift thought touched the Wisdom that abides over all things in eternity. If this could continue, and other visions that were far inferior could be withdrawn, and could this vision ravish and absorb and envelop its beholder in inward joys, so that eternal life would be like that one moment of understanding for which we longed, then would this not mean: 'Enter into the joy of your Lord'?[66] And when would that be? When we shall all rise again, though we shall not all be changed?"[67]

[10.26] Such were the things that I was saying, and even if not exactly in this way or with those words, yet, Lord, You know that it was on that day when we were speaking, and as she and I spoke, this world with all its delights became contemptible to us, and she said, "My son, as for me, I no longer delight in anything in this life anymore. I do not know what I am still doing here, or why I am here now, since my hopes in this world have all expired. The one thing for which I wanted to linger a while longer in this life was that I might see you a true Christian before I died, but my God has granted my wish in greater abundance than I had sought, for I now see that you despise earthly happiness and have become His servant. What am I doing here?"

[11.27] I do not remember what I answered, but within five days, not much more, she fell sick of a fever, and one day in her illness she fainted and for a moment lost consciousness. We rushed to her side, but she was soon revived, and seeing me and my brother near her, asked, "Where was I?" And then, looking straight at us as we stood there stunned with grief, she said, "It is here that you will bury your mother." I remained silent, refraining from tears, but my brother spoke, saying he would be happier if she did not die in a strange land but in her own. Hearing his words, she looked at him anxiously, her eyes admonishing him because such things were still important to him, and then looking at me said, "Do you hear what your brother says?" and turning to us both, "Bury this body anywhere, and do not worry about such trifles. The only thing I ask of you is that wherever you may be, you will remember me at the Lord's altar." And having expressed her feeling in such words as she could still utter, she fell silent, overwhelmed by her growing illness.

[11.28] But as I thought of Your gifts, O invisible God,[68] which You plant in the hearts of those faithful to You and from which wondrous fruits spring, I rejoiced and gave thanks to You, recalling the worry that had burned within her about arranging and preparing a tomb next to her husband's body. Since they had lived together in great harmony, she had also wished to have this addition to that happiness and to have this commemorated among men—so slightly is the human mind able to embrace divine things—wishing that after her pilgrimage beyond the sea the same earth should cover her and her husband's earthly remains. I did not know when, through the wealth of Your goodness, these empty trifles had begun to subside in her heart, but I rejoiced, surprised at what she had divulged to me, even if in our conversation by the window, when she had said, "I do not know what I am still doing here," she no longer appeared to desire to die in her own country. I was to hear later, too, that while we

were at Ostia she had one day, when I was absent, spoken with a
mother's confidence to some of my friends about her contempt for
this life and the goodness of death. Amazed at the courage You had
given to a woman, they had asked whether she was not afraid to
leave her body so far from her own city, to which she replied: "Nothing is far away from God; nor is it to be feared that at the ends of
the earth He would not know from where He should resurrect me."
Then, on the ninth day of her illness, in the fifty-sixth year of her
life and the thirty-third of mine, that pious and religious soul was
freed from her body.

[12.29] I closed her eyes, and pouring into my heart was a vast sorrow that overflowed into tears, though my eyes, under the strict command of my mind, redrank the fountain dry, the struggle causing
great strife within me. At her last breath my son Adeodatus broke
into laments but, checked by us all, fell silent. In the same way, the
child within me strove toward weeping but was checked and silenced
by the voice of my heart, for we did not think it was fitting to celebrate the funeral with tearful cries and lamentations, as in this way
so many people lament the misery of the state of death, or death as
complete eradication, whereas she was neither unhappy in her death
nor entirely dead: of this we were certain because of the evidence of
the life she had led and her unfeigned faith.[69]

[12.30] What was it that was hurting me so grievously within if not
the fresh wound caused by the sudden shattering of the sweetest and
most beloved custom of our life together? I was delighted with her
words when, in her final illness, she countered my attentions with
endearments and said that I was an affectionate son, avowing with
great emotion and love that she had never heard from my mouth a
single harsh or reproachful word against her. And yet, my God Who
has made us, what comparison could there be between the esteem I
showed her and her selfless servitude to me? My soul was wounded,

losing such a great solace in her. It was as if my life were torn in two, since her life and mine had been as one.

[12.31] My son having been stopped from weeping, Euodius took up the Psalter and began to chant, our whole household answering him: "I will sing of mercy and justice to You, O Lord."[70] The news spread, and many brethren and religious women gathered, and while those whose office it was began to prepare the burial, I withdrew to another part of the house where, with friends who deemed I should not be left alone, I could aptly speak about matters suitable to the moment. The balm of truth soothed my torment that was known to You but unknown to them, and they listened to me intently, supposing that I felt no sorrow. But in Your ears, where none of them could hear, I blamed the weakness of my feelings and restrained my flow of grief, which for a while ceded to my will; yet its force overcame me once more, though not as tears bursting forth or my countenance changing. But I knew what I was suppressing within my heart. I was extremely unhappy with myself that these human matters, which in the due order and lot of our condition inevitably fall to us, could have such power over me, and with new grief I grieved over my grief, and so was consumed by a double sorrow.

[12.32] When her body was carried out for burial, we went and returned without tears. I did not weep during the prayers we poured forth to You when the sacrifice of our redemption was offered for her, nor during the prayers when her body was placed beside the tomb before being interred, as is the custom; but the entire day I was profoundly sad within, and with troubled mind prayed to You as best I could that You would heal my sorrow, though You did not, impressing by this lesson upon my memory, I believe, the strength of the chains of habit upon the mind, even when it does not feed on deceit. It seemed also good to me to go and bathe, having heard that the Latin word for bath, *balneum*, had its name from the Greek *balaneion*, casting anguish from the mind.[71] This too I avow to Your mercy, Father of orphans,[72] that I bathed and was the same as I had been before I bathed, for the bitterness of sorrow did not exude from my heart. Then I slept, woke up, but found that my grief had not softened at all. Alone as I lay in my bed, I remembered those true verses of Your Ambrose, for You are

> God, Creator of all things,
> Ruler of Heaven who vests
> The day with beauteous light
> The night with reposing sleep
> Loosening man's limbs in rest
> Restoring them, refreshed for labor
> Relieving the minds of the wearied
> Untangling the sorrows of the distressed.[73]

[12.33] Then gradually I returned to my former thoughts of Your handmaid, remembering her pious attachment to You and the holy helpfulness and tenderness to us of which I was suddenly deprived: and I wanted to weep in Your sight for her and on her account, for myself and on my account. And I released the tears I had restrained, letting them pour forth, strewing them out so that my heart could rest in them, and my heart found repose, for I wept before Your ears, not those of man, who would have eyed my tears with scorn. And now, Lord, I confess this to You in writing: let him read it who will and interpret it how he may, and if he finds it to be sinful that I wept for my mother for a few minutes, the mother who was now dead to my eyes and who for many years had wept for me that I might live in Your eyes, let him not scorn me, but rather, if he is a man of great love, let him weep for my sins before You, the Father of all the brethren of Your Christ.

[13.34] Now, my heart healed of that wound in which I could be blamed of a fleshly state of mind, before You, our God, I shed very different tears for Your maidservant, tears flowing from a spirit shaken by the thoughts of the danger every soul that dies in Adam faces, though she had been made alive in Christ[74] even before she was released from the flesh; for she had lived so that Your name would be praised in her faith and the life she led. But I do not dare claim that from the moment You regenerated her through baptism[75] no word against Your precepts issued from her mouth. Your Son, the Truth, has said, "Whoever shall say to his brother 'you fool' shall be in danger of the fire of Gehenna."[76] And woe even to commendable lives of men, if You should examine their lives casting mercy aside. But because You do not fiercely scrutinize our sins, we hope with confidence to find some place with You. But whoever enumerates his real merits to You is merely enumerating Your gifts. If only men would know themselves to be but men, and that he who glories would glory in the Lord.[77]

[13.35] Therefore, God of my heart, my Praise and my Life, laying aside for a while my mother's good deeds for which I give thanks to You with joy, I now beseech You for her sins. Hear me by the Healer of our wounds Who hung upon the cross and sits at Your right hand interceding with You on our behalf![78] I know that she always acted with compassion, and from her heart forgave her debtors their debts.[79] Forgive her debts too, Lord, if she contracted any in the many years since she received the water of salvation. Forgive, Lord, forgive, I beseech You, and enter not into judgment with her.[80] May mercy exalt above justice,[81] since Your words are true and You have promised mercy to the merciful.[82] That the merciful be so was Your gift to them, You Who will have mercy on whom You will have mercy and will have compassion on whom You have compassion."[83]

[13.36] And I believe that You have already done what I am begging of You, but accept, Lord, the willing offerings of my mouth,[84] for as the day of her release was imminent she gave no thought to having her body sumptuously wrapped or embalmed with perfumes; nor did she ask for an excellent monument or seek to be buried in her native land. She did not enjoin us to do these things, but asked only to be remembered at Your Altar at which she had served without missing a single day, for she knew that it is there that the holy sacrifice is dispensed through which the handwriting of the decree against us is blotted out.[85] It is there that the enemy summing up our sins and seeking with what to charge us is vanquished, finding nothing in Him in Whom we are victors. Who will restore to Him His innocent blood?[86] Who will repay Him the price with which He bought us[87] and so take us from Him? To the Sacrament of this price Your handmaid bound her soul by the bond of faith. Let none sever her from Your protection. Let neither the lion nor the dragon[88] interpose themselves by force or trickery. She will reply that she owes nothing, lest she be refuted and seized by the wily accuser. She will reply that her debts have been forgiven her by Him to Whom none can repay the price that He, Who owed nothing, paid for us.

[13.37] So may she rest in peace with the husband before and after whom she had no other, whom she served bringing forth with patience fruit unto You,[89] that she might also gain him for You. Inspire, my Lord, my God, inspire Your servants my brethren, Your sons my masters, whom I serve with voice and heart and pen, that all who read this may at Your altar remember Monnica Your maidservant, with Patricius who was once her husband, by whose flesh You brought me into this life, how I do not know. May they all remember with pious affection those who were my parents in this transient light and all my brethren under You our Father in our mother the Christian Church, and my fellow citizens in that eternal Jerusalem for which Your wandering people are yearning from their exodus to their return. This way my mother's last request of me will, through my confessions, be far more abundantly fulfilled by the prayers of many than by my prayers alone.

಄

NOTES

1   Psalm 115:7–8 (Vulgate), 116:16–17 (other translations). "O Lord, for I am thy servant: I am thy servant, and the son of thy handmaid. Thou hast broken my bonds: I will sacrifice to thee the sacrifice of praise, and I will call upon the name of the Lord." (Douay-Rheims Bible)

2   Psalm 34:10 (Vulgate), 35:10 (other translations).

>   "All my bones shall say,
>   'Lord, who *is* like You?'" (New King James Bible)

3   Psalm 34:3 (Vulgate), 35:3 (other translations).

4   Matthew 26:39.

5   Matthew 11:30.

6   This is the only instant in *The Confessions* where Augustine addresses Jesus Christ directly and by name.

7   The *feria vindemialis* lasted from August 23 to October 15 and was a time of harvesting grapes and preparing wine.

8   Psalms 119 through 133 (Vulgate), 120 through 134 in other translations of the Bible, each begin with the words "A song of ascents."

9   Psalm 119:3–4 (Vulgate), 120:3–4 (other translations).

10   Ezekiel 36:23.

11   Romans 14:16.

12   Psalm 45:11 (Vulgate), 46:11 (other translations).

13   Luke 14:14.

14   Psalm 67:16 (Vulgate), 68:16 (other translations).

15   The Roman provinces of North Africa. Nebridius was from near Carthage.

16   Luke 16:22.

17   A quotation from Psalm 26:8 (Vulgate), 27:8 (other translations).

18   Isaiah 40:4.

>   "Every valley shall be exalted
>   And every mountain and hill brought low;
>   The crooked places shall be made straight
>   And the rough places smooth." (New King James Bible)

19 2 Peter 3:18.

20 Psalm 28:5 (Vulgate), 29:5 (other translations).

> "The voice of the Lord breaks the cedars,
>   Yes, the Lord splinters the cedars of Lebanon." (New King James Bible)

See also Book VIII, 2.4.

21 Psalm 18:7 (Vulgate), 19:6 (other translations).

22 Psalm 4:1 (Vulgate), 4:3 (other translations).

23 A quotation from Psalm 4:3 (Vulgate), 4:3 (other translations).

24 Psalm 4:4 (Vukgate), 4:3 (other translations).

25 Ephesians 1:20.

26 John 14:16–17.

27 John 7:39.

28 Romans 8:34.

29 Psalm 4:5 (Vulgate), 4:4 (other translations).

30 Romans 2:5.

31 2 Corinthians 4:18. "While we do not look at the things which are seen, but at the things which are not seen. For the things which are seen *are* temporary, but the things which *are* not seen are eternal." (New King James Bible.) See also Plotinus, *Enneads* 1.6.8.

32 Psalm 4:7 (Vulgate), 4:6 (other translations).

33 John 1:9.

34 Ephesians 5:8. See also Book VIII, 10.22.

35 Psalm 4:7.

36 Psalm 4:8 (Vulgate), 4:7 (other translations).

37 Psalm 4:9 (Vulgate), 4:8 (other translations). "In peace in the selfsame I will sleep, and I will rest." (Douay-Rheims Bible)

38 1 Corinthians 15:54.

39 Malachi 3:6.

40 Psalm 4:10.

41 Psalm 138:21 (Vulgate), 139:21 (other translations). "Have I not hated them, O Lord, that hated thee: and pine away because of thy enemies?" (Douay-Rheims Bible)

42 1 Corinthians 2:9.

43 See Acts 15:15–17.

> "And with this the words of the prophets agree, just as it is written:
> 'After this I will return
> And will rebuild the tabernacle of David, which has fallen down;
> I will rebuild its ruins,
> And I will set it up;
> So that the rest of mankind may seek the Lord,

> Even all the Gentiles who are called by My name,
> Says the Lord who does all these things.'" (New King James Bible)

44 Justina had demanded that Bishop Ambrose of Milan relinquish several of his churches for Arian worship, which he successfully resisted by calling on his congregation to occupy the churches.

45 Luke 6:18.

46 Psalm 115:15 (Vulgate), 116:15 (other translations).

47 Song of Solomon 1:2.

48 Psalm 67:7 (Vulgate), 68:6 (other translations).

49 The Roman provinces of North Africa.

50 Psalm 22:4 (Vulgate), 23:4 (other translations).

51 Psalm 5:8 (Vulgate), 5:7 (other translations).

52 A quotation from Ecclesiasticus (Sirach) 19:1.

53 Virgil, *Aeneid* 7.53.

54 1 Timothy 5:9.

55 1 Timothy 5:4. "Let her learn first to govern her own house, and to make a return of duty to her parents: for this is acceptable before God." (Douay-Rheims Bible)

56 1 Timothy 5:10.

57 Galatians 4:19. "My little children, of whom I am in labour again, until Christ be formed in you." (Douay-Rheims Bible)

58 Philippians 3:13–14.

59 A quotation from 1 Corinthians 2:9.

60 Psalm 35:10 (Vulgate), 36:9 (other translations).

61 Psalm 4:9 (Vulgate), 4:8 (other translations). "In peace in the selfsame I will sleep, and I will rest." (Douay-Rheims Bible)

62 Romans 8:23.

63 Wisdom 7:27.

64 Plotinus, *Enneads* 5.1.2. "Let not only the enveloping body fall silent and the body's commotion, but everything around it: the earth silent, silent the sea and the air and the very heavens."

65 Psalm 76:18 (Vulgate), 77:17 (other translations).

66 Matthew 25:21.

67 1 Corinthians 15:51.

68 Colossians 1:15.

69 1 Timothy 1:5.

70 Psalm 100:1 (Vulgate), 101:1 (other translations).

71 It was a mistaken popular belief that the Greek word *balaneion* was made up of *bállo* (to cast) and *anía* (grief).

72 Psalm 67:6 (Vulgate), 68:5 (other translations).

73 See Ambrose's hymn "Deus creator omnium."

74 1 Corinthians 15:22. "For as in Adam all die, even so in Christ all shall be made alive." (New King James Bible)

75 Titus 3:5.

76 Matthew 5:22. "And whoever says to his brother, 'Raca!' shall be in danger of the council. But whoever says, 'You fool!' shall be in danger of hell fire." (New King James Bible)

77 2 Corinthians 10:16–17.

78 Romans 8:34.

79 Matthew 6:12.

> "And forgive us our debts,
> As we forgive our debtors." (New King James Bible)

80 Psalm 142:2 (Vulgate), 143:2 (other translations). "Do not enter into judgment with Your servant." (New King James Bible)

81 James 2:13.

82 Matthew 5:7.

83 In Romans 9:15 God says to Moses: "I will have mercy on whomever I will have mercy, and I will have compassion on whomever I will have compassion." (New King James Bible)

84 A quotation from Psalm 118:108 (Vulgate), 119:108 (other translations).

85 Colossians 2:14.

86 Matthew 27:4. Judas says, "I have sinned by betraying innocent blood." (New King James Bible)

87 1 Corinthians 6:20.

88 Psalm 90:13 (Vulgate), 91:13 (other translations).

89 Luke 8:15.

BOOK X

[1.1] May I know You Who know me; may I know You as I am known.[1] You are the power of my soul: enter it and fit it to Yourself so that You will have and hold it without spot or wrinkle.[2] This is my hope, which is why I speak, and in this hope I rejoice as I do when I am rejoicing over something sound, for the more the other things of this life are lamented, the less they merit being lamented over, and the less they are lamented, the more they merit lamentation. For behold, You have loved the truth,[3] since he who does the truth comes to the light.[4] This I want to do in my heart before You in confession, and with my pen before many witnesses.

[2.2] Even if I were not to confess, what in me could remain hidden from You, Lord, before whose eyes the abyss of man's conscience lies bare?[5] For I could only hide You from myself, not myself from You. But as my laments bear witness, I am now aggrieved at myself, and You shine forth and are so pleasing and longed for and beloved that I am ashamed of myself and forgo myself and choose You, and can neither please You nor myself other than in You. To You therefore, Lord, am I manifest[6] as whatever I am, and I have already said what the fruit of my confession to You is, nor do I confess with the words and sounds of the flesh but with the words of my soul and the cries of the thoughts that Your ear knows. For when I am bad, then to confess to You is nothing more than my being aggrieved at myself, while when I am good, confessing to You means that I do not ascribe that goodness to myself, since You, Lord, bless the righteous,[7] but only after You have made the ungodly righteous.[8] Thus, my God, I confess before You both silently and not silently, for in sound my confession is silent, but in love it cries out aloud. And I do not utter anything to men that is right which You have not first heard from me; nor do You hear anything from me that You have not first said to me.

[3.3] Why should I care that men hear my confessions, as if men could heal all my weaknesses,[9] a race so eager to learn about the lives of others but so slow to amend their own? Why do they want to hear from me what I am when they will not hear from You what they are? And how can they know whether what I say is true when it is from me they hear about myself, since no man knows what is in man except for the spirit of the man that is within him?[10] But if they hear from You about themselves, they cannot say, "The Lord is lying." To hear from You about oneself is to know oneself, but who knows himself yet still says, "It is false," unless he is a liar? But as love believes all things,[11] at least among those whom love has bonded to itself and made one, I will also, Lord, confess to You in a way that those can hear to whom I cannot prove that my confessions are true. But they whose ears will be opened by love shall believe me.

[3.4] But reveal to me, my innermost Healer, what the fruit of my doing this shall be. For when people read and hear the confessions of my past sins—which You have forgiven and covered so that You might bless me in You,[12] changing my soul through faith and Your Sacrament—their hearts will be stirred so that they no longer will slumber in despair and vouch "I cannot," but will awaken in the love of Your mercy and the sweetness of Your grace. He who is weak is made strong when he becomes conscious through Your grace of his own weakness.[13] And good men delight to hear of the past evils of those who have now shed them, not because of the evils, but because the evils once existed and now do not. So what is the benefit, Lord my God, to Whom my conscience daily confesses and trusts more in the hope of Your mercy than in my conscience's own innocence, what is the benefit, I ask, in my confessing before mankind in this book and also before You what I am now, instead of what I once was? For I have already seen and spoken of the benefit of confessing the past. But many want to know who I now am at this very moment of my confessions, many who have known me personally and many who have not, or who have heard something from me or about me: but their ear is far from my heart where I am what I am. They wish to hear me confess what I am within, where neither their eye nor ear nor mind can reach; they wish it and want to believe, but will they know? For the love by which they are good tells them that I do not lie about myself in my confessions. The love within them believes me.

[4.5] But what benefit are they hoping for? Do they wish to join me in thanksgiving as they hear how near, by Your gift, I have drawn to You, and pray for me as they hear how much I am held back by my own weight? To such will I reveal myself. For it is no small benefit, Lord my God, that many should offer You thanks and entreat You on our behalf.[14] May a brotherly spirit love in me that which You teach must be loved, and lament in me that which You teach must be lamented. A brotherly mind may do this, not that of a stranger or the children of strangers whose mouths utter vanities, their right hand a right hand of iniquity,[15] but a brotherly spirit that delights when it regards me as good and is saddened when it regards me as bad: for whether it delights or is saddened, it loves me. To such will I reveal myself, and they will sigh with relief at what is good in me and sigh in despair at what is bad. What is good in me is Your work and Your gift, and what is bad are my transgressions, to be judged by You. May my brethren sigh with relief at the one, and with despair at the other, and may hymns and laments ascend from the hearts of my brethren, Your censers, before Your countenance, and may You, Lord, delight in the incense of Your holy temple and have mercy upon me according to Your great mercy[16] for Your own name's sake. You, Who never forsake what You have begun, perfect my imperfections.

[4.6] This is the benefit of my confessions: not confessing what I have been, but what I am, and not confessing this before You alone in secret exultation, trembling and with secret sorrow and hope,[17] but also before the ears of believing sons of men, sharers of my joy and comrades in my mortality, fellow citizens and fellow pilgrims, those who have gone before me, those who will go after me, and companions of my time on this earth. These are Your servants, my brethren whom You have willed to be Your sons and my masters, and whom You command me to serve if I seek to live with You and from You. Your Word would have meant little to me had it only been an order in words that had not first been preceded by deeds.[18] I therefore do this in deed and word; I do this under Your wing, and would be in great peril were not my soul subjected to You beneath Your wing,[19] my weakness known to You. I am a child but my Father will live forever, and I do not need more than my Protector, for He is the one who has begotten me and protects me. You are all that is good in me, You Who are almighty and are with me before I am with You. And so to those whom You command me to serve I will reveal not what I have been, but what I now am and continue to be. But neither do I judge myself.[20] That is how I seek to be heard.

[5.7] But You, Lord, judge me, because though no man knows what is in man except for the spirit of the man within him,[21] there is something of man that not even the spirit of the man within him knows. But You, Lord, who have made him, know him entirely. And yet I, though I despise myself before Your Countenance and consider myself dust and ashes,[22] know something of You that I do not know of myself, but we definitely see as if through a glass, darkly, still not face to face.[23] Therefore, as long as I am absent from You,[24] I am more present to myself than to You, and yet I know that You can in no way be violated,[25] though I do not know which temptations I can resist and which I can not. But there is hope, because You are faithful and will not allow us to be tempted beyond what we can bear, but together with the temptation You also make a way to escape so that we can bear it.[26] So I strive to confess what I know of myself and also to confess what I do not know of myself, because what I do know of myself I know from Your shining upon me, and what I do not know of myself I will not know until my darkness be made as noonday before Your Countenance.[27]

[6.8] I love You, Lord, without doubting and with steadfast certainty. You pierced my heart with Your word, and I loved You. Behold! Heaven and earth and all they contain bid me from all around to love You; nor do they cease to say so to all mankind so that they will be without excuse.[28] For You will have mercy more deeply on whom You will have mercy and more deeply compassion on whom You have compassion;[29] otherwise heaven and the earth sing Your praises to deaf ears. But what do I love when I love You? Not corporeal form, nor temporal splendor, nor brightness of the light in which the eye delights, nor sweet melodies of myriad songs, nor the fragrance of flowers and perfumes and spices, nor manna and honey, nor limbs that flesh delights in embracing: I do not love these when I love my God, and yet I do love a kind of light, a kind of voice and fragrance and sweetmeat, I love a kind of embrace when I love my God, a light, a voice, a fragrance, a sweetmeat and the embracing of my inner man, where that which is boundless fills my soul with light, and where a voice resounds that time cannot ravish, and where there is a fragrance that no wind can disperse, a taste no gluttony can diminish, and an embrace no sating can rend asunder. That is what I love when I love my God.

[6.9] "But what is it that I love?" I asked the earth, and the earth replied, "It is not me," and all that lives upon the earth declared the same. I asked the sea and its depths, and all the reptiles living there, and they replied, "We are not your God. Seek Him above us."[30] I asked the blowing winds, and the air and all that lives within it replied, "Anaximenes was wrong—I am not God." I asked the sky, the sun, the moon and the stars, and they replied, "Nor are we the God you are seeking." And I said to all the things outside the gates of my flesh, "Tell me of that God you are not. Tell me something about Him." And in a mighty voice they all cried out, "He made us."[31] My questions had arisen from looking at their forms, but their reply came from within their beauty. And I turned my thoughts to myself and asked, "Who are you?" And I replied, "I am Man." A body and a mind have been granted me, one outer, the other inner. But by which of these should I have sought my God, Whom I had already sought through the body from earth to heaven as far as I could send the beams of my eyes as messengers? Seeking Him through the mind is the better way. To the mind, as to a presiding judge, all the messengers of the body have reported the answers of heaven and earth and all that is within them, all saying, "We are not God, but He made us." The inner man knows this through the ministry of the outer man: I, the inner I, received these answers: I, I the mind, through the senses of my body asked the entire mass of the world about my God, and it replied, "I am not He, but He made me."

[6.10] Is this harmony not apparent to all whose senses are whole? Then why does it not speak in the same way to all? Animals great and small can see it but are unable to ask it, because reason does not preside over their senses to judge what their senses report. But men can ask so that the invisible things of God come to be clearly seen, being understood by the things that He created;[32] but in loving them they are subjected to them,[33] and the subjected cannot judge. Nor will what is created answer those who ask unless they can judge; nor will it change its voice, that is to say, its form. If one man only sees while another both sees and asks, it will not show itself one way to the first man and another way to the second, but will show itself the same way to both. Yet it will be mute to the former and speak to the latter: or, rather, it speaks to all, but only those will understand who compare its voice that comes from outside with the truth within themselves. For truth says to me: "Your God is not heaven, nor earth, nor any other body." This is what their nature declares: "You see? They are a mass, but a smaller part than in the whole." As for you, soul, you are greater, for you animate the mass of your body, giving it life, which no body can give to a body, but your God is the Life of your life.

[7.11] So what do I love, when I love my God? Who is He above the summit of my soul? By my very soul will I ascend to Him. I will pass beyond the force by which I am bonded to my body filling its whole frame with life. I cannot find my God with that force, for otherwise He could be found by horses and mules that have no understanding,[34] since it is the same force by which their bodies have life. There is another force: not only the one through which I animate my body, but also the one through which I endow my flesh with sense. The Lord fashioned it for me, commanding the eye not to hear and the ear not to see, but commanding that I should see with the former and hear with the latter,[35] and ordered each of the other senses to their particular place and function. Through their diverse functions I act as one mind. I will also pass beyond this force that I have, for the horse and the mule possess it too, for they too perceive through the body.

[8.12] So I will also pass beyond this power of my nature, ascending step by step to Him Who made me, coming to the fields and spacious palaces of my memory where there are treasures of innumerable images brought there from things my senses have perceived. There too is stored everything that we think, enlarging and reducing, or in whatever way varying the things with which the senses

have engaged, as well as whatever else has been deposited and preserved that oblivion has not swallowed up or buried. When I am
in the palace of my memory I demand that whatever I want must
be brought forth, and some things come immediately, while others
need longer to be sought out and are brought to me as if from some
more secret recess, and others again come rushing out in droves, and
though I am looking for a certain thing, they come springing forth
as if calling out: "Could it be me you want?" With my heart's hand I
chase them away from the face of my memory until what I have been
seeking is unveiled, emerging out of its place of hiding. Other things,
again, come easily and calmly in the order in which I call them up,
those in front ceding to those that follow, and as they cede they disappear, ready to reappear at my command. All this takes place when
I recount something from memory.

[8.13] There everything is preserved in different classes, each having arrived through its own entrance, such as light and all the colors and shapes through the eyes, every kind of sound through the
ears, all the smells by way of the nostrils, all the tastes by way of
the mouth, and what is harsh or mild by way of the sensation of the
whole body: what is hot or cold, smooth or rough, heavy or light,
and what is external or internal to the body. The vast recesses of
memory receive all these impressions into their unknown secret
reaches, but hold these impressions ready to be taken up again and
reconsidered when they are needed, each entering through its own
portal and then stored. It is not the things themselves, of course,
that enter: it is the images of the things perceived that are kept
there ready to be recalled by thought. Nobody knows how these
images are formed, but it is clear enough by which sense each has
been seized and brought within to be stored. For even were I to
dwell in darkness and silence I could, at will, bring forth colors in
my memory, distinguishing between black and white and whatever other colors I pleased. Nor do sounds interrupt and disturb the

image I am contemplating that my eyes have drawn in, though the sounds are also there, but as if lying hidden, deposited separately. Yet should I wish to call for these sounds they appear right away, and even if my tongue is in repose and my throat silent, I can sing as much as I like, while the images of colors, despite being present, do not interpose themselves or interrupt when another treasure that has flowed in through the ears is recalled. All the rest, too, that has poured in and been amassed by the other senses I can recall at my pleasure. I can without smelling anything distinguish the fragrance of lilies from that of violets, and I prefer honey to sweet wine, and what is smooth to what is rough: all this from memory, without tasting or touching anything at that moment.

[8.14] I do all these things within me, inside the vast palace of my memory. For there I have heaven, earth, and sea, and whatever sensations I was able to experience with them, as well as all I have forgotten. There I also come upon myself as I recall myself by when, where, and what I have done and the feelings I had at the time. There is kept all that I remember either through my own experience or through what others have confided in me. From that same supply I combine similar things I have undergone or heard about and believed on the basis of what I have experienced, and from the past surmise future actions, occurrences, and hopes, and reflect on all these as if they were present. "I will do this and that," I say to myself within that vast interior of my mind that is filled with so many and such great images of things. Much arises from this, and I say, "O if only this would happen, or that!" "May God avert this or that!" I say this to myself, and as I am speaking, the images of everything I speak of are present from the same treasury of memory; nor could I say a single thing if those images were lacking.

[8.15] Great is the power of memory, prodigiously great, my God, a vast and boundless chamber. Who has ever reached its inner depths?

And yet this is a power my mind has, a power that belongs to my
nature, though I myself cannot comprehend in full what I am. Is the
mind therefore too narrow to contain itself, and where would the
part be that it cannot contain? Outside itself, not within? But how
can it not contain itself? This truly astonishes me; I am filled with
amazement. Men will stand in wonder at tall mountain peaks, the
mighty waves of the sea, the great waterfalls of rivers, the expanse
of the ocean, and the paths of the stars, but will overlook themselves. Nor did they stand in wonder when I spoke of all these things
but did not see them with my eyes, though I could not have spoken about them if I were not seeing within my memory the mountains, waves, rivers, and stars that I myself had seen, or the ocean
about which I had heard, and seeing them in the same vastness as
if I was seeing them outside myself. And yet, when I had first seen
them I had not drawn them into myself when I was beholding them
with my eyes; nor are they themselves within me, only their images,
and I know through which of my senses each of these images was
impressed upon me.

[9.16] But this is not all that the immense capacity of my memory holds. There is also everything that I have learned and retained
from the liberal sciences, kept in some remote inner place that is no
place: nor are these things images of this learning but are the learning itself. What philology or the art of dialectics is, or what forms
of questions in rhetoric there are—everything I know about such
things exists in my memory. But not as if I had kept the image and
left the actual thing outside, ringing out and dissipating like a voice
that enters an ear and leaves a trace through which it can be recalled
as if it were still ringing out when it no longer does so; nor as a smell
which, as it passes and dissolves into air, affects the sense of smell,
conveying to memory an image of itself which we can call back when
we remember it; nor does it exist in memory like food that, once it is
in one's stomach, has no taste, though in one's memory it is as if its

taste remains; nor is it like anything that is felt through the body's touch, which when it is removed from us can be imagined by memory. The objects themselves are not introduced into the memory; it is only their images that with surprising speed are captured and then stored in wondrous storerooms from which memory can miraculously bring them forth.

[10.17] But when I hear that there are three kinds of question—"Is something? What is it? What is its nature?"—then I keep images of the sounds of which those words are made, but I know that those sounds carry through the air and are suddenly no more. But the things themselves that those sounds signify I never touched with any sense of my body; nor have I ever seen them anywhere but in my mind; and yet in my memory it was them I stored and not their images. If anyone can say how they entered me let them speak, for I have gone over all the entrances to my flesh but cannot find the ones through which they entered. For the eyes say, "If they have color, we have reported them." The ears say, "If they have sound, we disclosed them." The nostrils say, "If they smell, they passed through us." The sense of taste says, "If they lack flavor, do not ask me." The sense of touch says, "If it does not have a body, I did not touch it, and if I did not touch it, I did not report it." From where and how did these things enter my memory? This I do not know. For when I learned them I did not believe what came from another man's mind, but found them in my own and confirmed them as true, commending them to my mind as if storing them there so that I could bring them forth whenever I wanted. Hence they were already within me before I learned them, but were not in my memory. Thus when they were mentioned, how and from where did I recognize them and affirm, "That is correct, it is true," unless they had already been in my memory but stored away so deeply as if in hidden caverns, so that if another had not suggested that they be unearthed I would perhaps have been unable to think of them?

[11.18] And so we find that to learn the things whose images we do not draw in through our senses, but distinguish within ourselves without images just as they are, is simply the gathering together of the things that the memory already contained in scattered confusion; through thinking and through binding these together, and through close attention, we keep these things within reach in our memory, so that whereas they had been kept concealed before, scattered and disregarded, they now come forth naturally and with ease. My memory holds a great number of such things that have already been acquired and, as I have mentioned, placed within reach, things we are said to have learned and have come to know. And yet, if for a short period of time I stop recalling these things they sink away, gliding back down into the deeper recesses of my mind. They have no other place to go, so that if I am to know them again they must once more be called up in thought from there as if they were new. In other words, from their dispersion they must be gathered together (*conligenda*), from which the word "cogitate" (*cogitare*) is derived, for *cogo* (to gather together) and *cogito* (to ponder, to reflect upon) are related,³⁶ as are *ago* (to impel) and *agito* (to keep impelling), or *facio* (to do) and *factito* (to keep doing). The mind, however, has claimed the word *cogito* for itself, so that not what is gathered together in general, but what is gathered together in the mind is rightly said to constitute thought and reflection.

[12.19] The memory contains also the innumerable principles and laws of numbers and dimensions, none of which have been impressed on the mind by the bodily senses since they have no color, no sound, no taste, no smell, nor can they be felt by touch. I have heard the sound of the words by which they are identified when they are discussed, but the sounds are different from the things themselves, for the words have a different sound in Greek and in Latin, and the things themselves are neither Greek nor Latin, nor any other language. I have seen the lines drawn by architects, the finest lines that are like a spider's threads, but these too are not the thing itself: they are not the images of the lines that my eyes of flesh have shown me. Anyone could discern them within himself without thinking of any sort of object. I have also perceived through all the senses of my body the numbers we use for counting: but they too are different from what is counted; nor are they the images of those things, but exist in their own right.[37] Let him who does not see all these things mock me for saying this, and if he mocks me I shall pity him.

[13.20] All these things I keep in my memory, and I keep them there in the way in which I learned them, also retaining the many false arguments against them that I have heard and remember, which though they are false, it is not false that I remember them. I also remember that I discerned between the truths and the falsehoods that countered these truths, and I see that discerning this now is different from my remembering how I often discerned this in the past. Thus I both remember that I understood these things, and also store in my memory what I now discern and understand, so that in the future I will remember that I understand it now. Therefore I also remember that I remembered, since if I later recollect that I was now able to recall these things, I will be able to recall them by the power of memory.

[14.21] Memory also contains the emotions of my mind; though not in the way that my mind does in experiencing them, but quite differently and through an energy particular to itself. For without being joyful I can remember myself having been filled with joy, and without being sorrowful I can call to mind a past sorrow, and what I once feared I can recall without fear, and without desire I can remember a desire that has passed. Sometimes, on the contrary, I might remember with joy a past sorrow and remember a past joy with sorrow. This is not surprising when it comes to the body's feelings, for the mind is one thing and the body another; therefore it is not a surprise if while I am happy I can remember some past pain my body felt. But in this case the memory itself is the mind. When we tell someone to commit something to memory we say, "See that you keep that in mind," and when we forget we say, "It slipped my mind," and in doing this we call the memory itself the mind. This being so, how is it that when I remember a past sorrow with joy, my mind is joyful while the memory is sad? In this case, the mind filled with joy is joyful, yet the memory filled with sadness is not sad. But would anyone claim that memory does not belong to the mind? Hence the memory is something like the stomach of the mind, while joy and sadness are like sweet and bitter food, which when they are committed to memory pass like food into the stomach, where they are collected but have no taste. It might seem ridiculous to make such a comparison, and yet one could say that the two things are quite similar.

[14.22] But note, when I say that there are four emotions of the mind—desire, joy, fear, and sorrow—it is from my memory that I bring this forth;[38] and whatever I can put forward about these emotions, dividing and defining them according to their types and kinds, it is in my memory that I find what to say, and I bring forth from there what I say: yet am I not moved by any of these emotions when by recalling them I remember them. They were there before I recollected them and brought them back, which was why they could be remembered and brought back. Perhaps memories are brought forth from memory just as food is regurgitated from the stomach. Why then does not he who speaks and remembers taste in the mouth of his memory the sweetness of joy or the bitterness of sorrow? Or does the analogy here fall short because these things are not quite analogous? For who would want to speak of such emotions if whenever we mention sorrow or fear, we were forced to be sad or frightened? And yet we would not be able to speak of them if we did not find in our memory the sounds of the names related to the images that have been impressed on the memory by the senses of the body, and also the notions of the actual things themselves that we did not receive through any entrances of the flesh. It is the mind itself that perceived these through the experience of its own passions, depositing them in the memory; or the memory itself retained them without their having been deposited in it.

[15.23] Whether all this happens through images is not easy to say. I can refer to a stone and I can refer to the sun without their being present to my senses, but their images have been clearly preserved in my memory. I refer to a physical pain, but will not feel it if nothing at that moment happens to be hurting me; yet if the pain's image were not present in my memory I would not know what I was talking about, nor in discussing it would I be able to distinguish it from pleasure. I might refer to bodily health when I am healthy in body, the thing itself being present to me; but if its image were not also present in my memory I would not be able to recall what the sound of the words "bodily health" signifies. Nor would the sick recognize what is being spoken of when health is mentioned unless its image had been retained by the force of memory even though the thing itself was absent from the body. I speak the numbers by which we count, yet in this case it is not their images but the numbers themselves that are present in my memory. And if I refer to the *image* of the sun, then it is the image that is present in my memory, since I do not call up the image of its image, but the image itself. When I refer to memory, I recognize what I am referring to: and where would I recognize this if not in my memory itself? For would memory be present to itself through its image, and not through itself?

[16.24] What about when I refer to forgetting and here too recognize to what I am referring? How can I recognize it if I am not remembering it? I do not mean the sound of the word but the thing it signifies; had I forgotten this, I would be unable to recognize what the sound represents. So when I remember memory, memory is itself present to itself, but when I remember *forgetting*, then both memory and forgetting are present: memory, through which I remember, and forgetting, which I remember. But what is forgetting if not the privation of memory? So how can forgetting be present so that I remember it, since when forgetting is present I cannot remember? But we keep in memory what we remember, and so we cannot think "forgetting" without having retained it through memory; otherwise, hearing the word, we could never recognize the thing it signifies. Hence, forgetting is present so that we do not forget that which, when it is present, we forget. Are we to understand from this that when we remember forgetting it is present to the memory not through itself but through its image? For if it were present through itself it would cause us not to remember it, but to forget. Who can fathom this matter? Who can understand its essence?

[16.25] But I, Lord, am truly trying to fathom it, and to fathom myself. I have become a terrain of prodigious toil and sweat to myself, for we are not searching out the vault of heaven,[39] or measuring the distances between the stars, or inquiring the balances of the earth, but are inquiring into me, myself who am remembering, into me, the mind. It is not surprising that what I myself am not is distant from me. But what can be nearer to me than myself? And yet, I myself do not understand the power of my own memory, though I cannot say that I stand outside it. For what should I say as it becomes clear to me that I remember *forgetting*? Should I say that what I am remembering is not in my memory? Or should I say that forgetting is in my memory so that I will not forget? Both ideas are quite absurd. What third way is there? Could I say that the image of forgetting—and not forgetting itself—has been retained by my memory when I remember it? How could I say this, since a thing would have to have been present when its image was first imprinted on the memory, or else it could not have been imprinted? It is thus that I remember Carthage, that

I remember all the places I have been, the faces of men I have seen, the things reported by the other senses, the health or sickness of the body. When these things were before me, my memory received their images so that I might be able to consider them and bring them back in my mind as if they were present when I remembered them in their absence. Consequently, if forgetting is kept in the memory through its image and not through itself, then forgetting must clearly have itself been present at one time so that its image could be held fast. But when it was present, how did it inscribe its image in the memory, since forgetting, by its very presence, erases even what it finds already inscribed? And yet in some way, however incomprehensible and inexplicable this might be, I am certain that I also remember *forgetting*, through which what we remember is obliterated.

[17.26] Great is the power of memory, wondrous, my God, in its profound and infinite plenitude; and this is the mind, it is I myself. What am I then, my God? What is my nature? It is filled with varied and manifold life, exceedingly immense: behold the fields, caves, and caverns of my memory, innumerable and innumerably filled with countless kinds of things, either through images of any thing that has a form, or through the actual presence of things, such as those connected to the sciences, or those connected to what one might call notions or impressions, such as the emotions of the mind, which memory holds fast, even if they are not being experienced by the mind at that moment, though whatever is in the memory is also in the mind. Through all these depths of my mind I run and flit hither and thither, entering as far as I can, but there is no end. So great is the force of memory, so great the force of life in mortal man! What shall I do then, You Who are my true life, my God? I will transcend even this power of mine that is called memory; I will transcend it so that I may approach You, sweet Light. What are You saying to me? Behold, as I rise through my mind toward You Who ever abide above me, I transcend this power of mine that is called memory, seeking to reach You where You can be reached, and to cling to You where one can cling to You. For even beasts and birds have memory; otherwise they could not return to their dens and nests, nor do the many things that they are used to doing, for they could not be accustomed to anything except through memory. Hence I will transcend memory too, so that I may reach Him Who has separated me from the four-footed beasts and made me wiser than the birds of the sky.[40] I will pass beyond memory, but where will I find You, O true Goodness, O steadfast Sweetness? Where will I find You? If I find You outside my memory, then I will be unable to think of You, and how can I find You if I am unable to think of You?

[18.27] The woman who had lost her drachma coin and looked for it with a light[41] would not have found it unless she had remembered it. For when it was found, how would she have known that it was the same coin unless she remembered it? I myself remember to have looked for and found many things, by which I know that when I was looking for any of these things and was asked, "Might it be this?" "Might it be that?" I kept saying, "No, it is not," until the thing I was looking for was presented to me. Had I not remembered it, whatever it was, I would not have found it even if it were presented to me because I would not have been able to recognize it. It is always thus when we seek and find anything that has been lost. Even so, when any thing is by chance lost from one's sight, but not from one's memory—any visible form—its image is retained within, and it is sought until it is restored one's to sight; and when it is found, it is recognized through the image that is within. We do not say that we have found what was lost if we do not recognize it; nor can we recognize it if we do not remember it. It was lost to the eyes, but kept within the memory.

[19.28] But what if it is the memory that loses something, as when we forget and try to remember: where is it that we then search if not in the memory itself? And it is there that when something is prof-fered instead of what we are seeking, we reject it until what we seek appears, and when it does appear we say, "This is it," which we would not say if we did not recognize it, nor would we recognize it if we did not remember it. Hence it is certain that we had forgotten it. Or did perhaps the thing not elude us as a whole but only as a part, and with the part that we had seized we looked for the other part, because memory felt that it was not recalling what was usually a unit, and, limping as if robbed of its familiar crutch, it demanded the return of what was missing? We might see a man we know, or think of him, and, having forgotten his name, try to remember it: names might come up that we cannot connect with him because we were not in the habit of thinking of these names in connection with him, and so we reject these names until the one name appears that assuages our knowledge that has habitually linked it with him. But where does this name emerge from if not from memory itself? Even when we recall it because someone reminds us, it is still from our mem-ory that it emerges, for we do not consider it to be something new but, remembering it, confirm that the name mentioned is the right one. For had it been completely erased from our mind, we would not remember it even if we were reminded. We have not forgotten some-thing entirely that we remember we have forgotten. We cannot seek something as if it were lost once we have utterly forgotten it.

[20.29] How then am I to seek You, Lord? For when I seek You, my God, I seek a life of happiness. I will seek You so that my soul may live,[42] for my body lives from my soul, and my soul from You. How then am I to seek a life of happiness, which cannot be mine until I can say, "It is enough, this is it"? Now I should say how I seek it. Is it through remembering, as though I had forgotten it but recall that I had forgotten it? Or is it through desiring to understand what it is as something unknown that I have never known, or have forgotten so entirely that I do not remember having forgotten it? Is not a happy life what everyone wants? Is there anyone who does not want it? But how is it that they know that they want it so? Where did they see it so that they love it? We can surely have a life of happiness somehow: there are those who actually have it and so are happy, and then there are those who live in hope for it and so are happy. The latter have a lesser kind of happiness than those who actually have a happy life, but they are still better placed than those who are neither happy nor live in hope of happiness, though even they must hope for happiness in some way; otherwise they would not be striving for it. That they too want happiness is certain beyond doubt. I do not know how they have come to know of it and what kind of knowledge they have of it, and I must wonder if it is already in our memory, which, if it is there, means we have once been happy, either singly or all together in that man who first sinned in whom we all died[43] and from whom we are all born with misery. Yet that is not what I am seeking an answer to now, but only whether happiness is in our memory. For we would not love it if we did not know it. We hear the word "happiness" and we all grant that we desire it, and it is not the mere sound of the word in which we delight, for when a Greek hears it in Latin, he is not delighted since he does not know what is being said; but we speakers of Latin delight in it, and he would too if he heard it in Greek, because the thing itself that Greeks and Latins and men of other tongues long to possess is neither Greek nor Latin. It is therefore known to all, for if they were asked in a single voice if they would want to be happy, they would answer without doubt that they would. This can only be if the thing itself to which the word "happiness" refers has been retained in their memory.

[21.30] But is it like a memory such as the memory someone has of Carthage who has seen that city? It is not. For since it does not have a form, a life of happiness cannot be seen with the eyes. Is it the way we remember numbers? It is not. For he who knows them does not strive to attain them, but we know a life of happiness and therefore love it, but we strive to attain it so we will be happy. Is it the way we remember eloquence? It is not. For when people hear the word "eloquence," there are those who call eloquence to mind who are not yet eloquent, though many long to be so; from this it is clear that they already know eloquence: for through their bodily senses they have observed others being eloquent and were delighted and so want to be eloquent, though it could only be out of some inner knowledge of it that could lead to their delight; nor would they want to be eloquent if they had not been delighted. As for a life of happiness, we do not experience it in others through any bodily senses. Is it the way we remember joy? It might be that: for even when I am sad I remember my joy as a life of happiness while I am unhappy. Nor did I ever with bodily sense see, hear, smell, taste, or touch my joy, but I experience it in my mind when I am joyful, and the knowledge of it adheres in my memory so that I am able to recall it, sometimes with disdain and sometimes with longing, according to the nature of the things in which I remember myself to have been delighted. If repulsive things somehow immerse me in joy, I now recall these things with disgust and abhorrence, and if I recall good and virtuous things with longing, though they might no longer be present, it is with sadness that I recall my former joy.

[21.31] Where and when did I experience my life of happiness for me to remember it, and love it, and long for it? Nor is it I alone, or a few others besides, who want to be happy: we all want to be happy. If we did not know this with such certainty we would not want it with such steadfast will. But how is it that if two men are asked if they would go to the wars, one might answer that he would and the other that he would not, yet if they were asked if they would want to be happy, both would immediately and without any doubt say that they would. And it is in fact to find happiness that one man would go to the wars and the other not. Is it that one man seeks his joy in one thing, while another seeks it in another? But both agree that they want to be happy, as they would if they were asked if they would want to have joy, and this joy they call a happy life. So although one acquires this joy by one means and another joy by another, they both strive toward the single goal of attaining happiness. And as this is something that all men say that they have experienced, it must therefore be found in the memory and recognized whenever the words "a life of happiness" are mentioned.

[22.32] Far be it, Lord, far be it from the heart of Your servant who here confesses to You, far be it that whatever joy I felt should lead me to think myself happy. For there is a joy that is not granted to the impious but only to those who love You for Your own sake, whose joy You Yourself are. And this is the life of happiness, to rejoice to You, in You, for You; it is this, there is no other. For they who think that there is another pursue some other joy that is not the true one. Yet their will is still drawn to some image of joy.

[23.33] Thus it is not certain that everyone seeks to be happy, for they who do not seek to find joy in You, which is the only life of happiness, do not truly desire a happy life. Nor do all desire this, for the flesh desires against the Spirit and the Spirit against the flesh,[44] and as they cannot do what they want, they fall upon that which they can do and are content with it; because what they are not able to do, they do not want strongly enough to be able to do it. Anyone I might ask if he would prefer to have joy in truth or in falsehood will not waver, and will say, "joy in the truth," just as he would not waver in saying that he wants to be happy. A happy life is of course joy in truth, and this means having joy in You Who are the Truth, God my light, Salvation of my countenance,[45] my God. This is the happy life that all are seeking—it is this life alone that is happy. To delight in truth is what all are seeking. I have encountered many who want to deceive, but none who want to be deceived. From where did they know this life of happiness, if not from where they know the truth as well? And they love truth as well, for they do not want to be deceived, and when they love a happy life, which is nothing more than rejoicing in the truth, they also love truth, which they would not love if there were not some knowledge of it in their memory. So why do they not rejoice in truth? Why are they not happy? It is because they are more strongly preoccupied with other things that have more power to make them miserable than with their wavering memory of truth, which makes them happy. For a little while longer there is light in men: may they walk, walk, lest darkness overtake them.[46]

[23.34] But why does truth generate hatred,[47] with Your man preaching truth becoming an enemy to them[48] when they love a life of happiness, which is nothing more than rejoicing in the truth? It is because everyone loves truth so much that all who love something else want that thing which they love to be the truth, and since they do not want to be deceived, they do not want it proven that they have been duped. They hate truth for the sake of that which they love instead of truth, and so they love truth when it enlightens and hate truth when it refutes;[49] for since they do not want to be deceived but want to deceive, they love truth when it reveals itself to them and hate it when it reveals them. Truth repays those who do not want to be revealed by truth in that it both reveals them against their will and does not reveal itself to them. It is ever thus, that the mind of man, blind and ailing, foul and deformed, seeks to remain hidden but does not want anything to be hidden from it. But it achieves the opposite: it itself is not hidden from truth, but truth is hidden from it. Yet even in such a miserable state, it delights in truth rather than falsehood. Hence it will be happy when no hindrance remains and it can delight in that truth alone through which all things are true.

[25.35] Behold how far I have roamed in my memory seeking You, Lord, and I have not found You outside it. Nor did I find anything

from You other than what I have recalled from my memory ever since
I learned of You, for since I learned of You I have not forgotten You.
Where I found truth, there I found my God, Truth itself,[50] which
since I learned it I have not forgotten. Therefore since I learned of
You, You abide in my memory, and it is there that I find You when I
remember You and delight in You. These are my holy delights that
You have given me, as You gaze down upon my neediness in mercy.

[25.36] But where in my memory do You abide, Lord? Where in it
do You abide? What abode did You create for Yourself? What sanctuary did You build? You have bestowed the honor upon my memory
by condescending to abide in it, but in what part of it do You abide?
That is what I am trying to fathom. In thinking about You I passed
beyond such parts of the memory that beasts also have, for I did not
find You there among the images of corporeal forms. I then came
to those parts in which I kept the emotions of my mind, but I did
not find You there either. Then I entered the very core of my mind
that is located in my memory, since the mind remembers itself too,
but You were not there either, for as You are not a corporeal image,
nor the emotion of a living being, as when we rejoice, sorrow, desire,
fear, remember, forget, or have other emotions; You are not the mind
either, because You are the Lord God of the mind, and all these
things are mutable while You remain immutable above all things,
and yet since I have learned of You, You have condescended to abide
in my memory. And why do I now look for what place in which You
dwell as if there really were places there? It is certain that You dwell
there, for I have remembered You ever since I learned of You, and it
is there that I find You when I think of You.

[26.37] Where then did I find You so that I could learn of You? Nor
were You in my memory before I learned of You. Where then did I
find You so that I could learn of You if not in You above me? But
there is no place: we go backward and forward, but there is no place.

O Truth, You preside over all those who ask counsel of You, and You reply at the same time to all though they ask Your counsel on many different things. You reply with clarity, though not all hear You clearly. All consult You on what they want, though they do not always hear what they want. Your best servant is he who does not seek to hear from You that which he himself wants, but rather wants that which he hears from You.

[27.38] I was late in loving You, O Beauty so ancient and so new; I was late in loving You! And behold, You were inside and I was outside, and there I looked for You, deformed as I was, immersing myself among the beautiful forms You had made. You were with me, but I was not with You. These forms kept me far from You, forms that do not exist unless they exist in You. You called and shouted and pierced my deafness. You sparkled and shone, and dispelled my blindness; You were fragrant and I breathed in and now gasp for You. I tasted and now am hungry and thirsty for You; You touched me and now I burn for Your peace.

[28.39] Once I cling to You with my entire self there will be no pain or sorrow anymore for me, and my life will be lived entirely filled with You. You raise those whom You fill, but because I am still not filled with You I am a burden to myself. Lamentable joys clash with joyous sorrows, and I know not which of the two is to be victorious. What is lamentable and bad is clashing with what is happy and good, and I know not which of the two is to be victorious. Woe is me! Lord, have pity on me! Woe is me! Behold, I do not hide my ills—You are the Healer, I the diseased; You are the merciful, I the wretch. Is not the life of man upon earth a trial?[51] Who desires troubles and toils? Your command is that these be endured, not loved. No one loves what he endures, even if he might love to endure. He might delight in what he endures, but he would rather there were nothing for him to endure. In adversity I desire prosperity; in prosperity I fear adversity. Is there a middle ground between these two where the life of man is not a trial? Woe to the prosperity of the world, woe twice over, because of fear of adversity and corruption of joy! Woe to the adversities of the world, once, twice, and thrice over, because of the longing for prosperity, because adversity itself is harsh, and because it might well shatter our endurance! Is not the life of man upon earth a trial without respite?

[29.40] And all my hope is placed solely in Your great prodigious mercy. Give what You command, and command what You will. You enjoin us to be continent, and one man said:[52] "When I knew that no one can be continent unless God grants it, it was also a part of wisdom to know whose gift continence is." For it is continence that gathers us and brings us who have been dissipated back into one. Too little does the man love You who along with You loves things that he does not love because of You. O Love, You Who burn forever and are never extinguished, Love, my God, set me alight! You command us to be continent: give what You command, and command what You will.

[30.41] You sternly command me to continence from the lust of the flesh, the lust of the eyes, and the ambition of the world.[53] You commanded continence from concubinage, and You directed me from matrimony to something higher than matrimony, which You have allowed, but since You granted me something higher, I embraced it, even before I became a dispenser of Your Sacrament. But in my memory, of which I have spoken so much, images still live of such things as my former habits fixed in my mind[54] and which assault me, weakly when I am awake but powerfully when I am asleep, arousing pleasure and even almost obtaining my consent for what is very much like the lustful act itself. And the illusion of the image holds such sway over my mind and my flesh that when I am asleep false visions persuade me to do what true visions are unable to when I am awake. At such moments am I not myself, Lord my God? And yet there is so much difference between myself at the moment in which I pass from being awake into sleep and myself as I return from sleeping. Where is reason then that resists such suggestions when one is awake, remaining firm if the actual acts are urged upon it? Is it locked away as one's eyes close? Is it lulled to sleep with the senses of the body? And how is it that even in sleep we often resist and chastely adhere to our purpose, refusing to yield to such enticements? Yet the difference is so great that when it happens otherwise than we would wish in our sleep, we return to a peaceful conscience when we wake up, and through this very difference we discover that we did not actually do what we are regretting, but that it was in some way done within us.

[30.42] Is Your hand not strong enough, God Almighty, to heal all the ills of my soul and by Your even more abundant grace to extinguish the impure motions of my sleep? Lord, You will increase Your gifts within me ever more so that my soul, freed from the birdlime of lust, may follow me to You and not rebel against itself or commit even in dreams such debasing vileness through carnal images that lead to the emissions of the flesh or even to consenting to them. For it is not a great feat for You, the Almighty, Who are able to do more than everything that we pray for or can conceive,[55] to ensure that nothing of this kind should give the slightest pleasure, or at least not more pleasure than the chaste state of mind of a sleeper can repel; and this not only at some later point in my life, but even at my present age. What I still am in this form of my evil I have declared to my good Lord, rejoicing with trembling[56] over what You have given me and lamenting what I am still imperfect in, hoping that You will perfect Your mercies in me until I reach the fullness of peace that my inner and outer self shall have with You when death shall be swallowed up in victory.[57]

[31.43] There is another evil of the day that I wish would be sufficient unto it.[58] For we restore the dwindling of our bodies by eating
and drinking, until You destroy our food and our stomachs,[59] when
You will slay want with wondrous satiety, and will array this corruptible body with eternal incorruption.[60] But now I delight in the need
for food, and battle this delight so that I will not be taken captive
and wage a daily war of fasting, forcing my body back into subjuga-
tion. But my pains are repelled by pleasure, for hunger and thirst are
like pains, and burn and kill like a fever if the medicine of nourishments does not hasten to our aid; these nourishments exist through
the consolations of Your gifts with which land and water and air
minister to our weakness, and that is why calamity is called delight.

[31.44] You have taught me that I must take food like a medicine,
but as I pass from the distress of want to the ease of satiety, the snare
of concupiscence accosts me in that very passage, for this passage is
a pleasure; nor is there any other way of passing to where we must
pass. And though health is the reason for my eating and drinking, a
dangerous pleasure is close at heel, like a footman endeavoring more
often than not to overtake me, so that I end up doing for pleasure
what I declare I am doing or seeking to do for my health; nor is the
measure for pleasure and for health the same, for what is enough for
health is too little for pleasure, and often it is uncertain whether what
is seeking sustenance is the requisite care of the body or whether
a deceiving voluptuous greed has usurped its place and is demanding to be served. This uncertainty gladdens the unhappy soul, for
it offers an excuse with which it can protect itself, delighted that
the amount of nutrition that suffices for the sustenance of health is
unclear and that under the pretext of health it can obscure the presence of pleasure. These temptations I strive to resist every day, and I
invoke Your right hand: to You I refer the fervor of my mind because
my judgement on this matter is not yet settled.

[31.45] I hear the voice of my God commanding: "Let not your hearts be weighed down with drinking and with drunkenness." Drunkenness is far from me, and may Your mercy ensure that it shall not come near me. But at times drinking will creep upon Your servant, though may Your mercy ensure that it shall stay far away from me. No one can be continent unless You grant it,[61] and You granted us much when we prayed, and also whatever good we received before we prayed we received from You, which we later came to understand was also a gift from You. I was never a drunkard, but I have known drunkards who were turned into sober men by You. Thus it was Your deed that many never became what they were not, and it was also Your deed that many were not to remain what they were, and Your deed too that both the former and the latter knew whose deed it was. I heard Your voice again: "Go not after your lusts, but turn away from your pleasures."[62] The following too, which I have truly loved, I heard by Your gift: "Neither if we eat shall we be better, nor if we eat not shall we be worse,"[63] which is to say that neither will the one make me rich, nor the other wretched. And I heard another voice: "I have learned to be content in whatever condition I am, and I have known both abundance and how to endure need. I can do all things in Him Who strengthens me."[64] These are the words of a soldier of the heavenly host, not of the dust that we are. But remember, Lord, that we are dust,[65] and that of dust You have made man, and that he was lost and is found.[66] Nor was the Apostle Paul, able to do this of himself, he too being dust, he whom I so loved for saying within the breath of Your divine inspiration: "I can do all things in Him Who strengthens me." Strengthen me so that I can. Give what You command, and command what You will. The Apostle avows that he has received it from You, and that he who glories, glories in the Lord.[67] I have heard another begging for this benefaction: "Take from me," he said, "the lusts of the belly,"[68] from which it is clear, my holy God, that You grant us strength when we do what You command be done.

[31.46] You have taught me, good Father, that to the pure all things are pure,[69] but that it is evil for a man to eat with offense;[70] and that every one of Your creatures is good and that nothing is to be refused that is received with thanksgiving,[71] and that food does not commend us to God,[72] and that no man should judge us in food or drink;[73] let not him who eats despise him who does not eat, and let not him who does not eat judge him who eats.[74] I have learned these things, thanks be to You, praise be to You, my God, my Master, as You knocked at the door of my ears and filled my heart with light. Deliver me from all temptation.[75] I do not fear the impurity of meats, but the impurity of lust. I know that Noah was permitted to eat all kinds of meat that could be used for food,[76] that Elijah was restored with meat,[77] that John, endowed with wondrous abstinence, was not polluted by feeding on living creatures, on locusts,[78] and I know that Esau was beguiled by his craving for lentils,[79] and that David rebuked himself for desiring water,[80] and that our King was tempted not with meat but with bread.[81] And that is why the people wandering in the desert also deserved reproof, not because they longed for meat, but because in their longing for food they grumbled against the Lord.[82]

[31.47] Surrounded by these temptations, I battle every day the lust for eating and drinking, as it is not the kind of thing I can cast off once and for all, never touching food or drink again, as I could do with concubinage. The reins of the throat are to be held lightly with a grip that is relaxed but also firm, but what man, Lord, is not transported at least a little beyond the measure of need? Whoever this man is, he is a great man who glorifies Your Name. I am not like him, for I am a sinful man, but I too glorify Your Name. He who has overcome the world will intercede with You for my sins, numbering me among the weak members of His body, because Your eyes have seen what is imperfect in them, and in Your book all shall be written.[83]

[32.48] The enticements of aromas are not of great concern to me: when they are lacking, I do not seek them, and when they are present, I do not reject them. I am prepared to be deprived of them forever. That is how I perceive myself, but perhaps I am mistaken. For there is also a lamentable darkness in which the abilities within me are hidden from me, so that when my mind examines itself about its own powers it does not readily believe itself, because even what is within it is mostly hidden, unless experience should uncover it; and no one can be untroubled in this life, which has been called a single trial.[84] He who is capable of changing from worse to better is also capable of changing from better to worse. The one hope, the one confidence, the once certain promise, is Your mercy.

[33.49] The delights of the ear had entangled and subjugated me more firmly, but You released and freed me. I admit that I still find tranquility in the melodies into which Your words breathe life when they are sung by a sweet, skilled voice; but not so that I am enthralled, but can rise and free myself whenever I please. And yet, though these melodies seek to find a position of honor in my heart together with the words that give them life, I have trouble finding for them a place that is suitable. At times it seems to me that I give them more honor than is fitting, when I feel that our minds are raised more devoutly and fervently to the flame of piety by the holy words when they are sung in this way than when they are not; and that all the emotions of our spirit in their variety have their own proper measures in voice and song through some mysterious connection by which they are stirred. But physical pleasures to which the mind should never be surrendered and thus weakened often waylay me, for sensuality does not attend on reason, following patiently in its footsteps, but once admitted to its presence strives to overtake it and to lead. So in these things I sin unknowingly, and only afterward become aware.

[33.50] But sometimes when I guard against this very deception, I err because I become too severe, even reaching the point where I wish all the melodies and sweet chants with which we celebrate David's Psalter to be banished both from my ears and from those of the Church itself. At such times I hold safer the path that I have been told Bishop Athanasius of Alexandria chose, having the reader of the psalms use so slight an inflection of the voice that his reading was more like a proclamation than a chant. But when I remember the tears I shed when I heard the songs of Your Church at the outset of my regained faith, and how I am even now moved, not by the singing but by what is sung when it is sung in a clear voice and with great harmony, I acknowledge the great benefit of this practice. Thus I waver between the peril of pleasure and the experience of its healing attributes, but I am ever more inclined—without hereby pronouncing an irrevocable judgment—to approve of the practice of singing in the church, so that through the delight of the ears a weaker mind may rise to the feeling of devotion. Yet when I find myself more moved by the singing than by what is being sung, I admit that I am committing a sin that deserves punishment, and I would rather not hear the singer. That is how it is with me. Weep with me and weep for me, men who have goodness within you and act upon that goodness, for you who do not act will not be touched. But You, Lord my God, hear me: consider and see, and have mercy and heal me, You before Whose eyes I have become an enigma to myself;[85] that is my illness.

[34.51] There remains the pleasure of these eyes of my flesh that I include in my confessions for the ears of Your temple to hear—those pious, brotherly ears—so that we will have listed all the temptations of the lust of the flesh that still assail me, even as I groan and desire to be clothed with my habitation that is from heaven.[86] The eyes love beautiful, varied forms and bright, charming colors. May these not possess my soul: may God possess it Who made these things, and indeed they are very good,[87] but He is my good, not they. And forms and colors reach me every day in all my waking hours; nor am I ever granted rest from them as I might be from the sounds of a melody or an entire song when it falls silent. For light, the queen of colors, washes over all that we behold, enveloping me with a variety of forms wherever I am during the day, soothing me even when I am immersed in other things and my attention is elsewhere. So strongly does it seep into everything that when it is suddenly withdrawn I seek it fervently, my soul saddened if it is absent for too long.

[34.52] O Light that Tobias saw when, his eyes unseeing, he taught his son the right path of life,[88] himself walking before him along that path of charity, never erring; Light that Isaac saw when his fleshly eyes were heavy and dimmed by age and he was granted to bless his sons unknowingly, but by blessing them was granted to know them;[89] Light that Jacob saw when he too, blinded by age, with illumined heart poured light on the races of future generations embodied in his sons, and upon his grandchildren by Joseph he laid his hands, mystically crossed, not as their father sought to correct him by his outward vision, but as he himself inwardly discerned.[90] This is the Light, it is one, and all who see and love it are one. But the other corporeal light that I mentioned before seasons life for the blind lovers of this world with a waylaying and dangerous sweetness; but those who do know how to praise You for this corporeal light include it in Your hymn, "God Creator of All,"[91] and are not consumed by it in their sleep. That is how I would like to be. I resist the seductions of the eyes, lest the feet with which I walk upon Your path be ensnared; and I raise invisible eyes toward You that You will pluck my feet out of the snare[92] as You always do, for they keep being ensnared; You do not cease to pluck them out, while often I am caught in traps that have been laid all around me; for You Who keep Israel neither slumber nor sleep.[93]

[34.53] What innumerable things men have created by diverse skills and crafts to beguile their eyes: innumerable things in clothing, shoes, and every kind of artifact and implement; innumerable pictures and all kinds of images, everything far beyond what might be necessary and of pious and moderate use. Men outwardly follow what they themselves create, while inwardly they relinquish Him Who created them, destroying that for which they were created. But I also sing a hymn to You for these things, my God and my Glory, and offer praise to Him Who has sacrificed Himself for me, because those beautiful things that men's souls inspire their dexterous hands to create come from that Beauty that is above our souls, and for which my soul sighs day and night. It is from that Beauty that those who make and cherish these things of outward beauty gain a measure for judging them, but they do not gain a measure for using them; that measure is there, but they do not see it; otherwise they would not wander so far from it but keep their strength for You[94] and not scatter it in pleasurable depletion. But I, though I say this and see it, find my feet entangled in these beautiful things; but You pluck them out, Lord, You pluck them out because Your mercy is before my eyes,[95] for I am miserably trapped, but You pluck me out mercifully, sometimes without my discerning it when I had stepped only lightly into a trap; at other times you pluck me out painfully because I was stuck fast.

[35.54] To this we must add another temptation, one most dangerous for its manifold facets. Beside the concupiscence of the flesh that lies within the delight of all senses and pleasures whose slaves perish as they go far from You,[96] the mind has, through these same senses, a certain vain and curious desire not to delight in the flesh, but to experiment through the flesh under the auspices of knowledge and learning. As this is part of man's appetite for knowledge, and the eyes are the foremost instrument of the senses used in attaining knowledge, the Holy Writ has called it "the lust of the eyes";[97] this, because seeing is the domain of the eyes, though we use the word "seeing" of the other senses too when we employ these senses in seeking knowledge. We do not say, "Hear how it flashes!" or "Smell how it glimmers!" or "Taste how it dazzles!" or "Feel how it glitters!" For all these we use the word "see." Yet we do not only say "See how it shines!," something that only the eyes can perceive, but also "See how it sounds," "See how it smells," "See how it tastes," and "See how firm it is." This is why the Holy Writ has called the entire experience of the senses "the lust of the eyes," because the function of seeing is a prerogative of the eyes that the other senses take upon themselves because of the similarity of the action of their senses when they are exploring.

[35.55] Through this we can discern more clearly the different parts that pleasure and curiosity play in the action of the senses: pleasure seeks out what is beautiful, harmonious, fragrant, savory, and soft, while curiosity will also seek out sensations that are the opposite: not in order to experience things that are unpleasant, but from a desire to test and experience these things. What pleasure can there be in seeing a mangled corpse, the sight of which can only make one shudder? Yet a crowd will quickly gather if a corpse is lying somewhere, people seeking to be distressed and dismayed. They fear such a sight even in their dreams, but when they are awake it is as if someone is compelling them to see it, or as if a report of its beauty prevailed upon them. The same is true of the other senses, though listing examples would take much time. This disease of curiosity has led to the sensational sights we see in the arenas of the theater. It leads men to examine occurrences in nature that are beyond their grasp, the knowledge of which is of no use—but still they desire nothing more than to know. This same perverted quest for knowledge leads men to embrace the magical arts, and the same is true in religion when men strive to test God, demanding of Him signs and omens;[98] not for any good, but simply out of their urge to test.

[35.56] In this vast forest filled with snares and dangers I have smashed and cast from my heart so many traps, as You have granted me to do, God of my salvation! Yet when can I venture to say, with so many things of this kind flitting about us every day, when can I venture to say that nothing of this kind draws my attention or sparks an empty concern? It is true that the grand arenas no longer beguile me; nor do I seek to read the movements of the stars, nor did my mind ever seek answers from the dead; I detest all sacrilegious rites. Lord my God, to whom I owe pure and humble service, by what machinations and suggestions did the Devil prevail upon me to beg for some sign from You! But I beseech You by our King and by our pure and pious country, Jerusalem, that as any consenting to the Devil's prompts is far from me, so may it stay further and further away from me. But when I pray to You for the salvation of another, my aim and intention is very different, and You grant me and will grant me to follow You willingly, as You do with me what You will.

[35.57] And yet who can count the trivial and contemptible things that draw our curiosity every day and how often we give way to them? We tolerate inane stories so as not to hurt those with simpler minds, but little by little we start taking an interest in these stories. I might no longer go to the circus to watch a dog chasing a rabbit, but if I happen to come upon such a chase in the fields it will seize my attention, distracting me from even the weightiest thoughts; not that I would turn my horse and stop, but my heart will be drawn to the spectacle. And if You do not show me my weakness, swiftly admonishing me either to relinquish the sight and rise toward You by some other thought, or to scorn the sight and move on, I will linger there, staring foolishly. How is it that when I am sitting idly at home my attention is often drawn to a lizard catching flies, or a spider ensnaring them as they fly into her webs? Is my curiosity any different simply because these creatures are small? From them I move on to praise You, the wonderful Creator and Orderer of all things, but that is not what first draws my attention. It is one thing if we are quick to rise again after we have fallen, and another not to fall in the first place; my life is filled with things such as these, and my one hope is Your wondrous and great mercy. For when our hearts become the receptacle of such things and are filled with a copious host of inanities, our prayers too are often interrupted and thrown into confusion, and while in Your sight we direct the voice of our heart to Your ears, this momentous deed is interrupted by frivolous thoughts that come pouring in from all sides.

[36.58] We certainly cannot cast these things aside as trivial, but Your mercy, which I have known since You have begun to change me, fills me with hope: You know how much You have changed me, You Who first healed me of my sinful urge to justify myself so that You might forgive all the rest of my iniquities and heal all my weaknesses, redeeming my life from corruption, crowning me in mercy and pity, assuaging my desire with good things.[99] You restrained my pride through fear of You and subdued my neck to Your yoke, and now I bear that yoke and bear it with ease, for You promised it would be so and made it so, and so it was to be, though I did not know it when I feared to bear that yoke.

[36.59] But I ask You, Lord, You Who alone rule without pride because You are the only true Lord and have no lord above You: has the third kind of temptation[100] also fallen away from me, or will it ever fall away in my life, the temptation of striving to be feared and loved with no other aim than to find joy where there is no joy? Life is miserable and ostentation foul. This leads to man neither loving nor fearing You in purity, which is why You oppose the proud and give grace to the humble,[101] and You thunder upon the ambitions of the world, shaking the foundations of the mountains. Certain duties of society make it necessary to be loved and feared by other men, and so the Enemy of our true blessedness pursues us, spreading everywhere his snares of "Well done! Well done!"[102] As we avidly seek this praise we are seized unawares and no longer find our joy in Your Truth, but place it instead in the deceitfulness of men, content at being loved and feared not for Your sake, but instead of You. In this way, the Enemy makes man to be like him, and man is united with him not in the harmony of love but in the sharing of punishment, for the Enemy has set up his throne in the north, and in darkness and cold men serve him who in his corrupted perversion imitates You.[103] But we, Lord, are Your little flock. Possess us; stretch out Your wings and let us come fleeing to their safety. Be our glory! Let us be loved because of You, and let Your Word be feared in us. A man seeking to be praised by men when You reprimand him will not be defended by men when You judge him, nor delivered by men when You condemn him; and with this I do not mean a sinner praised in the desires of his soul, nor the unjust man blessed,[104] but a man praised for some gift that You have granted him, and rejoicing more in the praise than in the gift for which he is praised. This man will be praised by man and reprimanded by You, for better is the man who praised than the man who was praised, since the former was delighted by a gift that God granted a man, while the latter was more delighted by the gift of a man than by a gift granted by God.

[37.60] These temptations accost us every day, Lord; they accost us without respite. Our daily furnace is the tongue of men.[105] In this way too You enjoin us to be continent. Give what You command and command what You will. You know the cries of my heart and the streams that flow from my eyes, for I cannot surmise how far I am cleansed from this plague, and I greatly fear my secret sins that Your eyes know but mine do not.[106] When it comes to the other kinds of temptations, I am able to examine myself, but when it comes to this temptation barely at all. For I can see how far I have progressed in restraining my mind from the pleasures of the flesh and idle curiosity when I do without those temptations, either by choice or because they are unattainable; I then wonder if it is more disturbing or less disturbing not to have them. Men strive for wealth so that it may serve one of these three concupiscences—or two of them, or all three; if the mind cannot discern if it despises wealth once it owns it, it can renounce it in order to examine itself. But in turning our backs on all praise to ascertain our capabilities, must we not live a bad life, one that is so greatly dissipated that all who know us would detest us? What greater madness! If praise is the apt companion of a virtuous life and good deeds, we should not forgo praise any more than forgo the virtuous life itself. But unless a thing is absent, I cannot ascertain if I would be troubled or untroubled in forfeiting it.

[37.61] What am I to confess to You, Lord, for this kind of temptation? What can I confess, if not that I am delighted by praise, but even more delighted by truth itself? I know what I would choose if I had to choose between being irrational and wrong in everything but praised by all men, or being constant and unwavering in truth but disparaged by all. But I would not want another's words of favor to increase my joy over something good within me; yet I admit that it does increase it, and not only that, but words of disparagement diminish it. But when such misery vexes me I fall back on the excuse that I might be uncertain, but that You, God, know its value. You have commanded us not only to continence, that is, from which things to hold back our love, but have also commanded us to do justice, that is, commanded us where to bestow it. You have willed us to love not You alone but our neighbor too: often, when I am delighted by praise from a discerning man, I see myself as delighted by my neighbor's promise or adeptness, or am saddened by his failings when I hear him upbraid what he does not understand or what is good. For I am also sometimes saddened at praise that is leveled at me, either when qualities I dislike are praised in me, or when a good quality that is minor and slight is esteemed more than it should be. But again, how can I know if I am responding in this way because I do not want the person who is praising me to hold a view of myself that differs from my own? Not because I am being moved by thinking of his benefit, but because the same good qualities that I like in myself I like even more when they are liked by another person as well. It is as if I am not praised when my opinion of myself is not praised, or qualities are praised that I dislike, or qualities are praised more that I like less. Is it that when it comes to this I am uncertain of myself?

[37.62] In You, O Truth, I see that I must not be moved for my own benefit when I am praised, but for the benefit of my neighbor. But I do not know if this is so with me, for in this I know less of myself than I know of You. I beseech You, my God, reveal me to myself as well, so that I may confess to my brethren who pray for me what I discover within me to be damaged. Let me examine myself again more closely. If in my praise I am moved by the good of my neighbor, why am I less moved if someone else is unjustly blamed than if I am blamed myself? Why am I more sharply stung by an insult leveled at me than one leveled at another in my presence, though both insults be just as unfair? Is this something that I do not know either, or is it simply that I am deceiving myself and do not acknowledge the truth in my heart and tongue before You? Lord, send this madness far from me so that my words do not turn into the oil of the wicked for me and anoint my head.[107]

[38.63] I am poor and needy,[108] but I am better when I am aggrieved at myself with secret laments, and seek Your mercy until my failing is mended and am again restored to the peace that knows not the eye of the proud. But the words that issue from our mouths, and our deeds of which men hear, bring with them a most perilous temptation: the love of praise that strives to gather approbation and applause in order to assure one a certain superiority. This love of praise tempts me even when I reprove it in myself simply in that I am reproving it, for all too often the contempt of glorying in something leads to even greater glorying: one is not truly contemptuous of glorying in vainglory, for one does not disdain something when one glories in it.

[39.64] Within, deep within, lies another evil that springs from the same kind of temptation in which those who are pleased with themselves flounder. Others might not like them, might dislike them, but they do not aim to please others. But in pleasing themselves they very much displease You, not only taking pleasure in things that are not good as if they were good, but taking pleasure in what You bestow as if it were their own; or even if they acknowledge it as Yours, they act if they have received it through their own merits; or if they acknowledge having received it from Your grace, then they do not receive it rejoicing that their fellows receive it too, but envy it in others. In all these and similar perils and toils You see the trembling of my heart; I do inflict wounds upon myself, but You are quick to heal them.

[40.65] Where, O Truth, have You not walked with me, teaching me what to avoid and what to strive for when I turned to You and sought Your counsel on the things I could see here below? With my outward senses I examined the world as best I could, and appraised the life that my body has from me, as well as my senses. From there I entered the recesses of my memory, the winding depths wondrously filled with uncountable wealth; I beheld and stood aghast, and was unable to distinguish any of these things without You, nor finding any of them to be You. I was not their discoverer, though I had gone through them all, striving to distinguish and value everything according to its rank, perceiving some things through the report of my senses and studying them, sensing that other things were mixed with myself, distinguishing the messengers and counting them, and in the vast reaches of my memory scrutinizing some things, storing others, bringing forth still others. But it was not I myself who did this; in other words it was not my power that did it, nor was it You, for You are the abiding Light that I consulted in all these things: whether these things are what they are, or what their value is. I heard You teach and command me. I often meditate upon these things, for it delights me, and whenever I can free myself from necessary duties, I find refuge in this pleasure. Nor in all these things that I run through my mind, consulting You, can I find a safe place for my soul but in You, in Whom all that is scattered in me gathers, nothing of me receding from You. And sometimes You guide me to a most rare inner state, to some strange sweetness that, were it perfected in me, would not be of this world. But I sink back again through my wretched burdens, swallowed up by my former ways, and am held there, weeping bitterly; but I am held fast. So formidable is the burden of habit! Here I can prevail, but do not want to; there I want to prevail, but cannot. In both cases I am wretched.

[41.66] So I beheld the weakness of my sins in that threefold lust,[109] and invoked Your right hand to save me,[110] for with a wounded heart I beheld Your brightness, and driven back I called out, "I cannot reach there! I am cast away from before Your Eyes!"[111] You are the Truth presiding over all, but I in my covetousness did not want to part from You, but wanted to possess both You and a lie, just as no man would want to tell such lies that he no longer knows what is true. That is how I lost You, for You do not deign to be possessed together with a lie.

[42.67] Who could I find to bring me back to You? Should I have solicited the angels? With what prayers, what sacraments? Many have sought to return to You, but unable to do so of themselves have, I have heard, tried this and have fallen into desiring curious visions, and their recompense was delusion. Transported, they sought You through the pride of their learning, puffing up their chests rather than smiting them, and, their hearts in harmony with the powers of the air,[112] they drew these to themselves as conspirators and companions in pride who beguiled them with magical powers. They sought a mediator who would cleanse them, but there was none, for it was the Devil transforming himself into an Angel of light,[113] and it proved a great enticement to men of proud flesh that he had no body of flesh, for they were mortal and sinners. But You, Lord, to whom they proudly sought to be reconciled, are immortal and without sin. But a mediator between God and man must have some similarity to God and some similarity to man, lest being similar to man in both aspects he should be far from God, or if in both aspects like God then far from man, and so not be a mediator. The false mediator by whom in Your secret judgment pride deserved to be deluded has one thing in common with man, and that is sin; he wishes to appear to have something in common with God, for since he is not clothed with the mortality of flesh he vaunts himself to be immortal, but since the wages of sin is death,[114] he has in common with man that he is to be condemned to death with him.

[43.68] But in Your secret mercy You have revealed and sent to the humble the true mediator, that by His example they should learn humility. He is the mediator between God and man, the man Christ Jesus,[115] who appeared among mortal sinners and the Immortal Righteous One; mortal with men, righteous with God, because the wages of righteousness are life and peace.[116] In the righteousness by which He united with God, He voided the death of the ungodly turned righteous,[117] which He wanted to have in common with them. Hence He was revealed to ancient saints so that they might be saved through faith in His suffering to come, as we are saved through faith in His suffering that has been. Insofar as He was a man, He was mediator; but as the Word, He is not between God and man, because the Word is equal to God, and God with God, and yet one God alone.[118]

[43.69] How You have loved us, good Father, who did not spare Your only Son but delivered Him up for us, the ungodly![119] How You loved us, so that He Who thought it no robbery to be equal with You[120] was even made subject to the death of the cross.[121] He alone was free among the dead,[122] having the power to lay down His life and the power to take it up again:[123] for us he is both Victor and Victim before You, and therefore Victor because he is the Victim; for us he is both Priest and Sacrifice before You, and therefore Priest because he is the Sacrifice. He turns us from servants into sons before You in that He was born of You and served us.[124] My hope in Him is rightly strong, for through Him You will heal all my weaknesses,[125] through Him Who sits at Your right hand and intercedes with You for us;[126] otherwise I would despair. For many and great are my weaknesses, many and great, but Your medicine is greater. We might have thought that Your Word was far from any connection with man, and despaired of ourselves, had He not been made flesh and dwelt among us.[127]

[43.70] Terrified by my sins and the weight of my misery, my heart in turmoil, I considered fleeing to the desert, but You forbade it and strengthened me, saying, "Christ died for all so that those who live should live no longer for themselves, but for Him who died for them."[128] Behold, Lord, I cast my care upon You that I will live[129] and see wondrous things from Your law.[130] You know my ignorance and weakness: teach me and heal me. Your only Son in Whom are hidden all the treasures of wisdom and knowledge[131] has redeemed me with His blood.[132] Let not the proud speak evil of me, because I am aware of the price of my redemption, and I eat and drink and share it out, and poor as I am I seek to be sated by Him among those who eat and are sated, and they shall praise the Lord who seek Him.[133]

ᛣᛟᛊ

NOTES

1   1 Corinthians 13:12. "Now I know in part, but then I shall know just as I also am known." (New King James Bible)

2   Ephesians 5:27.

3 Psalm 50:8 (Vulgate), 51:8 (other translations).

4 A quotation from John 3:21.

5 Hebrews 4:13. "All things *are* naked and open to the eyes of Him to whom we *must give* account." (New King James Bible)

6 2 Corinthians 5:11.

7 Psalm 5:13.

8 Romans 4:5.

9 Psalm 102:3 (Vulgate), 103:3 (other translations).

10 A quotation from 1 Corinthians 2:11.

11 1 Corinthians 13:7.

12 Psalm 31:1 (Vulgate), 32:1 (other translations).

> "Blessed *is he whose* transgression *is* forgiven,
> *Whose* sin *is* covered." (New King James Bible)

13 2 Corinthians 12:9. "And He said to me, "My grace is sufficient for you, for My strength is made perfect in weakness." (New King James Bible.)

14 2 Corinthians 1:11.

15 Psalm 143:11 (Vulgate), 144:11 (other translations). "Deliver me, And rescue me out of the hand of strange children; whose mouth hath spoken vanity: and their right hand is the right hand of iniquity." (Douay-Rheims Bible)

16 Psalm 50:3 (Vulgate), 51:1 (other translations).

17 Psalm 2:11.

> "Serve the Lord with fear,
> And rejoice with trembling." (New King James Bible)

18 The deeds of Jesus Christ. See John 13:15. "For I have given you an example, that you should do as I have done to you." (New King James Bible)

19 Psalm 61:2. (Vulgate), 62:2 (other translations). "Shall not my soul be subject to God?" (Douay-Rheims Bible)

20 1 Corinthians 3:3–4: "In fact, I do not even judge myself. For I know of nothing against myself, yet I am not justified by this; but He who judges me is the Lord." (New King James Bible)

21 A quotation from 1 Corinthians 2:11.

22 Genesis 18:27. "Then Abraham answered and said, "Indeed now, I who *am but* dust and ashes have taken it upon myself to speak to the Lord." (New King James Bible)

23 Augustine quotes 1 Corinthians 13:12, but slightly altering the meaning: "For now we see through a glass, darkly; but then face to face: now I know in part; but then shall I know even as also I am known." (King James Bible)

24 2 Corinthians 5:6.

25 See Book VII, 1.1. "I preferred without hesitation that which cannot be

violated to that which is violable, and knew that what was immutable was better than what had to undergo change."

26   1 Corinthians 10:13. "But God *is* faithful, who will not allow you to be tempted beyond what you are able, but with the temptation will also make the way of escape, that you may be able to bear *it*." (New King James Bible)

27   Isaiah 58:10.

> "*If* you extend your soul to the hungry
> And satisfy the afflicted soul,
> Then your light shall dawn in the darkness,
> And your darkness shall *be* as the noonday." (New King James Bible)

28   Romans 1:20. "For since the creation of the world His invisible *attributes* are clearly seen, being understood by the things that are made, *even* His eternal power and Godhead, so that they are without excuse." (New King James Bible)

29   In Romans 9:15 God says to Moses: "I will have mercy on whomever I will have mercy, and I will have compassion on whomever I will have compassion."

30   Job 28:13–14. In Job's Discourse on Wisdom:

> "Nor is it found in the land of the living.
> The deep says, '*It is* not in me';
> And the sea says, '*It is* not with me.'" (New King James Bible)

31   Psalm 99:3 (Vulgate), 100:3 (other translations).

32   Romans 1:20. "For since the creation of the world His invisible *attributes* are clearly seen, being understood by the things that are made." (New King James Bible)

33   See Plotinus, *Enneads* 5.1.1. "Pursuing and admiring these is to admit inferiority, inferiority to things that are born and perish."

34   Psalm 31:9 (Vulgate), 32:9 (other translations).

35   See Plotinus, *Enneads* 5.5.12. "The appropriate organ is required for perception: the eye for one kind, the ear for another."

36   Marcus Terentius Varro, *On the Latin Language* 6.43. "*Cogitare* (to cogitate) is derived from *cogere* (to collect), the mind collecting into one place several things from which it can choose."

37   See Aristotle, *Physics* 4.11. "For 'number' is used in two ways: for what is counted or countable, and for that with which we count."

38   Cicero, *De finibus bonorum et malorum* 3.10.35. "All in all there are four types of emotion, with several subdivisions: sorrow, fear, desire, and a term the stoics use in relation to both the body and the mind—*hedone* (delight)—which I prefer to call joy, meaning the sensuous elation of the mind in a state of delight."

39   From Ennius' lost tragedy *Iphigenia*, quoted by Cicero in *On Divination* 2.30 and *Republic* 1.30. "No one inspects what is before his feet when he is searching out the vault of heaven."

40   Job 35:11.

> "But no one says, 'Where is God my Maker,
> who gives songs in the night,
> who teaches us more than he teaches the beasts of the earth
> and makes us wiser than the birds in the sky?'" (New International
>   Version)

41   Luke 15:8.

42   Isaiah 55:3.

> "Incline your ear, and come to Me.
> Hear, and your soul shall live." (New King James Bible)

43   1 Corinthians 15:22. "For as in Adam all die, even so in Christ all shall be made alive." (New King James Bible)

44   A quotation of Galatians 5:17.

45   Psalm 42:5.

46   John 12:35. "Then Jesus said to them, "A little while longer the light is with you. Walk while you have the light, lest darkness overtake you." (New King James Bible)

47   Terence, *Andria* 1.1.41, "Obsequiousness generates friends, truth generates hatred."

48   The Apostle Paul in Galatians 4:16. "Have I therefore become your enemy because I tell you the truth?" (New King James Bible)

49   John 3:20. "For everyone practicing evil hates the light and does not come to the light, lest his deeds should be exposed." (New King James Bible)

50   John 14:6. "Jesus said to him, 'I am the way, the truth, and the life. No one comes to the Father except through Me.'" (New King James Bible)

51   A quotation of Job 7:1.

52   King Solomon. The quotation is from Wisdom 8:21.

53   1 John 2:16. "For all that *is* in the world—the lust of the flesh, the lust of the eyes, and the pride of life—is not of the Father but is of the world." (New King James Bible)

54   See Book VIII, 5.10. "A thwarted will gives rise to lust, and whoever serves lust turns it into something customary."

55   Ephesians 3:20. "Now to Him who is able to do exceedingly abundantly above all that we ask or think, according to the power that works in us." (New King James Bible)

56   Psalm 2:11.

> "Serve the Lord with fear,
> And rejoice with trembling." (New King James Bible)

57   1 Corinthians 15:54. "And when this mortal hath put on immortality, then shall come to pass the saying that is written: Death is swallowed up in victory." (Douay-Rheims Bible)

58 Matthew 6:34. "Take therefore no thought for the morrow: for the morrow shall take thought for the things of itself. Sufficient unto the day is the evil thereof." (New King James Bible)

59 1 Corinthians 6:13. "Foods for the stomach and the stomach for foods, but God will destroy both it and them." (New King James Bible)

60 1 Corinthians 15:53. "For this corruptible must put on incorruption, and this mortal *must* put on immortality." (New King James Bible)

61 Wisdom 8:21. See Book X, 29.40.

62 Sirach 18:30. "Go not after thy lusts, but turn away from thy own will." (Douay-Rheims Bible)

63 1 Corinthians 8:8. "But food does not commend us to God; for neither if we eat are we the better, nor if we do not eat are we the worse." (New Revised Standard Version Catholic Edition)

64 Philippians 4:11–12. "Not that I speak in regard to need, for I have learned in whatever state I am, to be content: I know how to be abased, and I know how to abound. Everywhere and in all things I have learned both to be full and to be hungry, both to abound and to suffer need."

65 Psalm 102:14 (Vulgate), 103:14 (other translations).

"For He knows our frame;
He remembers that we *are* dust." (New King James Bible)

66 Luke 15:32.

67 1 Corinthians 1:31. "He who glories, let him glory in the Lord." (New King James Bible)

68 Ecclesiasticus 23:6.

69 Titus 1:15. "To the pure all things are pure, but to those who are defiled and unbelieving nothing is pure; but even their mind and conscience are defiled." (New King James Bible)

70 Romans 14:20. "All things indeed are pure, but it is evil for the man who eats with offense." (New King James Bible)

71 1 Timothy 4:4. "For every creature of God *is* good, and nothing is to be refused if it is received with thanksgiving." (New King James Bible)

72 1 Corinthians 8:8. "But food does not commend us to God; for neither if we eat are we the better, nor if we do not eat are we the worse." (New King James Bible)

73 Colossians 2:16. "So let no one judge you in food or in drink, or regarding a festival or a new moon or sabbaths." (New King James Bible)

74 Romans 14:3. "Let not him who eats despise him who does not eat, and let not him who does not eat judge him who eats; for God has received him." (New King James Bible)

75 Psalm 17:30.

76 Genesis 9:3–4. "Every moving thing that lives shall be food for you. I have given you all things, even as the green herbs. But you shall not eat flesh with its life, *that is,* its blood." (New King James Bible)

77 1 Kings 17:6. "And the ravens brought him bread and flesh in the morning, and bread and flesh in the evening, and he drank of tile torrent." (New King James Bible)

78 Matthew 3:4. "Now John himself was clothed in camel's hair, with a leather belt around his waist; and his food was locusts and wild honey." (New King James Bible)

79 Genesis 25:29–34.

80 2 Samuel 23:15. "And David said with longing, 'Oh, that someone would give me a drink of the water from the well of Bethlehem, which is by the gate!'" (New King James Bible)

81 Matthew 4:3. "Now when the tempter came to Him, he said, 'If You are the Son of God, command that these stones become bread.'"

82 Numbers 11:1.

83 Psalm 138:16 (Vulgate), 139:16 (other translations). "Thy eyes did see my imperfect being, and in thy book all shall be written." (Douay-Rheims Bible)

84 Job 7:1.

85 Psalm 12:4 (Vulgate), 13:3 (other translations). See also Book IV, 4.9.

86 2 Corinthians 5:2. "For in this we groan, earnestly desiring to be clothed with our habitation which is from heaven." (New King James Bible)

87 Genesis 1:31. "Then God saw everything that He had made, and indeed it was very good." (New King James Bible)

88 Tobit 4.

89 Genesis 27.

90 Genesis 48:18–19. "And Joseph said to his father, 'Not so, my father, for this one is the firstborn; put your right hand on his head.' But his father refused and said, 'I know, my son, I know. He also shall become a people, and he also shall be great; but truly his younger brother shall be greater than he, and his descendants shall become a multitude of nations.'" (New King James Bible)

91 Ambrose's hymn "Deus creator omnium."

> "God, Creator of all things,
> Ruler of Heaven who vests
> The day with beauteous light
> The night with reposing sleep." (See Book IX, 12.32)

92 Psalm 24:15 (Vulgate), 25:15 (other translations). "My eyes are ever towards the Lord: for he shall pluck my feet out of the snare." (Douay-Rheims Bible)

93 Psalm 120:4 (Vulgate), 121:4 (other translations). "Behold he shall neither slumber nor sleep, that keepeth Israel." (Douay-Rheims Bible)

94 Psalm 58:10 (Vulgate), 59:9 (other translations). "I will keep my strength to thee: for thou art my protector." (Douay-Rheims Bible)

95 Psalm 25:3 (Vulgate), 26:3 (other translations). "For thy mercy is before my eyes; and I am well pleased with thy truth." (Douay-Rheims Bible)

96 Psalm 72:27 (Vulgate), 73:27 (other translations). "For behold they that go far from thee shall perish." (Douay-Rheims Bible)

97 1 John 2:16. "For all that is in the world—the lust of the flesh, the lust of the eyes, and the pride of life—is not of the Father but is of the world." (New King James Bible)

98 Luke 11:16. "Others, testing *Him*, sought from Him a sign from heaven." (New King James Bible)

99 Psalm 102:2–5 (Vulgate), 103:2–5 (other translations).

100 1 John 2:16. "For all that is in the world—the lust of the flesh, the lust of the eyes, and the pride of life—is not of the Father but is of the world." (New King James Bible)

101 James 4:6.

102 Psalm 34:21 (Vulgate), 35:21 (other translations). The Enemy is Lucifer.

103 Isaiah 14:12–14.

104 Psalm 9:24. "For the sinner is praised in the desires of his soul: and the unjust man is blessed." (Douay-Rheims Version)

105 Proverbs 27:21. "As silver is tried in the fining-pot and gold in the furnace: so a man is tried by the mouth of him that praiseth." (Douay-Rheims Bible)

106 Psalm 18:13 (Vulgate), 19:30 (other translations). "Who can understand sins? from my secret ones cleanse me, O Lord." (Douay-Rheims Bible)

107 Psalm 140:5 (Vulgate), 141:5 (other translations). "Let a good man strike or rebuke me in kindness, but let the oil of the wicked never anoint my head." (Revised Standard Version)

108 Psalm 108:22 (Vulgate), 109:22 (other translations). "For I am poor and needy, and my heart is troubled within me." (Douay-Rheims Bible)

109 1 John 2:16. "For all that *is* in the world—the lust of the flesh, the lust of the eyes, and the pride of life—is not of the Father but is of the world." (New King James Bible)

110 Psalm 59:7 (Vulgate), 60:7 (other translations). "Save me with thy right hand, and hear me." (Douay-Rheims Bible)

111 Psalm 30:23 (Vulgate), 31:22 (other translations). "But I said in the excess of my mind: I am cast away from before thy eyes." (Douay-Rheims Bible)

112 Ephesians 2:1–2. "And you He made alive, who were dead in trespasses and sins, in which you once walked according to the course of this world, according to the prince of the power of the air, the spirit who now works in the sons of disobedience." (New King James Bible)

113 2 Corinthians 11:14. "And no wonder! For Satan himself transforms himself into an angel of light." (New King James Bible)

114 Romans 6:23. "For the wages of sin is death, but the gift of God is eternal life in Christ Jesus our Lord." (New King James Bible)

115   1 Timothy 2:5. "For there is one God and one Mediator between God and men, the Man Christ Jesus" (New King James Bible)

116   Romans 6:23. "For the wages of sin is death, but the gift of God is eternal life in Christ Jesus our Lord" (New King James Bible)

117   See Book X, 2.2. "You, Lord, bless the righteous, but only after You have made the ungodly righteous."

118   John 1:1. "In the beginning was the Word, and the Word was with God, and the Word was God." (New King James Bible)

119   Romans 8:32. "He who did not spare His own Son, but delivered Him up for us all, how shall He not with Him also freely give us all things?" (New King James Bible)

120   Philippians 2:5–6. "Let this mind be in you which was also in Christ Jesus, who, being in the form of God, did not consider it robbery to be equal with God." (New King James Bible)

121   Philippians 2:8. "And being found in appearance as a man, He humbled Himself and became obedient to *the point of* death, even the death of the cross." (New King James Bible)

122   Psalm 87:6 (Vulgate), 88:5 (other translations).

123   John 10:17–18. "Therefore My Father loves Me, because I lay down My life that I may take it again. No one takes it from Me, but I lay it down of Myself. I have power to lay it down, and I have power to take it again. This command I have received from My Father." (New King James Bible)

124   Galatians 4:7. "Therefore you are no longer a slave but a son, and if a son, then an heir of God through Christ." (New King James Bible)

125   Psalm 102:3 (Vulgate), 103:3 (other translations).

126   Romans 8:34.

127   John 1:14. "And the Word became flesh and dwelt among us, and we beheld His glory." (New King James Bible)

128   A verbatim quotation of 2 Corinthians 5:15.

129   Psalm 54:23 (Vulgate), 55:22. "Cast thy care upon the Lord, and he shall sustain thee." (Douay-Rheims Bible)

130   Psalm 118:18 (Vulgate), 119:18 (other translations). "Open my eyes, that I may see wondrous things from Your law." (New King James Bible)

131   Colossians 2:3.

132   Revelation 5:9.

133   Psalm 21:27. "The poor shall eat and shall be filled: and they shall praise the Lord that seek him: their hearts shall live for ever and ever." (Douay-Rheims Bible)

BOOK XI

[1.1] Since eternity is Yours, Lord, You are not unaware of what I am saying to You, for You see at the right time what occurs at that time. Why then have I laid out before You all these stories? Certainly not so that You might learn about them through me, but to foster my love as well as that of my readers toward You, so that we all may say, "Great is the Lord, and greatly to be praised."[1] I have said before and will say again, "I do this out of love for You." For we pray to You, and yet Truth has said, "Your Father knows what you need before you even ask Him for it."[2] Hence it is our love that we lay open before You, avowing our own miseries and Your mercies upon us so that You may free us entirely as You have already started to free us, that we may cease to be in misery in ourselves and be blessed in You. For You have called upon us to be poor in spirit, to be meek, to be mourners, to hunger and thirst after justice, to be merciful and clean of heart, and to be peacemakers.[3] Behold, I have told You many things, as I could and would, because You wanted that I first confess to You, my Lord God, for You are good, for Your mercy endures for ever.[4]

[2.2] But how can I suffice with the tongue of my pen[5] to declare all Your exhortations, all Your terrors and comforts, and the guidances with which You brought me to preach Your Word and dispense Your Sacrament to Your people? Were I to suffice in declaring them in an ordered way, the drops of time would run out.[6] For long now I have burned to meditate in Your law and to confess to You what I understand and of what I am ignorant—the first rays of Your enlightening me and the remnants of my darkness—until weakness be devoured by strength. And I do not want to spend on anything else the hours that I am freed from the necessities of restoring my body, the labor of the mind, and the service that we owe to men or which, though we do not owe, we still pay.

[2.3] Lord my God, hear my prayer and let Your mercy give heed to my desire that does not burn for me, but seeks to be of use to brotherly love. You can see into my heart that it is so. Let me offer in sacrifice to You the bondage of my thought and tongue, and grant what I seek to offer You, for I am poor and needy[7] and You are rich to all who call upon You,[8] Who are free of cares but care for us. Circumcise my inward and outward lips from all rashness and all lying. Let Your Scriptures be my chaste delight: let me not be deceived in them, nor deceive others with them. Lord, hear and have pity, Lord my God, Light of the blind and Strength of the weak, Light of the seeing and Strength of the strong! Hear my soul, and hear it crying out from the abyss. For if Your ears are not in the abyss as well, then where can we go? Where can we cry out? Yours is the day and Yours the night;[9] moments fly by at Your will. Grant in these moments a space for our meditations on the hidden things of Your law, nor shut Your law against us as we knock. It is not in vain that You willed so many pages of opaque secrets in Your Holy Writ; nor are the forests without their deer that withdraw into them to restore themselves, moving and feeding, resting and ruminating. O Lord, perfect me and reveal these secrets to me! Behold, Your voice is my joy; Your voice exceeds the abundance of pleasures.[10] Grant what I love, for I love, and it is You Who granted that love. Do not forsake Your gifts, nor despise Your plant in its thirst. Let me avow before You whatever I shall find in Your Scriptures, hear the voice of praise, and drink You in and consider the wondrous things of Your law,[11] from the begin-

ning where You created heaven and earth until the perpetual reign
with You in Your Holy City.

[2.4] Lord, have mercy on me and hear my ardent desire,[12] for I
believe it is not a worldly desire, not one for gold and silver or for
precious stones, not for splendid regalia, honors, and offices, nor for
the pleasures of the flesh or what we need for our body and this life
of our pilgrimage, all of which shall be given to those who seek Your
Kingdom and Your Righteousness.[13] My God, behold the origin of
my desire. The wicked have told me of delights, Lord, but not such
as Your law.[14] Behold from where my desire stems! See, Father, look
and see and approve, and may it be pleasing to You in the sight of
Your mercy[15] that I may find grace before You, that as I knock, the
hidden meanings of Your words shall be opened to me.[16] I beseech
You by our Lord Jesus Christ Your Son, the Man at Your right hand,
the Son of man whom You have confirmed as Your mediator and
ours,[17] through Whom You sought us who were not seeking You,[18] but
sought us so that we might seek You, and seek Your Word through
Whom You made all things, among them myself as well; I beseech
You by Your only Son through Whom You called to adoption the
people who believe,[19] myself as well; I beseech You by Him Who sits
at Your right hand and intercedes with You for us,[20] and in Whom
are hidden all the treasures of wisdom and knowledge.[21] These I seek
in Your Books. Moses wrote about Him—He said so Himself, the
Truth said it.[22]

[3.5] I seek to hear and understand how in the beginning You created heaven and earth. Moses wrote this; he wrote it and departed,
passing on from You back to You. He is not before me now, for if he
were I would stop him and ask; I would beseech him through You to
elucidate these things to me, and I would open my ears to the sounds
issuing from his mouth. Were he to speak Hebrew, the sounds would

strike my senses in vain, nor would any of them touch my mind, yet were he to speak Latin I would understand what he said. But how would I know if he were speaking the truth? If I knew this too, would I know it from him? It would be from within me, from inside, in the chamber of my thoughts, that the truth, neither Hebrew, nor Greek, nor Latin, nor barbarian, without the organs of mouth or tongue, without the sound of syllables, would say, "He speaks the truth," and I immediately would say with certainty to that man of Yours, "You speak the truth." But as I cannot ask him, I beseech You, O Truth Who filled him when he spoke, I beseech You my God to forgive my sins; and You, who granted him, Your servant, to speak these things will also grant me to understand them.

[4.6] Behold, heaven and earth exist! They proclaim that they were created, for they change and vary. Whereas whatever has not been created and yet exists has nothing in it that it did not have before, for if it were otherwise there would be change and variation. They also proclaim that they did not create themselves: "We exist because we have been created; we did not exist before we existed so as to be able to create ourselves." The voice of the proclaimer is its own evidence. You therefore, Lord, made them, You Who are beautiful, for they are beautiful; You Who are good, for they are good; You who are, for they are. Yet they are not beautiful, nor good, nor are they as You their Creator are, compared to Whom they are neither beautiful, nor good, nor are. We know this thanks to You, but our knowledge compared with Your knowledge is ignorance.

[5.7] But how did You create heaven and the earth? What machine did You use for such a great undertaking? It was not done as a human craftsman would do, his mind directing him to create one form from another, giving it the kind of shape his inner eye might see within itself. And how would he be able to do this unless You had created it? The craftsman gives it a form that already exists, and uses a substance such as earth, or stone, or wood, or gold, or materials of that kind. And where would these have been if You had not first created them? You created the body of the craftsman and the mind commanding his limbs, and You created the sub-stance with which he makes a thing; You created the ability with which he masters his art and sees within himself what he does outwardly. You created his bodily senses, through which, like an interpreter, he translates what he makes from mind to matter, and reports back to his mind what he has done, so that his mind can inwardly consult the truth that presides over it to ascertain if it has been well done. All these praise You, the Creator of all. But how do You make them? How, God, did You make heaven and earth? It was not in heaven or on earth that You made heaven or earth, nor in the air or in the waters, since these also belong to heaven and earth; nor in the entire world did You make the entire world, because there was no place to make it before it was made, so that it could exist. Nor did You hold anything in Your hand out of which to make heaven and earth: from where would You have taken what You had not made in order to make something? Everything that exists does so because You exist. Therefore You spoke and these things were made, and in Your Word You made them.[23]

[6.8] But how did You speak? Was it a voice coming out of a cloud saying, "This is my beloved Son"?[24] That voice rose and passed, began and ended, the syllables sounding and passing, the second syllable after the first, the third syllable after the second, continu-ing in their order until the last syllable passed after the others, and after it came silence. From this it is clearly evident that the voice was formed by the action of a creature, itself temporal, serving Your eternal will. And these words of Yours, which were created for a moment, the outward ear reported to the judicious mind whose inner ear was attentive to Your Eternal Word. But the judicious mind compared these words sounding for a moment with the silence of Your eternal Word, and said, "They are very different, so very different. These words are far beneath me, nor do they exist, because they hasten by and pass. But the Word of my Lord remains above me in eternity." If, then, in words that sounded and passed, You said that heaven and earth be made—and thus You made heaven and earth—there was a physical creation before heaven and earth through whose temporal action that voice passed in time. But there was no body before heaven and earth, or if there was, then You had certainly made it without using such a passing utterance, so that then You could make the passing utterance say that heaven and earth be made. For whatever it was that created such an utterance could not have existed at all unless it was created by You. But what Word did You speak that caused a body to be made by which these words were made?

[7.9] You summon us to understand the Word—God Who is with You God[25]—and the Word is spoken eternally, and through the Word all things are spoken eternally. For what was spoken did not come to an end with something else spoken after it so that everything can be said, but all things were said at once and eternally; otherwise we would have time and change and not true eternity or true immortality. I know this, my God, and give thanks. I know, I confess to You, Lord, and all know and bless You with me who are thankful for this certain Truth. We know, Lord, we know, since death and birth can only come about when there is something that is not which once was, and something that is which once was not. Nothing of Your Word recedes or succeeds because it is truly immortal and eternal, and therefore, together with Your Word, coeternal with You: You say at once and eternally all that You say, and whatever You say will be created is created, nor do You create otherwise than by saying; and yet not all things You create by saying are created together and eternally.

[8.10] I ask, Lord my God, why is this so? I can somehow glimpse it, but I do not know how to express it other than whatever begins to be and ceases to be does begin at the moment and ceases at the moment when the Eternal Reason, within which nothing begins or ends, deems that it must begin or cease. The Eternal Reason is Your Word, which is also the Beginning that speaks to us.[26] Thus in the Gospel the Word speaks through the flesh, and this has sounded outwardly to the ears of man so that it shall be believed and sought inwardly, and found in the Eternal Truth, where the good and only Master teaches all His disciples. There I hear Your Voice, Lord, speaking to me, because he who speaks to us teaches us, but he who does not teach us is not speaking to us even if he speaks. Who now teaches us if not the immutable Truth, for even when we are admonished by a mutable creature, we are being led to the immutable Truth where we truly learn as we stand and hear Him, and we rejoice greatly because the Bridegroom's voice[27] returns us to where we are from. And therefore He is the Beginning, because unless He abided, there would be no place for us to return to when we stray. But when we return from error, it is through knowing that we return, and He teaches us so that we will know, because He is the Beginning and He speaks to us.

[9.11] In this Beginning, God, You made heaven and earth in Your Word, in Your Son, in Your Power, in Your Wisdom, in Your Truth, wondrously speaking and wondrously making. Who can comprehend this? Who can articulate it? What is it that shines through me and smites my heart without injuring it? I am terrified and am roused: I am terrified insofar as I am unlike it, and I am roused insofar as I am like it. It is Wisdom, Wisdom that shines through me, cutting through the clouds within me that have returned to cover me as I falter within the fog that envelops me in punishment. For my strength is weakened through poverty[28] so that I cannot bear the good things granted me until You, Lord, Who have shown mercy to all my iniquities, will heal all my weaknesses. For You shall also redeem my life from corruption and crown me with mercy and compassion, sating my desire with good things because my youth shall be renewed like that of an eagle.[29] For we are saved by hope, and in patience we await Your promises.[30] Let him who is able to, hear You speaking within. I, confident of your divine announcement, will proclaim: "How wonderful are Your works, Lord. You have made all things in wisdom."[31] And this Wisdom is the Beginning, and in that Beginning You made heaven and earth.

[10.12] Behold, those who are still filled with their old self[32] ask us, "What was God doing before He made heaven and earth? If He was free of all action, doing nothing"; they ask, "Why did He not continue to be forever as he was before he began his works?[33] For if any alteration is to arise in God, and a new will to create a creature that He had never created before, how can that be a true eternity where a will arises that did not exist before? For the will of God is not a creation but is before creation, since nothing can be created unless the will of the Creator precedes it. God's will consequently belongs to His Substance. But if anything has arisen from God's Substance that did not exist before, then that Substance could not be truly called eternal. If the will of God has from eternity been that the creature should be, then why did this creature not exist in all eternity?"

[11.13] Those who speak this way do not yet understand You, O Wisdom of God, O Light of minds, they do not yet understand how the things are made that are made by You and within You. They strive to understand eternity while their mind still flits between things that change and have a past and future, and still are empty. Who will seize and hold that mind so that it will stay still for a moment, so that for a moment it might grasp the splendor of never-changing eternity, and compare it with the ever-changing times and see that they cannot be compared? Such a mind will see that a long stretch of time is only long insofar as it is made up of many passing motions that cannot be extended all at once, while in eternity nothing passes but the whole is present, whereas no time can be present all at once. Such a mind will see that what is past is driven on by what is in the future, and all that is in the future follows from the past, and all that is past and future is created and issues forth from that which is eternally present. Who will seize and hold the heart of man that it may stand still and see that eternity without future and past stands still and determines time with its future and past? Does my hand, or the hand of my mouth through words, have the strength to fulfill such a great task?

[12.14] This is my reply to those who ask, "What did God do before He made heaven and earth?" I do not answer in jest, eluding the weighty question as it is said someone once did, saying, "He was preparing hell for those who ask too many questions." It is one thing for us to make light, another to seek what is right. I would not answer in this way, for I would rather say that I do not know what I do not know than make light of one who asks such a weighty question, and be praised for a false response. But I say that You, our God, are the Creator of every creature, and if by "heaven and earth" every creature is to be understood, I will boldly say, "Before God made heaven and earth, He did not make anything." For if He had made something, what would He have made if not a creature? If only I could know all the useful things I seek to know with the same certainty as I know that no creature was made before any creature was made.

[13.15] If a darting mind flits through the images of passed times and wonders that You, the all-potent and all-creating and all-sustaining God, the Creator of heaven and earth, refrained for countless ages from such a great work before You ventured to undertake it, then let this mind awaken and realize that its wondering is false. For how could countless ages pass that You, the Progenitor and Maker of all ages, had not created? Or what times would have existed that were not made by You? How would they pass if they never were? Since You are the Maker of all times, if any time existed before You made heaven and earth, how can those people[34] say that You refrained from Your works? For You would have created that time; nor could any times pass before You created them. But if before heaven and earth there was no time, why are they asking what You were doing then? For there was no *then* when there was no time.

[13.16] You do not precede the times through time; otherwise You would not precede all times. But You precede all things past through the sublimity of an ever-present eternity, and surpass all things future because they are future, and when they come they will be past. But You remain the same, and Your years will have no end.[35] Your years neither come nor go, whereas ours come and go so that they will all come. Your years all stand together because they stand, nor are departing years driven away by coming years, since they do not pass. But our years will all be when they will no longer be. Your years are one day, and Your day is not any day, but *today*, for Your today does not cede to tomorrow, nor does it replace yesterday. Your today is eternity. It is therefore that You beget the Coeternal to whom You said, "This day have I begotten You."[36] You have made all times and You are before all times; nor was there a time when time did not exist.

[14.17] Hence there was no time when you had not made something, because You had made time itself. And no times are coeternal with You, because You abide, but if they were to abide they would not be times. For what is time? Who can explain this simply and in a few words? Who can comprehend it in thought so as to express it in words? And yet, when we converse, do we ever speak of anything with greater familiarity than of time? And we know what time is when we speak of it, just as we do when we hear another speak of it. So what is time? If no one asks me this, then I know; but if I am forced to explain it to someone who asks, then I do not know, though I will boldly maintain that I do know: that if nothing passed, there would be no past time; and if nothing were to come, then there would be no future; and if nothing is, then there would be no present time. So how do those two times—the past and the future—exist if the past does not exist now and the future does not yet exist? As for the present, if it were always present and never passed into the past, it would be not time but eternity. Thus if the present, in order to be time, only comes into being because it passes into the past, how can we maintain that it exists if the aim of its being is that it will not be? Can we in truth maintain that time exists because its aim is not to exist?

[15.18] And yet we speak of a *long* time or a *short* time, though only in connection with the past or the future. A long time ago, for instance, we call a hundred years past, and a long time in the future, a hundred years hence; but a short time ago, we might call ten days ago, and a short time in the future, ten days hence. But how can something be long or short that does not exist? The past does not exist now, and the future does not yet exist. So let us not say of the past "It is long," but "It was long," and of the future "It will be long." My Lord, my Light, does not Your Truth mock mankind here too? A past time that was long: was it long once it had passed or when it was still present? For in the past it could be long, as there still was some-thing that was long, but once it was past it no longer existed, and how can something be long that no longer exists? So let us not say, "The time past was long," as we will not find what has been long, for since it is past it does not exist. But let us say, "That present time was long," because when it was present, it was long: it had not yet passed so that it did not exist, and therefore there existed that which could be long; but after it was past, that which ceased to be also ceased to be long.

[15.19] So let us consider, O mind of man, if present time can be long, for it has been granted you to sense and measure the length of time. What will your answer be? Are a hundred years of the present a long time? But first consider if a hundred years can be present. If the first of these years is current, it is present, though the remaining ninety-nine years are in the future and so do not yet exist. But if the second year is current, one year is now past, another is present, and the remaining years are in the future. Consequently, whichever of the years among the hundred we suppose to be present, all the years before it are past, and all the years after it are future. Therefore a hundred years cannot be present. But consider then if the year that is now current can be present, for if one month is current, the rest are in the future, and if the second month is current, then the first month is already past, while the rest do not yet exist. Hence the current year is not present as a whole, and if it is not present as a whole, then the year is not present. A year, after all, is made up of twelve months, of which the current month is the one that is present, the rest being either past or future. And yet the current month is not present either, only one of its days. If it is the first day of the month, then the others are still in the future; if it is the last, then the others are past; if it is any of the middle days, then that day is between past and future days.

[15.20] We now see how the present time, which we had thought could be called long, is reduced to barely the length of a single day. But let us investigate that too, because a single day is also not present as a whole, since there are twenty-four hours of night and day, the first hour of which has the rest in the future, the last in the past, while any hour in the middle has hours behind it in the past and hours in front of it in the future. And an hour in itself has many tiny fleeting parts: whichever of these parts has flown by is past, and whatever remains is future. If we can conceive of an instant of time that cannot be further divided into infinitesimal parts of moments, that alone is what we may call the present, which itself passes with such speed from the future into the past that it cannot be prolonged by the minutest instant. For if it is prolonged, it must be divided into past and future. But the present has no actual expanse. So where is the time that we can call long? Is it in the future? But we do not say, "It is long," because it does not yet exist for it to be able to be long, but we say, "It will be long." Yet when will it be long? For even when it is in the future it cannot be long, because how can something be long that does not yet exist? But it will be long when from the future, which does not yet exist, it will begin to be, and so have become present, so that it exists and consequently could be long, though the present time will then cry out with the argument used above that it cannot be long.

[16.21] And yet, Lord, we perceive and compare intervals of times, and claim that some are shorter and some longer. We also measure how much longer or shorter one time is compared to another, and maintain that it is twice or three times as long, or just as long as the other. We measure passing time through our perception, but who can measure what is past and no longer exists, or future and does not yet exist, unless he will dare claim that he can measure what does not exist? Thus when time is passing it can be perceived and measured, but once it is past, it cannot, since it does not exist.

[17.22] I am seeking, Father, not asserting. Watch over me and guide me, my God. Is there one who will tell me that there are not three times—past, present, and future—as we learned as children and have taught children, but that only the present exists because the other two do not? Or do they also exist in that the future emerges from somewhere hidden as it becomes present, and again retires to somewhere hidden when from present it becomes past? For where did they who foretold the future see the things they saw if they did not yet exist? One cannot see that which does not exist. And those who relate past things could not relate them if they did not see them in their minds. If these things did not exist, they could not be seen. Thus both past and future do exist.

[18.23] Permit me, my Lord and my Hope, to seek further. Let not my quest be confounded. For if past and future things exist I want to know where they are, which if I am still unable to know, at least I know that wherever they are, they are not there as future or past, but as present; for if they are also there as future, they are not yet there, and if they are also there as past, they are no longer there. Thus wherever and whatever they are, they only exist as present. When true things are recounted from the past, it is not the past things themselves that are brought forth from the memory, but words generated from their images that, as they passed through the senses, were fixed as imprints in the mind. Hence my childhood, which now no longer exists, is in the past that now no longer exists: but as I recall and recount its image, I behold it in the present because it still exists in my memory. Whether there is a similar process in foretelling things of the future, if one can preview the images of things that do not yet exist, I confess, my God, I do not know. What I do know is that we often first think our future actions through, and that this thinking through is present, but the action we are thinking through does not yet exist because it is a future action. It is only once we have embarked on this action, and have begun to do what we were thinking through, that this action exists, because then it is no longer future, but present.

[18.24] Whatever the nature of this mysterious sensing of future things, nothing can be seen that does not exist. But what now exists is not future, but present. Thus when things of the future are said to be seen, it is not the actual things that are seen, which do not yet exist—that is, which are future—but perhaps what is seen is their causes or signs that already exist. Hence these things are not future but are present to those who see the things from which the future, being generated in the mind, is foretold. Such generated things already exist, and those who foretell the future behold them as present before them. Let me take one example from a great number of examples: I see daybreak and predict the rising of the sun. What I see is present, what I foresee is future—not the sun being future, as it already exists, but its rising, which has not yet occurred. If I could not imagine in my mind the rising itself, as I do now in speaking of it, I would not be able to foretell it. Yet the daybreak that I see in the sky is not the sunrise, though it precedes it, just as the imagining of it in my mind is not the sunrise either. Both of these are discerned as present, so that the future sunrise can be foretold. Hence future things do not yet exist, and if they do not yet exist, they do not exist and cannot be seen. But they can be foretold from things that are present, which do exist and so can be seen.

[19.25] Ruler of Your creation, how do You teach minds future things? For You taught Your Prophets. How do You reveal the future, You to whom nothing is future? Or is it that you teach what is present of the future, for what does not exist can in no way be taught? It is far beyond what I can understand; it is too high, I cannot attain it,[37] except through You if You will grant it, Sweet Light of my covered eyes.

[20.26] What is now clear and plain is that neither future things nor things of the past exist; nor can one rightly say, "There are three times: past, present, and future," though one might rightly say, "There are three times: a present of things past, a present of things present, and a present of things future." These three do in some way exist in the mind, for I do not see them anywhere else: the present of things past is memory, the present of things present is what I am seeing, and the present of things future is expectation. If I can express myself in these terms, I see three times, and I acknowledge that there are three. But we can actually say, "There are three times: past, present, and future." It is wrong, but that is how we say it. I do not take offense or find fault with what is said in this way if it is understood to mean that neither the future nor the past is present now. There is so little that we name correctly—most things we do not—but we do manage to impart what we mean.

[21.27] I mentioned above that we measure past times as they pass so that we might be able to say that this time is twice as long or just as long as another time, the same being true for other parts of time that we can measure and define. Thus, as I pointed out, we measure times as they pass, and if anyone should ask me how I know that, my reply would be: because we measure them and cannot measure things that do not exist, and things past and future do not exist. But how does one measure present time when it has no actual expanse? One measures it as it passes, but not once it has passed, for then there is be nothing to be measured. But from where, which way, and to where does it pass when we measure it? From where, if not from the future? Which way, if not by the present? To where, if not to the past? In other words, from that which does not yet exist, through that which lacks an actual expanse, into that which no longer exists. But what is it that we measure, if not time in some expanse? For when we refer to time in terms of single, double, triple, equal, or any other kind of measurement, then we are actually speaking of expanses of time. So in what expanse is it that we measure passing time? In the future, from where it comes? But we cannot measure that which does not yet exist. In the present, through which it passes? But there is no expanse in the present for us to measure. Or in the past, to where it passes? But we cannot measure that which no longer exists.

[22.28] My mind is burning to fathom this intricate enigma. Lord my God, good Father, I beseech you by Christ, do not shut the gates on these familiar though mysterious things, preventing my ardent

quest from penetrating them and being illumined by Your enlight-
ening mercy, Lord. Whom can I ask, and to whom can I confess my
ignorance more usefully than to You, Whom my ardent and fervent
exploration of Your Scriptures does not vex? Grant what I love, for
I do love, and it is a love that You have granted me. Grant me this,
Father, You Who truly know to give good gifts to Your children.[38]
Grant me this, for I have taken upon myself to understand this, and
I am facing much anguish until You open the gates. I beseech you by
Christ, in His Name, Holy of Holies, let no one impede my quest. For
I have believed, and that is why I speak.[39] This is my hope. I live that
I may gaze upon the delight of the Lord. Behold, You have made my
days old[40] and they pass, though how they pass I do not know. And
we talk of time and of times, "How long ago did he say this?" "How
long ago did he do this?" "How long has it been since I saw that?"
or "This syllable lasts twice the time that that single short syllable
does." This is how we say these things, and this is how we hear them,
and we understand and are understood. These things are so evident
and ordinary, but at the same time extremely obscure, and fathom-
ing them is a novel task.

[23.29] I heard a learned man say that the movements of the sun,
the moon, and the stars are what time is, but I disagreed. For in that
case why should time not be the movement of all bodies? If the lights
of heaven should cease and a potter's wheel is still turning, would
there be no time by which we could measure those turns and say
that the wheel either moved with uniform revolutions, or if it turned
at times faster and at times slower, that some revolutions were longer,
some shorter? And as we were speaking those words, would we not
also be speaking within time, some syllables in our words long, others
short—this because the former sounded for a shorter time, the latter
for a longer? God, grant to men that they see in a small thing notions
that are common to things that are small and things that are great.
The stars and the lights of heaven are there for signs and for seasons,

for years and for days.[41] This they are, but still I would not claim that the turning of that potter's wheel was a day; nor would the learned man claim that the turning of the wheel was no time at all.

[23.30] I want to understand the force and nature of time through which we measure the movement of bodies and might claim, for instance, that one movement is twice as long as another. I ask: the word "day" signifies not only the sun's period of time over the earth, according to which a day is one thing and a night another, but also signifies its entire circuit from east to east, according to which we say, "So many days have passed," in which "so many days" includes each day's night, the expanse of night not being counted separately. Hence, since a day is completed by the movement of the sun and its circuit from east to east, I ask if the day is constituted by the movement alone, or the period of time in which that movement is completed, or if it is constituted by both. For if it is constituted by the movement alone, a day would still be a day if the sun were to complete its course in a single hour. If it were constituted by the period of time, a day would not be a day if between one sunrise and another there were only a single hour, the sun having to circuit twenty-four times to complete a day. If it were constituted by both, we could not call that a day either: not if the sun would complete its entire circuit in the space of an hour, nor if, while the sun ceased moving, as much time were to pass as the sun usually takes to complete its entire circuit from one dawn to another. Thus I will not ask what it is that we call "a day." I will ask what time is, through which, measuring the circuit of the sun, we could say that it was completed in half the usual time if it happened to complete its circuit in a space of twelve hours and, comparing both times, would call the former "once the time" and the latter "twice the time," even if the sun were to complete its circuit from east to east sometimes in once the time, sometimes in twice. Hence, let no one tell me that the movements of the heavenly bodies are time, because when a man once prayed for the sun to stand still until he achieved victory in battle, the sun stood still, but time continued.[42] The battle was fought and completed in the space of time it needed. Thus, I see time as being a distention. But do I see this, or do I only think I see it? You will show me, O Light, O Truth!

[24.31] Do You command me to agree if someone were to claim that time is the movement of a body? You do not, for I hear that no body can move except in time; that is what You say. But I do not hear that the movement of a body is time; You do not say that. For when a body moves, it is by time that I measure how long it moves, from the time it begins to move until it ceases. And if I did not ascertain when it began, that it kept up its movement, and when it ended, I would not be able to measure its movement, except perhaps from the moment I noted it until I stopped. If I was looking for a long while, I could only report that it is a long time, but not how long, because when we state how long something is, we state it by comparison, such as, "This is as long as that," or "This is twice as long as that." But if we can observe the points from which and to which the body moves—or its parts, if it is moving around its axis—we can ascertain how much time the movement of that body or its parts took to proceed from one place to another. Thus the movement of a body is one thing, while that by which we measure the length of time it moves is another. Is it not clear which of the two should be called time? Furthermore, a body may sometimes move and sometimes be immobile, in which case we would measure not only the time of its movement but also the time of its immobility; and we might say, "It was immobile for the same amount of time as it had been in motion," or "It was immobile two or three times as long as it was moving," or some other kind of measurement we might make either through observation or by guessing, in which case we tend to say "more or less." Therefore time is not the movement of a body.

[25.32] I confess to You, Lord, that I still do not know not what time is, and again I confess to You, Lord, that I am aware that I have been saying all this within time, and having spoken for so long about time, this "so long" is only long within a period of time. How is it that I know this when I do not know what time is? Or might it be that I do not know how to express what I know? Alas, I do not even know what I do not know! Behold, my God, before You I do not lie.[43] As I speak, so is my heart. You will light my lamp, Lord, my God, You will light my darkness.[44]

[26.33] Does not my soul confess to You in all truth that I measure time? Is it, my God, that I am measuring and do not know what I am measuring? If I am measuring the movement of a body in time, am I not measuring time itself? Would I be able to measure the movement of a body, the duration of the movement, and how long it takes to move from one place to another, without measuring the time in which it moves? So how do I measure time itself? Do we use a shorter time to measure a longer time, the way we measure the length of a crossbar in cubits? We also tend to use the length of a short syllable to measure the length of a long syllable, calling it twice as long. We measure the length of poems by the length of the lines, and the length of the lines by the length of the feet, and the length of the feet by the length of the syllables, and the length of long syllables by the length of short. We do not measure the poem by its pages, for that way we would be measuring space, not time, but once we have declaimed the poem's words and they pass on, we say, "It is a long poem, because it is made up of so many lines; the lines are long, because they are made up of so many feet; they are long feet, since they stretch over so many syllables; it is a long syllable because it is twice as long as the syllable that is short." But even in this way we cannot determine a precise measurement of time, because it could be that a shorter line is spoken with more gravity and so takes up more time than a longer line declaimed with urgency. The same is true for a poem, a foot, a syllable. This has led me to believe that time is simply a distention, but of what I do not know, though it would be surprising if it were not of the mind itself. For I beseech You, my God, what is it that I am measuring, when I say either indefinitely, "This time is longer than that time," or definitely, "This time is twice that"? I know that I measure time, but I do not measure the future, because it does not yet exist; nor do I measure the present, because it does not extend over any expanse; nor do I measure the past, because it no longer exists. So what is it that I am measuring? Perhaps the passing times, not those that have passed? This is what I have said before.

[27.34] Keep seeking, O mind of mine, and keep striving with zeal! God is our helper;[45] He made us, and not we ourselves.[46] Strive on as truth begins to dawn. Suppose the voice of a body begins to sound—sounding and continuing to sound—and then stops: there is silence now; the voice is past and is no longer a voice. It was a future voice before it sounded, and could not be measured since it did not yet exist, and now it cannot be measured because it no longer exists. But it could be measured while it sounded, because then there existed that which could be measured. Yet even then it did not stand still, for it was passing and passed away. Could it be measured all the better for that, since as it passed it extended into another expanse of time and so could be measured, since the present has no expanse? Let us suppose that there is another voice that has begun to sound, and still sounds in one continued tenor without disruption. Let us measure it while it sounds. When it has ceased to sound, it will be past, and there will be nothing that can be measured. So let us measure it and state how long it was. But if it is still sounding, it can only be measured from its beginning, where it starts to sound, until its end, where it stops sounding. We are measuring the actual distance between a beginning and an end. There-fore a voice that has not yet ended cannot be measured so that one can say how long or short it is; nor can it be said to be equal to another, or that it is as long, or twice as long, or the like. But once it has ended it will no longer exist. How can it then be measured? And yet we measure times, though not those that do not yet exist, nor those that no longer exist, nor those times that do not extend over some period, nor those that have no end. Thus we do not measure future times, nor past, nor present, nor passing times; and yet we measure times.

[27.35] *"Deus creator omnium"*:[47] this eight-syllable line alternates between short and long syllables. The four short syllables—the first, third, fifth, and seventh—are single in relation to the four long syllables—the second, fourth, sixth, and eighth. The long syllables each have twice the time of the short; as I declaim them I ascertain that this is so to the extent that one can discern such things by ear, and it is to this extent that I measure a long syllable by a short one and discern it to be twice as long in time. But when one syllable sounds directly after the other, and the former is short and the latter long, how can I take the short syllable and apply it to the long one so that I can ascertain it to have twice the length, since the long syllable will not begin to sound unless the short syllable has already ceased sounding? And am I then able to measure the long syllable while it is present if I cannot actually measure it before it has ended? Once it has ended it is in the past. What is it, then, I am measuring? Where is the short syllable that I am using as a measure? Where is the long syllable that I am measuring? Both have sounded, have flown away, have passed on; they no longer exist. Yet still I measure, and, to the extent one can rely on a trained ear, I maintain with confidence that in the expanse of time one syllable is clearly single, the other double. I could not have accomplished this if the syllables had not passed on and ended. Thus it is not the syllables, which no longer exist, that I am measuring, but something in my memory that has remained imprinted.

[27.36] It is in you, my mind, that I measure time. Do not impede me, or rather do not impede yourself with a turmoil of impressions overwhelming you. I avow that it is in you that I measure time, using the impression that things leave in you as they pass by, the impression that remains even once they have passed. It is this which is still present that I measure, not the things that have passed and that have created those impressions. It is this that I measure when I measure time. Hence either this constitutes time, or I am not measuring time. What about when we measure silences, and state that one silence has lasted as long as a sound has? Do we not picture in our minds the measurement of a sound, imagining it sounding so that we can ascertain the lengths of silence in a given space of time? For even when our voices and mouths cease to sound, we can still in our thoughts go over poems, over lines, over every sort of conversation, ascertaining the length of their motion and the expanse of time they occupy, comparing one to another just as we would if we were speaking them out loud. Supposing a person were to emit a drawn-out sound, and had decided beforehand how long it was to last; in this case he would first pass over an expanse of time in silence and, committing this expanse to memory, begin to emit the sound, which will continue sounding until he has brought it to the end he has planned. Moreover, his sound has both sounded and is sounding, for as much of it as has passed has sounded, and the rest will sound. This is how it passes, until the person's present intention transfers the future into the past, the future diminishing, the past increasing, until through the expending of the future everything is in the past.

[28.37] But how can the future be diminished or expended when it does not yet exist, or the past be increased when it no longer exists? This comes about with three actions in the mind: the mind anticipates, observes, and remembers, so that what it anticipates passes through what it observes into what it remembers. Who will then deny that the future does not yet exist? And yet there is in the mind an anticipation of future things. Who will deny that past things no longer exist? And yet there is still a memory of past things in the mind. Who will deny that the present time has no expanse since it passes in an instant? And yet we are continually observing as what will exist passes to that which does not. So it is not future time that is long, since it does not exist, but a long future is a long anticipation of the future; nor is a time long that has passed, as it does not exist, but a long past is a long memory of the past.

[28.38] Suppose I will recite a psalm that I know. Before I begin, I will anticipate the entire psalm, but once I have begun, however much of the psalm I will have recited, and thus expedited into the past, will become part of my memory, and the essence of my action will now be divided between the memory of what I have recited and the anticipation of what I am about to recite. That which exists in the present is what is before me now: through it, what was future can be carried over and so become past. The more this continues, the more the anticipation is shortened and the memory prolonged, until the entire anticipation is expended when the entire action is concluded and has passed into memory. And that which takes place in the entire psalm also takes place in each of its parts and each of its syllables. This is also true of longer actions of which the psalm might be a part, and is true of the whole life of man in which all the actions of man make up parts, and is true of the whole age of the sons of men, in which all the lives of men make up parts.

[29.39] But because Your mercy is better than lives,[48] behold, as my life was dissipating, Your Right Hand received me in my Lord the Son of man,[49] the Mediator between You the One and us the many, steeped as we are in a mass of manifold things. Yet I make Him my own as I have been made His own,[50] and I am freed of my former days so that I can follow the One, forgetting the things that are behind, and not reaching forward toward things of the future that are transient, but toward those things that are ahead of me.[51] I reach out not in all directions, but strive intently for the prize of my celestial calling where I may hear the voice of Your praise[52] and see Your delight[53] that neither comes nor goes. But now my years are spent in sighs,[54] and You are my solace, Lord, my eternal Father; but I have been scattered amid times whose order I do not know, and my thoughts, to the deepest recesses of my mind, are shredded into a jumble and turmoil until I flow as one into You, melted and purified by the fire of Your love.

[30.40] And now I shall stand firm in You, in Your Truth, my mold, and I will no longer have to endure the questions of men who, in their punishing affliction, thirst for more than they can drink, asking, "What did God do before He made heaven and earth?" And "How did it come to His mind to make something when he had never before made anything?" Grant them, Lord, to weigh carefully what they are saying, and to find that they cannot say "never" where time does not exist. If they say that God "never created," it is the same as saying that "there is no time when God created." Let them therefore refrain from speaking nonsense and see that time cannot be without creation. Let them reach forward toward those things that are ahead[55] and understand that before all times You are the eternal Creator of all time, and that no times are coeternal with You, nor is any created thing, even if there is a creation above time.[56]

[31.41] Lord my God, how deep are the recesses of Your mysteries, and how far from them have I been cast by the consequences of my errors! Heal my eyes so that with Your Light I can rejoice! If a mind existed that was graced with such great knowledge and prescience so as to know all things past and future, the way I know a well-known hymn, that mind would be most miraculous and awe-inspiring, for nothing that has taken place and nothing that is to come in future ages would elude this mind, just as when I sing that hymn it would not elude me how much of it had passed since I had begun sing-ing, and what and how much of the hymn still remained. But far be it from You, the Creator of the universe, the Creator of minds and bodies, that You should know all things future and past in that way: You know them far more wonderfully and mysteriously. Someone who sings or hears a hymn he knows will feel his perception change and expand as he anticipates the words to come and remembers the words that have past. But this is not so with You Who are unchange-ably eternal, the eternal Creator of minds. Just as You knew in the Beginning the heaven and the earth without any change of Your knowledge, so You made in the Beginning the heaven and the earth without Your action expanding. Let him who understands confess to You, and let him who does not understand confess to You. How exalted You are, and yet You dwell in those who are humble in heart! You raise up all who are cast down,[57] and those whose sublimity You are do not fall.

✺

NOTES

1 Psalm 47:2 (Vulgate), 48:1 (other translations).

2 Matthew 6:8.

3 Matthew 5: 3–9.

> "Blessed are the poor in spirit: for theirs is the kingdom of heaven.
> Blessed are the meek: for they shall possess the land.
> Blessed are they that mourn: for they shall be comforted.
> Blessed are they that hunger and thirst after justice: for they shall have their fill.
> Blessed are the merciful: for they shall obtain mercy.
> Blessed are the clean of heart: for they shall see God.
> Blessed are the peacemakers: for they shall be called children of God."
> (Douay-Rheims Bible)

4 Psalm 117:1 (Vulgate), 118: 1 (other translations). " Give praise to Lord, for he is good: for his mercy endureth for ever." (Douay-Rheims Bible)

5 Psalm 44:2 (Vulgate), 45:2 (other translations). "My tongue is the pen of a scrivener that writeth swiftly." (Douay-Rheims Bible)

6 Augustine is referring to the clepsydra, or water clock, that was used to time orators in their speeches.

7 Psalm 108:22 (Vulgate), 109:22 (other translations). "For I am poor and needy, and my heart is troubled within me." (Douay-Rheims Bible)

8 Romans 10:12. "For there is no distinction between Jew and Greek, for the same Lord over all is rich to all who call upon Him." (New King James Bible)

9 Psalm 73:16 (Vulgate), 74:16 (other translations).

10 Psalm 118:72 (Vulgate), 119:72 (other translations). "The law of thy mouth is good to me, above thousands of gold and silver." (Douay-Rheims Bible)

11 Psalm 118:18 (Vulgate), 119:18 (other translations). "Open thou my eyes: and I will consider the wondrous things of thy law." (Douay-Rheims Bible)

12 Psalm 26:7 (Vulgate), 27:7 (other translations).

13 Matthew 6:33. "But seek first his kingdom and his righteousness, and all these things shall be yours as well." (Revised Standard Version Catholic Edition)

14 Psalm 118:85 (Vulgate), 119:85 (other translations). "The wicked have told me fables: but not as thy law." (Douay-Rheims Bible)

15 Psalm 18:15 (Vulgate), 19:15 (other translations). "And the words of my mouth shall be such as may please: and the meditation of my heart always in thy sight. O Lord, my helper, and my redeemer." (Douay-Rheims Bible)

16 Matthew 7:7. "Ask, and it will be given to you; seek, and you will find; knock, and it will be opened to you." (New King James Bible)

17 Psalm 79:18 (Vulgate), 80:17 (other translations). " Let thy hand be upon the man of thy right hand: and upon the son of man whom thou hast confirmed for thyself." (Douay-Rheims Bible)

18 Romans 10:20. " I was found by them that did not seek me: I appeared openly to them that asked not after me." (Douay-Rheims Bible)

19 Galatians 5:4–5. "But when the fullness of the time had come, God sent forth His Son, born of a woman, born under the law, to redeem those who were under the law, that we might receive the adoption as sons." (New King James Bible)

20 Romans 8:34.

21 Colossians 2:3.

22 In John 5:46–47, Jesus is quoted as saying: "For if you believed Moses, you would believe Me; for he wrote about Me. But if you do not believe his writings, how will you believe My words?"

23 Psalm 32:9. "For he spoke and they were made: he commanded and they were created." (Douay-Rheims Bible)

24 Matthew 17:5. "While he was still speaking, behold, a bright cloud overshadowed them; and suddenly a voice came out of the cloud, saying, 'This is My beloved Son, in whom I am well pleased. Hear Him!'" (New King James Version)

25 The Word (*Logos*) designates the Word of God and Jesus Christ. John 1:1. "In the beginning was the Word, and the Word was with God, and the Word was God." John 1:14. "And the Word became flesh and dwelt among us, and we beheld His glory, the glory as of the only begotten of the Father, full of grace and truth." (New King James Bible)

26 John 8:25. "They said therefore to him: Who art thou? Jesus said to them: The beginning, who also speak unto you." (Douay-Rheims Bible)

27 John 3:29. "The friend of the bridegroom, who standeth and heareth him, rejoiceth with joy because of the bridegroom's voice. This my joy therefore is fulfilled." (Douay-Rheims Bible)

28 Psalm 30:11 (Vulgate), 31:11 (other translations). "My strength is weakened through poverty and my bones are disturbed." (Douay-Rheims Bible)

29 Psalm 102:3–5 (Vulgate), 103:3–5 (other translations). "Bless the Lord, O my soul, and never forget all he hath done for thee. Who forgiveth all thy iniquities: who healeth all thy diseases. Who redeemeth thy life from destruction: who crowneth thee with mercy and compassion. Who satisfieth thy desire with good things: thy youth shall be renewed like the eagle's." (Douay-Rheims Bible)

30 Romans 8:24–25. "For we are saved by hope. But hope that is seen, is not hope. For what a man seeth, why doth he hope for? But if we hope for that which we see not, we wait for it with patience." (Douay-Rheims Bible)

31 Psalm 103:24 (Vulgate), 104:24 (other translations). "How great are thy works, O Lord? thou hast made all things in wisdom: the earth is filled with thy riches." (Douay-Rheims Bible)

32 Romans 6:6. "We know that our old self was crucified with him so that the sinful body might be destroyed, and we might no longer be enslaved to sin." (Revised Standard Version Catholic Edition)

33 In *On Genesis against the Manichaeans* 1.2.3, Augustine presents this argument as a Manichaean disputation. "The Manichaeans tend to find fault in the following way with . . . the words, "In the beginning God made heaven and earth." They ask, "In what beginning?" And they say, "If in some beginning of time God made heaven and earth, what was He doing before he made heaven and earth? And why did he suddenly decide to make what he had not previously made in eternal time?"

34 In *On Genesis against the Manichaeans* 1.2.3, Augustine further develops this riposte to the Manichaean disputation.

35 A verbatim quotation from Psalm 101:28 (Vulgate), 102:27 (other translations).

36 Psalm 2:7 (Vulgate), 3:8 (other translations). "The Lord hath said to me: Thou art my son, this day have I begotten thee." (Douay-Rheims Bible)

37 Psalm 138:6 (Vulgate), 139:6 (other translations). "*Such* knowledge *is* too wonderful for me; it is high, I cannot *attain* it." (New King James Bible)

38 Matthew 7:11. "If you then, being evil, know how to give good gifts to your children, how much more will your Father who is in heaven give good things to those who ask Him!" (New King James Bible)

39   Psalm 115:1 (Vulgate), 115:10 (other translations). "I have believed, therefore have I spoken." (Douay-Rheims Bible)

40   Psalm 38:6 (Vulgate), 39:5 (other translations). "Behold thou hast made my days measurable." (Douay-Rheims Bible) Augustine's quotation is closer to the older Latin translations of the Bible that follow the Greek Septuagint version. "Behold, thou hast made my days old." (Brenton Septuagint Translation)

41   Genesis 1:14. "Then God said, 'Let there be lights in the firmament of the heavens to divide the day from the night; and let them be for signs and seasons, and for days and years.'" (New King James Bible)

42   Augustine is referring to Joshua. Joshua 10:13. "And the sun and the moon stood still, till the people revenged themselves of their enemies. Is not this written in the book of the just? So the sun stood still in the midst of heaven, and hasted not to go down the space of one day." (Douay-Rheims Bible)

43   Galatians 1:20.

44   Psalm 17:29 (Vulgate), 18:28 (other translations).

45   Psalm 61:9 (Vulgate), 62:8 (other translations).

46   Psalm 99:3 (Vulgate), 100:3 (other translations).

47   Ambrose's hymn "God, Creator of All Things."

48   Psalm 62:4 (Vulgate), 63:4 (other translations). "For thy mercy is better than lives: thee my lips shall praise." (Douay-Rheims Bible)

49   Psalm 62:9 (Vulgate), 63:9 (other translations). "My soul hath stuck close to thee: thy right hand hath received me." (Douay-Rheims Bible)

50   Philippians 3:12. "Not that I have already obtained this or am already perfect; but I press on to make it my own, because Christ Jesus has made me his own." (Revised Standard Version Catholic Edition)

51   Philippians 3:13. "Forgetting those things which are behind and reaching forward to those things which are ahead." (New King James Bible)

52   Psalm 25:7 (Vulgate), 26:7 (other translations). "That I may hear the voice of thy praise: and tell of all thy wondrous works." (Douay-Rheims Bible)

53   Psalm 26:4 (Vulgate), 27:4 (other translations). "One thing I have asked of the Lord, this will I seek after; that I may dwell in the house of the Lord all the days of my life. That I may see the delight of the Lord, and may visit his temple." (Douay-Rheims Bible)

54   Psalm 30:11 (Vulgate), 31:10 (other translations). "For my life is wasted with grief: and my years in sighs." (Douay-Rheims Bible)

55   Philippians 3:13. "Forgetting those things which are behind and reaching forward to those things which are ahead." (New King James Bible)

56   Augustine is referring to angels.

57   Psalm 144:14 (Vulgate), 145:15 (other translations). "The Lord lifteth up all that fall: and setteth up all that are cast down." (Douay-Rheims Bible)

BOOK XII

[1.1] In my lowly existence my heart is perturbed when struck by the words of Your Holy Scripture. How often the poverty of human understanding is copious in words, because inquiring requires more words than discovering, requesting takes much longer than obtaining, and the hand that knocks toils more than the hand that receives. But as we have Your promise, who can bring it to naught? If God is for us, who can be against us?[1] "Ask, and it will be given to you; seek, and you will find; knock, and it will be opened to you. For everyone who asks receives, and he who seeks finds, and to him who knocks it will be opened."[2] These are Your promises, and who need fear deception when it is Your Truth that is making the promise?

[2.2] My tongue in its lowliness acknowledges before You on high that You made heaven and earth: this heaven that I see and this earth on which I tread, and which is this earth of which I am made and that You created. But where is the Heaven of Heavens, Lord, of which we hear in the words of the Psalm: "The Heaven of Heavens is the Lord's: but the earth he has given to the children of men"?[3] Where is that heaven that we do not see, before which all that we see here is earth? For this physical whole, that is not everywhere in its entirety, has received a beautiful form in its lowest parts, its utmost depths being our earth. Yet to that Heaven of Heavens even the heaven of our earth is only earth. It is not absurd to call both these great bodies earth in comparison to that unknown heaven that belongs to the Lord and not to the sons of men.

[3.3] This earth was invisible and unformed,[4] with I know not what profound deep upon which, because it was formless, there was no light. Therefore You commanded that it be written that "darkness was over the deep."[5] What else is this than the absence of light? For if there had been light, where would it have been if not over everything, rising high and illuminating all? Thus, since light did not yet exist, what was the presence of darkness if not the absence of light? Darkness was therefore over the deep because light was not over it, as when there is no sound there is silence. And what is it for there to be silence if not that there is no sound there? Have not You, Lord, taught this soul that is confessing to You? Have You not taught me, Lord, that before You formed and fashioned this formless matter there was nothing, neither color, nor shape, nor body, nor spirit? And yet it was not that there was nothing, for there was a certain formlessness without any shape.

[4.4] But what should it be called so that it can be understood by dull minds if not by some ordinary name? And what is closer to complete formlessness in the entire world than the earth and the deep? Because of their lowest rank, they have less form than all that is ranked higher and is pellucid and filled with light. Why then should I not assume that You created the formlessness of matter without shape so that You could create this world of shapes, which can suitably be conveyed to man through the words "invisible and unformed earth"?

[5.5] If our thoughts seek to fathom what our mind has touched upon, our thoughts will claim: "This is neither a form connected to intelligence, such as life or justice, because it is the matter out of which bodies are made, but nor is it a form connected to our senses, because being invisible and unformed, there is nothing in it that could be sensed or seen." Therefore, as man's thoughts ponder this, he seeks either to know it unknowingly or to be knowingly ignorant of it.

[6.6] Lord, if I am to avow before you by mouth and pen all that You have taught me about this substance, then I must avow that I had heard about it before without understanding, when those who do not understand[6] told me about it. I had understood it as having innumerable and diverse forms, and so had understood nothing. My mind had reflected upon repugnant and horrible forms that were in disorder, though I still called these "forms," while I called "formless" not what was lacking form, but what had a form that my mind shunned as unfamiliar and unsuitable, confounding me in my human weakness. Consequently, that which I was conceiving was not deprived of all form, but was formless in comparison to forms that were more harmonious, true reason now persuading me that I had to entirely remove all remnants of any kind of form if I wanted to conceive of the absolute formless, something that I was unable to do.[7] I could sooner imagine that something deprived of all form did not exist than conceive of something that existed between form and nothingness: something neither formed nor nothing, something formless that was almost nothing. Thus my mind stopped questioning my thoughts that were filled with the images of formed bodies that my thoughts could alter and change at will, and I began to focus on the bodies themselves, examining more deeply their mutability, through which they stop being what they are and begin to be what they are not. I now suspected that this movement from form to form passed through a formlessness, but not through absolute nothingness. But what I wanted was to know, not to suspect. Yet if my voice and pen were to avow everything before You, everything that You revealed to me in my search, what reader could endure to hear me out? But my heart shall never cease to honor You and sing hymns of praise for all that I am unable to express here. The mutability of mutable things can adopt all the forms into which these changeable things change. But what is this mutability? Is it mind? Is it body? Is it some aspect of the mind or of the body? If one could call it "a nothing something" or "that which is and is not," then that is what I would call it. And yet, it has in some way to exist for it to be able to adopt these visible and compound aspects.

[7.7] Yet where did this come from if not from You from Whom all things come insofar as they exist? But the further from You they are the less they are like You, though it is not a matter of distance. You therefore, Lord, Who are not one in one place and another in another but are the Selfsame, and the Selfsame, and the Selfsame, Holy, Holy, Holy, Lord God Almighty,[8] in the Beginning, which came from You, in Your Wisdom that was born of Your Substance, You created something and created it out of nothing. You created the heaven and the earth, though not out of Yourself, for then they would have been equal to Your Only-Begotten Son and thus to You as well, and in no way would it be right that anything that is not You should be equal to You. And there was nothing else besides You out of which You, God, One Trinity and Trinity in One, could have created these. And so out of nothing You created the heaven and the earth, a great thing and a lesser thing, for You are almighty and good and so make all things good, even the great heaven and the lesser earth. You existed, and there was nothing else out of which You created heaven and earth, two entities, one near You and the other near nothingness, one which You are above, the other below which is nothingness.

[8.8] The Heaven of Heavens is Yours, Lord, but the earth that You gave to the sons of men, an earth that could be seen and felt, was not as we now see and feel it. It was invisible and unformed, and there was a deep over which there was no light: or darkness was over the deep, that is, rather than *in* the deep. For this deep of waters, visible now, has even in its depths a light of its own kind, somehow visible to the fish and the creatures that creep over the seabed. But first that deep was almost nothing because as yet it had been entirely unformed, though there was already that which could be formed. For You, Lord, created the world from unformed matter,[9] creating out of nothingness an almost-nothingness from which You were to make the great things that we the sons of men behold in wonderment, for truly wondrous are the heavenly bodies that are the firmament between water and water:[10] on the second day, after You created light, You said, "Let it be made," and it was made. This firmament You called "heaven," but a heaven to this earth and sea, which You made on the third day by giving a visible aspect to the formless matter that You had made before all days.[11] For You had also made a heaven before all days, but it was the heaven of this heaven, because in the Beginning You had made heaven and earth. But this same earth that You made was formless matter, because it was invisible and unformed, and there was darkness over the deep, and out of this invisible and unformed earth, out of this formlessness, this almost-nothingness, You were to make all these things of which this mutable world is made but does not endure; its very mutability is apparent because time can be discerned and measured, for time is made by the change in things as their forms vary and transform, the matter they are made of being the invisible earth I have just mentioned.

[9.9] Therefore when the Spirit, the Teacher of Your Servant,[12] reveals that in the Beginning You created the heaven and the earth, the Spirit says nothing about time, is silent about days. For without doubt the Heaven of Heavens that You created in the Beginning is some kind of intelligent creation which, though it is in no way coeternal with You the Trinity, does share in Your eternity. Delighting in the blissful contemplation of You, the Heaven of Heavens keeps its own mutability in check, and, by adhering to You without having wavered since You first created it, it has risen beyond all the ever-altering and successive changes of time. Also not numbered among the days is the formlessness I have mentioned, the invisible and unformed earth, for where there is no shape or order, nothing comes or passes, and where nothing comes or passes there are no days nor any changes in the expanse of time.

[10.10] O Truth, Light of my heart, let not my darkness speak to me! I fell into that darkness and was blinded, but even from there, indeed even from there, I loved You. I went astray, but remembered You. I heard Your voice behind me, calling me back,[13] but I could barely hear it through the great din of those who hated peace.[14] And now, behold, I return burning and panting to Your fountain. No one can hold me back! I will drink from it, and so live. Let me not be my own life, for through myself I have lived badly. I was death to myself, but in You I find life once again. Speak to me, commune with me. I have believed Your Books, but their words are filled with mystery.

[11.11] Lord, already You have said to me in a powerful voice in my inner ear that You are eternal, as You alone have immortality[15] since You never change Your aspect or action; nor is Your will altered by time, since no will is immortal that one moment is one thing and another moment another. Before Your Countenance this is clear to me, and let it, I beseech You, become clearer and clearer, and as it does so may I abide serenely beneath Your wings. Lord, You have also said to me in a powerful voice in my inner ear that You have made all the elements and substances that are not what You are yet exist, and that only what does not exist is not from You; You have said to me that any movement of the will away from You—Who exist supremely—is a movement toward something that exists to a lesser degree than You, and such movement away from You is transgression and sin; You have also said to me that no man's sin either harms You or unsettles the order of Your Rule up above or down below. Before Your Countenance this is clear to me, and let it, I beseech You, become clearer and clearer, and as it does so may I abide serenely beneath Your wings.

[11.12] You have also said to me in a powerful voice in my inner ear that that creation, Your Heaven of Heavens whose bliss You alone are, is not coeternal with You but is sated by You with unwavering purity, in no place and at no time manifesting its innate mutability.[16] You are always present to the Heaven of Heavens, and it adheres to You with its entire love, neither having a future to expect nor sending anything it remembers into the past; it is neither altered by any change nor divided over future and past time. O blessed creation, if there be such, blessed for adhering to Your blessedness, blessed through You Who are its eternal Inhabitant and Enlightener! I cannot find a better name for Your House than "the Lord's Heaven of Heavens," a Heaven of Heavens that contemplates Your delights without wavering or falling away, a pure mind united in harmony in the steadfast peace of holy spirits, the citizens of Your city in the heavens above our heaven.

[11.13] Since it is thirsting for You, may this lead the soul, whose pilgrimage has been long and far, to understand, its tears having become its sustenance while every day it is asked, "Where is Your God?" The soul now begs of You one thing, and truly desires it, that it may dwell in Your House all the days of its life,[17] and what is its life but You? And what are Your days but Your eternity, as are Your years that will not end because You are always the same.[18] Through this may the soul that is able understand how high above all times You are, eternal, seeing Your House that never falls away, though it is not coeternal with You, yet by incessantly and unwaveringly adhering to You it does not suffer the successive changes of time. Before Your Countenance this is clear to me, and let it, I beseech You, become clearer and clearer, and as it does so may I abide serenely beneath Your wings.

[11.14] But who knows what kind of formlessness there is in the changes that the lowest and last things have undergone. Yet only a person whose empty heart leads him to pitch and turn among his delusions [phantasmatis / false phantasms & fn Manichaeans?] will claim that the successive changes of time are manifest when all shape has been so diminished and degenerated that only the formlessness remains through which a thing was changed from one form to another. This cannot possibly be, since there is no time without a series of movements, and where there is no change, there can be no form.

[12.15] As I weigh these things to the degree that You have granted, my God, to the degree that You have inspired me to knock and that You have opened to my knocking,[19] I find that there are two things You have made that are beyond the bounds of time, though neither is coeternal with You. The first of these is formed to abide in unceasing contemplation, with no interval of change: though it is changeable in itself, it remains unchanged and so delights in Your eternity and immutability. The second of these was so formless that it did not have shapes that could be changed from one form into another, whether in movement or in immobility, so that it would be subject to time. But You did not let it remain in such formlessness, because before You created all days, You created in the Beginning heaven and earth, the two entities I have just mentioned. "But the earth was invisible and unformed, and there was darkness over the deep."[20] It is through these words that formlessness is made known to us, and to help those gradually understand who cannot conceive that all absence of form does not necessarily lead to nothingness. A second heaven was created out of this formlessness, and a visible and formed earth, as well as the beautiful waters, and everything else that Your Scriptures recount were created along with the first days of creation. They were created as they were so that the successive changes of time could take place within ordered changes of movement and form.

[13.16] The following is my tentative understanding, my God, when I hear Your Scripture saying, "In the Beginning God made heaven and earth, but the earth was invisible and unformed, and there was darkness over the deep," without mentioning on what day You created them. My tentative understanding is that the heaven mentioned is the Heaven of Heavens, the intelligent heaven whose intelligence knows everything all at once, not in part, not darkly, not through a glass, but as a whole, clearly, face to face,[21] not one thing now, another later, but, as I have said, knowing everything at once, without being affected by the successive changes of time; and my tentative understanding is that the earth mentioned is the earth that is invisible and unformed, also unaffected by the successive changes of time where there might be one thing now, another later, because where there is no form there can be no now or later. About these two entities—one formed from the beginning and the other entirely unformed, the one being heaven, but the Heaven of Heavens, and the other being earth, but the earth that is invisible and unformed—about these two entities my tentative understanding is that Your Scripture says, without mentioning what day they were created, "In the Beginning God made heaven and earth." For right away Your Scripture adds of which earth it was speaking, and records that on the second day the firmament was created and called "heaven," making known to us which heaven had first been referred to without the mention of days.

[14.17] The depth of Your words is wondrous, their surface clear before us, beckoning to Your children, but what wondrous depth, my God, what wondrous depth! One is filled with awe as one looks upon it, an awe of honor and a shuddering love. I have hated its enemies with furor;[22] oh, if only You would slay them with Your two-edged sword so that they will no longer be its enemies.[23] But I would wish them slain so that they may live embracing You. But behold, there are others who do not find fault with the Book of Genesis, but praise it. And yet they say, "The Spirit of God, Who through His servant Moses wrote the Book of Genesis, did not want these words to be understood in this way. The Spirit of God did not want them to be understood the way you interpret them, but differently, the way we interpret them!" With You, God of us all, as judge, I give them the following answer:

[15.18] Will you gainsayers claim as false that which Truth says to me in a powerful voice in my inner ear about the eternity of the Creator, His substance in no way varying with time, nor His will distinct from His substance? He does not will one thing now and another later, but He wills all things that he wills once, and at once, and always, not again and again, nor now this, now that; nor does He will later what He did not will before, nor does He not will what He did will before, because such a will is mutable, and what is mutable is not eternal. But our God is eternal. Will you gainsayers claim as false what He tells me in my inner ear, that the expectation of things to come becomes manifest when they shall have come, and that the same manifestation becomes memory once they have passed. Moreover, every effort that varies in this way is mutable, and anything mutable cannot be eternal: but our God is eternal. I have gathered and brought these ideas together, and find that my God, the eternal God, has not created anything because of a new will, nor does His knowledge undergo anything transitory.

[15.19] What will you gainsayers say? Are these things false?

"No," they admit.

So is it false that every element that has been formed, or matter capable of form, can only come from Him Who is supremely good, because He is supremely good?

"We do not deny that either," they admit.

So then, do you deny that there is a certain sublime creation with such a pure love abiding by the true and truly eternal God, that although this creation is not coeternal with Him, it never sep-arates from Him to flow away into inconstancy and the successive changes of time, but reposes in the supremely truest contemplation of Him alone? For as this sublime creation loves You, God, as much as You command, You reveal Yourself to it and are sufficient to it, and therefore it does not turn away from You, nor toward itself. This sublime creation is the House of God, made not of earthly nor of heavenly mass, but spiritual, and partaking of Your eternity because it will never fall away. For You have established it for ever and ever—You have made a decree and it shall not pass away.[24] But nor is it coeternal with You, because it is not without a beginning, for it was created.

[15.20] But we find no time before this Heaven of Heavens, since wisdom was created before all things;[25] not Your Wisdom, which is equal and coeternal with You our God, its Father, the Wisdom by which all things were created and which was the Beginning in which You created heaven and earth, but that wisdom which is cre-ated: the intelligent nature that in contemplating light *is* light. And though it is created, it is also called wisdom. But there is as much difference between the light that illuminates and what is illuminated as there is between the Wisdom that creates and the wisdom that is created, and also between righteousness that forgives and righteous-ness that arises from forgiving. We are also called Your righteousness, for as a certain servant of Yours has said, "That we might become the righteousness of God in Him."[26] Therefore a certain wisdom was created before all things were created: the rational and intel-ligent mind of that pure city of Yours, our mother which is above and is free,[27] eternal in the heavens[28]—and in what heaven, if not in the heaven that praises You, the Heaven of Heavens that is also the Heaven of Heavens for the Lord? We find no time before this Heaven of Heavens, because it also precedes the creation of time, which was created before all things: yet the eternity of the Creator Himself existed before that Heaven of Heavens from Whom, being created, it received its beginning: not a beginning in time, for time itself did not yet exist, but the beginning of its condition.

[15.21] Therefore this Heaven of Heavens comes from You, our God, but in such a way that it is entirely different from You and in no way the same. Though we do not find time before it or even in it, as it is always able to behold Your countenance and never turn away, which is why it never varies or is never subjected to change, there is within it a mutability through which it could darken and grow cold if it did not adhere to You in great love like everlasting noon, shining and glowing from You.[29] O luminous and beautiful House, I have loved your beauty and the place where dwells the glory of my Lord,[30] your builder and possessor. Let my wandering sigh after you, and I beg Him Who made you, luminous House, to take possession of me too within you, since He has created me also. I have strayed like a lost sheep: but upon the shoulders of my Shepherd Who built you, I hope to be brought back to You.[31]

[15.22] What is your response, you gainsayers whom I have been addressing, you who also believe that Moses was the pious servant of God, and that his books are the oracles of the Holy Spirit? Is the Heaven of Heavens not the House of God, which is not coeternal with God, but still in its own way eternal in the heavens,[32] where in vain you seek a succession of times that you will not find? For it surpasses all expansion across time and all the expanses over fleeting years, as it is ever good to adhere to God.[33]

"It is the House of God," they say.

So then what do you dispute as being false of that which my heart has called out to my God when it inwardly heard the voice of His praise?[34] Is it that there was formless matter, where because there was no form there was no order? But where there was no order there could be no successive changes of time, and yet this almost-nothing, insofar as it was not entirely nothing, was certainly of the substance of which everything that is exists, insofar as it is something.

"This too," they say, "we do not deny."

[16.23] Those with whom I have been discoursing in Your presence, my God, concede everything about which Your Truth has not been silent in my inner mind. Let those who deny these things bark and roar as they will, but I will try to persuade them to be still and try to move them to open a path for Your Word to enter them. But if they refuse and repel me, I beg You, my God, do not be silent to me.[35] Speak the truth into my heart, for only You speak in this way, and I will leave these gainsayers outside, gasping in the dust and blowing it into their own eyes. But I will enter my chamber and sing to You songs of love,[36] sighing with sighs too deep for words[37] in my wanderings, and remembering Jerusalem with my heart lifted up toward it: Jerusalem my fatherland, Jerusalem my mother, and You Who rule over her, You the Enlightener, Father, Defender, Husband, her powerful and pure delight, her solid joy and all good things beyond compare, all this at once, for You are the one supreme and true Good. I will not flag until You gather all that I am from this dispersion and disorder into the peace of this dearest mother, where the first-fruits of my spirit[38] are, as well as the reason for my certainty, and You shape and strengthen it forever, my God, my Mercy. But those who do not claim that all this that is true is false, who honor Your Holy Scripture brought forth by holy Moses and who place it at the summit of authority that must be followed, and yet who still dispute us in some things, I will say this: You, our God, be the judge between my confessions and their disputations.

[17.24] For they say, "Though all this might be true, Moses was not thinking of those two things when, through the revelation of the

Spirit, he said, 'In the Beginning God made heaven and earth.' With the name 'heaven,' Moses did not mean the spiritual or intelligent creation that eternally contemplates the countenance of God, nor with the name 'earth' did he mean formless matter."

"What then did he mean?"

"He meant what we have claimed," they reply; "he meant what he expressed with those words."

"What is that?"

"With the names 'heaven and earth' Moses sought first of all to signify the entire visible world in both general and concise terms, so that he could then separate and enumerate the days, presenting the creation stage by stage, since it pleased the Holy Ghost to announce it in this way. Those Moses was addressing in the Book of Genesis were such rough and unspiritual people that he deemed it best to reveal to them only God's visible works."

These gainsayers do agree, however, that it is not incongruous to consider that it was out of the "earth that was invisible and unformed" and the "darkness over the deep," as the subsequent verses show, that all the visible things that we know were made and arranged during those days.

[17.25] But what if another were to claim that this same formlessness and disorder of matter was initially introduced by the name of "heaven and earth," because it was out of this that our visible world was created and perfected with all those elements that are evident, and that this world is now customarily called "heaven and earth"? And what if yet another were to claim that "heaven" and "earth" are suitable words for the invisible and visible entities, and that within these two words is included the universal creation that God made in His Wisdom, that is, in the Beginning? Yet all things were not made from the actual substance of God, but out of nothing, because they are not made of that which God is, and within them all there is a mutable nature, whether they abide as does the eternal House of

God, or whether they change as do the soul and body of man. Hence the shared matter of all things invisible and visible—still unformed though formable—out of which heaven and earth were to be made, in other words, the creation formed out of both what is invisible and visible, was announced with the names "heaven and earth." It was announced with the same names that had been given to the earth that was "invisible and unformed" and the "darkness over the deep," but with the difference that by the "earth that is invisible and unformed" is understood physical matter before it has been given form, and the "darkness over the deep" is spiritual matter before its unrestrained fluidity was restricted or was illumined by Wisdom.

[17.26] There might be another who will choose to say that where we read, "In the Beginning God made heaven and earth," the names "heaven" and "earth" do not signify entities that are already formed and perfected: these names refer to the inchoate state of things that were of material that was still unformed but capable of being formed and fashioned, because within them—in confusion and not yet distinct through their qualities and forms—were all the things that, once they were arranged into an order, were called "heaven" and "earth," the former being the spiritual creation, the latter the physical.

[18.27] Having heard and examined all these notions, I will not contend in words, for that is to no profit except for the subverting of the hearers.[39] But the law is good for edification if a person uses it lawfully,[40] for its purpose is love from a pure heart, from a good conscience, and from sincere faith.[41] And our Master knew on which two commandments He would have all the Law and the Prophets depend.[42] As I ardently acknowledge these things before You in secret, my God, Light of my Eyes, how can I be erring, since the words Moses wrote can be understood in many ways that are true? How can I be erring if my understanding of what Moses wrote differs from the understanding of another? All of us who read the Book

of Genesis are striving to fathom and understand what its author
wanted to say, and since we believe him to be speaking the truth,
we do not dare imagine him to have said something that we either
know or think to be false. While each of us strives to understand in
the Holy Scriptures what the writer understood, what evil is there in
a person understanding what You, the Light of all minds that speak
the truth, show that person to be true, even if the author he is reading understood something different, since the author also understood a truth, though a different truth?

[19.28] For it is true, Lord, that You made heaven and earth. It is
true that the Beginning is Your Wisdom in which You created all.
It is also true that the visible world has as its two great parts the
heaven and the earth, which bring together all created and fashioned entities. And it is true that everything mutable suggests to us
a notion of formlessness in which it adopts a form, or is changed, or
transformed. It is true that the mutable that abides by the Immutable
Form does not change despite being mutable. It is true that formlessness, which is almost nothing, is not prone to the successive changes
of time. It is true that the substance of which a thing is made might,
through our way of speaking, be called by the same name as the
thing of which it was made: hence the formlessness of which heaven
and earth were made might be called "heaven and earth." It is true
that of all things having form there is nothing closer to having no
form than the earth and the deep. It is true that You, of Whom are
all things,[43] made not only all that was created and formed, but also
all that is capable of being created and formed. It is true that all that
is formed out of what is formless was formless before it was formed.

[20.29] All these truths are not doubted by those whose inward eye
You have granted to see such things and who steadfastly believe Your
servant Moses to have spoken by the Spirit of truth. But out of all
these truths someone might choose one truth and say, "In the Begin-

ning God made heaven and earth; that is, God, together with His Word that is coeternal with Himself, made the creation that is intelligent and perceivable, or, if you will, spiritual and physical." Another will say: "In the Beginning God made heaven and earth; that is, God, together with His Word that is coeternal with Himself, made the entire mass of the physical world together with all the things it contains that are visible and known to us." Another will say, "In the Beginning God made heaven and earth; that is, God, together with His Word that is coeternal with Himself, made the formless matter of spiritual and physical creation." Another will say, "In the Beginning God made heaven and earth; that is, God, together with His Word that is coeternal with Himself, made the formless matter of physical creation within which heaven and earth were still in disorder, and which, now being ordered and formed, we today see as the entirety of this world." Another will say, "In the Beginning God made heaven and earth; that is, at the very start of His creating and working, God made formless matter that contained heaven and earth in disorder, which having been formed are now clear and are visible to us with all that is within them."

[21.30] As for the interpretation of the words that follow "In the Beginning God made heaven and earth," someone might choose one of the truths I have mentioned, and say, "The earth was invisible and unformed, and darkness was over the deep; that is, the physical creation that God made was still a formless matter of physical things, without order, without light." Another will say, "The earth was invisible and unformed, and darkness was over the deep; that is, the entirety that is called 'heaven and earth' was still a formless and dark matter of which the physical heaven and the physical earth were to be made with all that is within them that our physical senses can perceive." Another will say, "The earth was invisible and unformed, and darkness was over the deep; that is, this entirety that is called 'heaven and earth' was still formless and dark matter from which was to be made both the intelligent heaven, which I have also called the Heaven of Heavens, and the earth, that is to say, the entire physical world, including under that name also the physical heaven, in other words that out of which all visible and invisible creation was to be made." Yet another will say, "The earth was invisible and unformed, and darkness was over the deep, but the Scripture did not call that formlessness by the name 'heaven and earth.' The formlessness to which the Scripture referred when it said 'the earth was invisible and unformed' and 'darkness was over the deep' already existed, out of which the Scripture had already said that God had made heaven and earth: that is to say, the spiritual and physical creation." Another will say, "The earth was invisible and unformed, and darkness was over the deep; that is, there was already a certain formless matter out of which the Scripture had already said that God had made heaven and earth: that is to say the entire physical mass of the world, divided into two massive parts, an upper and a lower, containing within them all the creation that is familiar and known to us."

[22.31] Someone might try to counter the last two notions with the following response: "If you will not accept that the formlessness of matter might be called by the name 'heaven and earth,' then something that God had not made had to have existed out of which heaven and earth were to be made, for the Scripture does not state that God made such matter unless we understand it to be named 'heaven and earth,' or just 'earth,' when it states: 'In the Beginning God made heaven and earth.' In the verse that follows, 'But the earth was invisible and unformed,' which is how the Scripture signifies formless matter, we can only understand this as meaning that which God made, as is written in the first line of the Book of Genesis: 'In the Beginning God made heaven and earth.'" Here supporters of either of the last two notions[44] will doubtless reply, "We do not deny that God created this formless matter, God of Whom are all things that are very good.[45] But just as we state that what is created and formed is a greater good, so do we avow that what is made that is capable of creation and form is a lesser good, though still good. Yet just as the Scripture did not mention that God made this formlessness, it also does not mention the creation of many other things, such as the Cherubim and the Seraphim, or what the Apostle lists: 'Thrones, dominions, principalities, powers,'⁴⁶ all of which have clearly been created by God. Or if in the words 'He made heaven and earth' all things are supposed to be included, what about the waters 'above which the Spirit of God moved'?⁴⁷ For if the waters are supposed to be included in the word 'earth,' how can unformed matter be meant by 'earth' when we see the waters to be so beautiful? Or if it is to be understood as such, why is it written that out of that same form-lessness the firmament was made and called 'heaven,' yet nothing is written about the waters being made? For the waters are not formless and invisible, since we see them flowing in such beautiful form. But if they received that beauty when God said, 'Let the waters under the firmament be gathered together,'⁴⁸ and the gathering together was their forming, what can be argued about the waters above the firmament, where neither their being formless would have made them worthy of so exalted a seat, nor is it written by what command they were formed? Though Genesis may be silent about God mak-ing something, neither sound faith nor inquiring intellect will doubt that He did make it; nor will sober doctrine dare assert that these waters are coeternal with God, because we hear them mentioned in Genesis, but we do not hear when they were created. With Truth as our teacher, why should we not understand that formless matter, which the Scripture calls 'earth that was invisible and unformed,' and the 'darkness over the deep,' to have been created by God out of nothing and therefore can not be coeternal with Him, even if the Book of Genesis has omitted to state when it was created?"

[23.32] As I hear and examine these notions to the extent that my frail capacity permits, a frailness I avow before You my God Who knows it, I see two kinds of disagreements that might arise when something is revealed in mystical words by true heralds: the first disagreement is about the truth of what is being revealed, the second about what the herald is seeking to reveal. It is one thing to ask about the truth of the Creation, and another to ask what Moses, that illustrious servant of Your Faith, intended his reader or hearer to understand by his words. As for the first instance, may all those go far from me who believe themselves to know what is false, and as for the second, may those also go far from me who imagine Moses to have written things that are false. But, Lord, in You let me be brought together with those whose sustenance is Your Truth in the breadth of Your Love[49] so that with them I can delight in You: together with them we can draw near to the words of Your Book and seek in them Your will through the will of Your servant Moses, by whose pen You have bestowed them upon us.

[24.33] But who among us can find the one will of God among so many truths, which seekers see in those words that are understood in different ways? Who among us can confidently claim that Moses thought this or wanted to convey that, and just as confidently claim that something is true, irrespective of whether Moses thought one thing or the other? My God, I am Your servant and have pledged a sacrifice of confession in this book, and pray that through Your mercy I can pay my vows to You![50] I state with confidence that with Your immutable Word You made all things visible and invisible, but can I state with the same confidence that that is what Moses meant when he wrote, "In the Beginning God made heaven and earth"? I cannot state it with the same confidence, because though in Your Truth I see it as certain, I cannot be certain that that is what Moses thought when he wrote it. When he wrote "In the Beginning," he might have been thinking "At the start of His creating," and by "heaven and earth" he might have meant not a formed and perfected world, whether spiritual or physical, but a world inchoate and still without form. I know, of course, that either of these interpretations could be argued as true, but I do not know which interpretation Moses had in mind with those words. But irrespective of whether this greatest of men envisioned these meanings, or other meanings that I have not mentioned, when he uttered these words, I do not doubt that what he saw was true and that he expressed it rightly.

[25.34] Let no one trouble me[51] by claiming, "Moses did not mean what you are saying, but meant what I am saying." If this gainsayer had at least asked me, "How do you know that Moses thought what you are reading into his words?" I would have replied calmly and said what I have already said above, or explained it at greater length if the gainsayer was stubborn. But if he claims, "Moses did not mean what you are saying, but what I am saying," yet he also does not deny that what each of us claims may be true, then O God, O Life of the Poor, may You in Whose bosom there is no contradiction pour gentleness into my heart so that I can endure this with patience. These gainsayers are not telling me this because they are prophets and have seen what they are claiming in the heart of Your servant Moses, but they are saying it because they are proud, not knowing Moses' notion but loving their own, not because it is true but because it is theirs. Otherwise they would as much love another true notion as I love what they say when they say what is true, not because it is their notion, but because it is true: nor is it solely theirs because it is true. But if they love it because it is true, then it is both theirs and mine, as it is then common to all lovers of truth. But they contend that Moses did not mean what I say but what they say, and that is something that I reject, that I do not love: for even if it were so, their temerity would not be the temerity of knowledge but that of audacity, begotten not of insight but of pride. Therefore we must tremble before Your judgments, for Your Truth is not mine, nor his, nor another's, but belongs to all of us whom You publicly call to partake in it, warning us as we tremble not to strive to keep it for ourselves lest we be deprived of it.

He who claims for himself what You have placed before all to enjoy, and wants for his own what belongs to all, is driven from what is in common to what is his own, that is: from truth to lie, for he who speaks a lie speaks it from his own resources.[52]

[25.35] Hear, O Supreme Judge, God, You Who are Truth Itself, hear what I shall say to this gainsayer, hear! I say before You, and before my brethren who use Your law lawfully with love as their purpose:[53] "Hear and behold if what I shall say to this gainsayer will please You, for this is the word of brotherliness and peace that I will share with him: 'If we both see that what you are saying is true, and we both see that what I am saying is true, where, I ask, do we see it? Not I in you, nor you in me, but we both see it in the immutable Truth that is high above our minds.'" As we are not disputing with one another about the Light of our Lord God, why should we dispute about the thoughts of our neighbor, which we cannot see as we can see the immutable Truth? For even if Moses himself were to appear before us and say, "This is what I was thinking," we could still not see it but would have to believe it. Let us not be puffed up on behalf of one against the other beyond what is written,[54] but let us love the Lord our God with all our heart, with all our soul, and with all our mind, and let us love our neighbor as ourself.[55] Moses declared what he declared in his Books[56] based on these two commandments of love, and if we do not believe Moses, we make God a liar,[57] deeming in our fellow servant's mind other things than he taught us. See how foolish it is, in such an abundance of supremely true meanings as can be extracted from the words of Moses, to declare impetuously which of the meanings Moses particularly meant, and through hurtful disputes to strike at love itself, for the sake of which all this was said by Moses, the words of whom we are seeking to fathom.

[26.36] And yet, my God, You Who are the Height of my humility and the Repose of my toil, You Who hear my confessions and forgive my sins! Since You instruct me to love my neighbor as myself, I cannot believe that You gave a lesser gift to Your faithful servant Moses than I would have sought or desired You to have given me had I been born in the time that he was, and if You had put me in a place where by the service of my heart and tongue those Books could have been disseminated, Books that for such a long time after have benefited all peoples, and which with their great authority quell the words of all false and proud doctrine throughout the entire world. Had I been Moses in those days—for we all come from the same clay,[58] and what is man that You are mindful of him?[59]—had I been then what Moses was and been commanded by You to write the Book of Genesis, I would have wished to have been granted sufficient skill in expression and eloquence in composition. I would have wished this so that those who could not yet understand how God creates would not reject the words I would have written as being beyond their power of comprehension, while those who would already be able to comprehend, having attained a true understanding by whatever path of contemplation, would not find that what they have understood was being passed over in Your servant's meager words. And if another man were by the light of truth to perceive another truth in those words, then that truth too should not fail to be discernible.

[27.37] Just as a spring surging from a narrow fissure is more powerful, and supplies waters through many streams more amply than any of the single streams flowing from it over distant terrains, so too the verses written by Your servant Moses were to be of ample use to those who were later to preach them, streams of the clearest truth pouring forth from the narrow confines of a few words from which, all by longer digressions of discourse, can draw whatever truth they can on these matters for themselves, some one truth, others another. Some people, when they read or hear the words that Moses wrote, imagine God as being like a man, or as a mass possessing immeasurable power, and that through a new and sudden desire He decided to create outside Himself, and at a certain distance from Himself, heaven and earth, two great bodies above and below in which all things would be contained. And when they hear, "God said, 'Let it be made, and it was made,'" they imagine God's words beginning and ending, sounding in time and passing on, and that after the words had passed on, that which God commanded to exist instantly existed.[60] This and the like they imagine in their familiarity with things carnal, for they are still babes,[61] but the Scripture's humble words carry them in their frailty as if at a mother's breast, wholesomely nourishing their faith in which they are assured and certain that God made the entire world in its wondrous variety that their senses behold all around them. But should any man scorn the Scripture's words as being too lowly, leaning out of his nurturing cradle in proud frailty, he will alas fall, poor creature! Have mercy, Lord God, lest the unfledged chick be trodden by those who pass, and send Your angel to bring it back to its nest so that it will live until it can fly.

[28.38] But others, to whom the Scripture's words are no longer a nest but a bower, can see fruit hidden in the dim thicket, and, joyfully chirping, they fly around picking and plucking. For as they read or hear Your words, eternal God, they see that Your unwavering permanence surpasses all past and future times; they see that there is no temporal creation that was not made by You, and that Your will, because it is one with You, created all things: not by changing in any way, nor by suddenly arising not having existed before; they see that Your creation was not made out of You in Your own likeness, the form of all things, but out of nothing, an unlikeness that was formless and was to be formed by Your likeness, hurrying back to You, the One, each creature according to the capability granted its kind; they see that all things were made very good,[62] whether they abide close to You or are in gradations further from You in time and place, causing or sustaining beautiful alterations. They see these things and rejoice in the light of Your Truth in the limited way that they can.

[28.39] Another contemplates the words "In the Beginning God made heaven and earth," and perceives "the Beginning" to be Wisdom as the Beginning also speaks to us.[63] Another contemplates the same words, and by "the Beginning" understands the inception of created things: "In the Beginning He made" is understood as "First He made." But among those who understand "In the Beginning" to mean that in Your Wisdom You made heaven and earth, some believe that "heaven and earth" signifies the matter out of which heaven and earth were to be created and from which they received their name, while others believe that it signifies entities that were already formed and distinct; others again believe that "heaven and earth" signifies one formed entity under the name "heaven" that is spiritual, and a formless entity under the name "earth" that consists of physical matter. But those who perceive the names "heaven" and "earth" to signify matter that was still formless, out of which heaven and earth were to be formed, understand this in different ways as well: some, that it is the matter out of which the intelligible and sensible creation was perfected; others, that it is only the matter out of which the perceivable physical mass was to be made, containing in its vast expanse all the things that are clear and manifest to us. Nor do those who believe that "heaven and earth" signifies the creation that was already ordered and arranged have the same view, some considering it to be both the invisible and visible world, others the visible world alone, in which we can see our luminous heaven and the dark earth with all that is within them.

[29.40] But he who interprets "In the Beginning He made" as meaning "First He made" can only understand heaven and earth as being the matter out of which heaven and earth are made, in other words, the entire creation: that is, the intelligible and physical. For if he maintains that the entire creation was already formed, he might rightly be asked, "If God made this first, what did He make next?" Having made the entire creation, there was nothing left to make, and the next question will inevitably be, "How could God have made this first if after that He made nothing?" But were he to reply that God *first* made the formless, and *then* the formed creation, that is not unreasonable as long as he is capable of distinguishing what precedes in eternity, and what precedes in time, in choice, and in origin: in eternity, the way God precedes all things; in time, the way the flower precedes the fruit; in choice, the way the fruit is chosen before the flower; in origin, the way the sound precedes the song. Of these four kinds of precedence, the first and the last I have just mentioned are the most difficult to comprehend, while the two middle ones are the easiest to understand: since beholding Your eternity, Lord, immutable but creating the mutable and therefore preceding this creation is a rare vision that is most difficult to behold. But whose mind is so sharp as to be able to distinguish without great toil how the sound precedes the song, since a song consists of formed sound, and while a thing that is not formed can exist, that which does not exist cannot be formed. Consequently, matter precedes that which is made from it, matter preceding it not because it makes it, but rather because it is made; nor does it precede it by an interval of time, since we do not first utter formless sounds within time without singing, and then gather these formless sounds together to fashion them into the form of a song, in the way we might fashion wood into a box, or silver into a vase. Such materials precede within time the forms of the things that are made from them, but this is not so in singing. When a song is sung, the song's sound is heard: it does not first sound out formlessly, to then be formed into a song. For whatever will sound out will pass on: nothing remains to be gathered and skillfully fashioned. Thus a song is rooted in its sound, its sound being its matter, and it is this matter that is formed so that it can become a song. Therefore, as I have said, the matter of which sound consists precedes the form of the song, not preceding it by its capacity to create the song, for a sound cannot be the creator of the song, but rising from a body presenting a mind with the matter out of which to create a song. Nor is the sound first within time, for it is emitted together with the song; nor is it first in choice, for a sound is not preferred above a song, since a song is not only a sound but a beautiful one. The sound, however, is first in origin, because a song is not formed so that it will be a sound, but a sound is formed so that it will be a song. Through this example may those who are able understand how the matter of all things was created first and called "heaven and earth," because heaven and earth were made out of it, but it was not made first in time, because the forms of things are what gives rise to time, while it was without form, and only simultaneously with time became perceivable to us. And yet formless matter cannot be put into words other than by describing it as being first in time, whereas it is last in rank because formed things are superior to what is unformed and are preceded by the eternity of the Creator, so that out of nothing something can be created.

[30.41] In this diversity of the true interpretations, let Truth itself give rise to concord, and may our God have mercy upon us that we may use the law lawfully, the purpose of the commandment being pure love.[64] Thus if someone were to ask me which of all these interpretations Your servant Moses held, I cannot reply in my confessions other than to confess to You, "I do not know." But I do know that these interpretations are true, except the carnal ones about which I have spoken to the extent that I deemed necessary,[65] though there is still hope for the babes[66] who embrace those carnal ideas, for they are not frightened by the verses of Your Book, which are humbly profound and copious in their few words. But I avow that all we who see and speak out the truth delivered in those few words: let us love one another and together all love You, our God, Fountain of Truth, if it is for truth and not empty vanities that we thirst. Let us honor Your servant Moses, who, filled with Your Spirit, dispensed this Scripture to Your people, and let us believe that when through Your revelation he wrote these words, the meaning he intended was the one that is most exalted in the illumination of truth and precious benefit.

[31.42] So when someone says, "Moses meant his words as I interpret them," and another, "No, he meant them the way I interpret them," I believe it would be more pious to say, "Why not both interpretations, since both are true? And if there is a third or a fourth interpretation, if someone sees yet another truth in his words, why should we not believe that all these truths were seen by Moses, through whom the One God has tempered the Holy Scripture to the comprehension of many so that they will see true and diverse things? I speak boldly and with conviction from my heart that if I had to write words of such supreme authority, I would prefer to write them in such a way that whatever truth anyone could understand would resound from my words, rather than set down my own meaning so clearly as to exclude any other truths that could not offend me with any possibility of falseness. I therefore would not be so rash, My God, as to believe that Moses would merit any less from You: when he wrote those words, he most certainly meant and thought whatever truth we have been able to find, and other truths that we could not or have not yet been able to find, but which might be found in them.

[32.43] To conclude, Lord Who are God and not flesh and blood, even if men see less in the words that Moses wrote, could any truths remain hidden from Your good Spirit Who shall lead me to the right land,[67] any truths that You might reveal to future readers, even if Moses, through whom the words were written, held only one truth out of many? If this be so, let the interpretation that Moses held be more exalted than the rest. But to us, Lord, either reveal that same truth or any other that pleases You, so that whether You reveal the same meaning to us as You did to Your servant Moses, or some other meaning through the occasion of those words, You are nourishing us, and may no error entrap us. Behold, Lord my God, how much I have written on such few words of Scripture, oh how much! How would my strength suffice, or my time, if I endeavored to write in the same way on all Your Books? Therefore grant that I confess to You more briefly, and to have chosen one true, certain, and good interpretation with which You have inspired me, even though many have occurred to me wherever many could occur. I make my confession with the conviction that if I have managed to discover what Your servant Moses intended, then that is the right and the best interpretation— that is what I must strive for—but if I have not managed to do so, I strive to interpret that which Your Truth willed me to interpret in his words, since Your Truth also willed Moses to interpret what Your Truth revealed to him.

ᔕᓍ

NOTES

1   Romans 8:31.

2   Matthew 7:7–8.

3   Psalm 113:24 (Vulgate), 115:16 (other translations).

4   Genesis 1:2. Augustine's quotations of Genesis are closer to the older Latin translations of the Bible that follow the Greek Septuagint version.

5   Ibid.

6   The Manichaeans.

7   Plotinus, *Enneads* 1.8.9.

8   Revelation 4:8.

9   Wisdom 11:18.

10 Genesis 1:6. "And God said, Let there be a firmament in the midst of the water, and let it be a division between water and water." (Brenton Septuagint Translation)

11 Genesis 1:9. "And God said, Let the water which is under the heaven be collected into one place, and let the dry land appear, and it was so." (Brenton Septuagint Translation)

12 Moses, who was credited with writing the Book of Genesis.

13 Ezekiel 3:12.

14 Probably a reference to the Manichaeans.

15   1 Timothy 6:16.

16   See Book XII, 9.9.

17   Psalm 26:4 (Vulgate), 27:4 (other translations). "That I may dwell in the house of the Lord all the days of my life. That I may see the delight of the Lord, and may visit his temple." (Douay-Rheims Bible)

18   Psalm 101:28 (Vulgate), 102:27 (other translations).

19   Matthew 7:7. "Knock, and it will be opened to you." (New King James Bible)

20   Genesis 1:2.

21   1 Corinthians 13:12. "For now we see through a glass, darkly; but then face to face: now I know in part; but then shall I know even as also I am known." (King James Bible)

22   Psalm 138:22 (Vulgate), 139:22 (other translations). "I have hated them with perfect hatred; they were counted my enemies." (Brenton Septuagint Translation)

23   Psalm 149:6–7.

> "Let the high praises of God be in their mouth,
> And a two-edged sword in their hand,
> To execute vengeance on the nations,
> And punishments on the peoples." (New King James Bible)

24   Psalm 148:6. "He hath established them for ever, and for ages of ages: he hath made a decree, and it shall not pass away." (Douay-Rheims Bible)

25   Sirach 1:4. "Wisdom hath been created before all things, and the understanding of prudence from everlasting." (Douay-Rheims Bible)

26   The Apostle Paul in 2 Corinthians 5:21. "For He made Him who knew no sin to be sin for us, that we might become the righteousness of God in Him." (New King James Bible)

27   Galatians 4:26. "But the Jerusalem above is free, which is the mother of us all." (New King James Bible)

28   2 Corinthians 5:1. "We have a building from God, a house not made with hands, eternal in the heavens." (New King James Bible)

29   Isaiah 58:10. "Then shall thy light rise up in darkness, and thy darkness shall be as the noonday." (Douay-Rheims Bible)

30   Psalm 25:8 (Vulgate), 26:8 (other translations). "I have loved, O Lord, the beauty of thy house; and the place where thy glory dwelleth." (Douay-Rheims Bible)

31   Luke 15:4–5. " What man of you that hath an hundred sheep: and if he shall lose one of them, doth he not leave the ninety-nine in the desert, and go after that which was lost, until he find it? And when he hath found it, lay it upon his shoulders, rejoicing." (Douay-Rheims Bible)

32   2 Corinthians 5:1. "A house not made with hands, eternal in the heavens." (New King James Bible)

33   Psalm 72:28 (Vulgate), 73:28 (other translations). "But it is good for me to adhere to my God." (Douay-Rheims Bible)

34   Psalm 25:7 (Vulgate), 26:7 (other translations). "That I may hear the voice of thy praise: and tell of all thy wondrous works." (Douay-Rheims Bible)

35   Psalm 27:1 (Vulgate), 28:1 (other translations). "Unto thee will I cry, O Lord: O my God, be not thou silent to me: lest thou be silent to me." (Douay-Rheims Bible)

36   Matthew 6:6. "But thou when thou shalt pray, enter into thy chamber, and having shut the door, pray to thy Father in secret: and thy Father who seeth in secret will repay thee." (Douay-Rheims Bible)

37   Romans 8:26. "Likewise the Spirit helps us in our weakness; for we do not know how to pray as we ought, but that very Spirit intercedes with sighs too deep for words." (New Revised Standard Version, Anglicised Catholic Edition)

38   Romans 8:23.

39   A quotation of 2 Timothy 2:14. "Of these things put them in mind, charging them before the Lord. Contend not in words, for it is to no profit, but to the subverting of the hearers." (Douay-Rheims Bible)

40   1 Timothy 1:8. "But we know that the law *is* good if one uses it lawfully." (New King James Bible)

41   1 Timothy 1:5. "Now the purpose of the commandment is love from a pure heart, *from* a good conscience, and *from* sincere faith." (New King James Bible)

42   Matthew 22:40. "On these two commandments dependeth the whole law and the prophets." (Douay-Rheims Bible)

43   1 Corinthians 8:6. "Yet to us there is but one God, the Father, of whom are all things." (Douay-Rheims Bible)

44   The two notions presented in paragraph 21.30.

45   Genesis 1:31. "And God saw all the things that he had made, and they were very good." (Douay-Rheims Bible)

46   The Apostle Paul. Colossians 1:16. "For by him were all things created, that are in heaven, and that are in earth, visible and invisible, whether they be thrones, or dominions, or principalities, or powers: all things were created by him, and for him." (New King James Bible)

47   Genesis 1:2.

48   Genesis 1:9. "God also said: Let the waters that are under the heaven, be gathered together into one place." (Douay-Rheims Bible)

49   Ephesians 3:18–19. "You may be able to comprehend, with all the saints, what is the breadth, and length, and height, and depth: To know also the charity of Christ, which surpasseth all knowledge." (Douay-Rheims Bible)

50   Psalm 115:7–9 (Vulgate), 116:16–18 (other translations). "O Lord, I am thy servant; I am thy servant, and the son of thine handmaid: thou hast burst by bonds asunder. I will offer to thee the sacrifice of praise, and will call upon the name of the Lord. I will pay my vows unto the Lord, in the presence of all his people." (Brenton Septuagint Translation)

51 Galatians 6:17. "From now on let no one trouble me, for I bear in my body the marks of the Lord Jesus." (New King James Bible)

52 John 8:44. "When he speaks a lie, he speaks from his own resources, for he is a liar and the father of it." (New King James Bible)

53 1 Timothy 1:8. "But we know that the law *is* good if one uses it lawfully." 1 Timothy 1:5. "Now the purpose of the commandment is love from a pure heart." (New King James Bible)

54 1 Corinthians 4:6. "That you may learn in us not to think beyond what is written, that none of you may be puffed up on behalf of one against the other." (New King James Bible)

55 Matthew 22:37–39. "Jesus said to him, 'You shall love the Lord your God with all your heart, with all your soul, and with all your mind.' This is the first and great commandment. And the second is like it: 'You shall love your neighbor as yourself.'"

56 Guided by God's Spirit, Moses was believed to have written the first five books of the Bible.

57 1 John 1:10.

58 Romans 9:21. "Does not the potter have power over the clay, from the same lump to make one vessel for honor and another for dishonor?" (New King James Bible)

59 Psalm 8:5 (Vulgate), 8:4 (other translations). "What is man that thou art mindful of him?" (Douay-Rheims Bible)

60 See Book IX, 10.24.

61 1 Corinthians 3:1. "And I, brethren, could not speak to you as to spiritual people but as to carnal, as to babes in Christ." (New King James Bible)

62 Genesis 1:31. "And God saw all the things that he had made, and they were very good." (Douay-Rheims Bible)

63 John 8:25. "They said therefore to him: Who art thou? Jesus said to them: The beginning, who also speak unto you." (Douay-Rheims Bible)

64 1 Timothy 1:5. "Now the purpose of the commandment is love from a pure heart, *from* a good conscience, and *from* sincere faith." (New King James Bible)

65 See Book XII, 27.37,

66 1 Corinthians 3:1. "And I, brethren, could not speak to you as to spiritual people but as to carnal, as to babes in Christ." (New King James Bible)

67 Psalm 142:10. "Teach me to do thy will, for thou art my God. Thy good spirit shall lead me into the right land."

BOOK XIII

[1.1] I appeal to You, my God, my Mercy, Who created me and did not forget me though I had forgotten You. I appeal to You to enter my soul, which You are preparing to occupy through the longing that You have inspired within it. Do not forsake me as I call to You Who had come to me before I even called, and exhorted me with manifold and ever-louder calls so that I would hear You from afar, and turn around and call to You Who called to me. For You, Lord, wiped clean all the bad things that I did so as not to recompense my hands[1] by which I fell away from You; and You came before all the good things that I did so as to recompense Your hands with which You made me, because before I was, You were; nor was I anything to which You should grant existence. And yet, behold! I exist through Your goodness that came before all that You have made me to be and out of which You made me: nor did You have need of me; nor am I so good that I can be of use to You, my Lord and my God! I do not serve You as if You might tire in Your deeds or as if Your power might wane if You were to lack my service. I do not need to tend You like earth that in remaining untended would leave You unworshipped, but I serve and worship You so that goodwill come to me from You, from Whom comes my potential for goodness.

[2.2] It is out of the plenitude of Your goodness that Your creation exists, but Your creation is a good that in no way benefits You; nor is it of You and thus equal to You, but had the potential of being made by You. For what did heaven and earth, which You made in the Beginning, deserve of You? Let these spiritual and physical entities that You made in Your Wisdom reveal what they deserved from You. For on Your Wisdom depend even inchoate and formless things, whether spiritual or physical, though they move away from You toward disorder and increasing dissimilarity to You. But the spiritual, which is formless, is superior to the physical that is a formed body, and the physical that is formless, being superior to that which is nothingness and which relies on Your Word and remains in its formless state unless the Word calls it back to Your Oneness, giving it form. But all is made very good[2] by You, the One and supreme Good. But what did these formless things deserve of You to exist even in their formlessness, since but for You they would not have existed at all?

[2.3] What did physical matter deserve of You for it to exist even invisible and unformed, since it would not even be what it is if You had not made it? As it had not existed, it could not have deserved of You to exist. How could the inchoate spiritual creation deserve of You even to flow darkly *like* the deep and *unlike* you, unless the same Word had made it turn toward Him Who created it and, enlightened by You, become light: not equal to You but conformed to the Form that is equal to You?[3] Just as being a body is not equivalent to being beautiful; otherwise a body could not be deformed. So too for a created spirit to live is not equivalent to its living judiciously, otherwise it would be immutably judicious. But it is good for it always to adhere to You,[4] lest what light it has obtained by turning toward You it lose by turning away from You, relapsing into a life that is like the darkness of the deep.[5] For we too, who in regard to our souls are a spiritual creation, turned away from You, our Light, and were once darkness in that life.[6] And we still toil amid the remains of our darkness until we become Your Righteousness in Your Only Son[7] like the mountains of God, for we have been Your judgments like the great deep.[8]

[3.4] But when You said during the Beginning of the Creation, 'Let there be light,' and there was light,[9] I understand in this, not inappropriately, the spiritual creation, since there already existed a kind of life for You to illuminate. But just as this creation had not deserved of You a life that *could* be illuminated, once it had such a life it also did not deserve of You to *be* illuminated. Its formlessness could not please You unless it became light, and it became light not simply by existing, but by contemplating the illuminating Light and adhering to the Light so that it would live, and live in blessedness. This it owes alone to Your grace that led it to turn for better, toward what cannot be changed into worse or better, which You alone are because You alone simply are. For You alone it is not one thing to live and another to live in blessedness, since You are Your own blessedness.

[4.5] What then could You have lacked for Your good, which You are to Yourself, if Your Creation had either never existed or if it had remained formless? You did not create it out of any need but out of the wealth of Your goodness, embracing and converting it to form, not as if Your joy were to be completed by it. Perfect as You are, its imperfection displeased You, and consequently You perfected it so that it would please You: it is not that You were imperfect and by perfecting it You became perfect. For Your good Spirit was carried above the waters, not carried by the waters as if Your Spirit were resting on them. For those upon whom Your good Spirit is said to rest, the Spirit causes them to rest upon Himself.[10] But Your incorruptible and immutable will, sufficient unto itself in itself, was carried above that life that You had created and for which living is not the same as living in blessedness, for it lives also when it flows in its own darkness.

It remains for it to turn toward Him by Whom it was made, and to live ever closer to the fountain of life, and in His Light to see light, and so be perfected and filled with light and blessed.

[5.6] Now in a glass darkly[11] the Trinity appears to me, which You are my God, because You, Father, in the beginning of our wisdom, which is Your Wisdom born of Yourself, equal to You and coeternal with You—that is, in Your Son—You created heaven and earth. I have said so much about the Heaven of Heavens, and about the invisible and unformed earth, and about the dark deep with the flow and flux of its spiritual formlessness; once it turned toward Him from Whom it had the modicum of life that it had, it became through His illumination a beautiful life and the heaven of that heaven which God later placed between water and water.[12] And under the name "God" I now understood the Father who made these things, and under the name "Beginning" I understood the Son through whom He made them, and as I believed my God to be the Trinity, I kept searching in Your holy words fueled by my belief, and behold, I found Your Spirit moved above the waters, and behold, my God, I found the Trinity—the Father, the Son, and the Holy Ghost—the Creator of all creation.

[6.7] O truth-proclaiming Light! To You I raise my heart so that it will not teach me empty vanities! Dispel the darkness and tell me, I beseech You by our Mother Charity, tell me, I beseech You, the reason why Your Scripture only mentioned Your Spirit after it mentioned the heaven, and the earth invisible and unformed, and the darkness over the deep? Was it because the Spirit had to be introduced here so that it could be imparted that the Spirit was being carried above the waters, which could not be imparted unless the entity above which the Spirit could be understood to be carried was first mentioned? For the Spirit was carried neither above the Father, nor the Son, nor could the Spirit rightly be said to have been "carried above" if the Spirit was being carried above nothing. Thus it was first necessary to mention what it was that the Spirit was being carried above, and only then to mention the Spirit Who could not have been mentioned otherwise than as being carried above. But why could the Spirit not be mentioned otherwise than as being carried above?

[7.8] From this, let him who is capable follow the words of Your Apostle, where he says that Your love has been poured into our hearts by the Holy Spirit Who was given to us:[13] and, teaching us about spiritual things, the Apostle shows us the surpassing path to love, and bows his knees to You for us[14] that we may know the love of Christ that surpasses all knowledge.[15] And therefore the Spirit, surpassing from the Beginning, was carried above the waters. To whom can I express, and in what way can I express, how the weight of cupidity pulls us downward toward the deep, and how by love Your Spirit that was carried above the waters raises us up again? To whom can I express this, and in what way can I express it, for these are not entities into which one can be submerged and from which one can emerge. What can be more similar, what more dissimilar? It is our passions, different kinds of loves: the impurity of our spirit falling downward through love of worldly cares, and the holiness that is Yours raising us upward through love of serenity that we may raise and hold out our hearts to You where Your Spirit is carried above the waters, and reach that surpassing respite when our soul will have passed over the waters that are without substance.[16]

[8.9] Angels fell and man's soul fell, revealing that the dark depth could have engulfed the entire spiritual creation, had You not said in the Beginning, "Let there be light," and there was light,[17] and every obedient intelligent creation of Your Heavenly City adhered to You and rested in Your Spirit Who is carried immutably above everything mutable. Otherwise the Heaven of Heavens would itself have been immersed in the darkness of the deep, though now it is light in the Lord. For even in the wretched restlessness of the fallen spirits that revealed their own darkness when they were stripped of the vestments of Your Light, You abundantly divulge what a great rational creature You made. To this creature nothing less than You will suffice to yield a blessed respite, the creature not even sufficient unto itself. For You, our God, will illuminate our darkness. From You come our garments,[18] and our darkness shall be as the noonday.[19] Give me Yourself, my God, give back Yourself to me: I love, and if it be too little I will love more strongly. I cannot measure, and thus know, how much love I still lack for my life to fall into Your embrace, nor to turn away until it be hidden in the hidden place of Your Presence.[20] This alone I know: lacking You I am lost, lost both within myself and without, and all my wealth that is not my God is poverty.

[9.10] But was not the Father or the Son carried above the waters? If one understands this in a corporeal sense within a space, then neither was the Holy Spirit carried above the waters. But if one understands this as the greatness of the immutable Divinity being above all things mutable, then the Father and the Son and the Holy Spirit were carried above the waters. But why then is this only said of Your Spirit? Why is it only said of the Holy Spirit as if the Holy Spirit had been in a place that is not a place, and all that is said is that the Spirit is Your gift?[21] In Your gift we find respite: it is there we delight in You. Our respite is our place. Love carries us up there, and Your good Spirit raises our humble piety from the gates of death.[22] In Your goodwill is our peace. The body weighed down by its weight is driven toward its place. Weight pulls the body not only downward but also toward its place. Fire tends upward, a stone downward: they are driven by their weight; they seek their places. Oil poured into water is raised to the top of water, and water poured over oil sinks below the oil. They are driven by their weight; they seek their places.

Outside their order they are unsettled; within their order they are settled. My weight is my love; I am carried by it to wherever I am carried. Your gift sets us alight and carries us upward; we are incandescent and we fly. We ascend the ascent in our hearts and sing a song of ascents.[23] Your fire, Your good fire, enflames us and we fly, because we fly upward to the peace of Jerusalem, for I rejoiced in those who said to me, "We shall go into the house of the Lord."[24] A blessed will brings us there, so that we desire nothing else but to abide there forever.

[10.11] Blessed is the creation,[25] which has known nothing different, though it would have been different itself had it not—immediately upon its creation, with no interval in time—been raised through Your gift which is carried above all that is mutable, raised by Your summons when You said, "Let there be light," and there was light. For us there were separate times since we were darkness and have been made light;[26] but in the case of that higher creation Your Scripture only says what that higher creation would have been had it not been illumined, and what Your Scripture says is that it was in flux before, and dark so that the cause by which it was made different would appear, that is: by being turned toward the unfailing Light, it became light. Let him who is capable understand this, or pray for Your help: why should he trouble me[27] as if I could give light to any man coming into this world?[28]

[11.12] Who can understand the omnipotent Trinity? Many speak of the Trinity, but is it indeed of the Trinity that they are speaking? Rare is the man who in speaking of the Trinity knows of what he speaks. People contend and argue over the Trinity, but without calm no one can grasp it. I suggest that they seek three things within themselves. These three things are very different from the Trinity, but I shall speak of them so that people will experience, feel, and attune themselves to how far this triad is from the Trinity.

The three things I am speaking of are to be, to know, and to will. For I am, and I know, and I will. I am knowing and willing, and I know myself to be and to will, and I will to be and to know. In these three things, therefore, let him who is capable discern how inseparable they are: one life, one mind, and one essence. But let him also discern how distinct they are despite their being so inseparable. As man is an introspective being; let him look into himself and see and convey this to me. But when he does find something and conveys it, let him not believe that he has discovered what is above this triad and immutable: what immutably is, immutably knows, and immutably wills. He might wonder if this triad has led to the Holy Trinity, or if the triad is in each Person of the Trinity so that the whole triad belongs to each, or if both are true, wondrously simple yet manifold, infinite yet to itself finite; whereby the Trinity is and is known to Itself, and immutably suffices to Itself—the Selfsame—by the abounding greatness of Its unity. Who can envisage this simply? Who can put it into words in any way? Who would venture a rash pronouncement?

[12.13] Proceed in your confession, my faith! Say to the Lord your God, "Holy, Holy, Holy,[29] Lord my God, in Your Name we have been baptized, Father and Son and Holy Spirit;[30] in Your Name we baptize, Father and Son and Holy Spirit. For among us also did God in His Christ make heaven and earth, the spiritual and the carnal of His Church. And our earth, before it was given form by doctrine, was invisible and unformed,[31] and we were covered by the darkness[32] of ignorance. For You have corrected man for his iniquity[33] and Your judgments were like the great deep.[34] But because Your Spirit was carried above the waters, Your mercy did not abandon our misery, and You said, "Let there be light. Repent, for the Kingdom of Heaven is nigh.[35] Repent, let there be light." And because our soul was troubled within us we remembered You, Lord, from the land of Jordan, and from the mountain that is equal to You but became small for our sakes. Our darkness displeased us, and we turned toward You and there was light. And behold, we were once darkness, but now we are light in the Lord.[36]

[13.14] But still only by faith, not yet by sight,[37] for by hope we have been saved, and hope that is visible is not hope.[38] Still the deep calls to the deep, but now in the voice of your cataracts.[39] For even he who has said, "I could not speak to you as to spiritual people, but as to carnal,"[40] still does not consider himself to have comprehended, and forgets those things which are behind and reaches forward to those things which are ahead.[41] Burdened, the Apostle groans,[42] and his soul thirsts for the living God as the deer pants for the water-brooks, and he asks, "When shall I come?"[43] Seeking to be clothed with his habitation which is from heaven,[44] the Apostle calls to the lower deep, saying, "Do not be conformed to this world, but be transformed by the renewing of your mind.[45] And he says, "Do not be children in understanding, but be babes in malice and in understanding be mature."[46] And further, "O foolish Galatians, who has bewitched you?"[47] But now the Apostle no longer speaks in his own voice, but in Yours Who sent Your Spirit from above through Him who ascended up on high and opened the floodgates of His gifts[48] so that the force of His stream will make glad the City of God.[49] It is for that City that this friend of the Bridegroom sighs,[50] having now the first-fruits of the Spirit within him yet still groaning within himself, waiting for the adoption, the redemption of his body.[51] For that City he sighs, for he is a member of the Bride;[52] he loves her with zeal, as he is a friend of the Bridegroom; he loves her with zeal, not himself, since it is in the voice of Your cataracts and not in his own voice that he calls to that other deep, fearing his zeal for it lest, as the serpent deceived Eve through his craftiness, their minds should be corrupted from the purity that is in our Bridegroom, Your only Son.[53] What a beautiful light it will be when we shall see Him as He is, and the tears that have been my bread day and night will have passed, while they say to me every day, "Where is your God?"[54]

[14.15] I too ask,[55] "My God, where are You? You are here! In You I take breath a little[56] when I pour out my soul within me with a voice of joy and praise, the sound of one feasting.[57] And yet my soul is sad because it lapses and becomes the deep, or feels that it is still the deep. My faith, which You have kindled before my feet in the night, says to my soul, "Why are You sad, why are you troubling me? Hope in the Lord;[58] His word is a lantern to your feet![59] Hope and persevere until the passing of night, the mother of the wicked, and the passing of the Lord's wrath of which we too were children who were once darkness.[60] We bear its residue in our bodies that are dead because of sin[61] until the day shall break and the shadows flee away.[62] Hope in the Lord; in the morning I shall stand in Your presence and contemplate You;[63] I shall forever confess to You. In the morning I shall stand in Your presence and will see the health of my countenance,[64] my God, Who also will give life to our mortal bodies through the Spirit that dwells within us.[65] He has in mercy been carried above our inner dark and flowing deep. It is from Him we have received in this pilgrimage a pledge that we should now be light:[66] while we are saved by hope[67] and are the children of light and the children of the day, not the children of the night or of darkness[68] which we once were.[69] Between them and us in this uncertainty of human knowledge You divided,[70] You Who tested our hearts[71] and called the light day, and the darkness night. For who makes us differ from one another if not You, and what do we have that we have not received from You?[72] It is out of the same lump of clay that some vessels are made for honor and others for dishonor.[73]

[15.16] Who if not You, our God, made for us a solid firmament above us in Your Divine Scripture?[74] For heaven shall be rolled up like a scroll,[75] but now it stretches over us like a parchment.[76] Your

Divine Scripture has more sublime authority since the mortals through whom You dispensed it to us[77] died and passed away. And You know, Lord, You know how You clothed men with skins when they became mortal through sin.[78] Hence, like a parchment, You have stretched out the firmament of Your book, that is: Your words, which through the ministry of mortal men You have spread over us are always in agreement. And it was by the death of these men that this solid firmament of authority in Your words that were disseminated by them extended more sublimely over all that was beneath them, which while these men lived was not so sublimely extended. You had not yet spread the heaven above us like a parchment and had not yet enlarged in all directions the glory of their deaths.

[15.17] May we behold, Lord, the heavens, the work of Your fingers.[79] Disperse from our eyes the cloud You have spread before them. It is there that Your statutes are, making wise the simple:[80] my God, make perfect Your praise out of the mouth of infants and sucklings.[81] Nor do we know other books that so destroy pride, that so destroy the enemy and the defender[82] who resists Your reconciliation by defending his own sins. I do not know, Lord, I do not know any other such pure words[83] that so persuade me to confess and soften my neck to Your yoke,[84] and invite me willingly to serve You. May I understand these words, good Father: grant this to me who have submitted to them, for you have so solidly established them for those who have submitted themselves to them.

[15.18] I believe that there are other waters above that firmament[85] that are immortal and separated from earthly corruption. Let them praise Your Name; let the peoples above the heavens Your angels praise You. They have no need to gaze up at this firmament and to read so as to know Your Word, for they always behold Your face,[86] and there, without syllables within time, they read Your eternal will. They read, they choose, they love. They eternally read, and what they read never passes; for by choosing and loving they read the very immutability of Your intention. Their book is never shut nor their scroll rolled up, since You Yourself are this to them and exist eternally, because You have placed them above this firmament that You have firmly established over the infirmity of the people below so that they can look up and know Your mercy, announcing in time You Who made time. For in heaven, Lord, is Your mercy, and Your Truth reaches the clouds.[87] The clouds pass, but heaven abides. The preachers of Your Word pass from this life into another, but Your Scripture will be spread out to the people to the end of the ages. Even heaven and earth shall pass, but Your words shall not pass,[88] for the scroll will be rolled up, and the grass over which the scroll was spread shall pass away through its clarity and light. Your Word abides forever.[89] Now it appears to us darkly through the clouds as through a glass[90] of heaven, not as it is, because though we too are beloved by Your Son it has not yet been revealed what we shall be.[91] He looked through the lattices of our flesh,[92] and caressed us, and aroused us, and we ran after His fragrance.[93] But when He is revealed we will be like Him, for we shall see Him as He is.[94] As He is, Lord, will our sight be, but this is not yet given to us.

[16.19] How You are in entirety only You know, You Who exist immutably, and know immutably, and will immutably. And Your Essence knows and wills immutably, and Your Knowledge is and wills immutably, and Your Will is and knows immutably. You do not hold it right that as the immutable Light knows Itself, so should it be known by that which is illuminated and mutable. Thus my soul is like earth without water unto You,[95] because as it cannot illumine itself of itself, so it cannot satisfy itself of itself. For with You is the fountain of life, as in Your Light we shall see light.[96]

[17.20] Who gathered together the embittered into one place? Their single aim is a temporal and earthly happiness for which they will do anything, though countless cares make them drift and waver. Who, Lord, but You, said, "Let the waters be gathered together into one place, and let the dry land appear"[97] that thirsts for You? For the sea also is Yours, and You made it, and Your hands formed the dry land.[98] Yet it is not the bitterness of men's wills that is called the sea, but the gathering together of the waters, for You have bound the wicked desires of men's souls, and around them set bounds as to how far the waters may pass so that their waves will break,[99] and so You make this a sea by the order of Your rule over all things.

[17.21] But the souls that thirst for You[100] and appear before You have different aims that separate them from that gathering of the sea. Through a sweet and hidden spring You water the earth so that it will bring forth its fruit,[101] and it brings forth its fruit at Your command, the command of its Lord God. So too does our soul yield works of mercy according to its kind,[102] and we love our neighbor and seek to relieve his suffering, our soul containing seed in itself according to its likeness,[103] when from out of a sense of our own weakness we feel compassion to relieve those who are in need, helping them as we would hope to be helped if we were in similar need; helping not only in easy ways, like the grass yielding seed, but also in the protection of our help when given powerfully, like the tree yielding fruit,[104] that is, succor in delivering him who suffers wrong at the hand of those who are mighty, and offering him the shelter of protection through the power of just judgment.

[18.22] Thus, Lord, thus I beseech You, as You are the Maker, the Giver of joy and power. Let truth spring out of the earth and justice look down from heaven,[105] and let there be lights made in the firmament.[106] Let us deal our bread to the hungry and bring the destitute who have no shelter into our house. Let us clothe the naked and not despise those who are like our own flesh.[107] Since these fruits have sprouted from the earth, let us see that it is good, and let our

light break forth as in the morning.[108] May we from the lower fruits
of our good deeds reach the delights of contemplation, and may we
hold fast the Word of Life that is above and shines like lights in the
world,[109] adhering to the firmament of Your Scripture: for there You
explain to us so that we can distinguish between what is intelligible
and what can be sensed, such as distinguish between day and night,
or between minds, some of which are prone to things intelligible and
others to things spiritual, so that now it is not You alone who, as
before You made the firmament, distinguish in the mystery of Your
judgment between light and darkness. Since Your grace has been
manifested throughout the world, Your spiritual children are also set
and arrayed in the same firmament, and may they shine upon the
world and divide the day from the night and let them be for signs
and seasons.[110] Old things have passed away, and, behold, they have
become new![111] Our salvation is nearer than when we first began to
believe. The night is spent and the day is at hand,[112] and You bless
the crown of the year of Your goodness,[113] sending the laborers to
Your harvest[114] in the sowing of which others have labored,[115] sending them also into another field whose harvest shall be at the end.[116]
Thus You grant the prayers of him who prays, and bless the year
of the just; but You remain the same, and in Your years that will
have no end[117] You prepare a granary for the years that are passing.
By eternal counsel You bestow at the proper time heavenly blessings
upon the earth.

[18.23] To some the Spirit gives the word of wisdom, like a greater
light for those who cherish the illumination of truth as ruling of the
day;[118] to others the same Spirit gives the word of knowledge, like a
lesser light; to others the Spirit gives faith, to others gifts of healing,
to others the working of miracles, to others prophecy, to others the
discerning of spirits, to still others different kinds of tongues. And
all these are like the stars, for the same Spirit works all these things,
distributing to each one individually as He wills,[119] causing the stars

to appear manifestly to the advantage of all. But the word of knowledge that contains all the holy mysteries that vary in time is like the moon, and the knowledge of the other gifts that I have listed is like the stars, inasmuch as they are unlike that brightness of wisdom that rejoices in the day that I have mentioned before[120] and belong to the beginning of the night. For they are necessary to those to whom Your most prudent servant could not speak as to spiritual people, but as to carnal;[121] even he, who speaks wisdom among those who are perfect.[122] But the natural man,[123] like a babe in Christ and a drinker of milk until he is strengthened for solid food[124] and his eye can bear the light of the sun, let him not feel that he is steeped in darkness, but let him be content with the light of the moon and the stars. All this You explain to us with the greatest wisdom in Your Book, Your firmament, so that we can discern all things in admirable contemplation, though still in signs and seasons, and in days and years.[125]

[19.24] But first, wash yourselves and make yourselves clean, banish the evil from your souls and from before my eyes, so that dry land may appear. Learn to do good, judge the fatherless, plead for the widow[126] so that the earth will sprout grass for grazing and trees bearing fruit. Come now and let us reason together, says the Lord,[127] so that there will be lights in the firmament of the heavens, and they will shine upon the earth. There was the rich man who had asked the good Teacher what he should do to attain eternal life,[128] and the rich man was told by the good Teacher, whom he thought a mere man and nothing more—though He is good because He is God—that if he wanted to enter into life he had to keep the commandments:[129] he had to banish from himself the bitterness of malice and evil, and must not murder, nor commit adultery, nor steal, nor bear false witness, so that dry land would appear and the honoring of father and mother and the love of our neighbor would germinate.[130] "All this I did," he said. But then why are there so many thorns if the earth is fruitful? Go and weed out all the thorny thickets of avarice!

Sell what you own and be filled with fruit by giving to the poor,[131] and you will have treasure in heaven! Follow the Lord if you want to be perfect, and associate yourself with those among whom He speaks wisdom,[132] He Who knows what to apportion to the day and what to the night, so that you will also know it and so that there will be lights for you too in the firmament of heaven. But this will not come to be if your heart will not be there, nor if your treasure will not be there, as you have heard from the good Teacher; what will be there instead is a barren and saddened earth, with thorns choking the word.[133]

[19.25] But you, chosen generation,[134] you weak things of the world[135] who have left all so that you may follow the Lord:[136] go after Him and put the mighty to shame![137] Go after Him, beautiful feet,[138] and shine in the firmament so that the heavens may declare His glory,[139] distinguishing between the light of those who are perfect but not yet like the angels, and the darkness of those who are simple,[140] but not without hope. Shine over the entire earth and let the day, lightened by the sun, utter unto day the word of wisdom, and let night lit by the moon reveal unto night the word of knowledge.[141] The moon and stars give light to the night: the night does not darken them, but they illuminate it to the degree that they can. Behold, it is as if God were saying, "Let there be lights in the firmament of heaven,"[142] and suddenly from heaven there came a sound like the rush of a mighty wind, and there appeared divided tongues, as of fire, and a tongue rested on each of them.[143] And there were made lights in the firmament of heaven having the word of life.[144] O Holy Fires, beautiful fires, spread everywhere, for you are the light of the world, nor are you put under a bushel.[145] He to whom you adhere is exalted and has exalted you: spread everywhere and be known to all nations.

[20.26] Let the sea also conceive and bring forth your works: let the waters bring forth the creeping creature having life.[146] In separating the precious from the vile, you will be made the mouth of God,[147] saying, "Let the waters bring forth not the living soul that the earth brings forth,[148] but the creeping creature having life and the birds that fly above the earth.[149] For Your Sacraments, God, by the ministry of Your saints, have slowly advanced amid the waves of temptations of the world to imbue the nations in Your Name, in Your Baptism.[150] In the meantime many great and wondrous things were done,[151] such as great whales[152] and the voices of Your messengers flying above the earth close to the open firmament of Your Book that is set over them as the authority under which they are to fly wherever they may go. For there is neither speech nor language where their voice is not heard, as their sound has spread forth over all the earth and their words to the ends of the world,[153] because You, Lord, by blessing them have multiplied them.[154]

[20.27] Am I perhaps erring, melding all and not distinguishing between the clear knowledge of the things in the firmament of heaven and the material creations in the swelling sea beneath the firmament of heaven? For the knowledge of these things are fixed and defined without increase through the generations, such as the lights of wisdom and knowledge, yet the physical operations of these things are many and diverse, one thing growing out of another as they multiply through Your blessing,[155] God, You who have assuaged the aversion for mortal senses; so that a single thing in the understanding of our mind can be imagined and expressed in many ways through the motions of the body. The waters have brought forth these creations,[156] but through Your Word. The needs of the people alienated from the eternity of Your truth have brought them forth, but in Your Gospel, because the waters themselves cast them forth, the waters' dark bitterness being the reason why it was through Your Word that these creations were brought forth.

[20.28] And everything is beautiful because You have made it—but Lord, You Who have made everything are unutterably more beautiful. Had Adam not fallen from You, the brine of the sea would never have flown out of his loins, the human race so profoundly curious, so rabidly enraged, so fluid and fickle! There would then have been no need for Your stewards[157] to work in many waters,[158] presenting these mysterious actions and words in a corporeal and spiritual way—for that is how those creeping animals and birds of the air[159] now seem to me—while man, being instructed and initiated by corporeal mysteries, will not progress further unless his soul gains life spiritually on another level, and after the word of initiation looks toward perfection.[160]

[21.29] Yet it was not the depth of the sea but the earth having been separated from the bitter waters, which at Your Word brought forth not creeping creatures having life and the birds that fly, but the living soul that now has no need of baptism as the heathen does, and as it itself did when it was covered by the waters. For there is no other entrance into the Kingdom of Heaven than the one You appointed:[161] nor does the soul seek great and wondrous things in order to create faith; it does not need signs and wonders for it to believe,[162] since now the faithful earth is separated from the waters that were bitter with lack of faith; and tongues are for a sign not to those who believe, but to unbelievers.[163] Nor does the earth that You have laid out above the waters[164] need the creatures that fly which the waters brought forth at Your Word. Send forth Your Word to the earth[165] through Your messengers, for though we speak of the works of the earth, it is You Who make these works so that the earth can bring forth a living soul. The earth brings it forth because the earth has caused the living souls to be formed in her, just as the sea caused the creeping creatures that have life to be formed and the birds that fly under the firmament of heaven, creatures of which the earth has no need; yet it does partake of the fish raised out of the deep upon the table that

You have prepared before those who believe.[166] For the fish was raised out of the deep to nourish the dry land.[167] Birds are also progeny of the sea,[168] but they multiply upon the earth. Man's lack of faith was the cause for the first voices to preach the Gospels, yet the faithful are also exhorted and blessed by them so many times from day to day.[169] But the living soul has its origin from the earth. Only those already among the faithful find benefit in abstaining from loving this world so that their soul may live for You,[170] for their soul was dead while it lived in pleasures,[171] in deadly pleasures, Lord, for You are the life-giving pleasure of the pure heart.

[21.30] May Your ministers now work upon the earth; but not as upon the waters of faithlessness by proclaiming and declaring through miracles, mysteries, and mystic words in order to draw the attention of ignorance, the mother of wonderment with its fear of those secret signs. That is the gateway to faith for the sons of Adam who have forgotten You, while they hide themselves from Your face[172] and become an abyss. But may Your ministers now work as on dry earth that is separated from the whirling waters of the abyss, and let them be an example to the faithful by living before their eyes, inspiring the faithful to imitation: not only to hear, but also to do. Seek the Lord and your soul shall live,[173] so that the earth may bring forth a living soul! Be not conformed to the world,[174] but abstain from it. The soul lives by avoiding that which, in striving for, it dies. Abstain from the monstrous ruthlessness of pride, the torpid voluptuousness of luxuriance, and what is falsely called knowledge,[175] so that the wild animals will be calmed, the cattle tamed, and the serpents rendered harmless, for allegorically these animals represent the impulses of the soul. The haughtiness of pride, the delight in lust, and the poison of curiosity[176] are the impulses of a dead soul, for the soul does not lose all impulse in dying, since it dies by leaving the fountain of life and so is embraced by the passing world and conformed to it.

[21. 31] But Your Word, God, *is* the fountain of eternal life and shall not pass;[177] therefore in Your Word the departure of the soul is prevented when we are told, "Be not conformed to this world,"[178] so that the earth will bring forth a living soul in the fountain of life, a soul made continent in Your Word through the ministrations of Your Evangelists by imitating those who imitate Your Christ.[179] This is what "each according to their kind"[180] means, since a man will emulate his friend. "Be as I am," he [the Apostle Paul] says, "because I also am as you."[181] Thus in the living soul the beasts will have become good through the meekness of their manner, for You commanded: "Do your works in meekness, and you will be loved by all men";[182] and the cattle will be good in the living soul—if they eat they will not abound, and if they do not eat they will not lack; and there will be good serpents, not pernicious in their harmfulness but wise in their heed,[183] only exploring temporal nature to the extent that eternity can be clearly seen, being understood through the things that are made.[184] These allegorical beasts in the living soul obey reason when they are prevented from their deadly ways; they live and are good.

[22.32] For behold, Lord our God, our Creator, when our affections were prevented from loving the world through which we were dying by evil living, we began to be a living soul through good living. This was fulfilled by Your Word which You spoke through Your Apostle [Paul], saying, "Be not conformed to this world." And then there follows what You immediately added, saying, "But be reformed in the newness of your mind."[185] Though this is not each according to their kind[186] as though we could be reformed by imitating our neighbor who went before, nor as living under the authority of a better man, for You did not say: "Let man be made according to his kind," but You said, "Let Us make man in Our image, according to Our likeness,"[187] so that we might prove what Your will is.[188] It is for this reason that Your steward, who begat children through the Gospel[189] so that he would not forever have them as babes whom he must feed with milk[190] and cherish as a nurse,[191] exclaimed: "Be reformed in the newness of your mind, that you may prove what is the good, and the acceptable, and the perfect will of God."[192] That is why You did not say, "Let man be made," but "Let Us make man," nor did You say, "according to his kind," but, "in Our image, according to Our likeness." For someone who is renewed in his comprehension and beholds and understands Your Truth does not need a human guide in order to imitate his kind, but through Your guidance proves what is your good, acceptable, and perfect Will.[193] Now that he is capable, You teach him to see the Trinity of the Unity and the Unity of the Trinity. That is why it is said in the plural: "Let Us make man." After which is then added in the singular: "So God created man." Though also said in the plural is "in Our image," after which is added in the singular: "in the image of God."[194] Thus man is renewed in the knowledge of God according to the image of Him Who created him,[195] and having been made a spiritual man, he judges all things that are to be judged, but himself is judged by no man.[196]

[23.33] But "he judges all things" means the following: that man has dominion over the fish of the sea, over the birds of the air, and over all the cattle and wild beasts and the whole earth, and every creeping creature that creeps upon the earth.[197] Spiritual man judges through the capacity of his mind to understand, by which he comprehends the things of the Spirit of God;[198] for otherwise man, despite his position of honor, will not understand, and will be compared to the senseless cattle and will have become like them.[199] Therefore, our God, in Your Church—according to Your grace which You have bestowed upon it, for we are Your workmanship, created in good works[200]—in Your Church there are not only spiritual leaders, but also those who are spiritually subject to the ministers who lead; in Your spiritual grace You created man, male and female,[201] for in the sex of the body there is neither male nor female, just as there is neither Jew

nor Greek, neither slave nor free.[202] Spiritual people, whether those
who lead or those who obey, judge spiritually,[203] not judging the spiritual knowledge that shines in the firmament, for it does not behoove
them to judge so supreme an authority, nor Your Book, even if some
things in it might remain obscure, for we submit to it our capacity to
understand, and remain certain that even what is closed to our sight
is spoken rightly and in truth. Thus man, though now spiritual and
renewed in the knowledge of God after the image of Him Who created him,[204] should be a doer of the law, not a judge.[205] Nor must man
judge and distinguish between spiritual and carnal men, who are
known to Your eyes, our God, and who have not yet been revealed
to us by their works so that we might know them through the fruits
of their works. But You, Lord, know them and have already set them
apart and called them in secret before the firmament was made. Nor
does man, though he is spiritual, judge the confused people of this
world, for what has he to do with judging those who are outside,[206]
when he does not know which of them will be entering the sweetness of Your grace and which of them will continue in the perpetual
bitterness of impiety?

[23.34] Man therefore, whom You have created in Your own image,
was not granted dominion over the lights of heaven, nor over the
hidden heaven itself, nor over the day and the night that You called
into existence before the founding of heaven, nor over the gathering of the waters, which is the sea; man was granted dominion over
the fish of the sea, over the birds of the air, and over all cattle and
the whole earth, and every creeping creature that creeps upon the
earth.[207] Man judges, favoring what he finds to be right and condemning what he finds to be wrong: he judges the solemn rites of
the Sacraments by which those are initiated whom Your mercy seeks
out in many waters, and judges the solemn rite in which the Fish is
offered that is raised out of the deep and of which the devout earth
partakes;[208] he judges the preaching and the symbols within the

words spoken under the authority of Your Book that are like birds flying beneath the firmament, explaining, expounding, discoursing, explicating, praising, and appealing to You, bursting forth from the mouth as vocal symbols so that the people may answer, "Amen." The reason for all these words having to be pronounced physically is the abyss of this world and the blindness of the flesh that cannot see thoughts, so that the words must resound in the ears. Hence, though the birds were multiplied upon the earth, they had their origins in the waters.[209] The spiritual man also judges, favoring what is right and condemning what he finds to be wrong in the works and deeds of the faithful who give alms just as the earth brings forth fruit; he also judges the living soul, its impulses tamed by chastity, fasting, and pious meditations on the things perceived by the senses of the body. Of all this man is now said to judge that over which he also has power to set things right.

[24.35] But what is the line that follows, what is its mystery? You bless mankind, Lord, that it may be fruitful and multiply and fill the earth;[210] is there not something that you want to give us to understand? Why did You not also bless the light that you called day, nor the firmament of heaven, nor the lights, nor the stars, nor the earth, nor the sea? I would have said that You, our God, who created us in Your own image, I would have said that You had willed to bestow this blessing on mankind alone if You had not blessed in the same manner the fish and the whales that they should be fruitful and multiply and fill the waters of the sea, and that the birds should multiply on the earth.[211] I would also have said that this blessing was bestowed only on the species propagated from their own kind if I had found the blessing bestowed upon trees and thickets and the beasts of the earth. But neither the plants and trees, nor the beasts and serpents were told "Be fruitful and multiply," yet all these as well as the fish and birds and men propagate and increase their kind, preserving it.

[24. 36] What then shall I say, my Light, O Truth? That these are empty words without meaning? This they are not, Father of piety— far be it from a minister of Your Word to say such a thing! And if I do not understand what You mean by your words, let those who are better than I make better use of them, that is, those with more expertise than I, according to the extent of knowledge You have granted to each. But let my confession also be pleasing before Your Countenance, for I avow that I believe, Lord, that You did not speak these words needlessly, nor will I be silent on what this lesson suggests to me. It is true, nor do I see what should hinder me from understanding in the following manner these figurative words of Your Book. For I know that something can be expressed by the body in many ways that is understood in only one way by the mind, and that something can be understood in many ways by the mind that is expressed in only one way by the body. Behold how the simple love of God and our neighbor is expressed in corporeal ways in such manifold sacraments and innumerable languages, and in each language in innumerable ways. This is how the offspring of the waters are fruitful and multiply. Reconsider these words, my readers, behold what the Scripture presents in only one way, the voice resounding: "In the Beginning God created heaven and earth." Is it not understood in many different ways, and not through deceitful errors, but by a number of possible interpretations?[212] Thus man's offspring is fruitful and multiplies.

[24.37] If therefore we consider the natures of these things literally and not allegorically, then the words "Be fruitful and multiply" apply to all things that are propagated by seed. But if we approach the words as spoken figuratively, which I feel to be the intention of the Scripture, since surely it would not have needlessly bestowed this benediction on the offspring of fish and man alone, then we find a multitude of spiritual as well as corporeal creatures to be represented by heaven and earth; we find just and unjust represented by light and darkness; we find the holy authors through whom the Laws have been ministered represented by the firmament that has been established between the waters and the waters,[213] and the society of people made bitter[214] represented by the sea; we find the zeal of pious souls represented by the dry land, and works of mercy within this present life represented by the plants bearing seed and the trees bearing fruit; we find the spiritual gifts given to each for the profit of all[215] represented by the lights of heaven, and passions curbed by temperance represented by the living soul. In all these things we find multitudes, fruitfulness, and increase, but that something will grow and multiply in such a way that it can be expressed in many ways and a single expression be understood in many ways, we find only in signs that are corporeally expressed and in things conceived through the intellect. The signs put forth corporeally are generated in the waters, caused inevitably by the depths of the flesh, while things devised through the intellect by human generations are caused by the fruitfulness of reason. Therefore we believe that You said to these two kinds, "Be fruitful and multiply." For in this blessing, as I understand it, You have granted us the faculty and power to express in many ways what we understand in a single way, but also to understand in many ways that which we read and which is expressed obscurely but in a single way. Thus the waters of the sea are filled, swelling only on account of manifold meanings, and thus the earth is filled by human generations, the earth's dryness manifested in man's zeal and its dominion manifested in reason.

[25.38] I also want to say, Lord my God, what the following Scripture impresses upon me. I will say it without fear, for I will speak the truth, since You are inspiring me with what You will me to say about those words. Nor would I believe myself to be speaking the truth if it was by any other inspiration than Yours. You are the Truth and every man a liar,[216] therefore he who speaks a lie speaks of his own,[217] which is why for me to speak the truth I will speak of Your Own. Lord, You have given us for food every herb that yields seed upon all the earth, and every tree whose fruit yields seed.[218] And You have given these not to us alone, but also to all the birds of the air and to the beasts of the earth and to all serpents,[219] yet to the fish and to the great whales You have not given these. We were saying that the fruits of the earth signified and allegorically figured the works of mercy that are provided for the necessities of this life out of the fruitful earth.[220] Pious Onesiphorus, to whose household You granted mercy, was such an earth, because he often refreshed Your Paul, and was not ashamed of his chain.[221] The brethren did the same, and they garnered the same fruits, for out of Macedonia they supplied what he was lacking.[222] But how he grieved over some trees that did not grant him the fruit owed him, when he said, "At my first defense no one stood with me, but all forsook me. May it not be charged against them."[223] For such fruits are owed to those who minister the rational doctrine to us through their understanding of the divine mysteries, and they are owed these fruits as men; but they also are owed these as the living soul, offering themselves to be imitated in all continence, and they are owed such fruits as flying creatures because of their blessings that are multiplied upon the earth, since their sound has gone forth into all the earth.[224]

[26.39] But only they who rejoice in these fruits are fed by them, while those whose God is their belly[225] do not rejoice in them. To those who offer these fruits, it is not the fruits that are the gift but the spirit with which they give them. I therefore clearly see why the Apostle Paul was filled with joy in serving God and not his own belly,[226] I see it, and ardently rejoice with him. For he had received from the Philippians what they had sent him through Epaphroditus.[227] I see why he was filled with joy, since what gave him joy also fed him; he spoke sincerely when he said, "I rejoiced in the Lord greatly that now at last your care for me has flourished again; though you surely did care, but you had become weary."[228] The Philippians had grown weak in their prolonged weariness as if the fruit of a good work had withered them, and the Apostle rejoiced for them that they flourished once more, not rejoicing for himself that they had relieved his need. Therefore he continues, "Not that I speak in regard to need, for I have learned in whatever state I am to be content. I know how to be abased, and I know how to abound. Everywhere and in all things I have learned both to be full and to be hungry, both to abound and to suffer need. I can do all these things in Him who strengthens me."[229]

[26.40] In what then are you rejoicing, great Paul?[230] In what are you rejoicing, on what are you fed, O man renewed unto the knowledge of God according to the image of Him Who created you,[231] a living soul of such great continence, a winged tongue speaking mysteries? It is to such creatures that this nourishment is owed. What is it that feeds you? Joy. Let us see what words follow in the Scripture: "Nevertheless," the Apostle says, "you have done well that you shared in my distress."[232] This is in what he rejoices, this is on what he feeds, that they had done a good deed, not that his suffering was eased, for he says to You, "You have relieved me in my distress,"[233] for he knew both how to abound and how to suffer need in Him who strengthens him.[234] "Now you Philippians also know," the Apostle said, "that in the beginning of the Gospel when I departed from Macedonia, no church shared with me in giving and receiving but you alone. For even in Thessalonica you sent aid for my needs once and then again."[235] He now rejoices that they have returned to these good works, and delights that they are flourishing like fields sprouting in abundance once more.

[26.41] But had the Apostle meant his own needs when he said, "You sent aid for my needs"? Was he rejoicing on that account? He was not. But how do we know this? Because he himself says right away, "Not that I seek the gift, but I seek the fruit."[236] I have learned from You, my God, to distinguish between gift and fruit. A gift is the thing itself that he gives who bestows on us necessary things, such as money, food, drink, clothing, shelter, and help. The fruit on the other hand is the good and right will of the giver. For the Good Master did not only say, "He who receives a prophet," but added, "in the name of a prophet." Nor did He only say, "He who receives a righteous man," but added, "in the name of a righteous man." So naturally the one shall receive the reward of a prophet, the other the reward of a righteous man.[237] Nor did He only say, "Whoever gives one of these little ones only a cup of cold water," but added, "in the name of a disciple," and then added, "Assuredly, I say to you, he shall by no means lose his reward."[238] The gift is the receiving of a prophet, the receiving of a righteous man, a cup of cold water given to a disciple; the fruit is to do this for a prophet, for a righteous man, for a disciple. It was fruit when Elijah was fed by the widow who knew that she was feeding a man of God and therefore fed him; but when he was fed by the raven was he fed with a gift.[239] Nor was Elijah's spirit fed, but only his body, which for want of such food might have perished.

[27.42] So I shall say what is true before Your countenance, Lord, that when uninformed and unbelievers,[240] who to be initiated and won over need Sacraments of initiation and great miracles, which we believe to be represented by fish and whales, when such people undertake to provide bodily refreshment, or otherwise help Your children with something useful for this present life, they do not know why this must be done and for what reason. Thus neither do they nourish Your Children, nor are Your children nourished by them, because neither do the former do this out of a holy and right will, nor do the latter rejoice in their gifts, since there is still no fruit to behold. For the mind only feeds on that in which it rejoices, and therefore the fish and the whales do not feed upon foods that the earth has brought forth after it became separate and apart from the bitter waves of the sea.

[28.43] You saw all the things that You made, God, and they were very good,[241] and we too see them, and they are all very good. With each of Your works, when You said that they should be made and they were made, You saw that each of them was good. I counted that it is written seven times that You saw that what You had made was good, and the eighth time it is written that You saw all that You had made: and, behold, You saw not only that it was good, but very good, when You saw everything together.[242] Separately they were only good, but together they were both good and very good. The same can be said of all beautiful bodies, for a body consisting of beautiful parts is far more beautiful than the parts themselves by whose well-ordered gathering together the whole is perfected, even though the parts are in themselves beautiful too.

[29.44] Thus I carefully verified whether it was seven or eight times that You saw that Your works were good when they pleased You, but in Your seeing I could not find the times through which I could understand that You had seen what You had made so often. And I said, "O Lord, is not Your Scripture true since You are true, and being Truth have declared it? Why then do You say to me that there is no time in Your seeing, while Your Scripture tells me that what You created on each day You saw that it was good, and in counting these I ascertained how often." You answered me, for You are my God and speak with a powerful voice into the inner ear of Your servant, breaking through my deafness, and You pronounced, "O man, what My Scripture says is what I say. It speaks in terms of time, though My Word does not accede to time, because My Word exists as I do in eternity. The things that You see through My Spirit I see, just as what You speak through My Spirit I speak. But though you see those things in terms of time, I do not, just as when You speak in terms of time, I do not."

[30.45] I listened, Lord my God, and drank in a drop of sweetness from Your Truth, and understood that there are those who dislike Your works and say that You created many of these works compelled by necessity, such as the fabric of the heavens and the constellation of the stars.[243] They say that You created them not out of what was Yours, but that they had been created elsewhere and from another source, and that You gathered them and assembled and put them together, when having defeated Your enemies You raised the ramparts of the universe so that held back by these ramparts Your enemies could not rise against You once more. The rest, they claim, You did not create nor even put together, such as all flesh, the tiniest creatures, and all that by its roots clings to the earth, but that some hostile spirit, another nature not created by You and contrary to You, begot and fashioned these things in the nether regions of the world. It is madmen who say this, because they cannot see Your works by Your Spirit, nor do they recognize You in them.

[31.46] But they who by Your spirit see Your Works, it is You who are seeing from within them. Therefore when they see that these things are good, You see that the things are good, and whenever something pleases us because of You, it is You who pleases us in it, and what through Your Spirit pleases us, pleases You in us. "For what man knows the things of a man, except the spirit of the man which is in him?" the Apostle asks. "Even so, no one knows the things of God except the Spirit of God. Now we have received, not the spirit of the world, but the Spirit who is from God, that we might know the things that have been freely given to us by God."[244] And at this I ask, "Certainly nobody knows the things of God except the Spirit of God, but how do we ourselves know what gifts God has given us?" The answer I am given is that even the things that we know by His Spirit no one knows but the Spirit of God.[245] For just as it is rightly said to those who speak by the Spirit of God, "It is not you who speak,"[246] so is it rightly said to those who know through the Spirit of

God, "It is not you who know," and no less is it rightly said to those who see by the Spirit of God, "It is not you who see." Thus whatever they see by the Spirit of God as good, it is not they, but God Who sees that it is good. It is therefore one thing to think that something is evil that is good, as do those who I have mentioned above;[247] it is another thing to think that what man sees to be good is good in the way that many are pleased by Your creation because it is good, though it is not You Who please them in Your creation, since they prefer to delight in Your creation rather than delight in You; and it is yet another thing to think that when a man sees something that is good, God within him sees that it is good, so that He is loved in that which He has made, He Who cannot be loved other than through the Spirit He has given, because the love of God has been poured out in our hearts by the Holy Spirit who was given to us.[248] It is through this Spirit that we see that whatever exists in any degree is good, for its existence is from Him who Himself does not exist in degree, since HE IS WHO IS.[249]

[32.47] Thanks be to You, Lord. We see the heaven and the earth, the upper and lower corporeal parts or the spiritual and *corporeal* creation. For the adornment of these, of which the entire mass of the world consists, or rather the whole creation in its entirety, we see light created and divided from darkness; we see the firmament of heaven, either that first body of the world between the spiritual waters above and the lower corporeal waters below, or that space of air—since this is also called heaven—through which fly the birds of the air between those waters that are borne above them in vapors, which on clear nights are scattered as dew; we see the heavy waters that flow on the earth; we see the beauty of the waters gathered together in the fields of the sea,[250] and the dry land bare, then shaped, so as to be visible and formed, the mother of plants and trees. We see the lights shining from above, the sun sufficing to imbue the day, the moon and the stars comforting the night, time marked out and indicated by them all. We see wet nature all around, fecund with fish and beasts and birds, the thickness of the air strengthened by the exhalation of the waters carrying the flight of winged creatures. We see the face of the earth embellished with earthly creatures and with man who was created in Your image according to Your likeness[251] and set above all irrational creatures through Your image and likeness, that is, through the power of reason and understanding. Just as within man's soul, there is one thing that seeks to dominate and another that submits so that it might obey; hence, corporeally, a woman has been made for man and in rational intelligence she is equal to man in nature, but in the sex of her body she is subject to the male sex, just as the desire for action is subject to the reason of the mind so that it will garner from it the capacity of acting correctly. These things we see, and separately they are good, and together very good.

[33.48] Your works praise You that we may love You, and we love You that Your works may praise You. They have a beginning and an end within time, a rising and a setting, an increase and a decrease, a form and a privation. Thus they have their succession of morning and evening, in part secretly, in part manifestly, for they were created out of nothing by You; they were not created out of You, nor out of any matter that is not Yours or that existed before, but they were created out of matter that was created by You at the same time and together with its form, because You gave form to its formlessness without an interval of time. The substance of heaven and earth is one thing, and the form of heaven and earth another. You created the substance out of nothing at all, but the form of the world You created out of substance without form: yet You created both together so that the form would follow the substance without interval or delay.

[34.49] I have also considered the reason for the figurativeness in Your will to create things in a certain order or for them to be related in Your Scripture in that order. And I saw that separately things are good, and together very good in Your Word, in Your Only Son, heaven and earth, the Head and the Body of the Church,[252] in Your predestination before all time without morning and evening. You began to execute within time what was predestined in order to reveal hidden things and to form that which was unformed, for our sins were weighing upon us and we had sunk away from You into the darkness of the deep. But Your good Spirit was carried over us to help us in a seasonable time,[253] and You justified the impious[254] and separated them from the wicked; and You established the authority of Your Book between superior men who were prepared to learn from You, and inferior men who would be subject to them. You gathered together the unbelievers into a single conspiracy so that the zeal of the faithful would appear and bring forth works of mercy, as the faithful distribute to the poor their earthly wealth so that they may obtain heavenly riches. Then You lit certain lights in the firmament,[255] Your saints holding fast the Word of Life,[256] shining with the sublime authority that the spiritual gifts have bestowed upon them. And then, to initiate the unbelieving peoples, You produced out of corporeal matter the Sacraments and visible miracles, and the words sounding out through the firmament of Your Book by which the faithful would be blessed. And then You formed the living soul of the faithful by curbing their passions through the vigor of continence, after which You renewed their mind in Your image and likeness to be subject to You alone, needing no human authority as a model, subjecting its rational actions to the preeminence of understanding, as woman is subjected to man. And for all Your ministers who must lead the faithful to perfection in this life You willed that the faithful must provide for the ministers' temporal needs and that this shall secure for the faithful future rewards. All these things we see, and they are very good, because You see them from within us since You have given us Your Spirit by which we can see them, and in them love You.

[35.50] Lord God, give us peace, for You have granted us all things,[257] the peace of rest, the peace of the Sabbath, and peace that has no evening, since all this most beautiful harmony of things that are very good will pass away once they have run their course, for in these things there is both morning and evening.

[36.51] But the seventh day is without evening, nor does it set, because You have sanctified it to an everlasting eternity. You rested on the seventh day after You created Your works that were very good, though You created them in repose, and the voice of Your Book foretells us that we too, after our works that are very good because You have given them to us, will rest in You in the Sabbath of eternal life.

[37.52] For then You will rest in us just as now You work in us, and so will that be Your rest through us, just as these are Your works through us. But You, Lord, always work and are always at rest. You do not see within time, nor move within time, nor rest within time, and yet You make things that are seen within time, and You make the times themselves, and the repose that results from time.

[38.53] We therefore see all the things that You have created because they exist, and they exist because You see them. We look out of ourselves and see that they are, and look into ourselves and see that they are good, but You saw them created there where You saw that they were to be created. We are now moved to do good after our hearts conceived of Your Spirit, but at a former time we were moved to do evil, forsaking You. But You, the one and good God, have never ceased to do good. Through Your gift we too have some good works, but they are not eternal: after them we hope to rest in Your great sanctification. But You, the Good that needs no good, are ever at rest because Your repose is You Yourself. What man can make another man understand this, what Angel another Angel, what Angel a man? Let it be asked of You, be sought in You, let it be knocked for, and thus shall it be received, thus shall it be found, thus shall it be opened.[258] Amen.

ɔↄ

NOTES

1   Psalm 17:21 (Vulgate), 18:20 (other translations). "According to the cleanness of my hands He has recompensed me." (New King James Bible)

2   Genesis 1:31. "And God saw all the things that he had made, and they were very good." (Douay-Rheims Bible)

3   Romans 8:29. "For whom He foreknew, He also predestined to be conformed to the image of His Son." (New King James Bible)

4   Psalm 72:28 (Vulgate), 73:28 (other translations). "But it is good for me to adhere to my God." (Douay-Rheims Bible)

5   Genesis 1:2.

6   Ephesians 5:8. "For you were once darkness, but now you are light in the Lord." (New King James Bible)

7   2 Corinthians 5:21. "For He made Him who knew no sin to be sin for us, that we might become the righteousness of God in Him." (New King James Bible)

8   Psalm 35:7 (Vulgate), 36:6 (other translations). "Thy justice is as the mountains of God, thy judgments are a great deep." (Douay-Rheims Bible)

9   Genesis 1:3.

10 Isaiah 11:2. "And the spirit of the Lord shall rest upon him: the spirit of wisdom, and of understanding, the spirit of counsel, and of fortitude, the spirit of knowledge, and of godliness." (Douay-Rheims Bible)

11 1 Corinthians 13:12. "For now we see through a glass, darkly; but then face to face: now I know in part; but then shall I know even as also I am known." (King James Bible)

12 Genesis 1:7. "Thus God made the firmament, and divided the waters which were under the firmament from the waters which were above the firmament; and it was so." (New King James Bible)

13 The Apostle Paul in Romans 5:5. "Now hope does not disappoint, because the love of God has been poured out in our hearts by the Holy Spirit who was given to us." (New King James Bible)

14 The Apostle Paul in Ephesians 3:14. "For this cause I bow my knees to the Father of our Lord Jesus Christ." (Douay-Rheims Bible)

15 Ephesians 3:19. "To know also the charity of Christ, which surpasseth all knowledge, that you may be filled unto all the fulness of God." (Douay-Rheims Bible)

16 Psalm 123:5. "Our soul hath passed through a torrent: perhaps our soul had passed through a water insupportable." (Douay-Rheims Bible)

17 Genesis 1:3.

18 Isaiah 61:10. "My soul shall be joyful in my God; For He has clothed me with the garments of salvation." (New King James Bible)

19 Isaiah 58:10.

> "*If* you extend your soul to the hungry
> And satisfy the afflicted soul,
> Then your light shall dawn in the darkness,
> And your darkness shall *be* as the noonday." (New King James Bible)

20 Psalm 30:21 (Vulgate), 31:20 (other translations). "You shall hide them in the secret place of Your presence from the plots of man." (New King James Bible)

21 Acts 2:38. "Then Peter said to them, "Repent, and let every one of you be baptized in the name of Jesus Christ for the remission of sins; and you shall receive the gift of the Holy Spirit." (New King James Bible)

22 Psalm 9:13 (Vulgate), 9:15 (other translations). "You who lift me up from the gates of death." (New King James Bible)

23 Psalm 119s through 133 (Vulgate), 120 through 134 (other translations), each begin with the words "A song of ascents."

24 Psalm 121:1 (Vulgate), 122:1 (other translations). "I rejoiced at the things that were said to me: We shall go into the house of the Lord."

25 Augustine is referring to the Heaven of Heavens.

26 Ephesians 5:8. "For you were once darkness, but now you are light in the Lord. Walk as children of light." (New King James Bible)

27 Galatians 6:17. "From now on let no one trouble me, for I bear in my body the marks of the Lord Jesus." (New King James Bible)

28 John 1:9. "That was the true Light which gives light to every man coming into the world." (New King James Bible)

29 Isaiah 6:3. "Holy, holy, holy is the Lord of hosts." (New King James Bible)

30 Matthew 28:19. "Go therefore and make disciples of all the nations, baptizing them in the name of the Father and of the Son and of the Holy Spirit." (New King James Bible)

31 Genesis 1:2.

32 Psalm 54:6 (Vulgate), 55:5 (other translations). "Fear and trembling are come upon me: and darkness hath covered me." (Douay-Rheims Bible)

33 Psalm 38:12 (Vulgate), 39:11 (other translations). "Thou hast corrected man for iniquity. And thou hast made his soul to waste away like a spider." (Douay-Rheims Bible)

34 Psalm 35:7 (Vulgate), 36:6 (other translations). "Thy justice is as the mountains of God, thy judgments are a great deep." (Douay-Rheims Bible)

35 Matthew 3:2.

36   Ephesians 5:8. "For you were once darkness, but now you are light in the Lord." (New King James Bible)

37   2 Corinthians 5:7. "For we walk by faith, not by sight." (New King James Bible)

38   Romans 8:24. "For we are saved by hope. But hope that is seen, is not hope. For what a man seeth, why doth he hope for?" (Douay-Rheims Bible)

39   Psalm 41:8 (Vulgate), 42:7 (other translations). "Deep calls to deep at the voice of thy cataracts: all thy billows and thy waves have gone over me." (Brenton Septuagint Translation)

40   The Apostle Paul in 1 Corinthians 3:1. "And I, brethren, could not speak to you as to spiritual people but as to carnal, as to babes in Christ." (New King James Bible)

41   The Apostle Paul in Philippians 3:13. "Brethren, I do not count myself to have apprehended; but one thing I do, forgetting those things which are behind and reaching forward to those things which are ahead." (New King James Bible)

42   The Apostle Paul in 2 Corinthians 5:4. "For we also, who are in this tabernacle, do groan, being burthened." (Douay-Rheims Bible)

43   Psalm 41:1–2.

"As the deer pants for the water brooks,
So pants my soul for You, O God.
My soul thirsts for God, for the living God.
When shall I come and appear before God?" (New King James Bible)

44   The Apostle Paul in 2 Corinthians 5:2. "For in this we groan, earnestly desiring to be clothed with our habitation which is from heaven." (New King James Bible)

45   The Apostle Paul in Romans 12:2. "And do not be conformed to this world, but be transformed by the renewing of your mind, that you may prove what is that good and acceptable and perfect will of God." (New King James Bible)

46   The Apostle Paul in 1 Corinthians 14:20. "Brethren, do not be children in understanding; however, in malice be babes, but in understanding be mature." (New King James Bible)

47   The Apostle Paul in Galatians 3:1. "O foolish Galatians! Who has bewitched you that you should not obey the truth, before whose eyes Jesus Christ was clearly portrayed among you as crucified?" (New King James Bible)

48   Malachi 3:10.

49   Psalm 45:5 (Vulgate), 46:4 (other translations). "*There is* a river whose streams shall make glad the city of God." (New King James Bible)

50   Jesus is the Bridegroom, and here the Apostle Paul is the friend of the Bridegroom. John 3:29. "He who has the bride is the bridegroom; but the friend of the bridegroom, who stands and hears him, rejoices greatly because of the bridegroom's voice." (New King James Bible)

51 The Apostle Paul in Romans 8:23. "Not only *that*, but we also who have the firstfruits of the Spirit, even we ourselves groan within ourselves, eagerly waiting for the adoption, the redemption of our body." (New King James Bible)

52 The Bride is the Church.

53 2 Corinthians 1:3. "But I fear, lest somehow, as the serpent deceived Eve by his craftiness, so your minds may be corrupted from the simplicity that is in Christ." (New King James Bible)

54 Psalm 41:4 (Vulgate), 42:3 (other translations). "My tears have been my bread day and night, whilst it is said to me daily: Where is thy God?" (Douay-Rheims Bible)

55 Augustine himself is now asking, as opposed to the Apostle Paul, whose questions Augustine has been citing in the previous paragraph.

56 Job 32:20. "I will speak and take breath a little: I will open my lips, and will answer." (Douay-Rheims Bible)

57 Psalm 41:5 (Vulgate), 42:4 (other translations).

>   "My tears have been my food day and night,
>   While they continually say to me,
>   'Where *is* your God?'
>   When I remember these *things,*
>   I pour out my soul within me." (New King James Bible)

58 Psalm 41:6–7 (Vulgate), 42:3–5 (other translations). "Why art thou sad, O my soul? and why dost thou trouble me? Hope in God, for I will still give praise to him: the salvation of my countenance." (Douay-Rheims Bible)

59 Psalm 118:105 (Vulgate), 119:105 (other translations). "Thy word is a lamp to my feet, and a light to my paths." (Douay-Rheims Bible)

60 Ephesians 5:8. "For you were once darkness, but now you are light in the Lord." (New King James Bible)

61 Romans 8:10. "And if Christ is in you, the body is dead because of sin, but the Spirit is life because of righteousness." (New King James Bible)

62 Song of Solomon 2:17.

63 Psalm 5:5 (Vulgate), 5:4 (other translations). "In the morning I will stand before thee, and will see: because thou art not a God that willest iniquity."

64 Psalm 41:6 (Vulgate), 42:11 (other translations). "Hope in God, for I will still give praise to him: the salvation of my countenance." (Douay-Rheims Bible)

65 Romans 8:11. "But if the Spirit of Him who raised Jesus from the dead dwells in you, He who raised Christ from the dead will also give life to your mortal bodies through His Spirit who dwells in you." (New King James Bible)

66 Ephesians 5:8. "For you were once darkness, but now you are light in the Lord." (New King James Bible)

67 Romans 8:24. "For we are saved by hope. But hope that is seen, is not

hope. For what a man seeth, why doth he hope for?" (Douay-Rheims Bible)

68   1 Thessalonians 5:5. "For all you are the children of light, and children of the day: we are not of the night, nor of darkness." (Douay-Rheims Bible)

69   Ephesians 5:8. "For you were once darkness, but now you are light in the Lord." (New King James Bible)

70   Genesis 1:4. "And God saw the light, that *it was* good; and God divided the light from the darkness." (New King James Bible)

71   Psalm 16:3 (Vulgate), 17:3 (other translations).

> "You have tested my heart;
> You have visited *me* in the night;
> You have tried me and have found nothing;
> I have purposed that my mouth shall not transgress." (New King James Bible)

72   1 Corinthians 4:7. "For who makes you differ from another? And what do you have that you did not receive?" (New King James Bible)

73   Romans 9:21. " Does not the potter have power over the clay, from the same lump to make one vessel for honor and another for dishonor?" (New King James Version)

74   Genesis 1:7. "Thus God made the firmament, and divided the waters which were under the firmament from the waters which were above the firmament; and it was so." (New King James Bible)

75   Isaiah 34:4. "All the host of heaven shall be dissolved, And the heavens shall be rolled up like a scroll;" (New King James Bible)

76   Psalm 103:1–2 (Vulgate), 104:1–2 (other translations).

77   Augustine is referring to biblical figures such as Moses and David in the case of the Old Testament, and Apostles such as Peter and Paul in the New Testament.

78   Genesis 3:21. "And the Lord God made for Adam and his wife, garments of skins, and clothed them." (Douay-Rheims Bible)

79   Psalm 8:4 (Vulgate), 8:3 (other translations). "For I will behold thy heavens, the works of thy fingers: the moon and the stars which thou hast founded." (Douay-Rheims Bible)

80   Psalm 18:8 (Vulgate), 19:7 (other translations). "The statutes of the Lord are trustworthy, making wise the simple." (New King James Bible)

81   Psalm 8:3 (Vulgate), 8:2 (other translations). "Out of the mouth of infants and of sucklings thou hast perfected praise." (Douay-Rheims Bible)

82   Sirach 30:6. "For he left behind him a defender of his house against his enemies, and one that will requite kindness to his friends." (Douay-Rheims Bible)

83   Psalm 11:7 (Vulgate), 12:6 (other translations). "The words of the Lord are pure words: as silver tried by the fire, purged from the earth refined seven times." (Douay-Rheims Bible)

84 Matthew 11:29–30. "Take up my yoke upon you, and learn of me, because I am meek, and humble of heart: and you shall find rest to your souls. For my yoke is sweet and my burden light." (Douay-Rheims Bible)

85 Genesis 1:7. "Thus God made the firmament, and divided the waters which were under the firmament from the waters which were above the firmament; and it was so."

86 Matthew 18:10. "In heaven their angels always see the face of My Father who is in heaven." (New King James Bible)

87 Psalm 35:6. "O Lord, thy mercy is in heaven, and thy truth reacheth, even to the clouds." (Douay-Rheims Bible)

88 Matthew 24:35. "Heaven and earth shall pass, but my words shall not pass." (Douay-Rheims Bible)

89 Isaiah 40:6–8.

> "The grass withers, the flower fades,
> Because the breath of the Lord blows upon it;
> Surely the people are grass.
> The grass withers, the flower fades,
> But the word of our God stands forever." (New King James Bible)

90 1 Corinthians 13:12. "For now we see through a glass, darkly; but then face to face: now I know in part; but then shall I know even as also I am known." (King James Bible)

91 1 John 3:2. "Beloved, now we are children of God; and it has not yet been revealed what we shall be." (New King James Bible)

92 Song of Solomon 2:9. "Behold he standeth behind our wall, looking through the windows, looking through the lattices." (Douay-Rheims Bible)

93 Song of Solomon 1:3. "Draw me: we will run after thee to the odour of thy ointments." (Douay-Rheims Bible)

94 1 John 3:2. "But we know that when He is revealed, we shall be like Him, for we shall see Him as He is." (New King James Bible)

95 Psalm 142:6. "I stretched forth my hands to thee: my soul is as earth without water unto thee." (Douay-Rheims Bible)

96 Psalm 35:10 (Vulgate), 36:10 (other translations). "For with thee is the fountain of life; and in thy light we shall see light." (Douay-Rheims Bible)

97 Genesis 1:9.

98 Psalm 94:5 (Vulgate), 95:5 (other translations). "For the sea is his, and he made it: and his hands formed the dry land." (Douay-Rheims Bible)

99 Job 38:10–11. "I set my bounds around it, and made it bars and doors: And I said: Hitherto thou shalt come, and shalt go no further, and here thou shalt break thy swelling waves." (Douay-Rheims Bible)

100 Psalm 62:2. "For thee my soul hath thirsted; for thee my flesh, O how many ways!" (Douay-Rheims Bible)

101 Genesis 1:12. "And the earth brought forth grass, the herb *that* yields

seed according to its kind, and the tree *that* yields fruit, whose seed *is* in itself according to its kind." (New King James Bible)

102   Ibid.

103   Ibid.

104   Genesis 1:11. "Let the earth bring forth grass, the herb *that* yields seed, *and* the fruit tree *that* yields fruit according to its kind." (New King James Bible)

105   Psalm 84:12 (Vulgate), 85:11 (other translations). "Truth is sprung out of the earth: and justice hath looked down from heaven."

106   Genesis 1:14.

107   Isaiah 58:7. "Deal thy bread to the hungry, and bring the needy and the harbourless into thy house: when thou shalt see one naked, cover him, and despise not thy own flesh." (Douay-Rheims Bible)

108   Isaiah 58:8. "Then shall thy light break forth as the morning." (Douay-Rheims Bible)

109   Philippians 2:15–16. "In the midst of a crooked and perverse generation, among whom you shine as lights in the world, holding fast the word of life." (New King James Bible)

110   Genesis 1:14. "Then God said, "Let there be lights in the firmament of the heavens to divide the day from the night; and let them be for signs and seasons, and for days and years;" (New King James Bible)

111   2 Corinthians 5:17. "Therefore, if anyone is in Christ, he is a new creation; old things have passed away; behold, all things have become new." (New King James Bible)

112   Romans 13:11–12. "Now *it is* high time to awake out of sleep; for now our salvation *is* nearer than when we *first* believed. The night is far spent, the day is at hand." (New King James Bible)

113   Psalms 64:12 (Vulgate), 65:11 (other translations). "Thou shalt bless the crown of the year of thy goodness: and thy fields shall be filled with plenty." (Douay-Rheims Bible)

114   Matthew 9:38. "Therefore pray the Lord of the harvest to send out laborers into His harvest." (New King James Bible)

115   John 4:38. " I sent you to reap that for which you have not labored; others have labored, and you have entered into their labors." (New King James Bible)

116   Matthew 13:39. "The enemy who sowed them is the devil, the harvest is the end of the age, and the reapers are the angels." (New King James Bible)

117   Psalm 101:28 (Vulgate), 102:27 (other translations). "But You *are* the same, and Your years will have no end." (New King James Bible)

118   Genesis 1:16. "Then God made two great lights: the greater light to rule the day, and the lesser light to rule the night." (New King James Bible)

119   1 Corinthians 12:8–11. "For to one is given the word of wisdom through the Spirit, to another the word of knowledge through the same Spirit, to another

faith by the same Spirit, to another gifts of healings by the same Spirit, to another the working of miracles, to another prophecy, to another discerning of spirits, to another *different* kinds of tongues, to another the interpretation of tongues. But one and the same Spirit works all these things, distributing to each one individually as He wills." (New King James Bible)

120 Mentioned in the previous paragraph. Romans 13:11–12. "Now *it is* high time to awake out of sleep; for now our salvation *is* nearer than when we *first* believed. The night is far spent, the day is at hand." (New King James Bible)

121 The Apostle Paul in 1 Corinthians 3:1. "And I, brethren, could not speak to you as to spiritual people but as to carnal, as to babes in Christ." (New King James Bible)

122 1 Corinthians 2:6. "Howbeit we speak wisdom among the perfect: yet not the wisdom of this world, neither of the princes of this world that come to nought." (Douay-Rheims Bible)

123 1 Corinthians 2:14. "But the natural man does not receive the things of the Spirit of God, for they are foolishness to him." (New King James Bible)

124 Hebrews 5:12–13. "For though by this time you ought to be teachers, you need someone to teach you again the first principles of the oracles of God; and you have come to need milk and not solid food. For everyone who partakes only of milk is unskilled in the word of righteousness, for he is a babe." (New King James Bible)

125 Genesis 1:14. "Then God said, 'Let there be lights in the firmament of the heavens to divide the day from the night; and let them be for signs and seasons, and for days and years." (New King James Bible)

126 Isaiah 1:16–17.

> "Wash yourselves, make yourselves clean;
> Put away the evil of your doings from before My eyes.
> Cease to do evil,
> Learn to do good;
> Seek justice,
> Rebuke the oppressor;
> Defend the fatherless,
> Plead for the widow." (New King James Bible)

127 Isaiah 1:18.

128 Matthew 19:16. "Now behold, one came and said to Him, 'Good Teacher, what good thing shall I do that I may have eternal life?'" (New King James Bible)

129 Matthew 19:17. "So He said to him, "Why do you call Me good? No one *is* good but One, *that is*, God. But if you want to enter into life, keep the commandments." (New King James Bible)

130 Matthew 19:19. "Jesus said, 'You shall not murder,' 'You shall not commit adultery,' 'You shall not steal,' 'You shall not bear false witness,' 'Honor your father and your mother,' and, 'You shall love your neighbor as yourself.'" (New King James Bible)

131   From Luke's version of the parable of Jesus counseling the rich young ruler. Luke 18:22. "Sell all that you have and distribute to the poor, and you will have treasure in heaven; and come, follow Me." (New King James Bible)

132   1 Corinthians 2:6. "Howbeit we speak wisdom among the perfect: yet not the wisdom of this world, neither of the princes of this world that come to nought." (Douay-Rheims Bible)

133   Matthew 13:7. "And some fell among thorns, and the thorns sprang up and choked them." (New King James Bible)

134   1 Peter 2:9.

135   1 Corinthians 1:27. "God has chosen the weak things of the world to put to shame the things which are mighty." (New King James Bible)

136   Matthew 19:27. "Then Peter answered and said to Him, 'See, we have left all and followed You.'" (New King James Bible)

137   1 Corinthians 1:27.

138   Isaiah 52:7. "How beautiful upon the mountains / Are the feet of him who brings good news." (New King James Bible)

139   Psalm 18:2 (Vulgate), 19:1 (other translations). "The heavens shew forth the glory of God, and the firmament declareth the work of his hands." (Douay-Rheims Bible)

140   Psalm 18:8 (Vulgate), 19:7 (other translations). "The law of the Lord is perfect, converting the soul; / The testimony of the Lord is sure, making wise the simple." (New King James Bible)

141   Psalm 18:3 (Vulgate), 19:2 (other translations). "Day unto day utters speech, / And night unto night reveals knowledge." (New King James Bible)

142   Genesis 1:14. "Then God said, 'Let there be lights in the firmament of the heavens to divide the day from the night.'" (New King James Bible)

143   Acts 2:2–3. "And suddenly from heaven there came a sound like the rush of a violent wind, and it filled the entire house where they were sitting. Divided tongues, as of fire, appeared among them, and a tongue rested on each of them." (New Revised Standard Version Catholic Edition)

144   Philippians 2:15–16.

145   Matthew 5:14–15. "You are the light of the world. A city seated on a mountain cannot be hid. Neither do men light a candle and put it under a bushel." (Douay-Rheims Bible)

146   Genesis 1:20. "God also said: Let the waters bring forth the creeping creature having life." (Douay-Rheims Bible)

147   Jeremiah 15:19. "And if thou wilt separate the precious from the vile, thou shalt be as my mouth: they shall be turned to thee, and thou shalt not be turned to them." (Douay-Rheims Bible)

148   Genesis 1:24. "And God said: Let the earth bring forth the living creature in its kind." (Douay-Rheims Bible)

149   Genesis 1:20.

150 Matthew 28:19. "Go therefore and make disciples of all the nations, baptizing them in the name of the Father and of the Son and of the Holy Spirit." (New King James Bible)

151 Psalm 105:21–22. "They forgot God, who saved them, who had done great things in Egypt, / Wondrous works in the land of Cham." (Douay-Rheims Bible)

152 Genesis 1:21. "And God created the great whales, and every living and moving creature, which the waters brought forth." (Douay-Rheims Bible)

153 Psalm 18:4–5 (Vulgate), 19:3–4 (other translations). "There are no speeches nor languages, where their voices are not heard. Their sound hath gone forth into all the earth: and their words unto the ends of the world." (Douay-Rheims Bible)

154 Genesis 1:22. "And God blessed them, saying, 'Be fruitful and multiply, and fill the waters in the seas, and let birds multiply on the earth.'" (New King James Bible)

155 Ibid.

156 Genesis 1:20. "God also said: Let the waters bring forth the creeping creature having life." (Douay-Rheims Bible)

157 1 Corinthians 4:1. "Let a man so consider us, as servants of Christ and stewards of the mysteries of God." (New King James Bible)

158 Song of Solomon 9:7.

159 Acts 11:6.

160 Hebrews 6:1. "Therefore, leaving the discussion of the elementary principles of Christ, let us go on to perfection." (New King James Bible)

161 John 3:5. "Jesus answered, 'Most assuredly, I say to you, unless one is born of water and the Spirit, he cannot enter the kingdom of God.'" (New King James Bible)

162 John 4:48. "Jesus therefore said to him: Unless you see signs and wonders, you believe not." (Douay-Rheims Bible)

163 1 Corinthians 14:22. "Therefore tongues are for a sign, not to those who believe but to unbelievers; but prophesying is not for unbelievers but for those who believe." (New King James Bible)

164 Psalm 135:6 (Vulgate), 137:6 (other translations).

165 Psalm 147:15. "Who sendeth forth his speech to the earth: his word runneth swiftly." (Douay-Rheims Bible)

166 Psalm 22:5 (Vulgate), 23:5 (other translations). "Thou hast prepared a table before me against them that afflict me."

167 In Luke 24:36–42, Jesus appears after the Resurrection among his disciples and partakes of fish. The New Testament Greek word for fish, *ichthys*, was used as an acronym for *Iēsous Christos Theou Yios Sōtēr*, "Jesus Christ, Son of God, Savior."

168 Genesis 1:20. "God also said: Let the waters bring forth the creeping creature having life, and the fowl that may fly over the earth under the firmament of heaven." (Douay-Rheims Bible)

169   Psalm 60:9 (Vulgate), 61:9 (other translations). "So will I sing a psalm to thy name for ever and ever: that I may pay my vows from day to day." (Douay-Rheims Bible)

170   2 Corinthians 5:15. "And He died for all, that those who live should live no longer for themselves, but for Him who died for them and rose again." (New King James Bible)

171   1 Timothy 5:6. "For she that liveth in pleasures, is dead while she is living." (Douay-Rheims Bible)

172   Genesis 3:8. "And when they heard the voice of the Lord God walking in paradise at the afternoon air, Adam and his wife hid themselves from the face of the Lord God, amidst the trees of paradise." (Douay-Rheims Bible)

173   Psalm 68:33 (Vulgate), 69:32 (other translations). "Let the poor see and rejoice: seek ye God, and your soul shall live." (Douay-Rheims Bible)

174   Romans 12:2. "And be not conformed to this world; but be reformed in the newness of your mind, that you may prove what is the good, and the acceptable, and the perfect will of God." (Douay-Rheims Bible)

175   1 Timothy 6:20. "Guard what was committed to your trust, avoiding the profane and idle babblings and contradictions of what is falsely called knowledge." (New King James Bible)

176   *Curiositas* as eagerness for knowledge about things other than God.

177   Matthew 24:35. "Heaven and earth shall pass, but my words shall not pass." (Douay-Rheims Bible)

178   Romans 12:2.

179   The Apostle Paul in 1 Corinthians 11:1. "Imitate me, just as I also imitate Christ." (New King James Bible)

180   Genesis 1:21.

181   The Apostle Paul in Galatians 4:12. "Be ye as I, because I also am as you." (Douay-Rheims Bible)

182   Sirach 3:19. "My son, do thy works in meekness, and thou shalt be beloved above the glory of men." (Douay-Rheims Bible)

183   Matthew 10:16. "Be ye therefore wise as serpents and simple as doves." (Douay-Rheims Bible)

184   Romans 1:20. "For the invisible things of him, from the creation of the world, are clearly seen, being understood by the things that are made."

185   Romans 12:2. "And be not conformed to this world; but be reformed in the newness of your mind, that you may prove what is the good, and the acceptable, and the perfect will of God." (Douay-Rheims Bible)

186   Genesis 1:21.

187   Genesis 1:26.

188   Romans 12:2. "And be not conformed to this world; but be reformed in the newness of your mind, that you may prove what is the good, and the acceptable, and the perfect will of God." (Douay-Rheims Bible)

189   The Apostle Paul in 1 Corinthians 4:15. "For though you might have ten

thousand instructors in Christ, yet you do not have many fathers; for in Christ Jesus I have begotten you through the gospel." (New King James Bible)

190 1 Corinthians 3:1–2. "And I, brethren, could not speak to you as to spiritual *people* but as to carnal, as to babes in Christ. I fed you with milk." (New King James Bible)

191 1 Thessalonians 2:7. "But we became little ones in the midst of you, as if a nurse should cherish her children." (Douay-Rheims Bible)

192 Romans 12:2.

193 Ibid.

194 Genesis 1:26–27.

195 Colossians 3:10. "The new man who is renewed in knowledge according to the image of Him who created him." (New King James Bible)

196 1 Corinthians 2:15. "But the spiritual man judgeth all things; and he himself is judged of no man." (Douay-Rheims Bible)

197 Genesis 1:26. "Then God said, 'Let Us make man in Our image, according to Our likeness; let them have dominion over the fish of the sea, over the birds of the air, over the cattle, over all the earth and over every creeping thing that creeps on the earth.'" (New King James Bible)

198 1 Corinthians 2:14. "But the natural man does not receive the things of the Spirit of God, for they are foolishness to him." (New King James Bible)

199 Psalm 48:13 (Vulgate), 49:12 (other translations). "And man being in honour, understands not: he is compared to the senseless cattle, and is like to them." (Brenton Septuagint Translation)

200 Ephesians 2:10. "For we are his workmanship, created in Christ Jesus in good works, which God hath prepared that we should walk in them." (Douay-Rheims Bible)

201 Genesis 1:27. "So God created man in His own image; in the image of God He created him; male and female He created them."

202 Galatians 3:28. "There is neither Jew nor Greek, there is neither slave nor free, there is neither male nor female; for you are all one in Christ Jesus." (New King James Bible)

203 1 Corinthians 2:15. "But the spiritual man judgeth all things; and he himself is judged of no man." (Douay-Rheims Bible)

204 Colossians 3:10. "The new man who is renewed in knowledge according to the image of Him who created him." (New King James Bible)

205 James 4:11. "But if you judge the law, you are not a doer of the law but a judge." (New King James Bible)

206 1 Corinthians 5:12. "For what have I to do with judging those also who are outside?" (New King James Bible)

207 Genesis 1:26.

208 See Book XIII, 21.29.

209 Genesis 1:20. "God also said: Let the waters bring forth the creeping

creature having life, and the fowl that may fly over the earth under the firmament of heaven." (Douay-Rheims Bible)

210   Genesis 1:28.

211   Genesis 1:22. "And God blessed them, saying, 'Be fruitful and multiply, and fill the waters in the seas, and let birds multiply on the earth.'" (New King James Bible)

212   Genesis 1:1. See Book XII, 28.38 to 29.40, in which Augustine discusses the various possible interpretations of the first line of the Book of Genesis.

213   Genesis 1:7. "Thus God made the firmament, and divided the waters which were under the firmament from the waters which were above the firmament; and it was so." (New King James Bible)

214   See Book XIII, 17.20.

215   1 Corinthians 12:7. "But the manifestation of the Spirit is given to each one for the profit of all." (New King James Bible)

216   Romans 3:4. "But God is true; and every man a liar, as it is written." (Douay-Rheims Bible)

217   John 8:44. "When he speaketh a lie, he speaketh of his own: for he is a liar, and the father thereof." (Douay-Rheims Bible)

218   Genesis 1:29. "And God said, "See, I have given you every herb that yields seed which is on the face of all the earth, and every tree whose fruit yields seed; to you it shall be for food." (King James Bible)

219   Genesis 1:30. "Also, to every beast of the earth, to every bird of the air, and to everything that creeps on the earth, in which there is life, I have given every green herb for food." (King James Bible)

220   See Book XII, 17.21.

221   In the New Testament, in Apostle Paul's Second Epistle to Timothy, Onesiphorus' help is mentioned when Paul was imprisoned and in chains. 2 Timothy 1:16. "The Lord grant mercy to the household of Onesiphorus, for he often refreshed me, and was not ashamed of my chain." (New King James Bible)

222   The Apostle Paul in 2 Corinthians 11:9. "And when I was present with you, and in need, I was a burden to no one, for what I lacked the brethren who came from Macedonia supplied." (New King James Bible)

223   2 Timothy 4:16.

224   Psalm 18:5 (Vulgate), 19:4 (other translations). "Their sound hath gone forth into all the earth: and their words unto the ends of the world." (Douay-Rheims Bible)

225   Philippians 3:18–19. "They are the enemies of the cross of Christ: whose end is destruction, whose god is their belly, and whose glory is in their shame—who set their mind on earthly things." (New King James Bible)

226   Romans 16:17–18. "Now I urge you, brethren, note those who cause divisions and offenses, contrary to the doctrine which you learned, and avoid them. For those who are such do not serve our Lord Jesus Christ,

but their own belly, and by smooth words and flattering speech deceive the hearts of the simple." (New King James Bible)

227 Philippians 4:18. "Indeed I have all and abound. I am full, having received from Epaphroditus the things sent from you, a sweet-smelling aroma, an acceptable sacrifice, well pleasing to God." (New King James Bible)

228 Philippians 4:10.

229 Philippians 4:11–13.

230 Augustine is punning on the apostle's name Paulus, which in Latin means "small."

231 Colossians 3:9–10. "Stripping yourselves of the old man with his deeds, and putting on the new, him who is renewed unto knowledge, according to the image of him that created him." (Douay-Rheims Bible)

232 Philippians 4:14.

233 Psalm 4:2 (Vulgate), 4:1 (other translations).

234 Philippians 4:11–13.

235 Philippians 4:15–16.

236 Philippians 4:17. "Not that I seek the gift, but I seek the fruit that abounds to your account." (New King James Bible)

237 Matthew 10:41. "He who receives a prophet in the name of a prophet shall receive a prophet's reward. And he who receives a righteous man in the name of a righteous man shall receive a righteous man's reward." (New King James Bible)

238 Matthew 10:42. "And whoever gives one of these little ones only a cup of cold water in the name of a disciple, assuredly, I say to you, he shall by no means lose his reward." (New King James Bible)

239 1 Kings 17:1–17.

240 1 Corinthians 14:23.

241 Genesis 1:31.

242 Augustine's count reflects the text of the Septuagint translation of the Book of Genesis, whereas the Vulgate translation, on which most modern Bible translations are based, omits from the line concerning the creation of the firmament in Genesis 1:8 "and God saw that it was good."

243 Augustine is referring to the Manichaeans and their doctrines.

244 The Apostle Paul in 1 Corinthians 2:11–12.

245 1 Corinthians 2:12. "Now we have received, not the spirit of the world, but the Spirit who is from God, that we might know the things that have been freely given to us by God." (New King James Bible)

246 Matthew 10:19–20. "But when they deliver you up, do not worry about how or what you should speak. For it will be given to you in that hour what you should speak; for it is not you who speak, but the Spirit of your Father who speaks in you." (New King James Bible)

247 The Manichaeans.

248 Romans 5:5. "Now hope does not disappoint, because the love of God has been poured out in our hearts by the Holy Spirit who was given to us." (New King James Bible)

249 Exodus 3:14. "God said to Moses: I AM WHO AM. He said: Thus shalt thou say to the children of Israel: HE WHO IS, hath sent me to you." (Douay-Rheims Bible)

250 Virgil, *Aeneid* 10.214.

251 Genesis 1:26.

252 Colossians 1:18. "And He is the head of the body, the church, who is the beginning, the firstborn from the dead, that in all things He may have the preeminence." (New King James Bible)

253 Psalm 31:6 (Vulgate), 32:6 (other translations). "For this shall every one that is holy pray to thee in a seasonable time." (Douay-Rheims Bible)

254 Proverbs 17:15.

255 Genesis 1:14.

256 Philippians 2:15–16. "Children of God without fault in the midst of a crooked and perverse generation, among whom you shine as lights in the world, holding fast the word of life." (New King James Bible)

257 Isaiah 26:12. "Lord, thou wilt give us peace: for thou hast wrought all our works for us." (Douay-Rheims Bible)

258 Matthew 7:7–8 "Ask, and it shall be given you; seek, and ye shall find; knock, and it shall be opened unto you: For every one that asketh receiveth; and he that seeketh findeth; and to him that knocketh it shall be opened." (King James Bible)